PILOTS   12 ^{00}

Nothing about "blind" or cloud flying
without gyro instruments

133-136

191

275

280
282

GYRO!

GYRO!

The Life and Times of Lawrence Sperry

WILLIAM WYATT DAVENPORT

CHARLES SCRIBNER'S SONS
New York

Copyright © 1978 William Wyatt Davenport

Library of Congress Cataloging in Publication Data

Davenport, William Wyatt.
  Gyro: the life and times of Lawrence Sperry.

  Includes index.
  1. Sperry, Lawrence Burst, 1892–1923.   2. Aeronautics—United States—Biography.   I.   Title.
TL540.S687D38   629.13'0092'4 [B]   78-17826
ISBN 0-684-15793-4

.3 5 7 9 11 13 15 17 19   V/C   20 18 16 14 12 10 8 6 4 2

PRINTED IN THE UNITED STATES OF AMERICA

Grateful acknowledgment is made to:

The New York Times for permission to reprint articles © 1916, 1917, 1922,
1923, 1924.

The Philadelphia Inquirer for permission to reprint from *The Philadelphia
Public Ledger,* © 1914.

I.H.T. Corporation for permission to reprint from *The New York Tribune,*
© 1915.

TITLE PAGE: Flying boat. Lawrence conceived and built this first amphibian triplane
for the U.S. Navy in 1919.

To Nesta Obermer, O.B.E.

WHO LEAVES A TRACE OF WINGS

Acknowledgments

IN WRITING the biography of Lawrence Sperry I have had the indispensable help of many people who personally knew this gallant airman. I have also been aided by official experts and archivists as well as by members of Lawrence Sperry's family who have provided me with letters, photographs, and personal reminiscences. Of the scores of men and women who have made it possible to realize this project, I would like to single out the following: Mr. Lawrence B. Sperry, Jr., Mrs. Helen Sperry Lea, Mr. Elmer A. Sperry III, Mr. Sperry Lea, Gen. James H. Doolittle, Gen. Ira Eaker, Mr. Paul Garber, curator emeritus of the Air and Space Museum of the Smithsonian Institution, Mr. Robert Meyer, curator of the Smithsonian Museum in charge of Aircraft Engines, Mr. John Lea, and Miss Katherine Scott, librarian of the National Air and Space Museum.

For personal memories of Lawrence Sperry, I am especially indebted to Mr. Archie Roosevelt, Mr. John E. Taylor and Mr. Peter Laugessen, both of the National Archives, the late Grover Loening, the late Mr. F. Trubee Davison, assistant secretary of War for Air, 1926–1932, Mr. Preston Bassett, aviation historian and former president of the Sperry Gyroscope Company, Mrs. Joseph Parsons, Mrs. William V. Hester, Miss Betty Turner, and Professor Thomas Parke Hughes.

I am also indebted to Mr. Charles Colvin, air instrument pioneer, who helped with personal recollections of Lawrence Sperry's contributions in the same field; to Mr. Powell Griffis, a personal friend and fan of Lawrence in the early days of aviation; to Mr. "Casey" Jones, who remembers Lawrence as a keen competitor in early air races and who still runs an aviation school near La Guardia Airport on Long Island, and to Mrs. Andrew Underhill for her gracious collaboration and encouragement.

As in every life that has been lived to the hilt, there are hiatuses, documents that have been lost or suppressed, the ambiguities of reality, questions that have not been answered, problems that have not been solved. In such cases, in my attempt to gather up the radiance of a dynamic personality, I have been authorized to indulge in some judicious speculation and have occasionally asserted poetic truths where actual facts were missing.

—WILLIAM WYATT DAVENPORT

Foreword

by General James H. Doolittle

THIS BIOGRAPHY is a welcome addition to the history of aviation, of which Lawrence Sperry has been one of the unsung heroes. We are in his debt every time a plane takes off, lands, or flies in darkness or in fog.

I knew and greatly admired this dashing and creative aviator. I became especially aware of his accomplishments back in the 1920s when assigned to the "flying torpedo" project at old McCook Field in Dayton, Ohio. My job then was to make a comprehensive study of past experiments with automatic controls in order to project the future. It became evident at once that, beginning with Lawrence Sperry's invention of the automatic stabilizer as early as 1914, his was a peerless contribution to the kind of precise control of aircraft that we take for granted today.

Lawrence's work was outstanding. He invented such basic instruments as the automatic pilot, the turn indicator, the bank indicator, and an improved magnetic compass, and he insisted on demonstrating them himself. Every pilot today should recognize his signal contributions to air safety and be grateful for them.

Certainly I was, especially on two occasions. The first was on September 24, 1929, when I had the honor of making the first blind flight in history. It was at Mitchel Field, Long Island, New York. My Consolidated training plane was equipped with instruments that were then something of a novelty: a sensitive altimeter, a directional gyro, a gyro turn indicator, a rate-of-climb indicator, and a radio direction finder. All these instruments had been conceived, invented, or developed by Lawrence Sperry. With the help of his brother Elmer and the instruments I was ready for a new kind of pioneering flight. For the little plane was also equipped with a hood which was closed over the cockpit before takeoff. It was not possible to see outside the plane. It was rather an eerie feeling to take off in broad daylight with only the pale light of the instrument panel illuminating the inside of the plane; then to climb steadily, make a wide turn, fly downwind, then turn again and descend slowly on a long slanting approach, absolutely blind, using only the radio direction finder and other flight instruments. I—or rather my plane and its instrumentation—felt cautiously for the ground as we let down gingerly and finally touched down. Preston Bassett, describing this demonstration in his book *Long Island, Cradle of Aviation,* called this "a long moment" for both the pilot and the observer. I remember the thrill and the relief as those wheels touched the ground and I rolled to a stop. Within a year of this "long moment," blind flying instruments were installed in all U.S. air-mail planes. A new era in aviation safety had begun.

The second occasion when I felt particularly indebted to these sophisticated Sperry instruments was in 1942, one of the darkest moments in World War II, when we made our raid in B-25s over Tokyo and proceeded to China, arriving at night in very bad weather.

Lawrence was a mechanical genius, the son of a genius, Elmer Ambrose Sperry, whom I was also privileged to know. Father and son were much alike and often in conflict. The elder Sperry loved and admired his son but tried to restrain his impetuousness, to keep him on the ground. It was like trying to ground an eagle. Lawrence was offered a comfortable desk job in the paternal business, the Sperry Gyroscope Company. He turned it down. He was mettlesome and he wanted to make it on his own—in the air.

Quite apart from his inventive genius, Lawrence Sperry had a passion for flying that was contagious. Although airplanes were undeveloped in those days, sometimes even dangerous, he was convinced that they would be the chief mode of transport in the future, and his little Sperry Messenger did more to popularize flying than any other plane I can think of until Lindbergh's *Spirit of St. Louis.*

Lawrence's personality played an important role in promoting aviation, for he was handsome, absolutely fearless, and a favorite with newspaper reporters. He was full of what his father called, with some trepidation, "dash and bang." In other words, a bit on the wild side.

"Just as agreeably crazy as an aviator should be," said one of his British colleagues who knew him in 1922, when Lawrence was campaigning in his Messenger plane for both the Liberal and Conservative parties. This was to prove that aviation was above politics.

Lawrence was very impatient with ponderous bureaucrats in both the political and military establishments. This caused additional friction, I remember, between Lawrence and his father, who frequently felt constrained to announce that the opinions of Lawrence B. Sperry were quite independent of those of the Sperry Gyroscope Company. But Lawrence's independence won him the respect and affection of fellow mavericks like Eddie Rickenbacker and Billy Mitchell.

Another great figure in aviation who admired Lawrence was the late Grover Loening. "Lawrence Sperry was a lovable, delightful character," he wrote. "One of the most outstanding pioneering contributors to the aviation progress of the world, he had every bone in his body broken at least twice. There are countless legends about this eccentric and brilliant flyer. He was one of the first to make parachute jumps for fun! And it was no joke in those days. Once out in Dayton . . ."

But I have no wish to steal the author's thunder. This book is an accurate account of Lawrence Sperry's contribution to aviation. More than that, it resurrects a personality from a welter of documents in the Library of Congress, the Smithsonian Air and Space Museum, and the U.S. Patent Office. Since that personality vibrates in the memory of men still alive, myself among them, it is good to have the free spirit of Lawrence Sperry restored "in his habit as he lived."

—JAMES H. (JIMMY) DOOLITTLE

Greatness of name in the father oft times
overwhelms the son; they stand too near one
another. The shadow kills the growth.

—BEN JONSON

Lawrence Sperry, known to his fellow aviators
as "Gyro," refused to be killed by a shadow.

GYRO!

1

TO JUMP or not to jump: that was one of the most hotly debated questions of 1918. Safety for aviators depended on parachutes. German airmen had them; Americans did not. The results were painfully apparent in the casualty figures. When the Germans lost a plane, they didn't lose a pilot.

Some famous people were involved in the controversy—Thomas Alva Edison and Elmer Ambrose Sperry of the U.S. Naval Consulting Board—and some younger men who would become famous: Eddie Rickenbacker, Billy Mitchell, and Lawrence "Gyro" Sperry.

The last three had much in common. They were friends and they were fearless, not only of physical danger but of authority, especially if it got in the way of aviation progress. When mavericks attack the Establishment they usually accuse it of complacency at best, criminal negligence at worst. Rickenbacker, Mitchell, and Lawrence Sperry all used this latter term in their impatience with what Lawrence called "marble heads in marble halls."

Billy Mitchell's impatience was the most notorious. He was court-martialed for insubordination after declaring that "air accidents are the direct results of incompetency, criminal negligence, and the almost treasonable administration of U.S. national defense and aviation policies."

Eddie Rickenbacker's outburst was relatively restrained. He had been taken to France in 1917 as General Pershing's chauffeur. It was too sedate a job for him. He transferred to the air service, commanded the 94th Aero Pursuit Squadron, and personally shot down twenty-six enemy planes in dog fights over the western front. He gallantly saluted the German airmen as they bailed out safely with their parachutes, and he lambasted the U.S. high command for their "absolutely criminal failure" to provide American pilots with them.

A major, comfortably ensconced behind a desk in the Paris headquarters of the U.S. Air Service, said that the service did not "believe" in parachutes. "If you pilots had parachutes," he told Rickenbacker coldly, "you'd use them on the slightest pretext, and the Air Service would lose planes that would otherwise be brought down safely."

"I got so mad," Rickenbacker recorded in his autobiography, "I started hollering at him. Other officers broke it up. It was a good thing I had a few ribbons on my chest. Otherwise I would have been court martialled."

Meanwhile, back on Long Island, Lt. Lawrence Sperry, the first civilian to be commissioned in the Naval Aviation Flying Corps, was busy inventing the first American seat-pack parachute and echoing Billy and Eddie's blasts at the top brass.

"You're damnably selfish in permitting all these accidents to happen," he wrote to Admiral Gleaves of the Naval Flying Service. "I would like to see *you* court-martialled for criminal negligence."

No matter how justified by the appalling rate of air accidents, this was not the tone in which a lieutenant was expected to address an admiral. It was an embarrassment to his father, Elmer Ambrose Sperry of gyroscope fame, even more embarrassing since the senior Sperry was a member of the Naval Consulting Board, and most embarrassing in September of 1918 for a number of interlocking reasons.

The Naval Consulting Board had ordered a series of parachute tests at McCook Field as part of the Dayton Air Show. Lawrence had been invited to submit his newly invented parachute for demonstration but had been grounded by the Navy after an accident with the aerial torpedo and specifically and officially notified by his father that he was not to demonstrate the parachute himself. The Navy had plenty of competent pilots for that.

Lawrence was determined to demonstrate it himself. It was a matter of honor and policy with him; he had demonstrated all his inventions, from the automatic stabilizer to the aerial torpedo.

Father Sperry was equally determined that Lawrence should knuckle under for once and obey official orders.

The clash of wills between father and son, "Daedalus and Icarus," as the newspapers called them, involved a third party, Winifred Allen Sperry, the movie star, Lawrence's bride. They had been married seven months, the first bride and groom to have an "aerial honeymoon." Winifred did not want Lawrence to risk his life jumping from planes. But she was aware of an equal risk in the powerful and domineering personality of her illustrious father-in-law. In any conflict between father and son she would have to be on her husband's side.

The conflict had reached its climax at the Dayton Air Show of September 1918. Lawrence had refused to relinquish his parachute to the Naval Consulting Board for demonstration. In a final drastic step to bring his son to heel, Father Sperry, with the connivance of such VIPs as Edison, C. F. Kettering, and Colonel Deeds, had bribed two McCook Field mechanics to seize and hide the parachute. And now, in the words of an aviation journalist, "they sat back at the Dayton Air Show with sly smiles."

They did not anticipate the power of a woman's smile; but let us pause for a moment to place the Dayton Air Show in the perspective of history. It was a moment of great optimism. The most popular philosopher of the day, Emile Coué, had convinced Americans that physical, moral, and spiritual improvement could be attained by daily repetition of the phrase "Day by day in every way I am getting better and better."

How simple it was! How true! Gurus and mantras were not required in those days.

Coué, a French chemist turned philosopher, admired "American know-how." "The French," he said, "like to argue about principle. The American mind, on the other hand, puts the principle to work and discovers its practical adaptability to everyday life. That's why this young nation is a success, the most gigantic success story in history."

In France, General Pershing was proving the point. Having found Allied troops bogged down in the trenches while the high command argued about the pros and cons of trench warfare, he rejected the principle of trench warfare completely and mobilized 700,000 American doughboys in the great September 1918 offensive against the German redoubts of Saint-Mihiel and the Argonne Forest.

So at the Dayton Air Show thousands of spectators were shading their eyes against the September sun with newspapers proclaiming Pershing's success in jubilant headlines:

HUN ON THE RUN

HAD YOUR FILL,
KAISER BILL?

The *Dayton Journal Herald* and *Daily News* vaunted the war effort of their city, "cradle of American aviation, the most airminded metropolis in Christendom." Special features were devoted to McCook Field, "where Dayton mechanical genius has assembled the De Havilland planes to hurl death and destruction on the Hun, where Dayton pilots have driven them through the clouds on their maiden trips, where Dayton has trained 5,000 fliers to defend democracy."

Now those De Havilland planes darkened the September sky as they flew above the grandstands in a grand parade of aerial power. Great things happened, wonderful aspirations were realized. The crowd craned their necks, strained their eyes as Maj. R. W. Schroeder flew his Bristol 1300 Hispano plane so high that it vanished from sight, and there was a collective gasp of admiration when the loudspeakers announced that he had set a new world altitude record: an incredible 28,899 feet.

Even more exciting, because it could be seen at close quarters, was the demonstration of the recently invented Nelson gun control. A target was set up at one end of the field, and Lt. John Reddy zoomed down in his Lepere Liberty 400 plane and scored a dozen bull's eyes with a burst of machine-gun fire, perfectly synchronized through the spinning propeller. The crowd swarmed out onto the field to verify the perforated target, evidence of a perfect demonstration of this amazing invention.

The subsequent test flights of Charles Kettering's pilotless "Bug" with its preset controls were an anticlimax, though, especially to airplane buffs who knew about Lawrence Sperry's prior invention of the aerial torpedo, prototype of the guided missile.

What the crowd was waiting for was Lawrence himself, the most dashing aviator of the day, and the grand climax of the show: a parachute jump to demonstrate his most recent invention: the first all-American pack chute. Nobody at McCook Field, except for Lawrence and his entourage, knew about the private battle between Lawrence and the Naval Consulting Board. And no one could have imagined the family drama of the hidden parachute.

Six feet two inches tall, blue-eyed and blond, Lawrence was easily identifiable in his leather flying jacket. Usually smiling, today he looked serious, doubtless anticipating the perils of the coming demonstration. He sat in the box reserved for VIPs with his diminutive wife, Winifred Allen. The crowd recognized her too. Her last picture, *For Valour,* a stirring saga of the war, was a hit in Dayton. She had given up her career to marry Lawrence, "much to the disappointment," wrote a society reporter, "of many a New York debutante who had set her cap for Lawrence Sperry, a handsome figure who might have stepped from the pages of a novel. But debutantes were not very keen on flying, and Winifred Allen, a petite and beautiful girl, loved to fly."

In the box with Winifred and Lawrence were two other young women, smartly turned out like Winifred in the latest New York fall fashion: long, fur-trimmed suede coats that showed three buttons of their boots, and fur-trimmed cloche hats that hid the forehead and emphasized the eyes in a rather daring way. They all had the glamorous look of career women from New York, capital of art, fashion, and film. May Allen, Winifred's half sister, was an actress. "Too beautiful for her own good," she had once made headlines by running away from a fashionable eastern boarding school with the scion of a prominent New England family. The third young woman in the box was Betty Turner. She was an artist; she had been a classmate of Winifred's at the Art Students League in New York and now designed exotic jewelry. Exotic was the word for both these creatures. They both approved of high-flying Lawrence and Winifred's marriage to him, but they took a dim view of her giving up her career.

While the Kettering "Bugs" shuttled back and forth above the field, movie-struck girls and air-minded boys asked Lawrence and Winifred to sign their programs. They obliged, Winifred resolutely signing her married name, Winifred Allen Sperry.

Behind Lawrence and his bevy of women sat four of the most brilliant and influential men in the United States. Deaf as a stone, deep as the sea, Ohio's own Thomas Alva Edison was the most famous inventor in the world. A living legend, this silver-haired, radiantly intelligent man of seventy-one had had only three months of formal education in a public school, where the teacher dismissed him as a dunce. He remained the despair of intellectuals, since he was always saying corny things such as "Genius is one percent inspiration and ninety-nine percent perspiration."

Next to him sat another genius, fifty-eight-year-old Elmer A. Sperry, Lawrence's father, a handsome, dapper man with more than a thousand patents to his credit, including the gyroscopic devices that had leveled the seven seas and brought him fame and fortune. Next to him sat Charles F. "Boss" Kettering, forty-two. He had made *his* fame and fortune by inventing the self-starter and selling it, along with his services, to General Motors. Next to Boss Kettering sat Dayton's most prominent citizen, Col. Edward A. Deeds, head of the National Cash Register Company, a director of forty-eight other companies, organizer of the Pratt & Whitney Aircraft Corporation, czar of the Cuban sugar industry, and chief of Aircraft Procurement for the U.S. Army.

It was these last three powerful figures, with Edison as a silent witness, who had formed a coalition against Lawrence, hidden his parachute in locker 13 of hangar 13 at McCook Field, and were now sitting back with their "sly smiles."

Father Sperry had his reasons, dictated by love and anxiety, reinforced by a will that was used to having its way. Lawrence had been having accidents since the age of seventeen. The last one had almost been fatal. He had already made his mark in aviation. Now that he was twenty-six, and married to "a dear little wife," it was time for him to settle down and stop risking his fool neck. The Navy had been quite right to ground him. His services as an inventor and a teacher were far more important than continuing his "mad stunts." How stubborn he was, refusing to hand over the parachute to the properly constituted authorities! Defiance like that was not to be condoned. Kettering and Deeds agreed with Father Sperry, though it was regrettable to be obliged to go to such extremes to curb Lawrence's ungovernable will. But what was Edison up to? Father Sperry wondered.

Thomas Alva Edison, who was attracted to youth and especially young women until the day of his death at eighty-four in 1931, had risen from his seat and joined Lawrence and Winifred in the front row of the box.

Quite apart from Winifred's good looks ("One of the prettiest actresses I ever directed," said Allan Dwan), she had, as a silent film actress, an attribute that greatly appealed to Edison, who had been stone deaf for many years. She had perfect diction. He had read her pretty lips on the silver screen that he himself had invented. Now it was a pleasure to read them in reality under the warm rays of the September sun.

"I am interested in your invention," Edison told Lawrence. "One of my first experiments was with flying. I was eleven years old. I had read that balloons fly because they are filled with gas. I persuaded a chum of mine to take a triple dose of Seidlitz powders. I was sure that as soon as that boy's stomach filled with gas, he would start flying."

"What happened?" said Winifred, articulating each syllable and turning the full radiance of her brown eyes on this marvelous old man's beautiful face.

"Well," Edison said, "his stomach filled with gas, all right, but instead of rising from the ground he just lay down on it. It was a great disappointment. Tell me about your parachute," he said to Lawrence. "Is it foolproof?"

Lawrence nodded his head.

"Ab-so-lute-ly fool-proof," Winifred said, carefully enunciating each syllable as she did in the movies. She stood about five feet tall in her boots between these two giants, interpreting Lawrence's remarks for Edison's delighted eyes.

She told him that Lawrence had already tested the parachute by jumping from the roof of their house on Long Island. She explained that the pack parachute had been designed to stream out only after the aviator had fallen beyond reach of the slipstream that could tangle him up in the plane's tail. He had also included a foolproof safety belt. "One object of the invention," she said, quoting directly from Lawrence's patent application, "is to provide a safety belt which may be easily put on and which the aviator cannot fall out of."

She laughed, thinking of Lawrence's bluestocking sister, Helen. She had objected to Lawrence's ending a sentence with a preposition.

Thomas Alva Edison was enchanted by the configurations of that laugh. His blue eyes shone with delight in this young person's presence. Winifred knew how to lead an audience on, even a distinguished one like this.

Now she gave Edison a melting, adoring look, and, without uttering a sound, her lips formed the syllables of an essential question: "Where have they hid-den Law-rence's pa-ra-chute?"

Down came Edison's silver head, brilliant as the moon, and he whispered in her ear, "Hangar thirteen. Locker thirteen."

Down came Lawrence's blond head, and she whispered in his ear, "It's in hangar thirteen, locker thirteen."

Lawrence gazed up at the blue sky. Now all he needed was a plane. The Naval Consulting Board had been powerful enough to deny him the use of a U.S. Navy plane, but Lawrence also held a commission in the U.S. Army Aviation Reserve, having passed their test in 1916 by flying from Governors Island to Mineola. Lawrence also had the help of a close collaborator and friend, McCook Field's ace test pilot, Lt. John Reddy of the U.S. Air Service, who had just given a sensational demonstration of the Nelson gun control. Lawrence had told John Reddy about his woes with Father Sperry and the Naval Consulting Board, and Reddy had promised to check with him during the course of the afternoon in case the parachute turned up.

Reddy was just Lawrence's age, twenty-six. Like Billy Mitchell, Jimmy Doolittle, and "Gyro" himself, he was ready for any adventure that would advance the cause of aviation, and he was only too eager to outwit the old guard.

Now just as Father Sperry was congratulating himself on how well Lawrence had accepted his disappointment, John Reddy came taxiing up to the dignitaries' box in his little twin-cockpit Lepere Liberty.

"Gyro, how about a little ride?" he called to Lawrence.

"Lawrence has been grounded, placed on inactive status by the United States Navy," said Elmer A. Sperry to Lt. John Reddy.

"Sir," Reddy replied, "this is a United States Army plane, and Lawrence is fully licensed to fly it. Besides," he added, "he's only going as a passenger."

"And only partway," said Lawrence under his breath.

With that he kissed his wife, executed a graceful high jump from the grandstand, vaulted into the rear cockpit of Reddy's plane, donned his leather helmet and goggles, and waved to the enchanted crowd. They gave him a standing ovation. Only Reddy heard the magic formula: "Hangar thirteen. Locker thirteen."

Reddy knew McCook Field like a map. He made a beeline across the tarmac.

Father Sperry descended to the first row of the box and put a protective arm around his tiny daughter-in-law, while Edison stood there silent as the sphinx with an inscrutable smile on his face.

"Don't worry, Winnie," Father Sperry said. "Lawrence is not such a fool as to jump *without* a parachute."

"Oh, but he has done that," Winifred said coyly. "It's to test his reactions in the unlikely event that the parachute doesn't work."

Father Sperry looked perplexed, alarmed.

"Lawrence has jumped without a parachute?"

"Oh, yes," said Winifred. "From the roof of the house."

On the other side of the field John Reddy had taxied to a stop in front of hangar 13. The two airmen got out of the plane. As they entered the hangar they heard the loudspeaker squawking out the news:

"Ladies and gentlemen, your attention please. We regret to announce that the demonstration of the Lawrence Sperry pack parachute and seat belt, patent application serial number 235,188, scheduled at this time, has been canceled due to circumstances beyond our control on orders of the United States Naval Consulting Board."

The announcement, Lawrence was pleased to note, was greeted by a collective groan of dismay followed by a chorus of boos and catcalls.

"There it is," John Reddy said, indicating locker 13 and handing Lawrence a crowbar. "I work here," he added. "You'll have to take the responsibility of damaging government property."

Lawrence pried the door open and put his arms around the parachute, neatly folded in its bag. Then he and Reddy ran out of the hangar.

"Take a message to the announcer," Lawrence said to a mechanic, as he and Reddy climbed back into the plane. "Say that the demonstration *will* take place, that we're already in the air and ready to jump."

"The smiles of Mr. Sperry, Mr. Kettering, and Mr. Deeds froze in surprise a few minutes later," an eyewitness journalist reported, when the loudspeakers announced: "Correction, ladies and gentlemen. Lawrence Sperry is in the air and about to jump."

The crowd roared.

"There he is!" they shouted as the plane flew over, low enough so that they could see Lawrence waving and return his wave before pilot Reddy banked and began a steep climb. Winifred Sperry waved. Thomas Alva Edison waved. The rest of the present contingent of the Naval Consulting Board looked at one another in consternation.

Four thousand feet up in the air, Lawrence was in his element, even though it was a novelty to be a passenger. He looked down at McCook Field, at the huge hangars, now as small as scale models, at the dark runways painted with great white arrows pointing the compass courses to Chicago and all the main cities on the airways radiating from Dayton. The crowd in the grandstands was now a tawny blur, matching the fields of ripe wheat in the valley of the Miami River. He saw the colossal earthen dam, like an Egyptian pyramid, defending the valley from the river that had flooded Dayton in 1913, and he rejoiced in the sight of the town itself, its geometric streets, the spires of its 132 churches, the forest of chimneys of this vibrant middle western "City of a Thousand Factories."

At 4,000 feet, Reddy and Lawrence felt the cold north wind buffeting their little plane. Looking down, they saw that this stiff breeze was corrugating the silver surface of the Miami and Still-water rivers, which converge at the northern confines of McCook Field.

"I'll head north a mile or so," Reddy shouted, but Lawrence had already locked his safety belt and looped the leg harness around his thighs. He was cradling the parachute in a small, neat rectangular bag in his arms. Now he checked the attachment of the safety belt to the strings of the parachute. Everything was in order. He was ready to jump.

He stepped out of the plane ("Like he was getting off a bus," Reddy reported later), dragging the parachute out of its bag as he did so. He plummeted down for five long seconds, then yanked the cord. The parachute started to stream out, safely clear of the slipstream. Then he felt the reassuring pull as it opened, a dome of white silk, defying gravity, braking his fall.

"It was a beautiful performance, the whole thing," Reddy recorded later. "Lawrence dragged that parachute out of the bag like pajamas out of a suitcase. Never saw anybody so calm. I circled and volplaned down a few hundred feet. There was Lawrence sitting in his harness like a baby in a swing, holding onto the shrouds with his hands, swinging his feet, and grinning through his goggles.

"But my worst fears about that north wind were coming true," he continued. "Lawrence was being wafted south beyond the field toward the Mad River. He was headed for downtown Dayton."

On the ground the crowd was delighted. "But where's he gonna land?" they wanted to know.

Having bailed out brilliantly—even Father Sperry shouted, "Bravo, boy!"—Lawrence was drifting south at alarming speed 2,000 feet above the field. In a few moments he had left McCook and his audience behind and was now almost out of sight.

As though hypnotized by that vanishing figure, Father Sperry, Winifred, May Allen, Betty Turner, Boss Kettering, and Colonel Deeds walked silently and speedily to the parking lot and piled into Deeds's seven-passenger custom-built Cadillac, fully equipped with Kettering's self-starter and automatic ignition.

"Where to?" said the chauffeur.

"Follow that man with the parachute," Colonel Deeds commanded.

"Boss," said the chauffeur, "I driven you a million places. First time you ask me to go up in the sky."

"There he is," Boss Kettering shouted.

Lawrence was now sailing over the spires of the city.

"Step on the gas," said Colonel Deeds.

Winifred and Father Sperry sat tight-lipped, as though holding their breath, uttering no sound. May held one of Winifred's hands and Betty held the other as the Cadillac sped through the outskirts of Dayton and into the city, down Perry Street, across First, past Ludlow, to Main.

Now there was no sign of Lawrence, but Main Street was suddenly thronged with people on foot, on bicycles, on motorcycles. The chauffeur scattered all before him by squeezing the tube of the brass horn. Suddenly they heard the wail of a siren, and the bright red, gleaming steam fire engine of the City of Dayton came clanging down Main Street.

"Follow that fire engine," Colonel Deeds ordered.

The chauffeur did what he could, but the streets of downtown Dayton were so jammed at this point that he was forced to stop. There was nothing to do but get out and follow the crowd on foot.

"Look," shouted Boss Kettering, "there he is, the crazy fool. It's the maddest thing I ever saw."

Lawrence's parachute had caught on the cornice of the Dayton Savings and Trust Company, eleven stories above the street, and there he dangled helplessly, sitting in his seat harness, as thousands of eyes looked upward, focusing on this unique apparition.

"Leave it to Lawrence to choose a place like that," said Colonel Deeds.

Headquarters of the U.S. Aeroplane Production Department and the Aircraft Experimental Depot, the Dayton Savings and Trust was also known as the Air Service Building, "a towering structure of modern design." Five hundred experts from Washington worked there, and every one of them was now leaning backwards out of the office windows staring at Lawrence and shouting advice: "Sit still! Don't move! Wait for the firemen!"

The firemen in their gleaming, burnished helmets now made their way through the mesmerized mob, carrying a huge round net. They moved it to the base of the building, and twelve men held it. Meanwhile the fire chief dispatched six men to the roof of the building to disentangle the parachute from the cornice.

"Don't move, stay where you are," he bellowed at Lawrence through a megaphone.

Lawrence had other ideas. He had been training at his home in Garden City for just such an emergency. He had nearly driven Winifred to distraction, jumping from the roof of the house, rolling himself into a ball like a Chinese acrobat on contact with the ground.

Now Winifred opened her mouth to implore him not to move. But, as in a nightmare, she tried to scream but could not utter a sound.

"What's the gosh-darned fool doing now?" Boss Kettering said.

It was obvious what Lawrence was doing. He had decided not to submit to the humiliation of being rescued by the Dayton Fire Department, and he was hauling himself up, hand over hand by the shrouds of the parachute, in an effort to reach the cornice.

"Atta boy! Go on Gyro!" the crowd shouted.

They sensed what he was doing, and they were delighted.

"Lawrence, please! Stay where you are," Winifred managed to shout, but it was a lone female voice unheard in the roar of the crowd.

"He's made it. He's done it," they shouted, as Lawrence reached the cornice and sat there with his legs dangling 150 feet above the street.

"All right. Just sit there," the fire chief bellowed through his megaphone.

Lawrence responded to this by standing up on the cornice.

It was a purely decorative cornice, one foot wide. Its architect had never conceived of it as a parachute hook.

Lawrence waved reassuringly to the crowd, which had fallen suddenly silent. Then he bent over and began to disentangle the shrouds and the yards of Japanese silk that were caught on the angle of the cornice.

Down in the street, Winifred began to talk very quickly and intensely to Betty and May, who were watching Lawrence with a kind of petrified fascination.

"He's perfectly safe, perfectly safe," Winifred kept insisting. "You see, Lawrence really believes in Dr. Coué's theory of *will* over imagination. Suppose that cornice is just a plank on the ground. We'd all be willing to walk on it, wouldn't we? But, when you put it up in the air, you *imagine* you're going to fall."

"Yes, that's right," said Betty.

"That's right," said May.

"So you see," Winifred went on, "it's imagination that makes us afraid."

"That's right, that's right," Betty and May agreed nervously.

"Now, to Lawrence," Winifred said, "that cornice might just as well be on the ground. He isn't afraid because he *wills* it that way."

"Good grief," said May, "look what he's doing now."

Lawrence had gotten the chute pretty well disentangled. A puff of the north wind had inflated a section of it. The shrouds were free of the cornice. The helmeted firemen appeared on the roof. They were lowering a ladder to the cornice.

Lawrence was having none of that. He flexed his knees. He sat down again on the cornice, grasping the shrouds of his parachute. He edged his leather bottom along that narrow shelf of stone until he was straddling the corner. The silk streamed out, the air rushed into the parachute, and he let it drag him off the cornice.

"Stand back, everybody," the fire chief yelled. "Get that net under him."

The twelve firemen holding the net moved into position. They flexed their knees, awaiting the impact of a hurtling body. But Lawrence floated down, light as a thistle under the canopy of his parachute. The firemen caught him in their net. He bounced up once, as though in slow motion, then settled into the net under billows of silk.

The crowd rushed forward and grabbed him.

"Be careful of my parachute," he said.

But they were already tearing it to shreds. The first successful pack parachute in America made a thousand souvenirs. Un-buckling Lawrence's safety belt, they pulled him out of the leg harness and lifted him to their shoulders. Lawrence leaned down and picked up Winifred and held her in his arms while the citizens of Dayton carried them around the Air Service Building in a spontaneous snake dance. Then they picked up Betty and May for good measure.

Father Sperry watched all this with mixed emotions. There was no question that Lawrence had dramatized his invention in a unique way. He had won his private battle against authority, scaring everyone who loved him half to death.

"Mr. Sperry nearly fainted," a journalist reported, "when he saw the wind carry his son's chute over the city, and he nearly fainted again when Lawrence landed on the cornice, and a third time when the parachute dragged him off. Ever after that he was apprehensive about opening telegrams."

"I think we all need a drink," Father Sperry said when the crowd finally released Lawrence and the three ladies. Since the invitation appeared to include ladies, May Allen and Betty Turner were amazed. Even in New York women did not drink in public. Ready for anything new, they followed the old man eagerly.

He led them all to Dayton's most elegant ice cream parlor.

"What'll it be?" he asked. "I'll have a double chocolate soda, two scoops."

Enthusiastic about everything he put his mind to, Elmer Sperry was an ardent prohibitionist. Sipping his chocolate soda through the cool straws, he looked at his son with a quizzical expression, a subtle combination of affection, new respect, lingering disapproval. Lawrence had got the better of him this time, and the old man loved a winner. Icarus had disobeyed Daedalus, flown too high—and survived.

Winifred held her husband's hand and watched her straw turn a translucent red as she sipped her raspberry soda. It was wonderful to be sitting there with Lawrence like a normal middle-class wife in the cool comfort and security of an ice cream parlor.

Her half sister, May, sat next to her.

"I see what you mean about life with Lawrence being more exciting than the movies," she said, "but I think I'll settle for a stockbroker."

2

WHAT WERE THE ORIGINS of this genius, this maverick, this agreeably crazy good lad, this cliff-hanging sensation?

Lawrence Burst Sperry, whose middle name bore an inevitable light baggage of puns, burst upon the world and vice versa on December 22, 1892, in Chicago. He was the third child of Elmer Ambrose Sperry and Zula Goodman Sperry.

The Sperrys were of old American Puritan stock; their forebears were with John Davenport at the founding of the New Haven Colony in 1638. They moved west to Cortland, New York, in the nineteenth century. There, on January 1, 1860, Stephen Sperry, "a sober and industrious farmer, not addicted to lude or nude company," married a young woman named Mary Burst.

Mary Burst was a schoolteacher who had gone to college, an extraordinary thing for a girl to do in those days. She was graduated from Rutgers with honors in math and science. She died on October 21, 1860, while giving birth to a male child who would become one of the world's great inventors, Elmer Ambrose Sperry. She left him a great astronomy chart and science books, copiously annotated in her own hand. These were symbols of a genetic heritage, for Elmer Sperry was a scientific genius, one of the prodigies of American progress, and so was his son Lawrence. Their accomplishments recall the sapient observation of Alexis de Tocqueville that "in democratic America, inventions which add to the amenities of life seem the most magnificent effort of human intelligence."

Two geniuses in the Sperry family led to a lot of conflict, but that was another spur to progress. Progress was a matter of fact as well as faith in 1892. It was a self-confident year in which to be born. The Sioux Indians, who had so perversely resisted the onrush of civilization, had just surrendered to General Miles at

Wounded Knee, and homesteaders were poised for the land rush into the Cherokee Strip of Oklahoma, now conveniently cleared of redskins.

Scribner's Magazine was advertising lots in Florida for two dollars a month.

In far-off Vienna an obscure young doctor named Sigmund Freud was publishing his first studies on hysteria, a morbid state which he ascribed to "undischarged emotional energy."

Nobody in Chicago could imagine such a condition. Nobody needed psychotherapy when Phenix Phosphate calmed the nerves for a nickel, Orangeine Pain Alleviator cured all internal ills for the same price, and Kickapoo Indian Salve, made from buffalo tallow, erased every external eruption from pimples to piles.

Chicago was discharging its collective emotional energy in the World's Columbian Exposition, celebrating the four hundredth anniversary of the discovery of America. Congress had chosen the Windy City for this honor, and New York reacted with the petulance of an older woman scorned. "Porkopolis is a completely uncivilized place," said Ward McAllister, who personally selected the four hundred members of "True New York Society."

Stung by such eastern barbs, the denizens of despised Porkopolis transformed 666 acres of lakefront swamps and sandbars into the greatest fair the world had ever seen. There were 150 neoclassical buildings built of staff, a white composite of plaster of Paris and jute. They looked like a Latin grammarian's re-creation of imperial Rome. A few more recent items had been added. Full-size replicas of the *Pinta*, the *Niña*, and the *Santa Maria*, for example, floated in a man-made lagoon of Lake Michigan. The ships had been sent to Chicago by the queen of Spain, much to the annoyance of Ward McAllister. "Socially speaking," he said, "Christopher Columbus was an absolute nobody."

Mrs. Potter Palmer, queen of Chicago society and chairman of the fair's Board of Lady Managers, was more than a match for McAllister. She bought Saint-Gaudens's nude statue of Diana, considered too indecent for New York's Madison Square Garden, and, denouncing "the prudish nonsense of New York philistines," boldly installed the naked goddess in the Women's Building, which exhibited women's work from primitive times to the

present day, even though this daring sculpture was the work of a
man.

The Manufactures and Liberal Arts Pavilion exceeded anything
New York could do. It seated 300,000 people. It was the largest
building in the world, four times the size of the Colosseum in
Rome.

"This is the grandest civic event in history," proclaimed Halsey
Ives, chief of the Exposition's Department of Fine Arts. "It is the
spectacle of the centuries. All the highest and best achievements
of modern civilization are here, all that is beautiful, artistic, and
inspiring; a vast and wonderful university of the arts and sciences,
discovery and invention designed to stimulate the youth of this
and future generations, a collection of works of genius, an assembly of master spirits of the world."

One of these master spirits was Lawrence Sperry's father.
Elmer Ambrose Sperry was a person of insatiable curiosity about
the physical world and what made it work, and he believed in
improving it. His eyebrows were permanently raised in an expression of pleasure and wonder at the world about him, especially this microcosm of the universe which was the World's Co-
lumbia Exposition. His contributions to it included the Sperry
Electric Streetcar and the Sperry Electric Motor Car with Electric Brake, which ran the amazing distance of one hundred miles
on a storage battery. They were two of the hits of the Exposition.
"See them and run them yourself," a broadside announced, and
E. A. Sperry was pleased to note that people were lined up to do
so.

As an independent inventor-entrepreneur, Father Sperry was
chief stockholder in his own Elmer A. Sperry Company. He had
already applied for seventy-three patents. One of them was for
the first arc lights, which he had developed at the age of nineteen. He had already attracted national attention by illuminating
the Chicago Board of Trade and the Tribune Building with brilliant coronas of these lights. Now, at the great Exposition, the
Sperry electric arc lights were perfected. Powered by Sperry dynamos, they "turned night into day"; that was the phrase on the
admiring lips of all observers. More precisely, the arc lights
created the magic atmosphere of moonlight so that the pavilions

of staff became a gleaming alabaster city with its towers and cupolas casting shadows on the silver ground.

It was in the glistening aura of these arc lamps that Lawrence Sperry had his first "major outing" at the age of four months and nine days. Such events were duly recorded then by American families in "Baby's Record" by Maud Humphrey, which had a page for the first tooth, the first laugh, the first creeping, the first step, the first word, and the first lock of hair; Lawrence's was as blond as flax.

It was May 1, 1893, the opening night of the Exposition. Father Sperry had decided that the importance of the event warranted the full participation of the Sperry clan. "Even if Lawrence doesn't remember it," he said, "he will always be able to say he was there."

So there he was in his mother's arms, his blue eyes shining like his father's under the silver cloak of night, and nobody dreaming that the impressions and sensations of a four-month-old child could have the slightest effect on his future development; that was an idea that was ahead of its time.

Father Sperry, sporting a full beard to make him look older than his thirty-three years, held the hands of the other Sperry siblings, Helen, who was five, and Edward, two.

How confident and united they all were, their eyes full of wonder at the sights they were seeing. The Sperrys on that night were like the ideal family in *McGuffey's Reader*, where Lawrence and fifty million other Americans would learn spelling combined with sentiment (though Lawrence would favor sentiment over spelling):

> We are all here!
> Father, Mother,
> Sister, Brother,
> All who hold each other dear.

It remained for a more sophisticated age to prefer "Jump, Jane, Jump," and for a more disturbed age to challenge the validity of the nuclear family. As for women's liberation, President Grover Cleveland had settled that question for the moment: "The positions to be assumed by man and woman in the working out of our civilization were assigned long ago by a higher intelligence than ours."

Zula Sperry would have said amen to that. As she stood there with her dark curls shining under the arc lamps, she was a living rebuke to the obsessive pretensions of less secure women. The Sperry marriage conformed precisely to the simple formula in Thomas E. Hill's *Manual of Social and Business Forms:* "The husband should be strong, brave and wise, the wife confident in his bravery, strength and wisdom." As for a lady's comportment, that was ordained by Mrs. John Sherwood's *Manners and Social Usages:* "One should avoid even the remotest appearance of evil."

Born into a substantial Baptist family with the Bunyanesque name of Goodman, Zula must have been one of the least evil women who ever lived. People always assumed that Zula was a biblical name, indicating a fundamentalist familiarity with Scripture, but there is no Zula in the Bible, and nobody in the Sperry family could say where this strange name came from. It gave a unique quality to her, the only Zula ever known or heard of.

Elmer Sperry had first seen her playing the organ in the First Baptist Church of Chicago. He was so smitten that he went back to see her as Priscilla Alden in the church drama group's production of *The Courtship of Miles Standish.* She had a beautiful voice, clear and calm and soothing, and when she said, "Why don't you speak for yourself, John?" Elmer Sperry felt that these words were being addressed to him. They were engaged for a year, "a normal, decent interval" in those days, and married on June 28, 1887.

Zula had studied piano at Florenz Ziegfeld's Chicago Academy of Music, never dreaming that her teacher would create the notorious Ziegfeld Follies of New York. Zula had the catholic taste of a woman who really loved music. Her repertoire ranged from Schumann and Chopin to "Pale Hands I Loved Beside the Shalimar." Her favorite hymn was "Rock of Ages," but she also sang "After the Ball Is Over" and all the other popular songs that were published in the *Chicago Magazine of Fashion, Music and Home Reading,* which also told how to festoon the upright piano that was a fixture of every cultivated parlor of the Middle West. She was an accomplished pianist, a regular performer at the concerts of the Schumann Club. When Adelina Patti came to Chicago and her accompanist fell sick, Miss Zula Goodman was asked if she could fill in. She could and she did. Between Madame Patti's two groups of songs, she performed with appropriate dark fire the Prelude in C Sharp Minor of Rachmaninoff, a twenty-one-year-old virtuoso whose work would be banned forty years later in his native Russia as being "decadent, middle class, and especially dangerous on the musical front in the class war."

Such nonsense could not even be imagined by Father and Mother Sperry as they piloted their brood through the marvels of the Columbian Exposition. Zula stood in rapture before the clavichord of Bach and the original piano of Beethoven, while Lawrence fell asleep and Helen tugged at her mother's arm, pulling her in the direction of the Midway. Making a mental promise to return to the fair to hear Paderewski, Melba, and Emma Calvé's fiery rendition of *Carmen,* Zula yielded to the imperious pressures of a five-year-old daughter.

The Midway was a jumble of mosques, pagodas, Hawaiian grass shacks, and a Louis Tiffany confection called "a modern Byzantine Chapel." There was also a "Persian harem" and there were dancing girls from Brazil, Samoa, and other exotic places, luring the customers into a show called the Congress of International Beauty. The most sensational attraction was Little Egypt, who was said to rotate her belly amid swirls of chiffon that occasionally revealed her navel.

"No, Helen, we are not going in *there!*"

The Sperry family also eschewed "The Limit of the Marvelous": Miss Victorina, who swallowed an electric light that shone through her body, "making her flesh translucent to the astounded beholders."

"That," said Father Sperry, "is not the proper use of electricity."

The proper use was to be seen in the Hall of Electricity. Among the items on display were Sperry motors, Sperry dynamos, and Sperry electric mining machinery: an eclectric coal "puncher" that was a hundred times more powerful than a man with a pick, and an electric "mule," a squat, powerful locomotive that hauled the coal out of the mines.

The Ferris wheel was also acceptable as an appropriate wonder

of the electric age. Invented by G. W. Gale Ferris and illuminated with 2,500 lights supplied by the Sperry Electric Company,
it was a marvel of mechnical engineering. Nearly three hundred
feet high, the giant wheel carried thirty-six cars, each of which
could hold sixty persons. It was rather expensive, five cents per
ride, but Lawrence rode free as a babe in arms, and it was worth
it, not only for the vertiginous view of the white city reflected in
the mirror of the lake but also for the squeals of delight emitted
by Lawrence as the wheel swung the riders up to the dizzy summit of its trajectory. Then there was a frightening moment as the
car dropped a few feet and seemed to be dangling in the air. It
gave Zula and Helen an uneasy feeling in the pit of the stomach,
but Lawrence shrieked with joy and then cooed and made other
contented sounds that were duly recorded as "Baby's First
Laugh."

When the ride was over he began to bawl. He seemed to be
pointing at the Ferris wheel as he was carried away, and he
bawled and squalled and howled and would not be consoled until
Father Sperry gave in and they took another ride. "After all," he
reasoned, "this fair *is* the event of the century."

Lawrence's crying quickly gave way to more screams of joy as
the wheel swung the Sperrys once more up to the heights, and he
cried again when they came down, but didn't get away with it a
second time. Enough was enough. But now there was a more
urgent note in his bawling, a sustained, relentless tone of rage.
He was hungry. It was time to go home. Nobody nursed a baby in
public in 1893.

Helen, whose appetite for sensation had been whetted by the
Ferris wheel, wanted to shoot the chutes with scores of happily
screaming people who were sliding down a slope in gondola-sleds
that hit the water with a grand climactic splash.

But Lawrence would not stop crying. He was imposing his will
on the whole family.

"Helen, dear," said Zula gently, "stop pestering. You can see
that we must go home at once and feed the baby."

Eighty years after the fair Helen Sperry Lea remembered the
disappointment of not shooting the chutes. She loved her
brother, but this was typical: she was never able to control him.

In 1893 her trials as the older sister of two boys in a male-dominated family were just beginning. They would be exacerbated the following year by the birth of a third boy. This one, Elmer A. Sperry, Jr., was to become Lawrence's aider and abettor in adolescent experiments that would recall those of their father, who as a youth in Cortland, New York, once set fire to the front porch of his home while testing the powers of benzene vapors.

Lawrence's experiments would tend toward aerodynamics and defiance of the law of gravity. Posthumous psychoanalysis of Lawrence (he would never have dreamed of such a thing during his lifetime) has suggested that the vertiginous delights of the Ferris wheel gave him a lifelong zest for height and danger. Analysts have also stated that the brilliant panoply of Father Sperry's inventions at the fair symbolized what Lawrence would compulsively try to emulate as he grew up. All this must remain in the fascinating realm of speculation.

What is clear is that Helen and Zula Sperry had to cope with two geniuses in the family, Father Sperry and Lawrence. And when Elmer Jr. was born, Lawrence acquired a willing accomplice and devoted slave to assist him in experiments that kept the rest of the family in a state of constant apprehension.

3

LAWRENCE SPERRY'S FORMATIVE YEARS, from one to twelve, were spent in a spacious Victorian frame house at 855 Case Avenue in a "good" neighborhood in Cleveland, to which the Sperry clan migrated at the end of 1893. Cleveland was an "up and coming" industrial city. It boasted the first shopping center in America, a huge, four-tiered, glass-topped arcade housing 112 luxury shops. On Sunday, after worshipping God in the First Baptist Church and dining on good middle western roast beef, the Sperry family could revere Mammon without too much temptation (for the stores were closed on the Sabbath Day), window shopping along the four-hundred-foot esplanade while the sun streamed down through the prisms of glass and the grand music of the Cleveland Municipal Band reverberated under this commercial pleasure dome. The marches of John Philip Sousa and the *Light Cavalry Overture* of Franz von Suppé were enough to set the heart dancing with optimism on a Sunday afternoon.

In moving to Cleveland, Elmer A. Sperry had responded to the blandishments of eastern capitalists, among them Myron T. Herrick, who became ambassador to France. The eastern capitalists had set up an organization called the Sperry Syndicate of Cleveland. They were impressed by Elmer Sperry's "uncanny knack for being in the right place at the right time with the right invention." While leaving him free to invest the profits of "one queer dream in the next queer dream," they offered him $5,000 a year as a consulting engineer to help them develop and sell the mining machinery and electric streetcar he had patented.

Five thousand dollars a year was a handsome fee in those days. Eggs were a penny apiece; sirloin steak, ten cents a pound. For a nickel, thanks to the Edison Moving Picture Machine, one could see motion pictures "so life-like, so true to nature that the audience could scarcely believe that what they saw was a picture and not reality."

Spectators ducked as railroad trains rushed toward them at full speed on the screen and gasped with admiration as Eugene Sandow, "the modern Hercules," flexed the biggest biceps ever seen. It was the beginning of grand popular entertainment, suitable for all the family. One was urged to bring the children, but a good Baptist family is apt to take a dim view of entertainment for its own sake, and it was more adventurous for the Sperry children to bounce over the cobblestones of Cleveland in their father's electric horseless carriage than to watch the flickering facsimiles of progress on the silver screen.

The Sperry family was proud of the elegant electric carriage that Father Sperry was perfecting for the Sperry Syndicate. He, the inventor, sat, immaculately dressed as though for church, at the "tiller" or control lever that he had designed himself. He steered the carriage by a lateral movement of the lever, increased the speed by depressing it, and applied the four-wheel brakes (which he was the first to invent) by pulling the handle up hard, as one would rein a horse.

Beside her husband on the front seat sat Zula, elegantly draped in a long, flowing veil and white linen duster. Behind their parents, in a cramped area that would eventually evolve into a back seat, stood the children, with Helen holding Lawrence and young Elmer in a viselike grip as they both struggled to lean out as far as possible to watch the revolving wheels.

The neighbors gathered to watch these excursions, and crowds materialized whenever there was a breakdown. These were fairly frequent, but the Sperry children, each clutching an emergency nickel, could always go home on the Sperry Electric Streetcar, which had won a gold medal for its ability to climb hills. The Sperry Syndicate appears to have cornered both public and private transportation in Cleveland.

Lawrence's formative years! In 1898, when he was six, his Sunday School teacher at the Euclid Avenue Baptist Church was a spare, wizen-faced, keen-eyed, fifty-nine-year-old man who inculcated moral precepts about investing one's talents and not hiding one's light under a bushel. His name was John D. Rockefeller.

He had just retired as chairman of the board of the Standard Oil Trust, which controlled nearly all the oil refining and distribution in America. Some of the older boys at Sunday School said he was the favorite lamb of the Good Shepherd, who had anointed his head with oil.

Having ruined all his rivals by price fixing in collusion with the railroads, John D. had been the chief target of the Sherman Anti-Trust Law of 1890, and he was now confounding critics of his ruthless practices by the unheard-of amplitude of his philanthropies. His "expiatory generosity," as subversive specialists called it, was not attenuated by a graduated income tax; it would be another fifteen years before the federal government got around to that source of internal revenue. Meanwhile John D. Rockefeller was the richest man in the United States, Cleveland's most famous citizen, and an exemplary Sunday School teacher. When he said, "Take therefore the talent from him, and give it unto him that hath ten. For verily I say unto you, unto him that hath shall be given, but unto him that hath not, shall be taken away even that which he hath," his listeners sat up and took notice.

Mellowing as he approached his seventh decade, he vowed that, with the aid of temperance and mild exercise, he would live to be a hundred (he missed this goal by only two years, dying in 1937 at the age of ninety-eight), and he stored up goodwill and respect by handing out shiny new dimes to people he deemed worthy, among them six-year-old Lawrence Burst Sperry.

Father Sperry thought John D. should invest some of these shiny new dimes in a shiny new Sperry Electric Motor Car. The great oil tycoon had never ridden in a horseless carriage and accepted Father Sperry's invitation. The whole family helped shine up the car for this occasion, and the "Waverly," as the Sperry Syndicate had romantically named the car, performed quite well, racing along at twelve miles an hour on the hills and curves of Cleveland's fashionable Shaker Heights.

"There will be millions of these horseless carriages," Father Sperry told Rockefeller as they rolled along. "They will be all over the place. Even women will drive them."

"What a ghastly prediction," Rockefeller replied, "almost blasphemous."

When Father Sperry offered the controls to his distinguished passenger, Rockefeller declined, not wishing to take responsibility for what might happen in this newfangled contraption.

After the ride, Rockefeller, always mindful of the oil interests, urged Father Sperry to cash in on his electric cars and experiment with gasoline. Sperry did experiment with an internal-combustion vehicle, but he hated the vibration and fumes. He was against noise and air pollution nearly a century ahead of his time. Besides, the two-cylinder gas-powered model he built caught fire and burned down one of his workshops in 1896. "That's what I got for being unfaithful to electricity," he said.

Shortly after the Rockefeller ride, Father Sperry took six of his electric horseless carriages to Paris for the International Exposition of 1899. The first American to drive an American car in the streets of Paris, he created a sensation with his Sperry storage battery that got one hundred miles per charge as against only thirty provided by the nearest European competitor.

He was also the first American to be arrested in Paris for reckless driving. In the enthusiasm of one of his demonstrations, he ran into a vegetable cart, was arrested during the ensuing uproar, and settled the matter out of court by offering to pay damages of fifty francs. "I tried to help the fellow pick up his onions and tomatoes," he told Zula later, "but he kept screaming, '*Ne touchez pas.*' I got the impression he didn't want me to touch them. They are a strange race, but they certainly have a beautiful city."

He described the moving sidewalks of the Exposition, the glass and iron palaces, the bridge built in honor of Czar Alexander III, the first bridge in Europe to have electric lights. He was delighted by the Eiffel Tower, the tallest structure in the world and still a novelty in Paris. A committee of three hundred French artists and writers were demanding its demolition, but Father Sperry anticipated posterity's approval of this structural masterpiece, as light as lace, as strong as steel.

Pleased with an order for 110 of his cars and the sale of the patent rights for France, Father Sperry came home to Cleveland like a returning hero. For Zula and Helen he brought plumed straw hats, the kind one sees in Renoir paintings. They were the rage of

Paris. Equipped with chin straps to keep them on in the wind, they were perfect for motoring.

For each of his boys, Father Sperry brought a model Eiffel Tower and gyroscopic toy tops that were popular in France. He was also the first to import a new word into the United States: the French with their genius for linguistic precision had called his electric car an *automobile*.

Lawrence, who was now seven, was entranced by this word. He and five-year-old Elmer kept shouting it over and over again until Helen thought she would scream.

"Here, write it down," she said. "See if you can spell it."

They couldn't, of course, though Lawrence was already going to school and painfully learning Spencerian penmanship by copying from the blackboard such homilies as "Deserve success and you shall command it."

This is why the word *automobile* made such a hit. It was a concrete term. He knew what it was. It was what his father made and took them riding in. Formal schooling and abstract argument were more or less irrelevant to Lawrence's aims.

It was much more interesting to build bridges and dig tunnels in the backyard. Lawrence built houses for all his pets, a menagerie of goats, guinea pigs, rabbits, and pigeons. He was fascinated by his fantail pigeons and the way they baffled the cat. The pigeons would strut around while the cat stalked them. Then, just as the cat sprang, the pigeons flew to the safety of the dovecote he had made them, while the earthbound cat lashed its tail in frustration. Lawrence patted his pigeons and felt their wings.

"I wish I could fly," he said.

"You'd better go over and get your goat," said Helen. "He's nibbling the wallpaper in the Harrisons' front hall. And be careful with that fire. I don't see the point of burning up potatoes in the backyard when mother is baking them in a perfectly good oven."

Helen's recollections of the house in Cleveland are vivid. "On the street side," she recalled, "it was perfectly respectable. Our front lawn was as well manicured as the neighbors'. But the backyard was something else. It was full of messy building operations, fearfully flimsy structures, tunnels, pits, deep boy-made gullies. Those boys walked on the fences, climbed the trees, and hung upside down from the highest branches. Lawrence was always the ringleader. He saw no reason why he shouldn't fly like the pigeons, and he and Elmer jumped down from the branches with open umbrellas to emulate the doves. *Some* experimental things went on in that backyard to which ladies were not admitted. Mother believed in letting the children express themselves. Nowadays such an understanding of the need of children to work out their schemes is called progressive education."

Lawrence was delighted with his model Eiffel Tower and gyroscopic top. These were objects he could feel and manipulate. They could also be juxtaposed in various ways.

One evening when he was supposed to be asleep (he had said his prayers and blessed everyone in the family and every goat and guinea pig and dove by name), his parents heard him cry out from his room. Zula put down the chemistry book she was reading aloud to Father Sperry, in accordance with a theory he had that the ear absorbed more knowledge than the eye. She got up and walked swiftly up the stairs. She opened the door of Lawrence's room, then called Father Sperry.

Lawrence was sitting on the floor, his blue eyes shining in the lamplight. He held the bronze Eiffel Tower in his right hand, and the gyroscopic top was spinning on its summit. Gently he raised the tower, then tilted it slowly from side to side. The glistening gyroscope remained spinning, balanced at the same fixed angle, no matter how he shifted the position of the tower.

"Daddy, look at this," the boy said. "Isn't this wonderful?"

"Yes, Lawrence," his father replied. "It *is* wonderful."

4

NEW YEAR'S DAY, 1900, found America in the grip of an intellectual controversy. Was this the beginning of the twentieth century, or merely the first day of the last year of the nineteenth? By January 1, 1901, the arguments had simmered down.

Father Time was shown on the editorial page of the *Cleveland Plain Dealer* bequeathing to the New Year such problems as the Boer War and the "Chinese Imbroglio." But there was no problem, the editor said, that could not be licked by science and modern progress.

The recently invented electric iron, vacuum cleaner, and typewriter were there to prove it. A girl using one of these machines could get ten dollars a week working only sixty hours. Now a woman's place was in the office as well as in the home, where the hours were never counted.

President McKinley had been elected to a second term on the issue of prosperity, for which the Republican party assumed full credit. We had beaten Spain, freed Cuba, and acquired Puerto Rico and the Philippines as the spoils of war. The United States had emerged as a world power.

The nation was shocked on September 14, 1901, when McKinley was assassinated by an anarchist in the Temple of Music at the Pan American Exposition in Buffalo, but prosperity did not stop and optimism never flagged.

"God has marked the American people as His chosen nation to regenerate the world," said Senator Albert Beveridge of Indiana. "We are trustees of the world's progress and guardians of its righteous peace." This senatorial confidence was echoed in the pulpits of the land. "Art, industry, invention, literature, learning and government are captives marching in Christ's triumphant procession," said the Reverend Dwight Hillis, one of Father

Sperry's favorite preachers. "Laws are becoming more just, rulers more humane, music sweeter, and books wiser." He was referring to such works as *Janice Meredith* by Paul Leicester Ford and *The Master Christian* by Marie Corelli, Queen Victoria's favorite novelist. Zula read it aloud to Father Sperry at night, and they shared the general optimism. As for dissenting voices, *Vogue* magazine disposed of them in short order: "Avant garde writers, Ibsen, Shaw, and Zola, are not fit to read."

Prosperity was not conducive to social criticism, and the turn of the century was a prosperous time. "If you didn't make money last year," said the *Cleveland Press*, "you're just a hopeless case."

The Sperrys had every reason to be hopeful. There were eight thousand registered automobiles in the country, and customers were clamoring for more. Elmer A. Sperry now had eighty patents to his credit, including lucrative recent ones on his storage batteries, motor vehicles, railway actuating devices, power gears, and an "apparatus for governing and controlling marine or other engines."

Theodore Roosevelt, succeeding the slain McKinley, vowed to maintain prosperity as he took the oath of office as America's twenty-sixth president. At forty-two, the rough-riding hero of San Juan Hill was the youngest president in our history. Some people, including Mark Hanna, who thought he had shelved Roosevelt in the vice-presidency, found this "cowboy" downright childish.

"You must always remember," a British diplomat said, "that the president is only six years old."

But the Sperrys were united in their support of T.R. "He is doing a whale of a job as president," they said.

Lawrence Burst Sperry, now nine, did not share in the general complacency. He was going to grade school in Cleveland, where he was already making a name for himself as an atrocious speller and where he was required to ponder such subjects as igloos: "Can an ice house keep an Eskimo warm?"

Lawrence was not interested in the comfort of the Eskimos, even less in English orthography. He seemed to be allergic to reading, except for one book that was not on the school reading list. This was *The American Boy's Handy Book* by Dan Beard, and it taught boys everything they really needed to know—such as how to make a boomerang: "Allow the wood to remain in scalding water until it is pliable enough to bend."

"Helen, look out!"

His sister had inadvertently interrupted the course of the finished product with her knee, thus preventing the boomerang from completing its return circuit to the launcher.

"Helen, I did not hit you with the boomerang. You got in its way."

"I do not intend to be confused with an Australian aborigine," said Helen, rubbing her damaged leg.

"Give me back my boomerang, Helen."

"Are you sorry, Lawrence, truly sorry?"

"Yes. I cross my heart. I didn't do it on purpose."

To make amends he offered to make something for her: a beeswax candle in a walnut boat; the recipe for this was also in the *Handy Book*. But Helen, who was now fourteen, declined, especially when Lawrence spoke of getting the beeswax directly from the bees. She settled for a safe-conduct pass to cross the no woman's land of the backyard. Boomerang practice became one of the experiments to which ladies were not admitted.

What a relief! Lawrence did not want to make a beeswax candle in a walnut boat. What really interested him was the most fascinating chapter in the *Handy Book*: "Maintaining Your Bicycle."

There it was—a picture of a beautiful two-wheeler with diagrams of all the component parts: the major sprocket and chain, the minor sprocket, ball bearings, coaster brakes, adjustable handlebars, cushion saddle, a headlight, a taillight, a battery, a bell, and a rack above the back wheel in case you wanted to pack a lunch or peddle newspapers.

"Father, I want a bicycle."

"Splendid idea. Have you investigated the price?"

"Yes, sir."

"And how much might that be?"

"Eleven dollars and ninety-five cents."

"And how do you propose to finance this project?"

"By peddling newspapers."

"Is that a pun, Lawrence?"

But Lawrence was in no mood for idle persiflage. He wanted that bicycle more than he had ever wanted anything in his life. He wanted to possess it, ride it, take it apart, and put it together again; it was an intense mental and physical yearning. He also wanted to make money. He had heard Zula reading that piece from the *Press* aloud to his father: "If you didn't make money last year, you're a hopeless case."

"I want to make money," the boy said. "I don't want to be a hopeless case."

"Have you already picked out the wheel you want?" Father Sperry asked.

He had indeed. It was the Elgin King. Very high grade, he assured his father, steel frame with nickel joints, rubber pedals, a mud guard, and a chain guard.

"The price includes a genuine leather tool bag," Lawrence said, "with a wrench, a pump, and a tube of special cement for quick tire repair."

"Eleven ninety-five is not exactly cheap," Father Sperry mused. "I don't see how you can raise a sum like that selling newspapers."

"I'll get a penny a week for every paper I deliver. I can get a *Press* route with two hundred customers on the East Side; Mr. Scripps said so. Dad, that is *two dollars* a week. *If* I have a bicycle," he added.

He must have pictured himself speeding down the geometric avenues of Cleveland—Euclid, Carnegie, Case, Superior—breezing along Memorial Shoreway on his Elgin King as the dawn came up over Lake Erie.

"But why a bicycle?" Father Sperry wanted to know. "You could pull your papers in your wagon."

"A *wagon?*" said Lawrence. "You couldn't handle two hundred customers with a wagon. Father, this is a machine age."

The old man could hardly have denied that.

"Mr. Rockefeller says a bicycle is a good investment," Lawrence said, pressing his advantage with the highest moral support. "He said so right in church last Sunday. Can I, Father? Please!"

"*May* I," Helen corrected. "You can but you *may* not."

A bicycle for Lawrence had become the subject of a family confab.

"Can he? Can he?" chimed in Elmer Jr. Lawrence had already promised to carry him around on the handlebars.

"*May* he? *May* he?" Helen corrected, but it sounded like an additional plea.

Father Sperry consented to look at the merchandise. Lawrence, a gangling nine-year-old, almost as tall as his father, escorted the dignified older man as swiftly as possible down Case Avenue in the direction of Ferguson's Bicycle Shop, with little Elmer running to keep up with them.

"Lawrence, how do you know you can even ride a velocipede?" Father Sperry asked.

"Oh, I can, Dad, I really can."

Mr. Ferguson, he confessed, had already given him several demonstrations. In fact, when they arrived at the bike shop, Mr. Ferguson showed no surprise. He was standing outside the shop, waiting with a shiny new Elgin King.

Lawrence mounted it with the greatest of ease and took off. He rode around the block and dismounted in a state of exhilaration, keeping his hands firmly on the handlebars. This splendid object was going to be his.

"It's like you are riding a gyroscope," he said. "You have got to keep those wheels spinning; then the bike can't fall over. Watch this, Dad; look at this, Elmer."

He took off again, raising his bottom above the saddle, pumping vigorously with his long, thin legs; then, coasting and leaning to the right, he swung around in a wide arc and back to his worshipful brother and melting father.

What could Father Sperry say? His son had just given a flawless demonstration of two basic gyroscopic forces: inertia and precession. Baptist principles against buying something before you had the means crumbled before the optimistic imperative of science and the irrational force of a father's love.

"I'll advance you the money," Father Sperry said. "You can pay me back out of your earnings."

It must have been the happiest moment in the first nine years of the life of Lawrence Burst Sperry.

The bike and the paper route were a great success. Lawrence woke before dawn every morning to the shattering clamor of an alarm clock and rode off, with Elmer on the handlebars, to pick up his two hundred papers, still smelling of ink from the press. He strapped them on the rack above the back wheel and parceled them out to Elmer, whom he had trained to roll up each paper and toss it up onto the Victorian verandas of Cleveland's East Side homes as they sped by. Many subscribers appreciated the added service of being awakened by the thud of the morning paper on the porch. Others objected. At the homes of these more effete clients, Lawrence stopped the Elgin King while Elmer scrambled down from the handlebars and placed the paper quietly on the doormat.

Lawrence paid Father Sperry back at the rate of a dollar a week. In three months the bicycle was his inalienable property. Elmer's reward for faithful service was free lessons, facilitated by thick wooden pedals which Lawrence made to accommodate his brother's shorter legs.

By the end of 1903, when Elmer was nine—"going on ten," he said—he had a bike of his own and had also inherited the paper route. For something happened in the closing days of that year that focused Lawrence's attention on more important things than selling papers. On December 18 of that year, just three days before Lawrence's eleventh birthday, there was a small item in the *Cleveland Press* with a curious dateline: Kitty Hawk, North Carolina. It said that Orville and Wilbur Wright had flown a distance of 284 yards in an airplane from a sand dune called Kill Devil Hill. It was the first free flight of a power-driven, heavier-than-air machine in history.

"The age of flight has come at last," Orville Wright proclaimed. This, the paper pointed out, was Mr. Wright's answer to the noted astronomer Simon Newcomb. As chief of the National Observatory in Washington, D.C., Newcomb had said just a few weeks earlier that "aerial flight is one of those problems with which man can never cope. Even if an aeroplane darted through the air at a speed of several hundred feet per second," he went on, "how is it ever going to stop, since only speed sustains it?"

The news item in the *Press* concluded with the information that the Wright Brothers had designed and built their airplane and its gasoline-powered motor in their bicycle repair shop in Dayton, Ohio.

A few days later, on his eleventh birthday, Lawrence announced to the family that he had decided to turn the newspaper route over to Elmer and open a bicycle repair shop in the basement.

5

THE SPACE AGE had dawned in that momentous fifty-nine-second flight, but, strangely enough, Father Sperry was not especially impressed. He tended to agree with one of his favorite authors, H. G. Wells, who predicted, optimistically but inaccurately, that "the exasperating stench of automobiles will soon be refined away, but I do not think it at all probable that aeronautics will ever come into play as a serious modification of transport."

Father Sperry's initial lack of enthusiasm for the airplane must have been colored by his commitment to transportation by land and sea. He had already made a small fortune with his electric automobiles, streetcars, mining machines, and railroad equipment. He would make a far larger one and acquire world fame with his application of gyroscopic principles to marine navigation, with the gyroscopic compass, which made the old, unreliable magnetic compasses obsolete; with the gyropilot to steer ships automatically; and with the giant gyroscopes that steadied the rolling of the great steel ships that would dominate ocean transport for another thirty years.

Back in 1903, eleven-year-old Lawrence was a more avant-garde dreamer than his forty-three-year-old father. The growing conservatism of success would make the Sperrys wary of flying as a career for one of their sons, and Lawrence's passion for flying would eventually be the source of great tension and great tenderness, of pride and despair, of comedy and tragedy in the Sperry family. In 1904 nobody could foresee the strength and depth of his determination. Lawrence was just one more American boy dreaming of flying and building airplanes in the backyard. He would get over it, his parents thought. In the meantime, they were happy for him to express himself.

Lawrence was the "dynamo" among the children, Father

Sperry said with accurate prescience, just as Edward, Lawrence's older brother, was "a born businessman." Edward, or "Ad," as he was called, was a handsome child who grew up to look like the man in the Arrow Collar ad. He did all the correct and conventional things, went to a good college (Cornell), joined one of the best fraternities, and, upon graduation, was perfectly content to work in a junior executive position in his father's corporation; he was an early prototype of the "company man." Lawrence was quite different. Alone among the Sperry children, he inherited that rare and mysterious capacity for creative and original conceptions commonly called genius, and the family agreed that this should be encouraged.

Up to a point, Helen might have added. She too was an exceptional person of great intelligence, strength of will, and character. She had to be, for destiny and the conventional mores of the day had cast her in the role of the elder sister of three boys and, perforce, the assistant to her remarkable mother in an essentially patriarchal family dominated by a benevolent male despot whose authority no one but Lawrence ever dared to question. Helen was conscious of a certain imbalance in this male-dominated household. She felt shut out of the "shop talk" of her father and brothers, but her memories of Cleveland and Lawrence are tinged with more tenderness than bitterness.

"In Cleveland," she recalled when she was in her eighties, "Lawrence already had the look of a dreamer. But he was the ringleader of the brothers, the first to climb the chimney or hang upside down from the apple tree. Then the others, Ad and Elmer, had to imitate him. They did it on purpose, all hanging from the eaves of the house, to terrify poor Aunt Mattie Burst when she came to visit.

" 'Zula, how can you let your children do such things?' Aunt Mattie said, and Mother smiled and calmly replied, 'After all, they *are* boys.' Mother was, in her own quiet way, the center of that household," Helen said. "When things got too tense, in too much of a turmoil, she would go to the piano. She still played beautifully. Brahms's 'Lullabye' had a most calming effect.

"But those boys ran in a pack, tearing through that house that had such a sedate exterior appearance. They would chase me and

corner me, and I would jump up onto my bed. That was sacro-
sanct. They knew then that I had had enough. It was time to stop.

"I had two major responsibilities, getting the brutes to Sunday
School and to dancing school. On Sundays they insisted on chewing gum, a revolting habit. They knew Mother and I detested it.
But one day I have to admit it paid off. Elmer dropped his collection money through a grate in the sidewalk on Euclid Avenue.
Lawrence promptly got a long stick, stuck a wad of gum on the
end, and got the money back. I had to admit it was clever.

"Of course, they loathed dancing school. Ad and Lawrence
spent all their time in the men's dressing room. They wouldn't
come out. I was mortified.

"That was an intense, busy household on Case Avenue. Mother
tried to organize it, but it was hard. Some things had to be
shrugged off. One thing was certain: our father's life took prece-
dence over things that happened to us, and Lawrence's life followed a similar pattern. When I finally married Bob Lea [in 1921]
I was happy to escape into the calm of *une vie ordinaire.*"

Zula, from all reports, never lost her cool. Self-sacrifice for her
was self-fulfillment, and both were unconscious and automatic.
But Father Sperry did not take her for granted. (Indeed, when
she died, he survived her for less than a hundred days; it was as
though, losing her, he lost the will to go on.) He was cognizant of
her extraordinary qualities and said so, notably in a letter written
to her from Europe in 1911:

> Dear Precious Heart,
>   I was never so entirely lonesome on leaving you in my life. I can
> hardly stand it.
>   Serenity and patience are the crown jewels in your coronet.
> Through all the strife of battle we all have you to lean upon. . . .
> You are the most necessary person in the world to a lot of rustlers
> and they resemble nothing short of a mob at times, yet you will
> notice it all centers about you.

When Father Sperry's expanding interests ordained that the
family should move to New York in 1905, it was typical of Zula to
say, "You go on ahead and find us a house; I will take care of all

this." "All this" consisted of the accretions of a decade of life in
Cleveland, ranging from Helen's piano and musical scores to Elmer's pony and electric trains. Everybody in the family had
books, even Lawrence, and though his library was the smallest,
because of his highly selective reading habits, his chisels, saws,
and drills, his pumps and wrenches and winches, his sprockets
and chains and Bunsen burners had to be packed as carefully as
the family china.

Somehow the earthly possessions of half a dozen Sperrys were
packed into cartons, crates, and trunks and transported to the
railroad station by horse and wagon; there were no moving vans
in those days. Then everything, including Elmer's pony,
Kimbo, for whom Lawrence had built a special traveling stall, was
stashed into two baggage cars.

Somehow the family got to the station on time, arriving grandly
in two Sperry Waverly electric cars. There were scores of friends
and neighbors on the platform of Union Station to see them off.
Helen and Zula were in the Pullman compartment, unpinning
their hats and looking forward to the delicious moment when they
could collapse at last with the latest copies of the *Ladies' Home
Journal* and the *Chicago Magazine of Fashion, Music and Home
Reading.* Everybody was waving on the platform. The conductors
were shouting, "All aboard." Zula, Edward, and Helen were blow-
ing kisses from the open window, when Zula, turning around,
suddenly noticed that something was missing.

"Helen, where are those boys?"

Lawrence and Elmer were not in the compartment. They were
not in the parlor car. They had disappeared.

"Try to find them, Helen. I shall notify the conductor. We can't
go without them."

Helen pinned her hat back on. She adjusted her smart traveling costume: long skirt and shirtwaist, high buttoned shoes, and
kid gloves as tight as a second skin. Descending from the Pullman, she walked through the crowd on the platform, craning her
neck, looking for those boys, as the conductor began his final in-
cantation: "All aboard for Youngstown, Beaver Falls, Pittsburgh,
Harrisburg, Johnstown, Reading, Philadelphia, Trenton, Perth
Amboy, Newark, Hoboken, New York, and points in between."

Where on earth were those boys? Perhaps they had gone to re-assure Kimbo, Helen thought; they think more of that pony than they do of their mother and sister.

But the baggage cars were locked, and there was no sign of the boys on the platform.

"Better get on board, Miss," a smiling black porter suggested.

"I'm looking for my brothers," Helen wailed. "Have you seen two boys, thirteen and fourteen?"

"Yes ma'am. Two well-dress young men. They was down by the locomotive while ago talkin' with the engineer."

Helen ran toward the head of the train. The boys were no-where in sight. They were not down *by* the locomotive. They were up in it, right in the cab with the engineer, who was show-ing them how the throttle let steam into the cylinders.

"Lawrence, Elmer, come down here immediately. The train is leaving."

"But we're *on* the train," said Lawrence gaily. "Tell Mother not to worry. We're going to ride up here."

"No, you are not," said Helen firmly. "Come down this in-stant."

To her relief, the engineer backed her up. He was not permit-ted to have passengers in his cab during a trip. He descended with the two boys and squatted down to show them the pilot wheels and driving wheels. As he was explaining how the pistons make the wheels turn, Helen grabbed each of her brothers by the hand.

"I do not like to interrupt this fascinating lesson, boys, but *the train is leaving!*"

"Aw, Helen, how can the train leave without the engineer?"

The engineer climbed back into his cab and delighted his pupils with two ear-piercing blasts of the whistle.

"All aboard, boys," he said. "Come back and see me at the whistle stops."

Whistle stops, jerkwater towns: these were big-city words in the American vocabulary for those lonely spots along 200,000 miles of railroads where steam locomotives, like panting prehis-toric monsters, had to stop every forty miles for water.

Helen dragged her brothers back to the plush-upholstered

splendors of the Pullman. Lawrence and Elmer sat there glumly as the train started, knowing that it would be forty long miles before the first whistle stop. Helen was glum for a corresponding reason. All she wanted to do was enjoy the scenery, read the *Ladies' Home Journal,* and plan the decor of her new bedroom in Brooklyn, but now she would have to check up on those boys at every town between Cleveland and New York.

6

NEITHER GRAND CENTRAL nor Penn Station existed in 1905 when the Sperry family moved to New York, and the boys took a dim view of their arrival in the decadent and backward East. Their train had left Cleveland's splendid new Union Station. Now it came into what Elmer Jr. described as "a dinky little shed in Hoboken."

"From here we transferred to a ferry boat that dumped us off at a crummy landing near Canal Street, New York City," he said. "It was even more of a comedown when we boarded a *horse-drawn* trolley car to cross Manhattan to the Brooklyn Bridge. There we boarded a train run by a wheezing little steam locomotive. We disembarked in Flatbush somewhere near Newkirk Avenue and took a horse and buggy to the corner of Foster and Ocean avenues where we entered our new home—an old three-story house with a barn in back. Needless to say, we were ready to go back to Cleveland."

Kimbo, the pony, did not survive his displacement. He just keeled over in the barn the next morning and died. Elmer blamed it on Brooklyn and was inconsolable for several weeks.

Things picked up a few months later when the Sperrys moved to a newer and grander house (it had four bedrooms), still standing at 100 Marlborough Road. Helen was enchanted by the fan-crowned classical doorway and the white fluted Doric columns of the front porch, signs of the Greek Revival, about which she was learning at Packer Collegiate Institute. Packer was Brooklyn's most fashionable school for young ladies, noted for its "solid curriculum and its refined and elevating influences."

As for the boys, who were consigned to the relative rough and tumble of Public School 139, they liked the new house too. It had a big backyard, a huge attic big enough to build an airplane in, and a large basement, which Lawrence immediately claimed for his bicycle repair shop.

The bicycle shop was an instant success. Lawrence became the local agent for the Elgin King and Pierce bicycles. He made friends with Mr. Jones, the bicycle repairman just five blocks away on Snyder Street. Mr. Jones taught him how to spoke a bicycle wheel, and Lawrence and Elmer Jr. could soon do this in jig time. When Mr. Jones went to Detroit to take a job with the Ford Motor Company at the unheard-of wage of five dollars a day, Lawrence inherited his business. He installed a motor-driven line shaft in the basement of 100 Marlborough Road and belted a drill press and grinder to the shaft so that he could perforate metal and sharpen ice skates. His older brother Edward made a cash drawer from a design in *Popular Mechanics* magazine. It was a secret drawer, cleverly concealed under a workbench, and had a combination that only the proprietors knew.

Lawrence had promotional handbills printed, and young Elmer saturated the neighborhood with them. The handbills announced:

LAWRENCE B. SPERRY
Bicycles, Roller Skates and Doorbells
Repaired at Reasonable Prices
Also a Full Line of Bicycle and Roller Skate
Supplies and Parts
Prices the Lowest in the City

His line of merchandise included coaster brakes, pedals, handlebars, rubber grips, lamps, pumps, tires, skate wheels, chain grease, graphite, Cleveland glue, Never Leak patches, and Three-in-One Oil: "Cleans, Lubricates, Rustproofs!"

Lawrence also made a deal with Mr. Wilcox, who sold motorcycles on Flatbush Avenue. Wilcox agreed to make Lawrence his official repair agent if Lawrence would buy the spare parts from Wilcox. This worked out very well. The business flourished and expanded. Customers traipsed through the house, driving Zula and Delia, the Irish maid, out of their minds. When the motorcycle repairs began, Zula took a stand, and Lawrence and Elmer built a ramp so that motorcycles could be taken down the cellar stairs from the backyard.

Helen has a vivid memory of all this, seventy years after the fact: "I wonder how Mother stood it. Those two boys [Edward had gone off to school at Phillips Exeter Academy] always reeked of oil from their homemade engines. The motorcycles spit, coughed, gasped, trembled with a mighty ague, and they stank. The fumes! Oil trickled on the cellar stairs as the cycles were tugged up and down, and the oil under those boys' fingernails was ineradicable. Fortunately, our Irish maid, Delia, was young, healthy, and tolerant. Lawrence could get away with anything just by smiling at her. She had the patience of an Irish saint and nerves of solid cast iron."

Like his father before him, Lawrence Burst Sperry invested the profits of one queer dream in another queer dream. By 1907, when he was fifteen, he had made enough from his repair shop to buy his own Marsh-Metz motorcycle. His parents didn't realize it was his, since he was repairing so many others.

Then one fine day in April they found a note on the dining room table:

Dear Parents,
  I have gone to visit Uncle Herbert on my motorcycle. Don't worry. I'll be back for Easter Sunday dinner.
                                                              Love, Lawrence

A perfectly normal filial letter, but Uncle Herbert Goodman, Zula's brother, lived in Chicago, more than a thousand miles away.

"That was typical of Lawrence," Helen recalls. "He did as he pleased. He made his schemes in private, then suddenly confronted the family with a *fait accompli.*"

Lawrence arrived in Chicago four days later, coated with grease and the dust of half of America. His Uncle Herbert recalled that he looked like a photographic negative with his piercing blue eyes shining through a black face. He also remembered Lawrence's spirit of enterprise; he had paid the expenses of his trip by giving rides to the Chicago kids at fifteen cents a go. Uncle Herbert sent Lawrence and the motorcycle back to New York on a crack new train, the Lakeside Limited.

Back in Brooklyn, Lawrence and his accomplice, Elmer, had

their first motorcycle accident. As they were taking a curve too fast on the high-crowned roads of Prospect Park, one of the pedals hit the ground and sent the two boys sprawling in the dust. The motorcycle was minus a pedal, and the boys, though uninjured, were minus the right legs of their trousers. When they got back to Marlborough Road in this state, a family moratorium was declared on motorcycling.

To console them, their Uncle Will Conger, head of the delivery system of the American Can Company, gave them a mustang horse named Rex. Why not ride Rex, he said, instead of that infernal coughing machine? Briefly shaken by their motorcycle mishap, Lawrence and Elmer consented to this regression to the horse-and-buggy age. They kept the horse in Kimbo's old stall in the family stable on Ocean Avenue, and they rode it in Prospect Park. Rex had a peculiarity: he was irresistibly attracted to water. As soon as he saw the lake, he galloped right into it, taking his riders with him whether they were on his back or in the buggy. This gave an exciting new dimension to equestrian sport, especially since it was forbidden by law to swim in the park lake. Lawrence took advantage of these predictable accidents to practice a few strokes of the crawl, recently imported from Australia. When the police arrived, Lawrence and Elmer went home, soaking wet. Zula was relieved when winter came and the boys were skating on the frozen pond.

That was good for business too. Lawrence's repair shop sharpened most of the ice skates of Flatbush. Rex also contributed to Lawrence's growing income. At Christmastime he was hitched to his cart and delivered baskets of groceries from Hyman's Market to all the clients in that comfortable upper-middle-class neighborhood.

The educational focus of that neighborhood was one of the great high schools of America, Erasmus Hall, where Lawrence and Elmer were enrolled as soon as they graduated from P.S. 139. Erasmus had been founded in 1787 on land donated by the Flatbush Dutch Reformed Church. The original wooden building, still standing today, was funded by such celebrated Brooklynites as John Jay, Aaron Burr, and Alexander Hamilton. When the Sperrys arrived in Flatbush, Erasmus had just encompassed this venerable shrine with the neo-Tudor buildings of the Gothic Revival, forming a quadrangle reminiscent of the cloistered colleges of Oxford and Cambridge. The school had a strong classical curriculum, worthy of the great Dutch humanist for whom it was named, and it prided itself on "adapting its offerings to the ability, needs and ambitions of the student body."

Lawrence's abilities, needs, and ambitions must have presented Erasmus with the greatest challenge in its history. He and Elmer soon became more distinguished for their extracurricular activities than for their scholastic efforts.

Elmer, who remained small (his full-grown height was five feet eight inches, Lawrence's six feet two inches), was stocky, fast, and agile. He went out for football and had the thrill of hearing the old Erasmus cheer yelled from the grandstand in his honor:

> VIVO VAIVO VIVO VAIVO VESS
> E-R-A-S-M-U-S!
> Sperry! Sperry!!! SPERRY !!!

One Sperry exploit remains unique in the annals of Erasmus Hall. There was a girl named Mary Bacon who had a crush on Lawrence. She was one of the girls whom Helen deemed suitable for her brother. Mary was popular at Erasmus. She was running for student president. It looked as though the election was going to be close, so Lawrence and Elmer decided to help Mary's campaign.

In the bicycle shop in the family basement the two boys made a sign ten feet long and three feet high. Its message was simple and clear: VOTE FOR BACON.

At three o'clock on the morning of the election, Lawrence and Elmer got up quietly and carried the sign through the graveyard of the Flatbush Dutch Reformed Church across the street from Erasmus Hall. The church was locked, but Elmer, with a hundred feet of cord on his back and a weight in his pocket, climbed up the vines on the back of the church to the base of the steeple. Here he was able to loosen the screening wire and pry one of the louver boards loose so that he could squeeze through the louvers just above the ridgepole of the church. He then climbed the steeple from the inside to the base of the spire. He must have had the sure-footed balance of a mountain goat. He tied the weight to the end of the cord and lowered it for Lawrence, who was waiting in the predawn silence in front of the church a hundred feet below. Lawrence attached the cord to the sign, and Elmer hauled it back up and tied it to the steeple so that the sign hung from the platform at the base of the spire.

Dawn was breaking over Flatbush when the boys got home. They went to school early to observe the effect of their effort. It was most satisfactory. Everybody gawked at the huge sign, VOTE FOR BACON, and wondered how it got there. It had a hypnotic effect on the voters; Mary won the election by a landslide.

But after the lunch hour there were identical notes in the homerooms of Messrs. Lawrence B. Sperry and Elmer A. Sperry, Jr.: the boys were to report immediately to the office of Dr. Walter B. Gunnison, principal of Erasmus Hall.

"We know you did it," Dr. Gunnison said. "There is such a thing as carrying school spirit too far."

The boys admitted it and eagerly offered to make amends by taking the sign down.

Dr. Gunnison paled at this suggestion. "That will not be necessary," he said. "If you don't mind, we will have the sign removed by a professional steeplejack. Lawrence, I think it might be a salutary thing if you spent less time on electioneering and more time on your lessons."

He held Lawrence's semester report in his hand. "Ninety-five in mathematics is excellent," the principal said, "but fifty in English is less than satisfactory. After all, Lawrence, you come from an old American family; you are not the child of immigrants. Forty-five in German and thirty-seven in Latin are disgraceful. And your English teacher, Mr. Thistlewaite, informs me that your spelling is deplorable."

Lawrence's resolutely phonetic spelling was one of the scandals of the family. He had no patience with the absurdities of English orthography and spelled words the way they were pronounced: *sault, tekneak, electrolasiss.* Even when he became famous as the inventor of the airplane stabilizer, he spelled it *stabalizer.*

In the Tudor-Gothic halls of Erasmus these errors provoked a snobbish warning from Mr. Thistlewaite. "Lawrence," he said, "a poor speller might attain to the doubtful dignity of a grocer's clerk, but his aspiration to any higher station in life would be doomed to certain defeat."

Mr. Thistlewaite had no idea to what heights his aberrant pupil would aspire, nor was he aware that this worst of spellers was already an independent entrepreneur.

With the profits of the bicycle shop Lawrence bought a car. He found it in a secondhand automobile shop on Columbus Circle. It was a vehicle with a certain pedigree, a French Panhard that had belonged to the famous actor E. H. Sothern, who was costarring with Julia Marlowe at the Lyceum Theatre in *When Knighthood Was in Flower*. In a fit of temperament, E. H. Sothern had stripped the gears of the Panhard, so he sold it to Lawrence for $200.

The Panhard, according to Elmer Jr.'s notes, was "a gorgeous-looking automobile." It was one of the first closed-body coupés. It had a shiny black enamel finish, a great novelty in 1908. It had five forward speeds, a foot-pedal accelerator, a front bumper, and an electric horn and was so low-slung and daring in design that Elmer had to sit on two volumes of the *Encyclopaedia Britannica* to see through the windshield.

He went with Lawrence to get the car, and it took them three days to drive the Panhard from Columbus Circle to Flatbush. It broke down first on the Bowery, causing a sensation on that then fashionable street. A policeman helped them push it into a vacant lot, where they were obliged to leave it overnight. Returning at dawn the next day, Lawrence took out the transmission, removed the broken gears, cleaned out the chewed-up gear teeth, then proceeded toward Flatbush in second gear at a speed of four miles per hour; the top three speeds had ceased to exist. After a second breakdown in the middle of Brooklyn Bridge, they arrived in first gear at Mr. Wilcox's shop on Flatbush Avenue. Wilcox, who seemed to have mechanical connections all over the world, helped them obtain the necessary new gears.

At length, on a fine Saturday morning, the car was as good as new, and Father Sperry, sitting on the front porch, was dumbfounded to see his two younger sons drive up Marlborough Road

in the spiffiest car in Brooklyn, all black enamel and brass, pol-
ished to a dazzling mirror finish. His boys had acquired a gas-
combustion auto before he had.

"What kind of a vehicle is that?" he asked.

"It's a Chinese Mercedes," Lawrence replied.

Zula and Helen, though they greatly admired the looks of the
car, were not sure it was wise for the boys to keep it. Their grades
at Erasmus were so undistinguished that they were in danger of
flunking out.

Father Sperry was more sanguine. He looked over the engine
with an appraising eye. "If Lawrence has enough ingenuity to
keep that machine going," he said, "he certainly deserves to keep
it."

Lawrence had ingenuity all right, though to Mr. Thistlewaite's
distress, he spelled it *inginooity*. Lawrence had very specific
ideas as to what he intended to do with the Chinese Mercedes
(that name remained fixed in the annals of the Sperry family; the
car was never called anything else). In giving his blessing to this
startling purchase, Elmer A. Sperry had unwittingly contributed
to the history of aviation.

7

"WHEN LAWRENCE started on an idea, nobody could make him change his mind," wrote his younger brother and accomplice, Elmer A. Sperry, Jr., in a succinct and intimate memoir of Lawrence's monomania.

The obsession in the summer of 1910 was to build a full-size glider. The idea had been germinating since the first Mineola Air Meet of 1908 when Lawrence saw the great French ace Henri Farman fly his Voisin airplane for two minutes and actually make a turn in the air and return to the takeoff spot, as he had done earlier that year when he won the Grand Prix d'Aviation at Reims.

Lawrence had examined the Farman plane in minute detail and had shaken hands with the bearded French pioneer; it was like a religious experience. Now after two years of studying every photograph and diagram he could lay his hands on, he was ready to make his own plane, and he had the whole summer ahead of him to do it. School was out. "No more pencils, no more books, no more teachers' dirty looks," his classmates sang as they prepared to leave the hallowed halls of Erasmus for lake and seashore.

The Sperry family had discovered the charms of the nineteenth-century whaling port of Bellport, then "the chosen home of families of wealth and culture" on the south shore of Long Island. Zula and Helen, after a year of coping with the Sperry Bicycle Repair Shop, yearned for the tranquil haven of the Goldthwaite Inn, "a comfortable homelike house to which the same guests return season after season, drawn there by the irresistible attraction of the climate and the sea."

The proprietors of this five-story Victorian ark, Aunt Kate Maltby and Uncle Darwin Meserole, proclaimed that the climate of Bellport was the most salubrious in the United States. Although they were socialists, convinced that the Revolution was at hand, they ran a highly profitable hostelry for their seventy-five regular clients. Rates were admittedly high—from ten to twenty dollars a week for room and board—but the service, thanks to a black staff of twenty-five, was impeccable, and Aunt Kate and Uncle Darwin were perfect hosts.

Zula wanted Lawrence and Elmer to accompany her and Helen to the Goldthwaite Inn that summer. The swimming, sun, and sailing were just what Lawrence needed, but the boys had other ideas.

As soon as the rest of the family left for Bellport, the house on Marlborough Road became an airplane shop. With young Elmer's assistance, Lawrence built a steam box, ten feet long and a foot and a half square, in the basement. To provide steam for softening the wood, he disconnected the main steam line from the furnace and ran it into one end of the box. In the blistering heat of a Brooklyn July, he fired up the furnace, channeled the steam into his steam box, and steamed each piece of wood until it was pliable. Bending the wood to his will and design, he clamped each piece to a form he had nailed to the wooden floor of the laundry. When the wood was perfectly dry and shaped to his purpose, he removed each piece from the clamps. In the process of steaming the wood he cracked the furnace. He was sorry, but the ribs of his glider were done.

The long, narrow fuselage was also constructed in the basement. When Lawrence was applying the finishing touches, he had a visit from his business associate, Mr. Wilcox. Wilcox was genuinely impressed by the profesional look of the work in progress.

"What about an engine, Lawrence?" he asked.

"An engine?" Lawrence's temperature must have leaped a full degree.

"Yes," Wilcox said. "I could get you a good secondhand Anzani engine from France. That would turn your glider into a real machine."

Lawrence stood stock still, brush in hand, while the glue dripped on the cellar floor. He stared intently at the older man.

"A five-cylinder, sixty-horsepower, radial engine," Wilcox went on, "the same kind that Blériot used when he flew across the English Channel. Think of it: from France to England in thirty-seven minutes. You can't beat the Frogs when it comes to aeroplanes. You couldn't get a motor like that here," he added.

Lawrence's blue eyes took on a visionary gleam. His eardrums vibrated to the sound of an unseen motor. A propeller started spinning in his mind. A five-cylinder Anzani radial engine: he would have to have it. There was no question about it.

"How much would it cost?" he asked.

"Eight hundred dollars," Wilcox said.

"Elmer," said Lawrence, "how much have we got in the till?"

Elmer manipulated the combination of the secret cash drawer and began to count the oil-stained bills.

"Three hundred bucks," he reported.

"Shucks," said Lawrence.

His spirit had been soaring in the empyrean. Now he was back in the basement.

"Tell you what," said Wilcox. "I'll put up five hundred. You can put up the rest. I'll invest in your plane. I really have confidence in you, Lawrence."

"But how can I pay you back?" Lawrence said.

"Barnstorming," said Wilcox. "We'll take the plane to every county fair. Why, you'll be making as much as twenty-five dollars a day. You'll buy back my interest in no time."

Barnstorming! Lawrence was high in the sky putting his sixty-horsepower biplane through its paces, rolling, spinning, looping, swinging from side to side like a falling leaf, cleaving the blue air in a series of dazzling figure eights, swooping earthward and zooming back toward heaven in the nick of time while the roar of the crowd almost drowned out the resounding boom of his powerful Anzani engine.

"It's a deal," said Lawrence.

"I'll order the engine today," Wilcox said, shaking hands with Lawrence. "It'll be here in a month, by the time you finish the plane."

Fame is the spur! Exhilarated by the surging power of the engine that would be his, Lawrence took the dried wooden ribs from the cellar floor and carried them up to the attic to construct

and assemble the wings. He had decided on a biplane design, and
he and Elmer now began the delicate process of gluing the ribs to
the two wings to form the strutted panels so familiar from photographs of those early cratelike contraptions in which man first
defied the law of gravity in earnest.

All went well. It was a completely professional job. But when
the glue had dried, Lawrence suddenly realized that the wings of
the biplane were too large to be removed from the attic.

"Kiddo," he said to Elmer, "we're gonna need some tools."

"Like what, for instance?" Elmer asked.

"Screwdrivers, chisels, mallets, and crowbars," said Lawrence,
and Elmer got them from the basement.

Working as carefully as impatience and frustration would permit, the two boys pried away the frame of the attic door. Then
they were obliged to remove the attic rail, the banisters, and finally a section of the staircase itself.

Partial success: they were able to ease the wings down to the
second floor of the house. But they were unable to maneuver the
cumbersome panels and turn them in the upstairs hallway without damaging the wings.

Lawrence studied the situation. The most logical way to get the
wings out of the house was through the big bay window in their
parents' bedroom. But first they would have to widen the bedroom door.

"There's no other way," said Lawrence.

They removed the door frame, eased the bulky, fragile wings
into Mother and Father Sperry's bedroom, and began to take out
the casement window.

Working efficiently with the stoutest of screwdrivers, they first
pried the molding from the window frame. With the molding
gone, it was a relatively easy matter to unhook the sash weights
and chains of the double-hung windows, after which they removed the windows themselves.

The resulting aperture stubbornly refused to accommodate itself to the wings.

"Rats," said Lawrence. "We'll have to take out the window
frame."

With mallets and chisels, the boys worked their way from the
top to the sill of the window frame, removing both the inside and

outside trim. Then, plying their crowbars, they got rid of the frame itself.

There was now a large opening on the second floor of the Sperry house, punctuated by ragged holes where nails had once held the master bedroom windows in place. Success was in sight, but they were not quite there.

"We'll have to remove a few inches of the bay itself," said Lawrence.

With this decision, the boys found themselves in the throes of a major demolition. It involved ripping out a two-inch-thick coat of plaster with the lathing. That was easy enough, but the lath was nailed to thick two-by-four studs, and there was a lot of tar paper and other insulation in the way.

"Kiddo, we need a saw," said Lawrence.

"Good grief," said Elmer, trotting off to get it. "I had no idea this would be so complicated."

The lathing turned out to be springy and difficult to saw, and Lawrence found it very hard, especially in his impatience, to make a neat hole in the plaster partition that was stubbornly blocking the exit of his plane. But he finally reached the inch-thick clapboards of the exterior wall and managed to cut through the requisite square feet without splitting the house asunder. Everything considered, it was a pretty neat job, although there was a lot of debris, torn tar paper, white plaster powder, and sawdust in the Sperry master bedroom.

The boys now eased the wings of the glider through the ample space of what had been a bay window, and they worked together in the backyard, carefully and lovingly attaching the precious wings to the fuselage.

They had just about finished when Zula and Helen, marvelously refreshed from a cool July in Bellport, drove up to the front door in Zula's chauffeured Locomobile to see how the boys were getting along.

From the street side the house looked perfectly normal. Zula called out in her cheerful voice as she entered the front door, with its tranquil transom light and vertical side windows that always gave her and Helen such aesthetic pleasure, such a sense of composed order.

"Lawrence! Elmer! We're back. Are you home, boys?"

Helen, preceding her mother up the stairs, gasped as she reached the second floor.

"Mother, look!"

"My heavens to Betsy!" Zula cried.

One of the bedroom walls was almost gone. The summer sunlight streamed through the aperture. A swirl of white powder and sawdust rose as the two women walked to the gaping hole. Looking down, they saw Lawrence and Elmer standing proudly beside their glider.

"Mother, Helen," Lawrence said cheerfully, "how do you like it? Come down and see it up close."

As though mesmerized, mother and daughter obediently descended to the garden.

"How do you like it?" Lawrence repeated. "It's a real aeroplane."

"Isn't it keen?" said Elmer.

When Lawrence, who was now six feet tall, bent down to kiss his mother, he was puzzled by her behavior. She was crying, but she seemed to be laughing at the same time in an odd sort of uncontrollable way.

"Isn't it a beauty, Mother?" Lawrence said.

"A beauty," Zula sobbed. "Just a beauty," she giggled, and she went upstairs to pull herself and her perforated bedroom together.

Helen remained speechless. She looked at the glider, at the hole in the house, at her two grease-monkey brothers, and there were sparks in her blue eyes.

Finally she said, "You might at least get a broom and a dustpan and clean up Mother and Father's bedroom."

The boys were perfectly happy to oblige. Lawrence also offered to rebuild the demolished bay window, but Father Sperry, whose expressive eyebrows rose to new heights of astonishment when he saw the hole in his house, thought it advisable to have the assistance of a professional contractor.

The two ladies of the Sperry household consoled each other with the comfortable clichés of American middle-class life: Boys would be boys. Youth must be served. And Lawrence had gotten the glider out of his system.

So they thought. So they hoped. It *was* a remarkably professional-looking contraption, they had to agree. They had no idea that Lawrence intended to fly it, and they went back to Bellport to spend the month of August, leaving the boys to tinker with their toy in the yard and to survey the reconstruction of the bedroom wall.

8

LAWRENCE SPERRY WAS SEVENTEEN during that summer of 1910 when he built his glider and, though he had demolished part of the family home in the process of removing the biplane wings from the attic, he was not an inconsiderate person. Lawrence did not want to worry his mother and father and did not want to cope with parental interference, so he kept his flying plans a secret from everybody except his faithful younger brother and indispensable helper.

The glider was ready to fly. It was the first week in August. School would begin a week from Labor Day. They would have to work fast.

First they had to choose the site. Prospect Park was out. Too public. Fire Island and the other beaches of the South Shore would have made appropriate Kitty Hawks for Lawrence's great experiment, but they were already teeming with vacationists and accessible only by small passenger boats, the *Henry Ludlow* and the *Ripple*.

It was Elmer who hit on the idea of the Sheepshead Bay Race Track, just four miles south of Marlborough Road. The horse-racing season was almost over, and Lawrence agreed that this would be a perfect place to try out the glider. He took some photographs of the plane with his Brownie box camera, and they turned out so well that Elmer was sure they would command serious attention. "Absolutely keen" was his opinion.

The boys got in touch with Mr. Collins, manager of the Sheeps-head Bay Race Track, and made an appointment to show him the pictures.

"I'll never forget it as long as I live," Elmer noted in his memoir sixty years later, "our first important interview."

The boys drove to Sheepshead Bay in the Chinese Mercedes,

oblivious to the fact that they had acquired an unexpected ally in the person of the governor of New York, Charles Evans Hughes, who had just signed a bill outlawing all bookmaker betting on the race tracks of the state.

The Sheepshead Bay track was in a turmoil. Mr. Collins's office was thronged with jockeys and other nervous-looking characters, and the secretary told Elmer and Lawrence they would have to wait, as Mr. Collins was extremely busy with many prior appointments. They waited for hours in an atmosphere of heated, acrimonious discussion. They waited through the lunch hour and began to wonder if they had come on the wrong day.

"But Lawrence wouldn't give up," Elmer noted, "and just when everything seemed hopeless, Mr. Collins strode out of his office and said in a booming voice, 'Are you the boys that want to see me?' "

Lawrence, who had enough charm and persuasion to sell ice-boxes to the Eskimos, leaped up, pulled out the pictures of the glider, and said he wanted to fly his plane at the Sheepshead Bay Race Track.

Mr. Collins questioned Lawrence at some length about the glider. It turned out that he was an airplane buff. Lawrence explained how the ailerons would control the flight of the glider. He also showed Mr. Collins where an engine could be mounted on the forward part of the body longerons. In his fertile imagination Lawrence was already far ahead of mere gliding; he would duplicate and surpass the feats of Henri Farman.

Mr. Collins was much impressed. He picked up the phone and ordered a space reserved under the grandstand to accommodate the Sperry boys' glider. He arranged for them to have a key and free access to this storage area at any time.

"And let me know as soon as the glider arrives," he said.

Lawrence was worried about getting too involved with Mr. Collins and he wanted to know what the rent would be.

"Don't worry about that," Mr. Collins said. "The goddamn governor has taken care of that. That space would just be wasted anyway."

The goddamn governor! That sort of strong language had never been heard in the Sperry home.

Mr. Collins showed them the *Daily News*, a tabloid that was not seen in the Sperry home either. It had a full-page picture of Governor Hughes and a big headline:

BOOKIES BOLT AS
GOV NIXES BETS

Back home the two boys carefully stripped down the glider, causing Helen, who had come for the weekend, to remark that they might have done that in the first place instead of demolishing half the house.

"And what are you going to do with it now, may I ask?"

"We're putting it in storage," the boys replied.

That was good news. She went back to Bellport and reported to Zula that the boys had really gotten flying "out of their systems."

At the Sheepshead Bay Race Track, the boys reassembled the glider with loving care. The situation was ideal. The horses were being moved out, and except for a few stable boys, Lawrence and Elmer had the place to themselves, with a wide paved area of red brick in front of the stands on which to practice towing the glider. Elmer drove the Chinese Mercedes slowly and Lawrence followed on foot, observing the behavior of the plane. They added two wheels to the landing gear to make sure it would stand the strain.

Finally they were ready for the big experiment.

Lawrence installed himself on the flimsy plank that passed for the pilot's seat. Elmer attached the towline to the rear bumper of the Chinese Mercedes. He cranked up the car, got into the driver's seat, adjusted his bottom comfortably on the encyclopedias, and eased the car carefully into first gear. He could feel the line grow taut. He looked around. The glider was moving forward. Lawrence waved gravely; everything was all right. Elmer shifted quickly to second and third. The car gathered speed. Suddenly he saw the shadow of the plane on the ground in front of the car. A sudden puff of wind had lifted the glider 150 feet into the air, slackening the rope. Elmer jammed on the brakes. The towrope jerked taut and snapped. The glider soared up like a liberated bird, dipped dangerously to starboard, dropped, hit the ground on the starboard wing, flopped over on its back, and lay still.

Elmer jumped out of the car. There was no sign of Lawrence. He was underneath the plane. It was a long moment before he emerged. There was blood: his face was all scraped up. But his lanky limbs were miraculously intact, and there was a look of wild elation on his battered countenance.

"We flew," he shouted, "we flew!"

He grabbed his younger brother in a bear hug and the two of them did a jig of pure joy. The plane had weathered the crash remarkably well. The top wing had split and two of the struts were splintered, but the fuselage was all right, and it would be easy to repair the damage. The boys turned the plane back over and rolled it back into the storage bin under the grandstand. It had been a good day's work.

They spent the next week repairing the plane in order to make another trial flight. Lawrence recorded all this in his matter-of-fact way fourteen years later in an article in *U.S. Air Services:* "I would work all week repairing the damage in order to make another flight. The plane would usually be cracked up in landing and that kept me busy for the rest of the week getting ready for the next crash."

The most serious crash occurred at the end of August after the most successful flight. Except for the initial, involuntary flight when the towrope had snapped, Lawrence had not made a wholly unattached and independent flight. He did that one Saturday afternoon, to the delight of a crowd of about a hundred people, including a number of female admirers.

When Elmer got the Chinese Mercedes up to twenty-five miles an hour and Lawrence was speeding along at the same rate on a level with the car top, he took out his scout knife and calmly sliced the towrope. The glider sped forward on its own momentum, overtaking the Chinese Mercedes, and soared upward as the crowd cheered and watched it glide grandly over the race-track fence for more than two hundred yards. Then the plane dipped sharply to starboard, swept sideways by a gust of wind, and then it dropped, striking the marshy ground with the starboard wing before flopping over on its back with Lawrence underneath the wreckage.

With Elmer in the lead, the spectators rushed forward, climbed over the fence, sloshed through the marshy grass, and pulled the battered plane off the dazed and battered pilot.

"I'm all right," he said, despite the blood and mud. "Kiddo, did you see that baby fly?"

But he needed help. He fell down when he tried to walk. He had a lot of pain in his right wrist and his left foot, and he had to use Elmer as a crutch as he limped back through the marshes and across the race track to the jockeys' dressing room. Here one of the veterinarians diagnosed a sprained wrist and ankle, both of which he rubbed vigorously with Sloan's liniment before taping Lawrence's leg and arm as one would tape a horse's hoofs. Lawrence winced at this vigorous treatment, but no pain could erase the look of satisfaction from his battle-scarred face.

He cleaned himself up in the washroom, but the abrasions and contusions and sprains were difficult to explain at home. So were the girls who came to inquire about Lawrence's health.

The living room was full of them. Zula and Helen, who had returned from a healthy, wholesome summer at Bellport, were dumbfounded. Except for that nice Mary Bacon, they didn't know that Lawrence knew any girls. And such a heterogeneous lot. One of them had rouge on her cheeks; such a thing had never been seen in the Sperry parlor. Another chewed Wrigley's Juicy Fruit chewing gum, and another exposed her ankles, encased in green silk stockings.

Helen tried to be a good hostess.

"How do you do?" she said to one of these fast-looking creatures.

"Fine thanks, how's yasself?"

These were not the kind of young ladies who went to Packer Institute or even to Erasmus Hall. These were the fast females who hung around the Sheepshead Bay Race Track.

So the secret came out. Lawrence had flown and "nearly killed himself." Torn between pride and anguish, Zula was glad to relegate this exploit, part of growing up, to the past perfect tense.

Mr. Wilcox came to call, very concerned about the health of his "protégé."

"It's here," he whispered to Lawrence. "The Anzani engine arrived this morning. It's a beauty. And I've got my German carpenter, Otto, making the most beautiful propeller you ever saw."

"It's gonna work," Lawrence whispered back. "The race track, Monday morning, nine o'clock."

He lay back with a sublime look of contentment on his handsome, scraped-up face. His blue eyes burned with a gemlike flame, pure and concentrated as the blue dome of the sky where he wanted to spend the rest of his life. He had flown at the mercy of the wind. Now he would fly with the power of sixty horses harnessed to his will.

His parents were glad that he had "gotten it out of his system" and emerged alive. Zula was concerned about his health. The sweltering summer heat of Brooklyn had taken its toll. He had grown too fast, almost outgrown his strength. He was as skinny as a string bean and almost as green. And there was a feverish look about his eyes and dark rings under them that she found disquieting. But despite all the alarms and accidents, the summer had ended happily. It was optimistically presumed that Lawrence would now concentrate on his senior year at Erasmus and prepare himself for Cornell, where his older brother, Edward, was having "a whale of a time."

The illusion that Lawrence would settle down was strengthened when he and Elmer sold the Chinese Mercedes at a profit of $100 and returned to motorcycle transportation. They would ostensibly not be needing a car to tow that glider anymore.

They wouldn't need it because the glider was about to be equipped with a propeller and an engine, but Mother and Father Sperry remained in blissful ignorance of this development.

School opened on Monday, and the boys were reassuringly early for breakfast. Lawrence's wounds had scabbed over and his sprained wrist was sufficiently healed, Helen hoped, to enable him to obtain the final certificate of excellence in the Palmer Method of Business Writing, without which no cultivated person

could expect to graduate from Erasmus Hall and enter the college
of his choice.

But, in the process of downing a dozen of Delia's pancakes with
maple syrup, Lawrence was not thinking of penmanship; he was
impatient to install a new, six-wheel landing gear on his plane; he
had already dreamed this up to enable the plane to cross the little
drainage ditches of Sheepshead Bay without nosing over.

The boys picked up their schoolbooks and lunch boxes, kissed
Zula good-bye, and revved up their motorcycles. It did seem absurd to ride six blocks to Erasmus Hall, but it was the thing to do,
a sensible advertisement for the repair shop that still flourished in
the Sperry basement. Lawrence and Elmer had agreed to pay for
the reconstruction of the bay window out of the profits of the
shop. And if Zula or Helen noticed the fact that, on this first
morning of school, the boys each had three bicycle wheels
strapped behind their saddles, there was nothing untoward about
this; they were ostensibly returning repaired wheels to their
clients at school.

Only the Irish maid, Delia, was privy to the fact that the boys
stashed their schoolbooks in the milk delivery box before zooming
down Marlborough Road. They turned right on Albemarle as
usual, but instead of crossing Ocean Avenue in the direction of
Erasmus, they made a sharp right turn on this thoroughfare that
runs straight south to Sheepshead Bay.

"Somehow our motorcycles would go right to the race track instead of to school," Elmer noted sixty years later.

Mr. Wilcox was at the race track unpacking the Anzani engine.
He had brought Otto with him, and the propeller that would
transform the glider into the first tractor-type biplane to be built
in America. The boys were enchanted with that powerful radial
engine and the propeller, sanded, varnished, and waxed until it
gleamed like sculpture. They worked on the plane every day that
week, following the same routine, avoiding Flatbush Avenue and
Erasmus for Ocean Avenue and the irresistible marshes of Sheepshead Bay.

By Friday the plane had been repaired and strengthened down
to the last rib and strut. Lawrence had attached his six-wheel
anti-nose-over landing gear, and Elmer had recorded this ingen-

ious device for posterity with his Brownie camera. The Anzani engine and propeller were installed in front of the wings, a novelty in America, Mr. Wilcox pointed out, where pusher-type planes were favored. Lawrence made a final check of cylinders and pistons. Mr. Wilcox brought a pitcher of gasoline and poured it into the tank. Lawrence climbed onto the pilot's seat, which was nothing but a narrow board out in the open air with no floor below it and no windscreen in front of it. Otto caressed the shining propeller with loving hands, then pulled the blade down sharply. The Anzani motor sputtered, coughed, sputtered. The propeller began to turn slowly. Lawrence throttled the engine. It roared into life. The propeller responded, spinning rapidly like a high-speed fan.

"Kiddo," Lawrence yelled to Elmer, "it works. This time she's really gonna fly."

As the autumn wind whistled through the struts, the plane shuddered and wobbled, but the propeller whirled and the engine roared its defiance of nature. Even though the plane was trembling like a kite, Lawrence nosed it into the wind and started taxiing down the track. He could feel the propeller bite the air. He increased the "bite" by adjusting the pitch of those spinning blades, revved up that beautiful Anzani engine to the peak of its power, pulled back the stick, and felt the plane nose up. Suddenly, miraculously, he was in the air, "in high," commanding a team of sixty airborne horses. He was a hundred feet up, higher than his idol, Farman, on that memorable day in Mineola. Now, like Farman, he knew the hazards of *mauvaises conditions*. The plane swayed and dipped at the mercy of every gust of wind, at every current in the treacherous ocean of the air. But she responded to his control. When he moved the stick to the left he could feel the ailerons push the port wing down. Then, moving the stick to the right, he banked to starboard and managed to duplicate Farman's feat of turning in the teeth of the wind. He felt the plane surge forward with the added force of the tailwind, and he managed to climb to five hundred feet. At this point the plane leveled off and refused to climb higher, although Lawrence pulled the stick back as far as it would go. Something, some aerodynamic force, was pushing him down. Instinctively he pushed the stick forward. The plane responded to that. She nosed down. A few feet from the ground Lawrence pulled back lightly on the stick, and felt his bicycle wheels squish against the marshy ground like so many rubber cushions. The plane scudded and bumped along for a few hundred yards. Then Lawrence cut the motor and brought her to a stop.

Leaping from the pilot's plank, he kissed that smooth propeller in wild elation. Elmer, Wilcox, and Otto came sloshing through the marsh. They hugged Lawrence and hugged each other under the luminous clouds of the September sky.

"Congratulations," Mr. Wilcox said. "So far as I know, you have just made the first flight in America in a tractor plane."

"How long was I in the air?" Lawrence wanted to know.

"Six minutes," said Wilcox.

"Let's pray for calmer weather tomorrow," Lawrence said. "With a motor and a prop like that, we should be able to fly for an hour."

Carefully, tenderly, the two boys and the two men wheeled Lawrence's plane back to the race track and into the hangar under the creaking grandstand.

Wilcox had checked the weather reports. Northeasterly winds and stormy weather were predicted for the entire weekend.

"Rats," said Lawrence.

"Clearing on Monday," Wilcox said. "See you then. Ten A.M."

"It's a date," said Lawrence, and the two boys took off on their motorcycles, racing down Ocean Avenue as though they had sprouted wings.

When they got home they went to the milk box to retrieve their schoolbooks. The books were gone. Delia was sick. Helen had gone to the box to leave the empty bottles, found the telltale books, and removed them.

That night the Sperry family had a neighborly but professional visit from Dr. Gunnison, the principal of Erasmus Hall. Out of respect for the social position of the family, he had come himself, instead of sending the truant officer, to inquire why the two Sperry boys had missed the entire first week of school. He did hope the boys weren't sick.

"Mother and Father looked horrified," Elmer recalled in his memoir, "and the truth came out."

"Boys!" Zula called upstairs. "Will you come down please? Put on your bathrobes. Dr. Gunnison is here."

The jig was up. Zula's mouth remained open, as though spellbound on the opening note of "Rock of Ages," and Father Sperry's eloquent brows rose to new heights of baffled incredulity as Lawrence and Elmer admitted their juvenile deliquency.

Lawrence pleaded with his father. He went into a rhapsodic description of the Anzani radial engine, "the same kind that Blériot used when he flew across the Channel, Dad; *think* of it!" He described the propeller and the wheels that would keep the plane from nosing over.

"It works, Dad," he said. "The only reason I flopped before was because there was no motor. The engine changes the whole picture. I flew today. I flew for six minutes. I'm going to fly it on Monday," he went on. "It's a fixed date. I gave my word of honor to Mr. Wilcox . . ."

"Wilcox," Father Sperry interrupted, "what's he got to do with it?"

"He's my business partner," Lawrence said.

"He's real keen," Elmer put in loyally. "You'd like him, Dad. You would certainly approve of Mr. Wilcox."

"In what way is he your partner?" Father Sperry persisted.

Lawrence had to confess the terms of his agreement with Wilcox.

"But I'll pay off the debt, Dad. It's a beautiful engine; you'd really approve of that Anzani engine, Father, and it will belong to Elmer and me. It'll be Sperry family property."

"But how do you propose to pay back Wilcox's investment?"

"By barnstorming tours," Lawrence said, "with me as the pilot."

Zula, Father Sperry, and Dr. Gunnison were stupefied by this announcement. It must be remembered that this family drama took place in the summer of 1911, when would-be aviators and especially barnstormers were generally presumed to be suicidal maniacs, insane characters quite outside the pale of ordinary life. Sixteen years later the idea still persisted. As late as 1927, Charles A. Lindbergh, whose physical and temperamental resemblance to Lawrence has been frequently noted and who was to become a bulwark of the conservative American Establishment,

was called a "stunt merchant" and a "flying fool." In trying to understand the anguished concern of Mother and Father Sperry, it
is well to remember that the life of an American aviator depended
on the most fragile of threads, luck.

When "Lucky Lindy" took off from Roosevelt Field in the
pouring rain on May 20, 1927, his *Spirit of St. Louis* barely
cleared the treetops and telephone wires. He had one engine, no
radio, no parachute, one inflatable raft, a quart of water, and five
sandwiches. He flew by the polestar and his compass. Twenty-
eight hours from New York, he saw some fishing boats, circled
down, and shouted, "Which way is Ireland?"

There was no answer from the astonished fishermen.

At 10:20 P.M. he landed, guided by the lights of a great metropolis.

"Where am I?"

"Paris."

Asked how he felt, he replied, "I've been to eternity and back.
I know how the dead would feel to live again."

So much for the flying fool of 1927. Lawrence, who was only
seventeen at the time of this first crucial confrontation with his
family (Lindbergh was nine in 1911), must have appeared quite
unstable to his elders.

"Barnstorming with you as a pilot?" Father Sperry said. "But
you are not a pilot."

"I am a pilot. I have flown my plane," Lawrence said con-
fidently. "I'll be airborne for half an hour on Monday," he added.
"Mr. Wilcox says the weather will be perfect."

"No, Lawrence," Father Sperry said. "On Monday morning
you will be in school."

"I can have Mr. Keenan personally escort the boys to school,"
Dr. Gunnison interposed. Mr. Keenan was the truant officer of
Erasmus Hall; he handled cases of juvenile delinquency.

"Thank you, Dr. Gunnison, but that will not be necessary,"
Zula said. "The boys will be in school. Good night, Dr. Gunnison."

The boys looked at each other in tense silence; they were impressed by the firm authority with which their gentle, permissive
mother had dismissed the principal of Erasmus Hall.

Lawrence began talking very fast, very persuasively.

"Now I know I can fly," he said. "First I flew the glider."

"And you crashed," Father Sperry said drily. "A machine can be replaced, Lawrence, not a man."

"With an engine it's different," Lawrence persisted. "There's control. Dad, you've just about licked the problem of pitch and roll on the ocean, haven't you? What about the ocean of the air? Can't it be controlled too? I feel that it can. In the glider I felt that some kind of balancer could hold the plane in balance the way your gyroscopes control the balance of a ship. The glider tilted in an updraft. If we can lick that problem . . ."

Father Sperry gave his son a long, appraising, surmising look.

"You mean stabilize the plane?" he said.

"That's it," said Lawrence.

"These things take time," Father Sperry said. "Your plane is a remarkable achievement, Lawrence, and I am proud of it. But you need training if you want to be an engineer. You can get that at Cornell. But first you have to finish high school."

"I don't want to be an engineer," Lawrence said. "I don't want to go to Cornell. I don't want to finish high school. I just want to fly. I'm going to fly my plane on Monday like I promised . . ."

"Promised whom?"

"My sponsor," Lawrence said, "Mr. Wilcox."

"I'll take care of Wilcox," Father Sperry said. "You have other promises to keep to your parents and to yourself. There are enough of these wild, barnstorming fools killing themselves every day all over the country. Your mother and I didn't raise you for that."

Like most seventeen-year-olds, Lawrence did not perceive that this firming up of parental authority was dictated by affection and concern. It was the first of a series of crises between father and son, two imaginations, two wills, two temperaments that were remarkably alike. Lawrence was still too young to fear mortality. His father, at fifty, was more aware of the death that shadows glory.

The older man won out, and Lawrence knew the sickening pang of hope deferred. It was decided to separate "those boys." Elmer would go to Phillips Exeter Academy. Lawrence, who had taken on a green, cadaverous look and who, according to Zula's letters to her brother, "went completely wild every day or two when he thought about his aeroplane," was destined for a more distant exile: Arizona.

Dr. Evans's Desert School in Mesa had been highly recommended by President Theodore Roosevelt, who was sending his own son Archie there to build up his body and his character in the great outdoors. For the Sperrys, as for so many other solid Republican families, Teddy Roosevelt's opinion had the moral authority of Moses descending from Mount Sinai with the Ten Commandments.

The change of air and scholastic atmosphere would restore Lawrence's health, prepare him for Cornell, and get this mad obsession about flying "out of his system."

"It's 5,280 feet high," said Helen. "Most salubrious."

"I could fly that high without leaving Brooklyn," Lawrence grumbled.

In order to console him, a family pact was arranged. If, after obtaining his high school diploma from the Desert School, Lawrence still did not wish to enter college, his parents would not insist, and they would maintain an open mind about his future.

The whole family went to New York's splendid new Penn Station to see him off on the Lake Shore Limited. They took gaily wrapped presents, Helen remembers, "hoping to assuage his pangs at parting from his plane."

Zula and Helen stood at the end of the station clutching damp handkerchiefs. Elmer and Ad insisted on remaining aboard the train until the last minute. Finally Lawrence was alone on the rear platform of the observation car, very silent and subdued. It must have been a heart-wrenching relief for Zula when the train moved; she half expected her skinny, wayward boy to vault over the railing to freedom.

He may have thought of it, but, as the train pulled out, he contented himself by saying in a solemn and prophetic tone, "Mother, I know you mean well, but someday you will realize that you have ruined my life."

9

THE DESERT SCHOOL OF MESA, ARIZONA, to which
Lawrence was sent in 1911 was owned and run by an eccentric
Welshman, H. Davis Evans, one of whose avowed objectives was
"to put some strength into the fiber of the effete East." The
formula was horseback riding and camping in the great outdoors.

This kind of education attracted the rough-riding president of
the United States, Theodore Roosevelt, whose son Archie was at
Mesa during Lawrence's year there. Other "effete" eastern families who confided their sons to Dr. Evans included the Salton-
stalls, the Vanderbilts, the Duponts, the Lowells, and the Cabots.

Although David Riesman, the eminent sociologist who was an
alumnus of Mesa, said that Evans "was often more successful in
dealing with parents than their children," and although other
alumni opined that he was a cheerful, personable fellow who had
a way with rich old ladies and gentlemen and knew where the
cash lurked, it should be added that fame and fortune were not
the only requirements for admission to the school. Dr. Evans
turned down the application of Douglas Fairbanks, Jr., for example, because he "did not want those moving-picture characters
hanging around the school."

Most of the students had "problems," often connected with
health. Thomas D. Cabot, for example, was sent to Mesa because
he was "undersized, frail and too immature to enter Harvard although he had passed the entrance examinations when he was sixteen."

Lawrence Burst Sperry, Zula had written on his application,
was being sent to Mesa "to deter him from his obsessive interest
in aeroplanes. He loves to fly and has already had a number of
crashes in his home-made glider." Dr. Evans grandly ignored this

maternal anxiety and did nothing to deter Lawrence's "obsessive interest."

It seems unlikely that Father and Mother Sperry were fully aware of all the implications of the educational philosophy of the school. "Cleanliness and orderliness are more important than studies," Dr. Evans insisted. "Our idea is to give the boys as much freedom as possible, a taste of freedom and adventure, a rebellion against the dull, monotonous, conventional life usually looked upon as prerequisite to success.

"I am obsessed," he went on, "with two ideas: first that a school with but few rules, and those based on common sense, would teach a boy self-reliance, independence and initiative. Secondly, that life in the West, with its vision, distance and color, could kindle a boy's imagination, and leave him with that ethereal spark which might at any time burst into flame."

The obsessions of H. Davis Evans and Lawrence Burst Sperry thus appear to have been harmonious. Lawrence's taste for freedom and adventure and his rebellion against the dull, monotonous, conventional life were already quite manifest when he arrived at the school. As for his ethereal spark, it had long since burst into flame.

A typical day at Mesa was described by Donald Myrick, one of Lawrence's classmates: "Mornings were spent caring for our horses and attending to our studies. Early in the afternoons we were free to ride or do whatever appealed to us."

What appealed to "Sperrooch," as he was affectionately called by his classmates, was studying the flight of the buzzards that soared tirelessly all day in the vast Arizona sky. "He tried to figure out how and why they could glide so long," Archie Roosevelt recalled. "Then he built a glider himself, with wings shaped like the buzzards', and he made a flight from the top of a haystack. We all cheered as he flew a couple of hundred feet, but he was dissatisfied. He said it was a pretty paltry performance compared to what a buzzard could do. He was absolutely fearless, reckless. We laughed at his recklessness; we teased him. Life was too short for him. He thought he was immortal.

"Lawrence was a maverick," Archie went on in fond reminiscence sixty years after their school days together. "He was weird compared with the rest of us. He was a genius. There's no other word for it. Most of the boys at Mesa either had bad health or were hard to handle. Sperrooch was in the latter category, I guess, since he didn't like his other school. He was the tallest boy at Evans School. Everybody liked him, students and masters alike. He loved tinkering with the windmill and the water pump with Major Brady, second in command at the school, another eccentric. Brady helped Sperrooch shoot some buzzards so they could study the wingspread. That was Sperrooch's bag. He was allergic to academic matters. Latin was an unmentionable subject."

During the course of his year at Mesa, Zula wrote many letters touting the joys and advantages of higher education at Cornell, where Lawrence's older brother, Ad, was being rushed by a dozen fraternities and was on the freshman banquet committee. Zula did not allude to what Lawrence really cared about: the fate of his plane and its Anzani engine.

Lawrence replied faithfully with details he knew his mother wished to hear. He was gaining weight, the chili con carne was tasty, he had gone on a six-day pack trip to the Sun Flower Cattle Ranch, he had found Indian arrowheads in a cave, he had met Theodore Roosevelt (who was "bully") when the president had visited Archie at the school, he and Archie had become good friends, they had gone duck shooting together, and he had roped Archie with a lasso.

Lawrence did not mention gliders and other aerial distractions in letters to his parents. These were reserved for his younger brother. Two months after they had been separated, Lawrence wrote:

November 12, 1911

Dear Elmer

How are you kiddo? I suppose you are driving the car around by this time remember to take my girl for a ride just telephone 5510 Morningside and ask when you should come.

Be shur to destroy this letter so that mother wont see it because of the tales I tell you.

Last Tuesday I went up 2000 ft in a captive balloon it was swell, the second time up I sat on the edge of the basket and let my feet hang over just to see how it would be on the trapese of the hot air balloon.

I got aquainted with the lady parachute jumper and asked her to let me take her place the following day. She let a man do it who wanted to go into the business she was just about to let me when she found I was under age that queered it. I argued that if I got hurt it would be easier for her to get into trouble than to be hurt herself but she couldn't see it I would have taken a chance they have been doing it for 10 yrs without mishap.

Gee whiz but this school is a cinch I only study about 4 hrs a day at the most then am all thru.

There is a bird up here called the buzzard it shur can fly very seldomly moves its wing just soars all day long looking for decayed animals can soar up hill or down and like the wind I got a bird and wrote down a lot of data from its spread of wing is 5'8" weighs only 2½ lbs.

PS. Give me inside information about the aeroplane the folks keap putting me off I hope you will get the tools and everything if they move bring all those wheels propellar and all home won't you love

                                                        Lawrence

It is interesting to note that Lawrence's phonetic spelling re-mained uncorrupted by the instruction of Dr. Evans's school. He also showed a rejection of conventional punctuation and syntax that came naturally to him at a time when Gertrude Stein was striving, artfully and desperately, to achieve similar effects in far-off Paris.

The definitive letter home was written to his parents the fol-lowing spring. Although there are vestiges of Lawrence's phonetic spelling, this ten-page letter is so carefully organized and punc-tuated as to suggest a helping hand from Major Brady or Dr. Evans himself, who must surely have realized that Lawrence was not destined for conventional scholastic success. One word, *un-magnanimous*, very painstakingly penned and correctly spelled, suggests that Lawrence may have had editorial assistance. But the tone of urgency and earnestness are those of a nineteen-year-old youth on the verge of a major decision. The letter is a solemn declaration of desire, a poignant and persuasive plea for parental understanding, and an eloquent document, not only in the history of aviation but also in the evolution of a boy into a man:

April 5, 1912

Dear Mother and Father:

School will be over very soon, as you know.

Almost ever since I came here I have been thinking what I shall want to do, after I leave.

In making my decision, you can just wager that I have tried to consider your wishes and I know that you will agree with me when I tell you what I want to do, and why I want to do it.

The questions before I left were: shall I go to college, if not, what business shall I enter?

In the first place consider me; a youth, impetuous, anxious to do something that he wants to do, and which will advance him to that end, uncontented until he is busy at that something. A youth so built, that he has been contented in the west only because he knew he was doing his health perminent good, and who becomes rather desperate to do something, at times, when he finds from day to day he is no longer gaining in weight.

Then consider; I am not contented to go to school, and never have been so well contented at any school, as I was when I worked on the plane last summer.

College people say that the broadening influence of college and the friends one makes there are alone worth the four years. College people are liable to be a little narrow minded on this point. I consider that I was becoming broader and better last summer.

If one does not go to college he nead not box himself up from the world. In other words college is not the only means of becoming broad, nor the only place where you can gain friends.

One can get just as much good influence in business as at college, and then he doesn't have the chance of going to the bad, his mind being too taken up with other things. He also misses the opurtunity of learning to smoke and drink which every college man that I can think of has picked up, more or less as a habit.

The more I see of college men the less I think of the broadening influence of college training, and the more I think it is the fellow himself who makes the best of his opurtunities or doesn't. I have seen numbers of broad minded college men, and numbers who were quite the opposite. Place these two groups to work, without going through college, and in nine out of ten cases they would turn out the same, in that respect. Take for instance Ed Angle, the farmer who runs this ranch, compare him with the four college grads here. Ed did not have the education of these men, but he is as broad minded as any one of them.

I do not intend to be a regular engineer. I will take a different branch of work, and let the other fellow do the figuring. It is significant to notice that the leading aeroplane designers, for instance, are not college-trained engineers. They each probably employ a college man to work on details and figures, but it is they who accomplish the big things.

I could write a volume on why I think it would n't be a good idea for me to drag through 4 years of college, but I think these reasons will suffice.

I want to enter the aeroplane business. I know you have no objections to this save that you think the game has a poor future. As for me I have utmost confidence in a brilliant one, and think that it is near at hand. Already aeroplanes are used to carry mail and for light passenger service. The hydro-aeroplane such as Coffyn used in New York harbor insures the sale of it as a safe pleasure craft for the sportsman. If you doubt the future of aeroplanes you are, simply placing yourselves in the unmagnanimous position of those who doubted the future of the railroad and the automobile. The aeroplane is bound to become safe and practical. Already they know that if a certain relation between the rear elevator and the main supporting planes were made, longitudinal stability would take care of itself.

Where would aeronautics be today, if the Wright brothers and others had not had implicit faith in the future of it, then why should we, who have seen what can be done with the crude unscientifically designed machine of today, be afraid to plunge in?

Your attitude towards aeroplanes is just the same as the attitude of America towards them. The french as a nation have faith in aeroplanes. The great engineer Eifel, builder of the Eifel tower, is spending a fortune, and devoting his time, to aerodynamical research. America is unwilling to take hold and do anything until France has absolutely proved how practical the aeroplane is.

I want to learn to fly for the following reasons.

One: The first thing I want to do is to finish the plane. I shall never be satisfied until I do that, as it is only right that I should try to make good to Wilcox, and not be a quitter. I will be poorly qualified to adjust and fly his plane unless I really know how to fly. Mr. Wilcox has given me permission to do this.

Secondly: If I am in the aeroplane business I certainly shall not want to sit around watching them fly without knowing how they do it. If I am in the plane business I want to know as much about the game as possible. I cannot advance as fast unless I am a pilot.

The last reason: I want to know if I *can* fly. That is, I don't want to be in a business without knowing that I am wholly qualified to be in it.

You should not condem aeroplaning, as a dangerous pursuit, because a few reckless, and in fact ignorant men, wholly incompetent save as simply pilots are taking reckless, fool chances to make large financial returns. These men such as Regeneux, who purposely glided backwards, Moisant who went from Paris to London in the more crude machine of yesterday, bear no relation to sane flight. It is their ignorance which makes the aeroplane game widely and vigourously denounced by many.

Its just like riding broncos, as long as you don't know anything about them you are willing to get on anything, thereby taking chances. Even with my small experience in aeroplanes, I am not willing to do fool things for the sake of a crowd. There is a glider out here which I tried to fly in a wind with the proper precautions, but was willing to let the other fellow try fool stunts of hitching horses on first.

Glenn Curtiss, who probably knows as much about aeroplanes as anyone, and who frequently flies, wrote concerning the Page accident: "As long as men will continue to do such things as Page attempted, we shall have these deplorable accidents, just as shurely as accidents result from reckless automobile driving at high speed. Standard makes of aeroplanes are today safer than ever before, and flying is becoming safer all the time. It will continue to grow safer if aviators will avoid reckless flying and observe ordinary precaution."

You must remember that I am not tired of life, looking around for a means of committing suicide; consequently I am not going to do anything that is apt to shorten my life. The day of the aviator is here. Learning to fly in a hyrdro-aeroplane is devoid of danger. Straight non-exhibition flying is little or no more dangerous than automobiling. With me it is just the same as it was with the automobile. I wasn't satisfied that Edward should drive, and I not know how. When you finally let me learn, I didn't care about driving, very much. I know there will be no temptation with me to take risks, I will let the other fellow do that.

Dear Father and Mother, I do not wish to do anything against

your wishes, and I know, as I said before, that what I want to do
will be in accordance with them, if you only see it in the right
light. I am very determined to go into aeroplanes, and I think that
you should help me get started, as you promised to do last fall,
when you said, that if I returned still strong for aeroplanes you
would help me.

Lawrence had thought of every psychological persuasion; he
was a super salesman when he believed in the product, in this
case himself. It was clear that if Elmer A. Sperry opposed airplanes he would be placing himself in the "unmagnanimous" position of those who doubted the future of progress.

Lawrence lulled his parents into believing that he was the soul
of caution, one who would never take risk. (There was no mention
of dangling his legs from the basket of a balloon.) Finally, he
reminded them of a solemn promise and that he expected it to be
kept.

The letter hit home. Father and Mother Sperry accepted the
inevitable. In Lawrence's phrase, they saw things "in the right
light."

"If he doesn't want to go to college," Zula said, "there's nothing
we can do to make him."

Father Sperry, who by this time was the holder of more than
160 patents, including those for the most advanced ship gyroscopes and gyroscopic compasses, promptly bought out Wilcox's
controlling interest in Lawrence's airplane together with the Anzani engine. This was to be Lawrence's graduation present—with
one string attached. He would have to *learn* to fly.

Father Sperry also wrote to Capt. Washington Irving Chambers, head of the fledgling aviation section of the U.S. Navy,
suggesting that the Navy and the Sperry Company collaborate on
the development of an automatic stabilizer for naval aircraft.
Chambers replied that the Navy would order a hydroplane from
the Glenn Curtiss Aeroplane Company and Flying School in
Hammondsport, New York, for experimental use in developing
the stabilizer.

This was the situation when Lawrence got home from Arizona,
no longer a skinny adolescent but a handsome, fleshed-out young

man of nineteen, six feet two inches tall and radiating the superb self-confidence of a man who knew what he wanted and knew that he could get it.

After a big family homecoming dinner, father and son had a man-to-man talk. Father Sperry said, "Do you remember when you said a gyroscope should be able to keep a plane in balance the way it steadies a ship?"

Lawrence remembered.

"How would you like to work on that idea with Glenn Curtiss and the U.S. Navy as a sort of practical project engineer?"

"Gee *whiz*," Lawrence replied. "Can a duck swim?"

Left to right:
Edward ("Ad") Sperry, at twelve; "a born businessman," his father called him. A handsome child, he grew up to look like the man in the Arrow Collar ad. He was the cashier and controller for Lawrence's bicycle repair shop and became an executive in the Sperry Gyroscope Company, a perfect company (corporation) man.

Lawrence at ten in Cleveland, when he had his first bicycle and newspaper route. He carried his brother Elmer, eight, on the handlebars, after training him to throw the newspapers from that position onto the clients' front porches.

Elmer A. Sperry, Jr., Lawrence's devoted slave and accomplice, at eight, in Cleveland, 1902. The following year, Lawrence got interested in airplanes, and Elmer inherited his newspaper route.

Above: Helen Sperry with her three brothers in Cleveland in 1903. Lawrence, extreme left, was eleven years old and, in the wake of the Wright Brothers' first flight, had just decided to become an aviator.

Right: Two geniuses in the family: Lawrence Sperry (left) stands behind his father, Elmer A. Sperry, in the family home in Brooklyn in 1911. Lawrence, seventeen, had just built and secretly flown the first tractor biplane in America. Next to him stands his younger brother and chief "accomplice," Elmer A. Sperry, Jr. Elder brother Edward Sperry, sister Helen Sperry, and Mother Zula Sperry complete the family portrait.

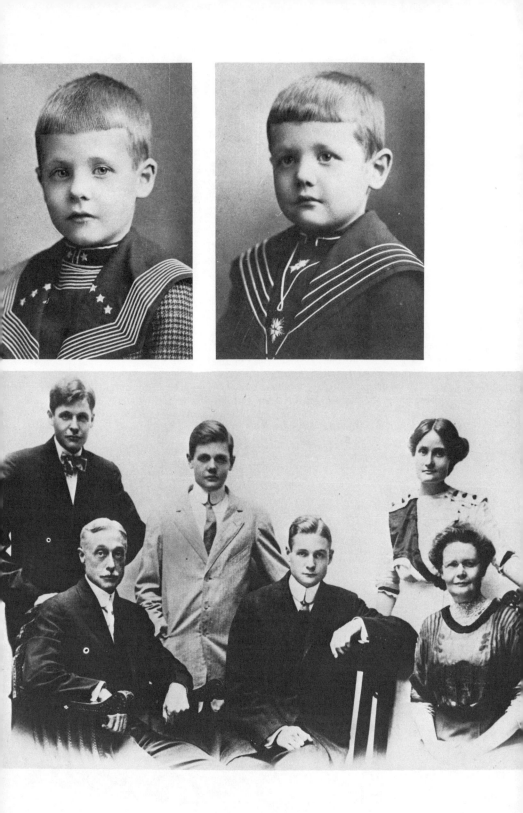

Above: Sixteen-year-old Lawrence at the wheel of the "Chinese Mercedes," his first car, acqui
with the profits of his bicycle repair shop in 1908.

Right: Lawrence puts finishing touches on the fuselage of his glider during the summer of 1910
upper right is the bay window he destroyed in order to get the wings out of the house.

Below: Lawrence tries out his glider without a motor at Sheepshead Bay, May 1911.

The first accident at Sheepshead Bay.

The six-wheel landing gear designed by Lawrence to keep the plane from turning over on rough ground.

On his way. Lawrence officially learns to fly in this Curtiss Pusher biplane with Pat Bellinger at the Glenn Curtiss School in Hammondsport in 1913. His first flights had been made surreptitiously three years earlier in a tractor plane of his own design and manufacture. *Courtesy of the Navy Department, the National Archives.*

Soloing at Hammondsport in the Curtiss Pusher biplane.

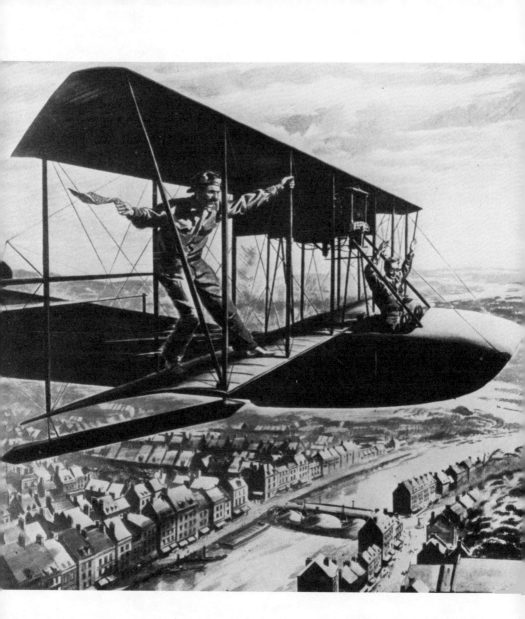

Top left: Contemporary and champion of Lawrence, Jimmy Doolittle, with his 1923 Curtiss Hawk at McCook Field, Dayton, the scene of Lawrence's cliff-hanging parachute jump. Like Lawrence, Jimmy was a stunt flyer whose "stunts" played a capital role in aviation research and testing.

Bottom left: Bezons, France, June 1914. Lawrence Sperry with his French mechanic, Emil Cachin, at the time of his prize-winning demonstration of the Sperry stabilizer, the first automatic pilot in aviation history.

Above: Artist's rendering of the triumphant demonstration of the stabilizer that won the $10,000 prize at Bezons, France. Lawrence, the pilot-inventor, was twenty-one.

Right: Father and son. Elmer A. Sperry, dapper in a derby, and Lawrence just before the demonstration of his stabilizer in 1914. Lawrence's physical resemblance to Lindbergh has often been noted.

Below: Lawrence developed this first American amphibian version of the Curtiss C-2 Flying Boat in 1915 at Amityville.

10

LAWRENCE had no formal engineering training. He studied birds, their weight, length, volume, and the relation of all this to their wingspread. His animal analogies were instinctive. He knew that seventy-six flyers had lost their lives in the course of a single year (1911) because of the instability of their planes in what Grover Loening, manager of the Wright Brothers Aeroplane Company, called "the treacherous and shifty character of the air ocean." In Mesa, Arizona, Lawrence had compared airplanes to bucking broncos that refused to acknowledge the right of man to master them. The planes had a tendency to nose-dive and ignore the wishes of the pilots. He was determined to change all that.

It was far above Keuka's waters (rather than Cayuga's) that Lawrence had his higher education under the direction of Glenn Curtiss, who, by 1912, had turned his hometown, Hammondsport, New York, into the most active aviation center in the United States. Curtiss Flying School was at Stonybrook Farm on the edge of Lake Keuka.

"There's nothing left at Hammondsport today but hallowed ground," Paul Garber, head curator of the Smithsonian Air and Space Museum, says. "But it really is hallowed. One of the greatest names in aviation is commemorated there in the Glenn Curtiss High School."

Lawrence, who was twenty when he went to Hammondsport, literally worshipped Glenn Curtiss. He was thirty-four and the most seasoned aviator in America. Like the Wrights, Lawrence himself, and so many other pilgrims of the air, Curtiss had begun his career with bicycles and motorcycles and graduated into flight. In 1908 he had won the *Scientific American* silver trophy for the first straight-line flight of one kilometer, flying a distance of 5,090 feet at Hammondsport. This performance also earned him Pilot License No. 1, issued by the Aero Club of America.

Going from strength to strength, Curtiss won the *Scientific American* trophy for the second time in 1909, flying his plane, the *Gold Bug*, twenty-five miles at Mineola. In August of that same year he achieved world fame by winning the James Gordon Bennett Prize for high speed in the first great international air meet at Reims, France. The following year Curtiss won the $10,000 Joseph Pultizer Prize by flying from Albany to New York City in two hours and fifty-one minutes, including refueling stops at Poughkeepsie and Spuyten Duyvel.

It was this flight, witnessed by millions of New Yorkers, that gave America a taste for exhibition flying. Glenn organized the Curtiss Exhibition Company, and his aviators made 541 flights in 210 cities during 1911 with gross receipts of nearly a million dollars.

Sending Lawrence to learn flying from Glenn Curtiss was thus like sending a seminarian to study under the pope. Glenn Curtiss found "Gyro," as he nicknamed Lawrence, the most apt of pupils, and absolutely fearless.

Grover Loening, four years older than Lawrence and destined, like Lawrence, to be a major force in the history of aviation, was at Hammondsport when Gyro arrived there.

"In the summer of 1913," he wrote in his personal papers, "there wandered into Hammondsport and over the flying field a miniature replica of an idealized Lincoln. Not so very miniature either for this boy had passed six feet in height before his 19th birthday. This boy's face had that combined expression of good humor, intelligence, bashfulness and diffidence one associates with the generally reproduced portraits of Lincoln. He had none of the lines marking the face of the Emancipator, of course. He was just a youthful, wistful, quite good-looking tall boy.

"His name was Lawrence Sperry, later to become known in the aviation world as 'Gyro' Sperry. A friendful youth who did not seem to take himself at all seriously, but who, for all his easygoing smile, had unlimited courage and perseverance. He was in Hammondsport at Glenn Curtiss' invitation for the triple purpose of experimenting with the gyroscopic stabilizer, demonstrating and developing it, and learning to fly.

"Young Sperry made an immediate conquest of Lieutenants Richardson and Bellinger, and received somewhat more grudging recognition from instructor Doc Wildman, who complained that the only trouble was that Sperry wanted to fly too fast and too high."

Lawrence's homemade tractor biplane crashed on the frozen surface of Lake Keuka that winter. The only things that were salvaged from the wreck were the Anzani engine and Lawrence himself. He slid several hundred yards across the lake on his leather backside, picked himself up, and said, "The trip lock of the stabilizer didn't work when I went back into manual control; that's why I couldn't get out of that thirty-degree angle of descent. I should have cut the motor sooner. Well, live and learn."

"You learn slower, you'll live longer," Doc Wildman said.

Glenn Curtiss then put one of his Curtiss Pusher biplanes at Lawrence's disposal. This was the famous flying boat in which Lawrence would make history.

"Take it easy, Gyro," Curtiss said. "Stick to grass cutting for a while."

Grass cutting meant low, relatively safe flying, but Lawrence couldn't manage to stay near the ground. Teacher had hardly turned his back when Gyro was a thousand feet up.

"That's mighty tall grass, son," Curtiss said when Lawrence returned to earth.

"We didn't have to teach Lawrence Sperry to fly," Curtiss recalled many years later. "He had no need of dual instruction. He took to the air like a bird; he was *born* to fly."

On October 5, 1913, two months before his twenty-first birthday, Lawrence officially got his "wings," receiving Federal Aeronautics Pilot License No. 11 from the Aero Club of America as a hydroplane pilot, having qualified with distinction in a Curtiss flying boat. This license was soon extended to cover all types of heavier-than-air flying craft. Gyro Sperry thus became the eleventh member of a proud and exclusive fraternity that included such pioneers as Orville and Wilbur Wright, Frank P. Lahm, Louis Paulhan, and Glenn Curtiss himself: Curtiss held Pilot License No. 1, much to the annoyance of the Wright Brothers and their partisans, but the Aero Club stuck to its guns. They considered Curtiss's invention and development of the flying boat even more important than the first flight at Kitty Hawk.

Fourteen years Lawrence's senior, Glenn Curtiss was one of the greatest pioneers of aviation. He had a bristling moustache and the burning, almost fanatical eyes of a prophet, eyes that saw an aviator's "vision of the world and all the wonder that would be." He also had a mordant sense of humor. When his mother, a chronic complainer, complained about the sand fleas at Coronado, where he was building her a house, Curtiss said, "After you've been there a year or so, you'll become distasteful to them."

Curtiss, looking for more clement weather than the freezing temperatures of Hammondsport, had established winter quarters for his school at North Island, a four-mile-long sandbar between San Diego Bay and the Pacific Ocean. It was separated from Coronado Island by a shallow bay, the Spanish Bight. Unlike Lake Keuka, the Spanish Bight never froze over. Curtiss and the Aero Club of San Diego negotiated a three-year lease with the Coronado Beach Company, which owned North Island. The clients of the fashionable Coronado Beach Hotel were delighted. In those days airplanes enhanced the environment.

Glenn Curtiss's success with the flying boat he had invented converted the U.S. Navy to a new interest in the possibilities of aviation. Congress appropriated $25,000 for the development of "a hydroplane capable of rising from or landing on land or water and capable of attaining a speed of at least 55 miles an hour, with a fuel supply for four hours' flight."

In the fall of 1913, twenty-year-old Lawrence Sperry, the youngest licensed pilot in America, followed Curtiss to North Island. Here, under the mentorship of Curtiss and U.S. Navy supervision, the Curtiss shop was put at Gyro's disposal. And here, according to Clara Studer in her book *Sky Storming Yankee*, Lawrence Sperry "worked for months trying to perfect his strange-looking invention, the gyroscopic stabilizer."

In perfecting the stabilizer Lawrence had to pit his wits against the inexorable forces of aerodynamics: gravity, lift, drag, and thrust. He was faced with major mechanical problems that could only be solved pragmatically by a skilled pilot who was not afraid to take chances. In spite of his father's objection that he should confine himself to the drawing board and let others risk their necks, Gyro could not work in that theoretical way. He *had* to use his practical experience and "seat of the pants" intuition to test the device he was creating. That it was worth creating he never doubted. He realized, without putting it into words, that the future of aviation depended on stability in flight, that a stable airplane must be developed to resist all the forces that could combine to change its flight position. He felt that this essential stability could and should be automatically assured. The stabilizer, once perfected, could actually eliminate human error. It could be counted on to keep a plane on course in bad weather conditions, even if the pilot's vision was reduced to zero.

Lawrence already knew from experience that once human control was relinquished, the plane would tend to roll and turn away from its set course, prey to "torque," the inevitable tendency of the aircraft to rotate in the opposite direction of the spinning propeller. He also knew, from having dared to take his hands off the joystick in full flight, that the plane would pitch up and down at the mercy of the wind, lose airspeed, stall, and crash. In certain air currents the aircraft would go into a "Dutch roll," turning, oscillating, zigzagging to left or right, floundering, totally out of control.

He would have to preclude all these potential disasters with his automatic pilot. He would also have to arrive at an exact determination of the aircraft's behavior around the three major axes: vertical and horizontal roll and horizontal pitch. In short, he had to devise a stabilizing system that would be as sensitive to all these hazards as the human pilot. The automatic pilot must do mechanically what the pilot did instinctively, and Lawrence was convinced that it could do it even better, since a gyroscope could not be disoriented as the human eye can when the horizon disappears in fog or darkness.

Lawrence decided that two gyroscopes would be necessary to stabilize the plane, one for the vertical axis, the other to regulate alignment in the horizontal pitch and roll axes. He conceived a vertical gyroscope to operate the ailerons and elevators of the plane and a horizontal gyroscope to control the rudder. The concept was brilliant and basically simple, but its practical application was complicated. First of all he rejected the unwieldy process of mounting the gyroscopes separately and suspending them like pendulums. Experience had taught him that they would swing and lurch with the motion of the plane. To avoid this liability, he decided to nest the two gyros on a single platform as near as possible to the center of gravity of the plane. In the Curtiss flying boat, this was on the floor of the hull just under the forward part of the engine.

Thinking more of his invention than of his own comfort, Lawrence removed the back of the copilot's seat so that he could turn and observe the action of the stabilizer in flight. He carefully suspended his two gyroscopes in gimbals, contrivances that permitted them to incline freely in any direction but still remain plumb when the plane pitched or rolled. The next step was to achieve perfect coordination between the gyroscopes and the rudder, ailerons, and elevator that control the aircraft's behavior. To effect this he installed three electric servomotors, equipped with cable reels.

"What's that strange-looking contraption?" Patrick Bellinger asked him. "It looks like a cross between an alarm clock and a fishing reel."

Bellinger, whom the Navy had designated as the official test pilot for the stabilizer-equipped Curtiss flying boat, was a good pilot but limited in imagination. He was suspicious of innovation. Although he visited Lawrence in the Curtiss shop and went through the motions of studying the stabilizer, he didn't really trust it. He liked to pilot an airplane, and he took a dim view of turning the controls over to a machine, especially since he was fond of stunting and buzzing the grandstands.

He watched Gyro attach these strange-looking "fishing reels" to the aircraft control cables. Thus attached, Lawrence explained to Bellinger, the servomotors replaced the pilot's control of joystick and rudder pedals and could automatically operate the rudder, elevators, and ailerons of the plane.

"Yeah," said Bellinger skeptically, "but what's gonna operate the servomotors?"

Lawrence explained that they were powered by an air-driven windmill-type generator mounted in the struts of the wing.

Gyro's use of this device was typical of his practical application of traditional principles.

Lawrence's next problem was to establish a communications link between the gyroscopes and the servomotors so that the gyroscopes would tell the motors what to do when human control of the plane was relinquished. He linked the gyro casings to the servomotors by means of an adjustable, sliding electric switch. He then devised a foot pedal for changing from manual to automatic control and back again, as the clutch of an automobile enables the driver to change speed.

With this adaptation of a familiar automotive principle to the new science of aeronautics, Lawrence achieved a typical mechanical breakthrough that was the culmination of a year's hard work.

"He's a chip off the old block," Zula Sperry wrote to her brother. "So full of energy and enthusiasm he's going his father's pace when his father was the same age."

The energy and enthusiasm infected all the flying students and naval personnel at North Island, except for Bellinger, who remained skeptical. But since the Navy was footing the bills for the testing of the stabilizer, Lawrence had to accept Bellinger, who incidentally was also suspicious of the Navy's spending so much money on a private venture. A first-rate flyer, Bellinger advanced eventually to the rank of admiral. It was his unfortunate destiny to be one of those admirals who were rudely awakened by the Japanese at Pearl Harbor in 1941.

Although Patrick Bellinger was a daredevil stunt pilot in his own right, he had reason to be wary of Lawrence's "contraption." Lawrence had supervised the installation of a lateral stabilizer on a flying boat for the U.S. Army, but its pilot, Lieutenant Goodier, smashed up the plane, fracturing his skull in the process. Another young Army pilot, Lieutenant Brereton, testing the longitudinal stabilizer, crashed on landing, destroying the plane and killing his passenger, Rex Chandler. Lawrence did not describe these accidents in letters home; he just hoped the folks wouldn't hear about them.

The Navy tests fared better. Lawrence installed the complete stabilizer on the Curtiss Flying Boat C-2. In the halcyon fall weather of North Island, Bellinger made fifty-two test flights with Lawrence aboard, his lanky frame contorted into the most difficult positions as he observed every action and reaction of the gyropilot. His concentration was so great that, on one occasion, sprawled on his stomach on the floor of the plane, he remained oblivious to danger as the flying boat slammed down into the water of the Spanish Bight. Finding himself underwater, Lawrence had the presence of mind to save the stabilizer as well as himself. He emerged, dripping wet, triumphantly brandishing his gyroscopes and "fishing reel" motors. Such bravery and his unswerving concentration won some grudging approval from Bellinger, who reported that Lawrence was "brilliant, hard-working, enthusiastic, but impetuous and young."

Problems accumulated. Every adjustment in the stabilizer disturbed the setting of the plane's controls. Resetting the controls disturbed the stabilizer. Lawrence discovered, among other things, that the vertical rudder of the plane had to be set five degrees off the neutral position to compensate for the rotation of the propeller. Once again, scientific theory was tempered by experience.

A major problem, from Lawrence's point of view, was Bellinger's tendency to grab the manual controls before Lawrence could determine the reasons for what appeared to be capricious deviations of the plane in flight. After the crash in the Spanish Bight, Bellinger was even more reluctant to relinquish manual control to Gyro's strange contraption. If the plane went into a turn, Lawrence would drop to the floor to make a compensatory adjustment with the lateral stabilizer, but Bellinger would switch to manual control so fast that the experiment was inconclusive.

There was a good deal of mutual exasperation. Lawrence felt that the stabilizer had not been given a fair chance to prove itself, especially in the matter of counteracting the plane's tendency to "hunt," or oscillate in the longitudinal sense.

As for Bellinger, *his* exasperation reached its apogee on one brilliant autumn day when Lawrence, in the midst of a flight, started to walk out onto the wing to test the stabilizer's ability to hold the plane in balance.

"Gyro, what the *hell* are you doing?" Bellinger yelled.

"Testing," Lawrence yelled back.

But the test was a failure because Bellinger had immediately
and instinctively pressed the foot pedal and grabbed the joystick
to resume manual control, thus preventing the stabilizer from
working.

"You're plumb crazy, Gyro," Bellinger shouted as the flying
boat dipped dangerously. "Get back in the cockpit or you'll kill us
both. And that's an order," he added in the best naval tradition.

Although he himself was not yet in the Navy, Lawrence obeyed
for the moment, but he bided his time. He understood now that
his major problem was to outwit Lieutenant Bellinger.

A minor problem was Bellinger's penchant for the ladies. The
nearby Coronado Beach Hotel was full of vacationing young
women who yearned to go up in a plane. Lieutenant Bellinger
preferred their company to that of Lawrence, especially during
the best weather for observation. Lawrence would eventually
outdo Bellinger in this department, sometimes with spectacular,
not to say scandalous, consequences.

In the fall of 1913, however, Lawrence had a spotless moral
reputation, worthy of his Baptist forebears. He was living with "a
gang of flyers and grease monkeys at North Island," Frank Bell,
one of his colleagues, recalled later, "but I don't think I ever saw
a *cleaner* boy than Gyro. That gang at North Island was really
tough in many ways, but Gyro was above it all. His head was in
the clouds and he had one fixed idea: that stabilizer, perfecting it
and publicizing it."

His efforts to perfect it often brought publicity. After fifty-two
test flights with Bellinger, Lawrence was convinced that the stabilizer had still not been given a fair shake; it had never been
allowed to function without Bellinger's interference. It was time,
he decided, to take desperate measures.

Though it went against the Sperry family's Baptist principles of
never working on the Sabbath, Lawrence chose a Sunday morning in late November of 1913 to do what he had to do. The "gang
of flyers and grease monkeys" had spent Saturday night wining
and wenching in the saloons of San Diego. The Glenn Curtiss
School, it must be admitted, had this reputation in Hammondsport as well as on North Island. The student pilots' motto
was "Water for frogs—wine for men."

Everybody was asleep in the barracks and cottages of North Island when Lawrence rose quietly at dawn on that particular Sabbath day. He got into his togs and, carrying his boots, stole past his snoring companions, silently opened the door, silently shut it, and breathed the fresh morning air. Quickly putting on his boots, he made a beeline for the great flying boat moored to the dock. He could see its huge bulk in the lemon-colored light of dawn, and the slap, slap of the water on its sledlike pontoon was music to his ears. No sound came from the waterfront shack, where the guard slept soundly. Stepping silently onto the pontoon, Lawrence gave an expert downward yank to the propeller. It spun at his touch. The motor sputtered, then roared, shattering the silence. He felt the vibration of the aeroboat in every fiber of his body. The plane was like a horse straining at its tether. No time to lose, no time to fool with knots. Lawrence cut the taut hawsers with two swipes of a knife. The boat was already moving as Lawrence climbed into the pilot's seat. He skimmed across the corrugated surface of the Spanish Bight, feeling the salt spray stinging his cheeks. Then he felt the bulky boat leap into the air like a sea gull. He was free.

On the ground people began to stir in their sleep. The guard woke up and rushed out onto the dock. He rubbed his eyes and strained them, as though in an effort to identify the early-bird Sunday morning pilot. What he saw he couldn't believe. There was no pilot visible. The plane appeared to be flying itself.

The incredulous guard ran to the bungalow where Glenn Curtiss, his wife, Lena, and their year-old son, Glenn H. Curtiss, Jr., were sleeping.

"Sir," said the guard, "there's a boat in the air and there's nobody in it. It's flying by itself."

"Man," said Glenn Curtiss, looking at him sternly, "you've been drinking. Better go back and sleep it off."

But the drone of the motor was unmistakable. There was no doubt that a plane was in the air, and it now appeared, banking and turning, swooping down toward the beach, then back up into the sky, then veering off toward the marshes, where it disturbed the flocks of pelicans and ducks that nested there. The sky was shattered by the silhouettes of these birds as Glenn Curtiss grabbed his field glasses and followed the antics of the wayward plane. It was true: no pilot was visible.

"Like I told you, sir," the guard said. "The plane is flying by its own self."

"Yes, it's flying by itself," Curtiss said as he followed every maneuver with eyes intense as fire, "but that doesn't mean there's nobody aboard. And if it isn't Gyro Sperry, then I'm not Glenn Hammond Curtiss."

"It's the maddest thing I ever saw," he said to Lena, who had joined him on the porch of the bungalow. "But, like it says somewhere in Shakespeare, there's method in it."

There was indeed. Lawrence was lying on the floor of the plane, working the foot pedal with his right hand, occasionally rearing up to grab the joystick, but concentrating most of all on his gyroscopes. Oblivious to danger, he exulted at last in the proof that his invention worked. When he deliberately veered to the right, the gyroscopes brought the plane back on course. When he went into a Dutch roll, the stabilizer calmed the bobbing plane like oil poured onto roiling water, and when he volplaned down toward the earth, the servomotors and the gyroscopes cooperated to level her out.

By this time everybody on North Island was awake. The students and the grease monkeys and the naval officers were all on the beach watching the "pilotless" plane.

Then the pilot appeared, tall in the cockpit, and then he got out and, grabbing the wooden struts, walked out onto the wing and waved to his colleagues below. The plane dipped, then righted itself.

"That's Gyro, all right," growled Bellinger. "Tried that damn fool stunt with me in the plane. If he was in the Navy he'd be court-martialed."

Everybody else cheered, except Glenn Curtiss, who had come down to the beach to watch Gyro land. Lawrence made a perfect landing on the water and taxied up to the dock in a burst of spray. His fellow students were irrepressible. They hoisted him onto their shoulders and did a little snake dance. Then they put him down before Glenn Curtiss, who did not look at all amused. In fact, the men, who regarded him as a comrade, had never seen him look so grim. His moustache bristled and there were sparks in his eyes.

"Gyro," he said sternly, "after a performance like that, I think you have just about exhausted the resources of North Island."

Silence on the beach, except for the shrieks of sea gulls. Lawrence was bewildered. All the men were looking at him, then at Curtiss.

"What do you mean, sir?" Lawrence managed to say.

"I mean that it's time to conduct these stabilizer experiments somewhere else."

"Like where?" Lawrence said. He was utterly dashed.

"Far from here," Curtiss replied. "Maybe in Europe."

"*Europe?*" Lawrence said.

"Matter of fact," Curtiss went on, "I was thinking of France."

"*France?*"

"The Aero Club of France and the French War Department have announced an international aeroplane safety competition," Curtiss said. "It'll be next June at a place called Bezons. That's near Paris," he added.

"They call this contest a *concours de sécurité*," Curtiss went on. "The prize is fifty thousand francs. That's ten thousand U.S. dollars."

The grease monkeys whistled. That was big money, all right.

Lawrence, looking very puzzled, was staring at Glenn Curtiss.

"I think you should enter that contest with your stabilizer," Curtiss said, "and I'll provide a Curtiss Flying Boat C-2 for the demonstration."

Lawrence didn't speak. He and the students and the other pilots and the mechanics were all looking at each other in varying degrees of wild surmise.

"The Aero Club of the United States will arrange for your entry as U.S. Pilot Number 11," Curtiss said. "And a graduate of the Glenn Curtiss Flying School.

"Well, Gyro, what do you say? Speak up. Will you enter the French safety contest?"

"Can a duck swim?" Lawrence said.

Curtiss smiled. He had cut the comedy. He advanced and put his arm around Lawrence's shoulders.

"Gyro," he said, "after your little matinee this morning, all the ducks on North Island are paralyzed."

Curtiss was as good as his word. In January 1914, just a week after his twenty-first birthday, Lawrence received a spanking new Curtiss flying boat. On January 20 the plane and Lawrence both appeared on the front page of the *New York Herald* under a banner headline:

SHIP AEROPLANE FOR BIG SAFETY
CONTEST IN FRANCE

Lawrence looked so handsome and eager: it was excellent publicity for Curtiss and aviation in general. Among the sports-minded millionaires who placed orders for planes and signed up for lessons with Curtiss were Harry S. Harkness, Harold F. Mc-Cormick of the International Harvester Corporation, and the Detroit publishing tycoon William B. Scripps.

Glenn Curtiss did try to attach one string to the flying boat he had provided for the contest. When Lawrence arrived in Paris in April he received a cablegram from Curtiss:

RECOMMEND YOU EMPLOY A PILOT TO FLY MACHINE
DURING TEST FLIGHTS AND FINAL DEMONSTRATION
BEFORE JUDGES

Remembering his trials with Bellinger, Lawrence wired back immediately:

PILOT WOULD BE IN THE WAY STOP I WILL FLY IT
MYSELF.

11

LAWRENCE ARRIVED in Paris in April of 1914 at that irrecoverable moment just four months before the husk of the Old World was split asunder by the First World War. The City of Light and the Valley of the Seine vibrated in a luminous haze. The noble vistas of Paris had yet to be spoiled by imitation American skyscrapers and other brutal excrescences of a less gracious age. Paris was still the most beautiful city in the world. Lawrence was well pleased with it, and it with him.

He stayed at the Hôtel Avenida at 41, rue du Colisée, just a block from the Champs-Elysées. Ultramodern, it boasted electric lights in every room and a bathroom on every floor. His room was equipped with a *cabinet de toilette,* with hot and cold running water, and something called a *bidet,* which he couldn't quite figure out.

Although he spoke no French, his linguistic accomplishments being limited to having flunked Latin and German at Erasmus Hall, Lawrence's good looks overcame this liability. He got along very well with his hosts, who pronounced him *beau et séduisant.* "Spéri" being such a *drôle de nom,* the hotel manager, Mme. Durand, referred to him as *le bel américain.*

He was taken into tow by Paul Jourdan, son of Commander Sauvaire Jourdan, who was the Paris agent of the Sperry Gyroscope Company. Paul knew all the hot spots of Paris. He took Lawrence to the *Folies Bergère.* There he saw unheard-of sights: women on stage, stark naked and shameless as Eve before the Fall. They were seductively deployed in a series of historic and aesthetic *tableaux vivants.* In Veronese's *Love Chamber of the Dogaressa,* Lawrence stared in delighted disbelief as the Doge's wife disrobed, dallied with her lovers, and pushed them into the Grand Canal. There was real water on the stage. They all emerged at the end, dripping wet in jockstraps, to take a bow. *Oh là là!* It was one of the first French phrases Lawrence learned.

Scenes like this could not be described in letters home. "We have a great deal of fun in the evening," Lawrence wrote to his mother. "The french certainly know how to have a good time." Writing to his sister Helen, he described such divertissements as *The Love Chamber of the Dogaressa* and *The Nights of Casanova* as "historical plays."

"I went to the Louvre," he wrote to Helen, "but I wish you were here to explain about the works of art I like to look at them but of course don't understand them. I can plainly see that Paris would be your Mecca."

His own Mecca was the village of Bezons on the Seine, northwest of Paris and adjacent to Argenteuil, a favorite spot of the Impressionist painters, who were fascinated by the shining river, wrapped in a gauzy shawl of vaporous light. Here at Bezons were the docks and hangars prepared for the air safety contest, and the village was abuzz with the activities of fifty-seven entrants. Though he spoke no French, Lawrence was instantly at home here in the grease-monkey atmosphere of French mechanics. He hired a mechanic named Emile Cachin, a tough little Parisian type with a superb moustache set with grease in a permanent twirl. Emile patted the flanks of the Curtiss flying boat as though it were a pet porpoise. *"Quel beau bébé!"* he exclaimed when he first saw it. "What a beautiful baby!" He and Lawrence treated it accordingly, easing the big aeroboat in and out of the Seine like two doting nursemaids. They understood the language of mechanics, and they had one other quality in common: neither of them knew the meaning of fear in any language.

Emile watched in admiration as Lawrence installed the stabilizer, and he had the instinctive mechanic's respect for *"le grand Gyro,"* who obviously knew what he was about.

"I've got a perfect mechanic," Lawrence wrote to his father. "Doesn't need to be told what to do he sort of senses it."

In this same letter Lawrence apparently felt the need to justify his wire to Curtiss about flying the plane without the aid of a pilot:

I have a good deal of experience around machines not so much flying alone but far more than the majority of men who went out with flying boats last winter at North Island. I am getting along very well going carefully of course and slowly at first. I have always been bothered by having to tell someone else what I wanted done in these experimental flights instead of doing it myself.

Yesterday I first flew with the lateral for ten or fifteen minutes. I made left turns and right turns each time the gyro keaping me from over banking. I then came down, disconnected the lateral and in its place connected the longitudinal. In the air I found that this worked equally well. I then connected the two together flying a long time solely with the gyroscopic control. Gyroscopic control certainly makes flying pleasant instead of having to be constantly on the alert the gyro does it for you. Current for the force impresser must be constantly supplied or else the gyros go off almost instantly, I did this when I throtled my motor too low. Today I have been rearranging belt shift so that I will always have current as long as the motor keaps running.

I think I am best off alone for many reasons. I can climb fast, much faster alone than with a passenger so I repeat another pilot would be in the way.

P.S. 1 Longitudinal gyros behave themselves on starting.

P.S. 2 Am deadbroke not having received any money from the company. Can you bring or send me some? I tried to telephone you but the french operator sounded like a hen on a hot griddle and I couldn't understand her except Ne quittez pas, that means don't quit but finely after about an hour I did.

Helen had urged Lawrence to learn French and live with a French family.

"You're right," he wrote her, "but it's impractical because with a french family you are obliged to pay even for meals you don't eat, and I am at Bezons most of the time and I do not have much time to learn French because I am so busy with the machine."

As a matter of fact he did learn French from his mechanic, Emile, who spoke no English. Lawrence explained the workings of the stabilizer to Emile in slow and careful English, and Emile caught on with the quick, vivacious intelligence of a French workman.

"Ah oui; le stabilisateur gyroscopique; c'est très logique ce truc là. Formidable. Ça permet au pilote le libre usage de ses mains."

"Oui, oui, oui," Lawrence replied. In two months' time he learned enough essential French so that he could deliver an irresistible sales talk for *le stabilisateur,* which, thanks to Emile, he now called *le truc* for short.

"Vous voyez ce truc là?" he would say to his audience. "Do you see that gadget there?"

They all did, and he could soon explain every *truc* of the stabilizer in French from *le générateur électrique* to the *servo-moteur.* He also picked up from Emile the habit of punctuating every phrase with an interrogation: *quoi?* or *n'est-ce-pas?* By the time Zula and Father Sperry arrived to witness Lawrence's performance in the contest, they were amazed at the fluency of their son, whom Erasmus Hall and the Desert School of Arizona had declared "ungifted for languages."

Every morning Lawrence took the trolley car from Paris to Bezons. He and Emile eased the C-2 out of its hangar onto the muddy bank of the Seine, slid it gently into the water, and climbed into the twin-seated open cockpit behind the snub nose of this cratelike biplane. Lawrence was determined to fly it under every possible atmospheric condition. He came to know the currents of the Seine as well as any man alive, and what a thrill it was to taxi down the river, paying special attention to the hazards of the bridges at Bezons and Argenteuil, and then to feel that heavy machine rise from the water. Lawrence got to know and love Paris from the air, picking out the landmarks of that concentric city widening out in circles from its historic nucleus on a little island in the Seine. It was like seeing the monuments of man with the eyes of God: Notre Dame, the Panthéon, the Ecole Militaire, the Invalides, and all the formal gardens and parks of Paris glistening through the hazy light of the Ile de France.

These were his happiest moments, when he was free to fly and to test the stabilizer, his only constraint being the machine itself. He loved the feeling of the shoulder yokes that made him feel the stabilizer's response, its sensitivity to every current of air, and its perfect lateral control. As soon as the machine began to tip in puffy weather, the yokes would move accordingly until the plane came back to level. Lawrence became a living part of the plane.

"It certainly is wonderful," he wrote, "to feel the moving frame against your body as all sorts of air puffs and biffs are being taken care of by the stabilizer. I think the greatest experience, however, is on turns where the plane banks itself and the apparatus holds the plane banked just right, stabilizing all the time and holding its new position against all puffs and irregularities of the wind and even pockets and holes in the air."

The Sperry stabilizer was last on the alphabetical list of the fifty-seven international entries in the Concours de la Sécurité en Aeroplane. Blériot was the first of the competing aviators. The tests of the Sperry apparatus were scheduled to take place after all the other carburetors, magnetos, self-starters, parachutes, compasses, and more conventional nongyroscopic stabilizers had been tested.

A few days before June 18, Zula and Father Sperry arrived in Paris and were given a royal welcome by Mme. Durand, the proprietor of the Hôtel Avenida: *"Tiens, la maman et le papa du bel américain si sympathique. Soyez les bienvenus, Monsieur et Madame Spéri!"*

Dapper, derbied, fifty-four-year-old Elmer A. Sperry had a sense of quiet showmanship and dignified publicity that now went smoothly into high gear. He and Reginald Gillmor, the head of Sperry's London office, had invited the American, French, British, and German naval attachés to the final day of the Concours. All ambassadors and consuls had been invited, and on the morning of June 18 an impressive cortege of black automobiles rolled up to the spot where the C-2 was standing on the north bank of the Seine between the bridges of Bezons and Argenteuil. The twenty distinguished gentlemen of the jury, including Commandant Barrès and M. René Quinton, president of the Ligue Nationale Aérienne de France, drove up in five automobiles and ensconced themselves in two grandstands that had been constructed at the edge of the river. There were reporters from all the Paris newspapers including the *New York Herald*, which reported that Lawrence was "nervous." Zula, on the contrary, pronounced her son "cool as a cucumber" and "happy and picturesque in his yellow blouse and trousers, very French."

If Lawrence was nervous it must have been because of the thousands of curious Frenchmen swarming around the Curtiss flying boat. There was hardly room for the Gaumont and Pathé newsreel cameramen to set up their cameras.

Finally, with all the judges and dignitaries seated, Lawrence and Emile Cachin were able to clear a path for the flying boat and ease it, with the enthusiastic if unsolicited help of numerous French youngsters, into the river. Lawrence and Emile climbed into the cockpit, waved to the crowd, and taxied upstream on the jade-green water of the Seine. Both left and right banks of the river were now thronged with people enjoying the intoxicating atmosphere of a perfect day in June, and the festive mood was accentuated by the firemen's band of Bezons-Argenteuil which essayed *The Star Spangled Banner* as the plane moved slowly on its pontoon upstream and out of sight.

After a long wait, the drone of the motor was heard on the summer air. The plane appeared just above the Argenteuil bridge.

"*Le voilà!*" somebody shouted. "Here it comes!"

Lawrence, in his own words, "disentangled himself from the control of the machine," and as the C-2 zoomed down right above the judges' stand, he stood up entirely away from the controls with both hands high above his head. The judges and the dignitaries ducked and gasped as the great volplaning machine righted itself on automatic control and soared back up into the sky.

Lawrence banked and turned, flew over the Argenteuil bridge once more, and made a second pass toward the north bank. This time, as he flew above the judges' stand, Emile Cachin got up from his seat and walked out seven feet on the lower starboard wing. The plane dipped momentarily to starboard, then righted itself immediately, thanks to the stabilizer, and the machine flew on completely by itself with Lawrence triumphantly repeating his no-hands gesture.

"*Mais c'est inouï,*" said Judge René Quinton—"absolutely unheard-of!"

It was dramatically clear that the disturbing force of the mechanic's weight on the wing had no effect on the plane's equilibrium as long as the stabilizer was operating.

Emile now returned to his seat. Lawrence resumed manual

control; then, as he approached the Bezons bridge, he put the machine on automatic again. As they flew low over the spectators again, both he and Emile stood up, gaily waving French and American flags.

When Lawrence deliberately let the motor drop below critical speed, the anemometer instantly changed the relation between the gyroscopes and the airplane so that the machine went into an automatic volplane of twenty degrees, which it maintained until Lawrence turned on the power for a third climb.

By this time the spectators were shouting, *"Bravo! C'est formidable! Remarquable! Extraordinaire!"* and other Gallic phrases of approbation, but they hadn't seen anything yet.

Approaching the spectators for the third time, Lawrence stood up on the seat of the plane while Emile crawled between the wings and out onto the fuselage "as close to the spinning propeller as possible without danger of being hit." The stabilizer automatically maintained the longitudinal balance of the plane.

Lawrence now repeated these dazzling demonstrations, flying even lower to enable the jury to see more clearly what was happening. In the culminating pass, Lawrence abandoned the pilot's seat entirely, strolled out onto the port wing, and waved the star-spangled banner while Emile did the same thing with the tricolor on the starboard wing.

The pilotless plane righted itself once more and soared above the heads of the delighted multitude.

"You must be very proud of your son," Mme. Sauvaire Jourdan said to Zula. "He is a fine aviator."

"Yes, it's a wonderful sight, and he made a beautiful landing," Zula said, and there were tears in her eyes after so many years of pent-up anxiety as she saw her smiling boy come skimming back across the Seine safe and sound.

But she couldn't get near him. As the prow of the flying boat touched the bank of the Seine, the crowd grabbed Lawrence and Emile, hoisted them to their shoulders, and carried them up and down the riverbank while the firemen's band burst into the *Marseillaise.* It was one of those spontaneous popular French tributes to the hero of the hour. Lawrence loved it all, but kept darting anxious looks in the direction of the plane, afraid the crowd might break it into bits as souvenirs. Fortunately it remained intact, and the triumphal snake dance up and down the riverbank ended abruptly for an imperative French reason: the clock struck twelve in the steeple of the Bezons church; it was time for lunch.

The judges now bussed Lawrence formally on both cheeks, requested private flights that same afternoon in the plane, and the Sperrys, the Jourdans, and various officials went off to Les Marronniers on the riverbank for a victory lunch under the flowering chestnut tree. It was a typical French country inn where Lawrence had been eating lunch for the past two months.

"Do not mention the Folies Bergère to my mother and father," Lawrence whispered to Paul Jourdan as they made their way to a table in the garden.

It was a wonderful lunch: pâté de foie gras, fresh salmon, those incomparable French green peas and potatoes, fresh strawberries with cream. "No wonder the French don't travel," sighed Zula. "How could they ever eat in America?"

"*Qu'est-ce-qu'il est beau, votre fils, madame,*" said Mme. Laroche, the proprietor of the restaurant, who, Zula noticed, was fond of ruffling Lawrence's hair and tweaking his ear.

"She says your son is beautiful," Mme. Jourdan translated.

"*Merci, madame,*" Zula essayed.

"*Je vous félicite,*" said Mme. Laroche. "*C'est vous qui l'avez fabriqué.*"

"What was that?" Zula asked.

"You're the one who manufactured him," said Mme. Jourdan.

"*Et le père aussi,*" said Mme. Laroche archly, batting her eyes at Father Sperry. She had blue eye shadow on, something the Sperrys had not seen before. It gave her the look of a raccoon.

"No wine, thank you," said Father Sperry. He thought the atmosphere was heady enough as it was.

Lawrence's triumph in demonstrating the stabilizer had had the air of a brilliant improvisation, of "dash and bang," to use one of Father Sperry's favorite expressions. The truth of the matter was otherwise. He had planned everything in advance and knew exactly what he was going to do, except for the grand finale when he and Emile both deserted the cockpit for their flag-waving stroll on the wings. On June 15, three days before the demonstration, he had sent a six-page memorandum to the president of the Aéro-Club de France outlining in minute detail precisely what he proposed to do. The Jury for the Competition was enormously impressed by this memorandum and by the way in which Lawrence carried out its promises to the letter. Their report is explicit about certain shortcomings of many of the competitors. The French pilot Lumière, for example, did not dare, as Lawrence did, to try the landing test with stopped engine. "Having lost his way between Buc and Chartres, he landed his spring-winged de Monge aeroplane unluckily in an alfalfa field, damaging both the landing gear and the engine so that he was out of the competition.

"Monsieur Sperry," the report went on, "was the only one who addressed to the jury a memorandum clearly indicating the experiments capable of demonstrating the qualities of its stabilizer. Monsieur Sperry carried out his program to the letter and complied with all the additional tests required by the jury."

The jury officially regretted that "the majority of the competitors did not even try to display to the jury the qualities of their machines in the wind." This was one of the "additional tests" imposed upon Lawrence. After the victory lunch at Les Marronniers, a number of the jurors flocked around the plane, and Lawrence explained the mechanism of the stabilizer in fluent French. As he talked the sky clouded over and a stiff breeze came up, ruffling the waters of the Seine. The jurors wanted to know if the stabilizer would work in unfavorable weather conditions.

"*Montez, messieurs,*" said Lawrence grandly. "I will take you up."

There was some hesitation. The breeze had become a high wind. It howled through the struts and wings of the flying boat, and the waves slapped the pontoons and set the C-2 rocking. Most of the judges looked at the scudding clouds with a wary eye.

"*Très mauvais. Dangereux,*" they said.

"I wouldn't risk it, Lawrence," said Father Sperry.

But one of the judges was as fearless as Lawrence: René Quinton, president of the Ligue Nationale Aérienne de France. The bad weather conditions were just what he wanted in order to make a final decision about the Sperry stabilizer.

"*Allez-houp,*" said Lawrence, and Monsieur Quinton, in his

dark suit and bowler hat, climbed into the cockpit. Lawrence revved up the motor, and the flying boat jiggled over the choppy waters of the Seine. Slap, slap, slap—the two men were drenched with spray, but dauntless, as the Curtiss flying boat rose from the whitecapped river into the threatening turbulence of the gusty air.

Quinton, the leading authority on aerodynamics in France, wrote a memorable signed article about this flight for *Le Matin* under a banner headline:

HISTORIC DATE IN AERIAL NAVIGATION
THE AEROPLANE THAT FLIES WITHOUT A PILOT
MARVELOUS DEMONSTRATION

This authoritative article clinched June 18, 1914, as one of the great dates in aviation history. Lawrence was awarded the first prize of 50,000 francs and became famous overnight. His handsome countenance appeared in the leading papers in Paris, London, Berlin, and New York and on the grainy screens of every movie theater.

Of the hundreds of newspaper articles on the stabilizer, the most comprehensive is the account by William L. Cathcart in the *Philadelphia Public Ledger:*

> The stabilization of the aeroplane is an accomplished fact. The human factor—to which in its history so many tragic deaths have been due—can now be entirely eliminated and replaced by an unerring apparatus, which will not let the aeroplane stray from any path the aviator may choose, which will guide it through eddies and gusts and over the dreaded "air holes" with serene unconcern for their existence, and, in short, will replace the hand control of the past, with its ever dangerous personal equation, by automatic governing in which nerveless discs and levers of steel will do the aviator's most pressing thinking and acting.
>
> Lawrence Sperry, a lad of 21, is the daring aviator who tried out this apparatus in thousands of hazardous flights until perfection was attained. Like many of the men who do these astonishing things in the world's progress, Lawrence Sperry, while genial and approachable on other subjects, is reticent as to his own exploits. A dialogue with him on this subject, I found, quickly resolved itself

into a monologue in which the details of his thrilling story were gathered only by a virtual cross examination endured by him with smiling resignation. . . .

The daring of Sperry and his French mechanic and their confidence in the stabilizer were shown by the fact that neither was strapped to the machine. Any defect in the operation of the apparatus would have meant instant death to both.

When I asked Lawrence Sperry how an aeroplane stabilized for horizontal flight could ascend or descend under automatic control, he answered smilingly, "We *fool* the gyroscopes. They continue to revolve in their original planes, but we move the connections. We're still in charge. But hereafter the pilot need only steer his machine: automatic control will do the rest."

Before Lawrence left France, the French War Department ordered thirty of the sensational new stabilizers for trial. The British immediately followed suit. Lawrence sailed for New York to fill the orders. On the crossing he painstakingly drew the figures for his patent application for the gyroscopic pilot for airplanes (No. 1,757,096).

He was welcomed home like a returning hero. According to the *Brooklyn Eagle* for July 9, 1914, he had "conquered the air. So completely satisfied is the United States Government with the success of the automatic aeroplane stabilizer invented by Elmer A. and Lawrence B. Sperry that it has been decided to install the apparatus on all the machines in Uncle Sam's aerial fleet.

"Two hundred members of the City Club welcomed the successful inventors at a lunch in their honor. Judge John B. Creighton, representing the Borough of Brooklyn, compared Lawrence Sperry's $10,000 prize to the Nobel prizes and said that his achievement had marked as great an era in the world's development as any prize in history.

"Henry Wodhouse, editor of *Flying*, said that the stabilizer had not only revolutionized flying but that it has brought aerial transportation close to hand and has linked the world into a large bond which practically makes economical wars impossible."

Just nineteen days after the expression of this wishful thought, the heir presumptive to the throne of the Austro-Hungarian Empire was assassinated at Sarajevo.

12

THE INITIAL AMERICAN REACTION to World War I was to stay out.

"We must be neutral in fact as well as name," President Wilson proclaimed.

"It would be folly to jump into war," said Theodore Roosevelt, and he spoke highly of the Germans as "a virile and masterful people."

In France, with the help of a fleet of taxicabs, General Joffre beat back the German invaders in the Battle of the Marne, September 1914. Paris was saved. The horrors of trench warfare began, leading to a murderous stalemate as antiquated as the American Civil War, a tactical situation that did not escape the notice of General "Black Jack" Pershing.

Henry Ford, apostle of benevolent neutrality, hired a steamship and filled it with an odd assortment of some 150 well-intentioned pacifists and preachers. The aim of this unofficial "peace ship" was to persuade the contending governments to call off the war and "get the boys out of the trenches by Christmas." Although nominally Christian, all the statesmen concerned rejected this idea as absurd.

Lawrence Sperry, who had fallen in love with France, tried to volunteer for the Lafayette Escadrille of the French Air Force. The American recruiters turned him down. For some mysterious reason, this elite group wanted only college graduates.

"There's no thorn without its rose," sighed Zula Sperry. "Now I'm glad he didn't go to Cornell."

Like many other American mothers, she played and sang one of the most popular songs of the day, "I Didn't Raise My Boy to Be a Soldier." She had no way of knowing that, within the year, her boy would be engaged as the sole volunteer in one of the most dangerous experiments in the history of flight: the development of the guided missile, which evolved from his automatic pilot.

The timing and the impact of Lawrence's invention of this flying bomb, or aerial torpedo, were momentous. On May 17, 1915, a German submarine sank the British liner *Lusitania* with a loss of 1,100 civilian passengers, including 128 Americans.

"If Teddy Roosevelt were in the White House, the Germans would not have dared to sink a ship with Americans aboard," said Father Sperry.

When Wilson said there was such a thing as being "too proud to fight," Theodore Roosevelt denounced him as a "Byzantine logothete."

"What the hell is a Byzantine logothete?" Lawrence Sperry demanded when this phrase appeared in the *New York Times*.

"I will tell you if you ask in a gentlemanly way," said his sister Helen.

"What the heck is a Byzantine logothete?" Lawrence corrected.

"A Byzantine logothete," Helen explained, "is an official of the Byzantine Empire who talks a great deal but does nothing."

Lawrence became rather fond of the phrase. It reflected his own impatience with bureaucratic bumbling. He spent the first half of 1915 perfecting and demonstrating the stabilizer, for which he became a persuasive salesman. He flew up and down the East River, skimming the water and the bridges in his flying boat. On one occasion he scared the wits out of one of his clients, an Italian generalissimo, by flying a little too close to the Statue of Liberty's torch.

"*Madonna mia!*" the general exclaimed, crossing himself.

"Nothing to fear with the automatic pilot," said Lawrence gaily.

Impressed—or possibly relieved—the general ordered three full sets of the gyroscopic stabilizer for the Italian Air Force.

This episode, like everything Lawrence did in 1915, made headlines.

While delivering the Italian general to the Navy Yard dock, Lawrence had one of those practical inspirations that were typical of his pragmatic genius. Why should the flying boat be restricted to water landings? What if he had to land on terra firma?

He set to work immediately to provide the plane with wheels

that could fold up against the pontoon. This was another important step in the development of the amphibian plane conceived two years earlier by Glenn Curtiss, Lawrence's teacher at Hammondsport.

"It's as easy as pie," Lawrence told the New York reporters after he had equipped his plane with the first retractable two-wheel landing gear. "The wheel gear can be attached by the pilot, just leaning over the side of the plane. It takes a minute. Then, when you don't want it, just pull it toward the boat and latch it into its socket."

This was duly recorded with appropriate photographs of the mechanism and its photogenic inventor. *Aerial Age Weekly* ran a series of pictures on March 29, 1915, with the following caption:

ALIGHTS ON LAND IN A FLYING BOAT

Lawrence Sperry, inventor of the Sperry Gyroscopic Stabilizer, who has been educating New Yorkers to the joys and safety of water-flying, recently landed on the land in his Curtiss flying boat without damage. This was the first demonstration of the possibility of alighting on terra firma in a flying boat without injury.

Even Lawrence's minor misdemeanors were reported in the press. On August 1, 1915, the *New York Times* published this item:

AUTOS SLOW TO SPERRY
Aviator So Used to Flying Fast,
Motor "Seemed to Crawl"

Lawrence Sperry, the young Brooklyn inventor and aviator, who makes frequent flights over the city and harbor from the Brooklyn Navy Yard, was charged in the Adams Street Court yesterday with overspeeding his automobile on the Brooklyn approach to the Manhattan Bridge. Patrolman Van Cleef of the motorcycle squad told Magistrate Voorhees that Sperry's auto was running at thirty-five miles an hour. The aviator seemed astonished at this.

"Why, I can hardly believe it," said he. "You see, I am used to flying through the air at sixty or seventy miles an hour, and it seemed to me that the automobile was just crawling along, so to speak."

Magistrate Voorhees dismissed the case with a warning to Mr. Sperry to avoid repeating the offense.

"He could even charm a judge," his sister Helen said. "I never got away with anything like that."

Lawrence much preferred the air to the road; there were no officious cops to inhibit his actions. The papers noted that he took the first lady passenger, a Mrs. Robert Saufley, aloft over New York City, circling the Statue of Liberty in the process. He also performed a feat that had been thought impossible: he looped-the-loop in a Curtiss flying boat.

"Lawrence," said his father sternly. "Is this sort of stunt necessary?"

"Yes, it is, Father," Lawrence replied firmly.

The old man was relieved when Lawrence sailed in September 1915 on the American liner *New York* for Liverpool in response to British interest in the perfected stabilizer.

"The night before we entered the War Zone lots of people on the ship stayed up all night," Lawrence wrote home from London on September 21. "They were nervous in case there might be an explosion. I thought that I was going to worry but found that it didn't concern me in the least, and I went to bed and slept.

"It's great to be in good old London once more. It certainly is a very fine thing that I can be here because I feel that I can do a lot of good. The Stabilizer is going finely with the British War Office. They are getting favorable reports from Headquarters of the results of our tests on the Maurice Farman Biplane at Calshot. We certainly have a good thing in this Stabilizer, and that this is true, there is no question."

The family was happy to have their wandering boy out of the headlines for a while. Not for long, however. Father Sperry knew about his son's pro-Allied sentiments. He was also privy to Lawrence's secret work on the aerial torpedo, a project already marked top secret by the U.S. Government. But Elmer A. Sperry was also the head of a major industry that employed hundreds of German-American workers, so he was taken aback by his son's military speculations when he read about them on the morning of October 21, 1915, on the front page of his favorite paper, the *New York Tribune*.

Aerial Torpedo Is Guided
100 Miles by Gyroscope

Sperrys Invent Self-Steering Plane Which
Can Carry Five Tons of Explosive—Compass and
Stabilizer Insure Great Accuracy

By GORDON BRUCE

(By Cable to The Tribune)

London, Oct. 20—A device which is likely to revolutionize modern warfare has been invented and tested, and will be ready for the market within a very short time. It is an aerial torpedo, and the men who have worked out the idea are Elmer A. Sperry, president of the Sperry Gyroscope Company, of Brooklyn, and his son, Lawrence B. Sperry.

Particulars of the newest and most destructive engine of death and the results of various tests were given to me today by Lawrence B. Sperry, who is in England in connection with the business the Sperry concern is doing with the British Admiralty.

If carried out on a large scale, the Sperry scheme would make possible the destruction of a whole town with a single torpedo, and the bombardment of cities as far distant as one hundred miles could be carried on without risk of a single life by the assailants.

What the plan amounts to is this: An aeroplane, complete with the exception of landing gear, is constructed and fitted with gyroscopic compass and stabilizer. The torpedo, bearing anywhere from five hundred pounds to five tons of tri-nitro-toluene, is set in place. From a specially arranged launching cradle the craft is sent into the air.

The direction to be taken by the flying bomb can be determined by scientific calculations, and the gyroscopic compass will insure a true course.

The stabilizer can be set and gauged that the plane will rise at any angle. At whatever height the adjustment of the stabilizer calls for, the machine will automatically assume a horizontal course, fly a predetermined distance along that course, and then descend at the desired angle. The machine can be made to take a perpendicular drop over a certain point. It can be launched from a battleship as well as from land.

For example, if a torpedo were to be discharged from a British vessel fifty miles from the Kiel Canal, the load of high explosive could be sent unerringly among the vessels of the German fleet there, and the only possibility of defense would be the exploding of the bomb in the air by gunfire. If the attack were made at night, even that possibility would be remote.

Great Accuracy Possible

Experiments with scale models show, Mr. Sperry said, that the following degrees of accuracy can be depended on with his device: One hundred miles, 8 miles; fifty miles, 2.3 miles; twenty miles, 0.8 mile; ten miles, 0.3 mile.

Thus, if a torpedo were discharged against a fortification or city a hundred miles distant, it could not diverge from its course enough to carry it more than eight miles wide of its mark. If set to land in the very heart of Berlin, for instance, it would explode within eight miles of that point. But, on the other hand, it might, and probably would, speed directly to its mark. And so on down, until a torpedo fired to explode at a point ten miles away would not vary more than three-tenths of a mile.

The principle is the same as that applied in the Sperry plan for the control of marine torpedoes. A recent test was made in San Francisco harbor with a torpedo (minus the war head), and the missile, equipped with a gyroscopic compass, was sent ten miles from shore and returned to within a few feet of the starting point, showing the accurate control lent by the compass.

Every warship of the British navy as well as every submarine, is fitted with Sperry compasses and stabilizers, as are the vessels of the United States. Germany has no stabilizers, but, according to Mr. Sperry, the German government bought one compass and proceeded to appropriate the idea, claiming that the Sperry instrument was an infringement of a patent already owned by Germany. He also called attention to the fact that an American never won a patent suit in Germany. Therefore the new torpedo would not be offered to the Germans under any consideration.

Can Carry Great Weight

As to the possibility of carrying the great weight which the new torpedo would require, it may be pointed out that the America, built by Glenn Curtiss and Lieutenant Porte to cross the ocean, lifted almost three tons, and with the improvements which have been made in motor construction since that time Mr. Sperry feels sure that five-ton burdens can be taken care of without any trouble. However, he says, two tons of tri-nitro-toluene would probably be sufficient for all purposes, although he makes no claim to a knowledge of chemistry.

The Sperry instruments are the subject of open admiration among British naval officers, and the inventor is cordially referred to in naval circles here as "the man who can do anything." He won the French government prize of 50,000 francs for his aeroplane stabilizer, and many of his instruments are in use in the royal air services of Great Britain.

Mr. Sperry told today of an amusing incident which occurred during the progress of his experiments with the aerial torpedo in the United States. After making trials with models, he said, he tried out the principle in a man-carrying machine and found that it worked perfectly.

However, he got into trouble when his propeller broke, carrying away the tail of his machine. The newspapers printed accounts of the accident, putting the blame on the stabilizer. Sperry said that he was content to let it go at that rather than disclose the nature of his flight.

Summed up, the new invention is a self-controlled aeroplane, flying without a pilot and loaded with death.

Practical admission of the fact that the Sperrys have such a device as the aerial torpedo was made yesterday to a Tribune reporter at the office of the Sperry Gyroscope Company in Brooklyn. An officer of the company, learning that The Tribune was in possession of the facts, asked that this newspaper defer their publication until Elmer A. Sperry was seen, on the ground that "the matter affected nations." But Mr. Sperry decided not to talk.

"Mind, I do not admit that we have such a device," said this officer. "You will have to publish the story on your own responsibility." But a little later he commented: "I declare, I don't see how in the world you got to know about this."

There was only one way the *Trib* could have known about it, Father Sperry decided: Lawrence had been shooting his mouth off.

He fired off a cable to Lawrence in London:

YOUR NEWSPAPER INTERVIEW VERY DAMAGING DO NOT TALK ANY FURTHER LETTER FOLLOWS

Lawrence was bewildered by this incomprehensible message. What was his father talking about? What article and in which newspaper? He, Lawrence, had never given an interview to the press.

Back in New York, Elmer A. Sperry was confronted by hundreds of his skilled German-American workers, all waving copies of the *New York Tribune* with the provocative article about speculative bombings of Berlin and Kiel.

A dozen employees resigned on the spot.

Beside himself, Elmer A. Sperry dictated a letter to his son:

October 22, 1915

Dear Lawrence:

The most serious situation that has ever been created in the personnel of our workmen was created by the interview you gave out in London, which was instantly published on the front page of the morning Tribune, copy of which is enclosed. Otto got on his desk twenty copies the first thing yesterday morning, and our workmen, the characteristics of whom you should be thoroughly acquainted with by this time, are very deeply disturbed. Just how many will join those who have already left owing to this terrible mistake of yours, I do not know. Will write on this later.

We at once cabled you that this interview was very damaging and not to talk any further, which I hope you will be very careful to heed and follow.

This is all I have time to get to you before closing our mail.

Sincerely,
E. A. Sperry

EAS-B Clipping attached

Meanwhile in London, Lawrence checked with the entire foreign press corps to track down the damaging interview referred to in his father's cable. Finding no trace, he cabled back:

CAN HAVE DAMAGING ARTICLE RETRACTED IF YOU CABLE NAME PAPER PRESS HERE SAY NO ARTICLES HAVE BEEN SENT

Unfortunately, thanks to the vagaries of "cablese," the word *retracted* got scrambled and came out in New York as *appreciated*.

When the old man read "CAN HAVE DAMAGING ARTICLE APPRECIATED," he nearly went through the oak-paneled ceil-

ing of the executive suite. Lawrence had taken leave of his
senses, he concluded, and he almost took leave of his own, especially when another article appeared in the *Tribune,* describing
Lawrence's visit to France, his sale of stabilizers to the French,
his sympathy for the *poilus* in the trenches of the western front,
and his participation as a voluntary rescue worker after a German
Zeppelin raid on London.

Trying to compose himself, he dictated another letter to
Lawrence:

October 30, 1915

Dear Lawrence:

Referring to your cable saying that you can have the damaging
article *appreciated,* which is taken to mean "apprehended," and that
all of the press in London say that no articles have been sent. Of
course you know as well as we do that this is rot, because the very
same day that this cable came there was another great, long article
in the New York Tribune telling about you finding the shoe with a
foot in it and tendons hanging to it, and that you had just come back
from France where you had put in a great many stabilizers, just in
time to see the "Zep raid" and how you turned in and helped carry
the dead men out, and a whole lot more talk about how you flew in
clouds, what the sensations were, etc., etc.

Now when you say that you don't talk for publication in London,
of course you can see that such a proposition is discredited by what
is published of what you say, so we appeal to you again to go carefully. I think it is very much better not to say anything because we
are still suffering from your first article and all these other things
simply corroborate, in the judgment of our people here, that this
firm is getting so pro-Ally that it is almost impossible.

Sincerely,

E. A. Sperry

The old man also wrote to Reginald Gillmor, head of the Sperry
office in London: "Please caution Lawrence against these extrava-
gant and reckless tendencies. We are hoping that as he grows older
he will acquire better judgment." This kind of secondhand parental
slapdown was not exactly soothing to a proud and earnest young
man of twenty-three.

It took more than a month for this mysterious and equivocal situation to clear up. It appears that Lawrence had a roommate in London, a friend named Charles A. Stiles, who wrote for the *New York Tribune* under the name of Gordon Bruce. Stiles had never sent the controversial "interview" by cable to New York. He had sent a letter to the *Tribune* editor with information on which a story could be written after consultation with the Sperry Company in Brooklyn. A hyperimaginative city editor or deskman had written the piece without consulting anyone and, to add to the confusion, made it appear as a cable dispatch from London.

The ambiguities were finally resolved in three more letters: one from Lawrence to his father, one from Stiles to his editor, and a final letter, written by Stiles, obviously at Lawrence's request, on Sperry Company stationery, explaining how the troublesome story happened to be written.

So the ambiguities were finally resolved. Despotic Daedalus was satisfied. Impetuous Icarus was innocent. But a gulf had widened between them.

13

LAWRENCE SPERRY returned to America early in 1916, his briefcase loaded with orders for the automatic pilot. There was no doubt that the Sperry stabilizer was a smashing success. Now the question was: how to stabilize Lawrence?

Now in his twenty-fourth year, he remained the idol of the New York press. He resumed flying, his chief recreation, and he was commissioned by the Navy to train young aviators. He also received letters from women, requesting lessons.

When a *Times* reporter asked Zula if it worried her much when Lawrence did his spectacular feats in the sky, she replied, "Well, I wouldn't want Lawrence to be an aviator by profession."

Father Sperry also felt that Lawrence had taken enough risks. As orders for the stabilizer poured in, Sperry prepared a contract for his son. An agreement was signed between the Sperry Gyroscope Company and Lawrence B. Sperry, employing the latter as manager of the Sperry Gyroscope Company's Stabilizer Department at a salary of $250 per month.

It was further agreed that "when the second party [Lawrence] has hired, trained or developed a competent man and aviator capable of making tests and exhibitions, and devotes himself exclusively to his duties as Business Manager, then the salary of the second party shall be doubled to the sum of 500 dollars per month."

The built-in blandishment was obvious, as was the anxiety of a devoted and increasingly conservative father. It was a repetition of the notion that Lawrence had "had his fling." He had performed brilliantly in the air; now it was time to settle down to a solid, substantial, conservative career on earth.

It was like trying to cage an aspiring bird, no idle analogy in Lawrence's case. For, as in his Arizona school days, he had a literal and poetic identification with the birds of the air. In describing the exploit of Bezons for the magazine *Flying* in August of that same momentous year, he wrote a memorable paragraph:

"In comparing a machine fitted with an automatic stabilizer to the bird fitted with Nature's stabilizer, we see that the gyro baseline corresponds to the bird's highly developed semi-circular canals, which instantly feel tipping about any axis; the air pressure device corresponds to the bird's muscular impressions, which instinctively feel speed, and the hand-setting device makes the aviator the equivalent of the bird's eyes, which tell it how to steer. The servo-motors correspond to the bird's muscles and the ailerons and rudders to its wing-tips and tail."

The man who wrote that, the young hero of the safety contest at Bezons, was never going to "devote himself exclusively to his duties as Business Manager," no matter how great the material incentives.

Lawrence seems to have had a great sense of audience, of dramatizing events according to how he wished people to regard them. This is shown by excerpts from three letters about his accident near Boston, in which he was lost at sea for fourteen hours, drifting five miles offshore. The first one is to a friend named Powell:

Dear Good, Old, Pal Powell—

I suppose you heard about the propeller blades flying off and cutting the tail in two pieces. I dropped 200 ft. but wasn't hurt even though the machine was smashed to bits only a pontoon left and no paddle. They simply will have to hang me for they will never get me that way.

Your pal,
Lawrence

The discoverer of the North Pole received a more formal letter:

Rear Admiral Robert E. Peary
Aero Club of America
New York City

Dear Admiral Peary:

In connection with your splendid work for coast guard, I was just thinking of an excellent example of the utility of the aeroplane for this purpose.

As you probably know, near Boston some time ago I was lost at sea for fourteen hours drifting five miles out from shore. In the morning four destroyers and two tug-boats were sent out by the Charleston Navy Yard—also two aeroplanes. The first aeroplane that left the shore came back in forty minutes and reported my position. The destroyers were out until three o'clock in the afternoon and did not find me at all.

I would say that planes are better than ships in coast guard rescue work.

Sincerely yours,
Lawrence Sperry

The most spirited letter, designed to tranquilize Lawrence's family, was written to his uncle Herbert Goodman, who had apparently written to the senior Sperry expressing alarm and anxiety about the accident:

Dear Uncle Herbert:

Now that the newspaper publicity has died down a little I thought I would drop you a line to tell you that your solicitude for my welfare was very much appreciated.

I am sorry that you wrote the letter you did of October 4th to father as a letter of this kind is apt to worry them. I expect always to fly. I am in the business and would not be in if I did not fly. As for the aeroplane business, it is the only business that I am interested in at present. Nothing can keep me from flying.

As for mother being worried, she is not. If people leave her alone and do not talk to her about the subject you will find that she is very little worried as she is used to exaggerated newspaper articles and is not in any way affected by them.

The next time you feel alarmed if you will simply write me or wait and find out the real facts from a more reliable source than the newspapers, I will very much appreciate it.

You should realize that there was no danger at any time. The machine ran out of gasoline during a 6 mile flight in which I was headed for the wrong light. The propeller fell off, but I was in no danger whatsoever, simply floating around the bay until I was picked up.

Yours as ever,
Lawrence

So much for the ambiguous nature of reality. The accident, a father's anxiety, and a son's persistence again recalled the analogy with Icarus and Daedalus, the classic inventor who built the famous Labyrinth of Crete.

Father Sperry's labyrinth was the huge Sperry Gyroscope Company Building, located at Manhattan Plaza, at the Brooklyn end of the Manhattan Bridge. He would have liked to change the name of Manhattan Plaza to Brooklyn Plaza; after all, it was in Brooklyn. A great booster of Brooklyn, of which he was now the most distinguished citizen, the senior Sperry took a dim view of Manhattan, declaring that it had been a nest of Tories in the Revolutionary War and Copperheads and Mugwumps in the Civil War period. Manhattan had always harbored an "old world element" that consistently resisted the tenets of Americanism. Brooklyn, on the contrary, remained a bastion of all that was admirable in the pioneer spirit. The new Sperry Gyroscope Building, whose eleven stories dominated the borough skyline, was a bulwark of Brooklyn in every sense of the word. It was a symbol of Elmer A. Sperry's success. It also marked his transition from a brilliant, independent inventor, "investing the profits of one dream in the next dream," to a corporate executive, head of a vast and complex Company, now always spelled with a capital *C*, an established organization of many departments, many vice-presidents, many managers, many committees, and thousands of employees.

When the Sperry Gyroscope Building was dedicated in 1916, everyone from the borough president to uniformed security guards was on hand to admire Helen's decor of the executive suite on the eleventh floor. Helen, like every other cultivated young woman of the time, had read and rejoiced in *Dorothy Vernon of Haddon Hall*, and she had re-created the baronial splendor of Haddon Hall in Brooklyn. The linenfold paneling of the executive suite would have done justice to the stateliest homes of England. There were fireplaces in Father Sperry's office and the board room, and there were two mullioned bay windows with commanding views of the Manhattan skyline, on which Father Sperry resolutely turned his back. On the oak-paneled wall of his office, framed in gold and hand-lettered in appropriate Old En-

glish script, like an illuminated manuscript, was a poem of pre-
sumably collective authorship. Its worshipful tone and uncertain
meter produced a ghastly combination, and when it was solemnly
read aloud to the assembled dignitaries and multitude, Helen
hissed at her brother, "Lawrence Sperry, wipe that smirk off your
face."

After the reading, Lawrence observed to one of his colleagues,
Charles Colvin, "This is no longer a Company; it's become a
Religion!"

To
ELMER AMBROSE SPERRY
Our Honored and Beloved President
on the occasion of the dedication of the
Sperry Building
1916

It is not oft that Nature gives to Earth
A man of great achievement and great worth;
At once possessed of fruitful, forceful mind,
Of humor rich, and heart most generous and kind,
Of wisdom deep, creative skill intense,
And personality that all must love and reverence.

The name of ELMER AMBROSE SPERRY needs
No words of praise or tribute, for his deeds
Have built for him an everlasting place
In that High Hall of Fame which none may grace
Save those who give their life's work willingly
To Art and service of Humanity.

But still a message coming from the heart
Of all thy friends and those who have a part
In thy great work, which helps the world progress,
May bring to thee the thoughts we can't express,
And on this day which crowns thy life's success,
We pray that God will all thy future bless.

God responded by increasing the net sales of the Sperry Gyroscope Company from $2 to $6 million within the course of the
next two years. Huge U.S. and Allied orders accounted for most

of the profits. Sperry gyroscopes and compasses stabilized the seven seas for a thousand battleships, submarines, and merchantmen. Sperry searchlights, developed by Preston Bassett and tested by Lawrence, drove the German Zeppelins so high above London that they could not hit their targets.

Lawrence's main job was to stabilize the air. His status in the huge hierarchy of the "religion" was that of manager and engineer of the Aeroplane Department of the Sperry Gyroscope Company, for which he had personally obtained, early in 1916, an order from the French government for forty additional stabilizers for its war planes. The hero of Bezons, who had asserted that "I am best off alone, that I have always been bothered by having to tell someone else what I want done," was now bothered by having to tell it to sixty-five employees. There were assistants and secretaries to deal with, draftsmen, mechanics, foremen, installation engineers, gyroscopic fitters, servomotor experts, generator specialists, and a "special testing and exhibition apprentice." This was Charles Colvin, the man Lawrence was supposed to train to make "tests and exhibitions" so that he, Lawrence Burst Sperry, son of the chairman of the board, could stay safely on the ground and devote himself to his duties as business manager.

Psychologically and temperamentally, Lawrence was almost incapable of doing this. He was bored to death with accounts receivable, accrued payroll, notes payable, notes discounted, and double-entry bookkeeping. He wanted to fly. In desperation he sent a telegram to his younger brother Elmer, now in his junior year at Cornell:

STOP WASTING YOUR TIME UP THERE STOP COME HOME AND HELP ME WITH MY AEROPLANES STOP LAWRENCE

Elmer promptly dropped out of Cornell. But Father Sperry was not about to encourage a resumption of this dangerous partnership. He was proud to have his boys working for the Company, but it would be necessary to divide and rule. Young Elmer was given the rather vague title of special assistant for research and development. Edward, the oldest brother, the only one to be graduated from college, was appointed supervisor of installation of a marine stabilizer for the yacht of Mr. H. M. Hanna, Jr., of Cleveland.

Keeping Lawrence under thumb was a much more difficult proposition, especially since the U.S. Army had put a plane at his disposal on Governors Island, and the Navy had offered him the use of a flying boat at the Brooklyn Navy Yard. The Sperry Gyroscope Company was just about midway between these two bases. Lawrence's office was on the third floor, and when he looked up from the avalanche of papers on his desk, his blue eyes gazed eastward past Manhattan Bridge to the Navy Yard, then westward beyond the Brooklyn Bridge to Governors Island. Between these magnetic poles, beckoning like the most irresistible of invitations, lay the sparkling surface of the East River. Above that was freedom: the air.

Although Thomas Morgan, sales manager of the Company, had also been assigned the task of "managing" Lawrence, he could not keep his bird in the many-splendored cage of the Sperry Building.

Preston Bassett, the brilliant chemist who eventually became president of Sperry Gyroscope, has a vivid recollection of Lawrence's spasmodic days as a business manager:

"Lawrence would sit there at his desk. He would accumulate a certain pent-up pressure that would burst out at two thirty P.M.

" 'I gotta go out,' he would say, and out he went. A few minutes later we would hear the sound of an airplane. The employees rushed to the windows. There was Lawrence zooming under the Brooklyn Bridge, then soaring up over the Manhattan Bridge, then down again under the Williamsburg Bridge, almost skimming the water. Then he would fly upside down for a while. He would come back to the office at four P.M. The pressure was off, and he would work like a Trojan on instrument design and production until closing time at five thirty.

"One day he really did an appalling stunt. *He did a loop-the-loop under and over the Brooklyn Bridge;* My heart was in my mouth. All the employees cheered from the windows.

"Another time he actually got the wings of his flying boat entangled in the cables of the Manhattan Bridge. He just walked calmly out on the wing, disentangled the machine, and came swooping down the river once more. The Sperry Building was like a grandstand on those days. All the workers adored Lawrence. The secretaries were goofy about him, but the Old Man up there on the eleventh floor was not pleased. Neither was the Executive Committee. Lawrence, of course, was not pleased that Tom Morgan had been set to spy on him."

There were stern parental remonstrances about unnecessary risks. Lawrence's old Arizona letter of 1912 was dragged out of the files with its promise that "I am not willing to do fool things for the sake of a crowd."

"It isn't for the sake of a crowd," Lawrence protested.

He hardly knew how to explain this "lonely impulse of delight," but he justified it in an article that appeared on the front page of the *Evening Sun:*

DOING STUNTS WITH AN AEROPLANE

One of the World's Most Daring Fliers Says You're Never
Safe in the Air Till You Know How to
Perform All the Thrillers

By Lawrence B. Sperry

On the ground that aviators are assuming unnecessary risks, much has been said and written against what is termed "stunt" flying. This usually conists of loops, stalls, tail slides, upside down flying and tail spins. It is not generally realized that these manoeuvres on the part of a pilot make for safety in flying, but in this country at least such manoeuvres are generally carried out for that definite purpose.

The object of this kind of flying is to teach the pilot to recover quickly from positions that would be dangerous if maintained for any length of time. How many pilots could have saved themselves from tail spins and their disastrous consequences had they known by actual experience how to recover quickly!

Some pilots are opposed to "stunting" because they fear to endanger their reputations as safe, sane, careful pilots. But the man who does not put his machine through its paces is not fit to fly a machine at all. Instead of "pussyfooting" around in a machine in a closed field, what we need in this country is "pep" in flying. The pilot should have the confidence that goes with handling his machine in all positions, and this can be gained only through actual practice. By practising every available manoeuvre beforehand, a man does not risk the danger of being helpless in an emergency and having the numbing effect of surprise added to a situation that requires all his faculties to effect a recovery in a dangerous situation.

The rest of the article is a manual of instruction on how to loop-the-loop, fly upside down, go into a tailspin and get out of it, and "reach the limit of which an aeroplane is capable."

Lawrence concluded this rational defense with a warning and one of the earliest recorded pleas for the use of the seatbelt:

"When going into upside down flying from a regular loop, centrifugal force tends to throw the pilot out of the plane instead of holding him in, and it is absolutely essential to be securely strapped in before attempting this manoeuvre. Of course none of these operations should be attempted too close to the ground."

He made no mention of water or such obstacles as bridges, but the message, though greeted with some reservation in the executive suite of the Company, was well received by the general public and the most forward-looking elements of the U.S. Armed Forces. Lawrence Sperry was now widely recognized, not only as "one of the world's most daring flyers," but as a pioneer in solving the problems of aerial navigation.

"The main serious attempt at instrument development in the United States during this period was being carried on by Lawrence Sperry," wrote Robert H. Sheppler in his *History of Aviation Instruments*. "Lawrence Sperry developed a completely automatic aeroplane which was gyroscopically controlled. In addition to operating all controls by means of a group of four gyros, he also directed the gyro operation by radio from the ground. This was the original 'guided missile' or 'Aerial Torpedo' which Lawrence patented in 1917."

Lawrence, whose spectacular activity appears to have placed him in the Tolstoyan category of "those who are too busy living to think," was actually one of the great inventors in the history of aviation. As early as 1916, in Sheppler's words, he was "one of a few far-sighted designers and flyers who were beginning to see the future uses of flight. These few also realized that instrumentation would soon play a large role in the overall development of aircraft."

Between 1915 and 1923 Lawrence filed twenty-six successful patents, some of which, like the aerial torpedo and the turn indicator, which made blind flying possible, changed the course of history. Lawrence had the extraordinary dual capacity of conceptualizing his inventions, then demonstrating them and perfecting them with a fearlessness that became legendary.

The most extraordinary example of this pragmatic-conceptual capacity was Lawrence's invention of the turn indicator. Only an active flyer could have done it, and he did it in the face of growing opposition, not only from his father but from the rest of the high brass of the Sperry Gyroscope Company, whose conservatism increased in direct ratio to increasing profits and salaries. They all agreed with the Old Man that Lawrence, as head of the Sperry Aeroplane Department, should settle down and stay at his desk in a corporate executive's role.

One day in 1917 Lawrence alarmed his father even more than usual by leaving the office and flying up out of sight into the roiling black clouds of a thunderstorm, a "mad stunt" that was considered almost suicidal at the time. Taken to task once more for taking "unnecessary risks," he explained that the risks were absolutely necessary, that it was essential, for him at least, to learn what it was like to fly under bad conditions.

On this day he learned something of signal importance that would later be confirmed by medical science: when pilots cannot see the horizon or the ground, they cannot depend on their senses to tell them the position or attitude of their plane. As Lawrence flew into the thunderclouds he became completely disoriented, as helpless as a blind man groping his way along the ragged edges of an abyss. It was an eerie feeling to be flying blind, out of visual touch with ground and horizon: to think he was sitting up straight when he was actually leaning to one side, to imagine he had turned when he hadn't, to feel he was flying a straight course through the clouds and then to discover, as he flew out of them, that he had actually turned. Scudding in and out of the shifting shadow and light, Lawrence had a revelation: "seat-of-the-pants" instinct was fine in fine weather; with poor visibility it was absolutely useless.

There was a second revelation at this lonely moment. The conventional magnetic compass was useless; it oscillated erratically, affected by the centrifugal force of each and every turn of the plane.

It was at this moment, while trying to navigate in the capricious currents of the storm-riven air, that Lawrence realized the necessity of an instrument that would tell a pilot flying under such blind conditions which way he was turning.

He spent the next few weeks, not at his desk, but at the Brooklyn Navy Yard, "tinkering" with his plane and taking it up "in the most reckless and perverse way," one of his colleagues noted, whenever the weather was bad. His first step was to install a small gyroscope on the primitive instrument panel of the flying boat. Not much bigger than a man's fist, the gyroscope was free to rotate horizontally around the aircraft's roll axis. He connected a pointer to this freely suspended gyro. He felt sure that the pointer would indicate any turn of the aircraft because the gyroscope would "precess," or tilt in relation to the horizontal roll of the plane. He went up in good weather and saw that he was right; he confirmed the gyroscope's indications with the evidence of his own eyes, and he knew that the indicator would perform rain or shine, day or night. He was as delighted with this discovery as he had been as a boy when he had first become aware of the precessive proclivities of his gyroscopic top.

But there were more technical problems to resolve before the turn indicator could be called a success. Although the pointer invariably indicated the turn, it stubbornly stayed at its new reading even when the pilot resumed a straight course. How could the pointer be brought back to its zero-turn reading when the plane had been "righted" and was flying straight? There must be a way, Lawrence reasoned, as he continued his dangerous flights, even venturing into the blackest storm clouds above the Poconos in his ongoing experiments.

The problem was paradoxical. The gyroscope indicated the turn because of its normal tendency to precess. Now, because the pointer would not return to its position, he had to find a way to restrain the gyroscope and to *inhibit* its tendency to precess. The answer came to him like a flash of lightning in a stormy sky: a *spring* would do the trick, a simple spring. Installed inside the gyro, it should act against the precession-caused rotation around the horizontal roll axis of the aircraft. It should, it would, and it did. Lawrence installed the spring and resumed testing. Sure enough, the pointer, having indicated the turn, now sprang back to its zero-turn reading when Lawrence came out of the turn and put the plane back on a straight course.

This was the crucial key to the turn indicator which, more than any other instrument, paved the way for blind flying. This was the breakthrough that liberated Lawrence and all subsequent aviators from the tyranny of visual reference to the horizon. Lawrence filed for a patent on May 21, 1920. It was granted in 1922. The Sperry turn indicator remains the prototype of a basic instrument in all aircraft from Piper Cubs to Jumbo Jets, where it still serves in a standby capacity. If all else failed, a 747 could be navigated by using the Sperry turn indicator without visual reference to horizon or ground.

Recognition of the importance of the Sperry turn indicator was immediate. It even preceded Lawrence's application for the patent. All the seaplanes that participated in the first nonstop transatlantic flight from Newfoundland to the Azores in 1919 were equipped with this amazing new device, and Lawrence had the pleasure of reading an eyewitness accolade by Commander H. C. Richardson, one of the pilots of that epoch-making flight:

"During the night of the flight from Newfoundland to the Azores there were many times before the moon rose when we were flying through darkness, and sometimes through fog when no horizon was available, and complete dependence had to be placed on the turn indicator. By its use we were enabled to keep from turning off our course; the turn indicator did it for us, apprizing us of our turns in the proper direction before the compass could have done so. The same conditions obtained when we ran into fog and squalls in the vicinity of the Azores. I feel that the Sperry Turn Indicator should be installed on every plane which has to fly through thick and hazy weather."

In the wake of this success, Lawrence turned his pragmatic-conceptual vision to a complementary improvement on the turn indicator. This was the bank indicator. He placed a ball in a glass tube filled with liquid and installed this tube horizontally on the instrument panel of his plane. It was a simple but imaginative device. Lawrence was sure that gravity and centrifugal force would do the rest, and he was pleased to note that the ball remained in the center of the tube when he executed a perfect bank and turn. But when he deliberately allowed the plane to slip, the ball moved toward the direction of the turn. If he let his aircraft skid or yaw, the ball moved away from the direction of the turn.

Combining the two instruments in one case, Lawrence effected the turn-and-bank indicator, now a standard item on the complex instrument panel of every modern aircraft.

After these pioneer achievements Lawrence was directly involved in the development and testing of all the early aircraft instruments manufactured by the Sperry Company under his supervision as head of the Aeroplane Department. The instruments included the airspeed indicator, the drift indicator, the altimeter, and the magnetic compass. Lawrence brought the Creagh-Osborne liquid-filled magnetic compass over from England as early as 1915. He set up production under British license, improved the compass on the basis of his own personal testing, and incorporated it into his drift indicator, which won the Collier Trophy for the Sperry Gyroscope Company.

Father Sperry was grateful for the precious collaboration of his son in the development of these instruments, but despite the obvious affinities between father and son, the organization men at Sperry Gyroscope did not share Lawrence's Tennysonian vision of the future: "the heavens filled with commerce, argosies of magic sails."

The big profits in 1916 came from the sea, not from the air. Sperry gyroscopes were being installed on every seagoing craft from private yachts to ocean liners, not to mention every man-of-war in the U.S. and Allied navies. The evidence of Charles Colvin, a Sperry employee, Lawrence's putative "test pilot," is conclusive in this matter.

"The powers at the Gyro Company just weren't interested in aviation," he said. "Reg Gillmor [general manager of Sperry Gyroscope] said, 'Just forget about this aviation thing. It's never going to amount to anything.'

"Lawrence and I were interested in air problems and we

weren't in the least interested in boats, so we said, well, we may be crazy but we'd simply rather go on our own and see what can be done with aircraft. I remember very well talking with Reg. He said, 'You're just out of your minds, but if that's what you want to do, go ahead. We can't stop you.' "

Nothing could. Charles Colvin started the Pioneer Instrument Company, which became the most important firm of its kind in America. Lawrence remained in the Sperry Company until 1917, but there were diversions from his desk work. He designed an optical drift-set in conjunction with the magnetic compass to correct the course of wind-drift. He devised a roller-type chart holder so that pilots could read maps at a glance. He was the first aviator to install landing lights on a plane and the first man in history to fly at night, making a fifty-mile hop in his Curtiss hydroplane from Moriches to Amityville, Long Island. He made a longer night flight from Amityville to Block Island in an hour and fifteen minutes and was the first to make a night flight over New York City.

The U.S. Army, deeply impressed by his night flights, enrolled him in its first Aviation Reserve Corps in 1916, and he was the only Army pilot to volunteer for night flying tests to determine the distance at which a powerful searchlight could pick out an airplane and hold it in its beam. In fact, it was this experience that had helped spark the development of the turn-and-bank indicator.

The development of aviation now took a military turn, sparked by events in Europe and on the Atlantic Ocean which had, until 1917, isolated the United States from the Old World.

In March German U-boats sank five American merchant ships. President Wilson and the nation were at the end of their tether. On April 6, 1917, Congress declared war on Germany.

Lawrence's active engagement had preceded this official entry by three months. On January 5, 1917, he became the first civilian to be commissioned an officer by the United States Navy Flying Corps. He was immediately called upon to train student pilots and took charge of thirty New York naval militiamen at Bayshore, Long Island. With his combination of courage and charisma, he turned out to be a most effective instructor. He was the rarest of teachers; he could practice what he preached; he could demonstrate in the air what he explained on the ground.

At that time the greatest danger in flying was the tailspin; it had taken a heavy toll of students and war pilots, including the American aviators of the Lafayette Escadrille. Lawrence wasn't afraid to go into a tailspin to show how to get out of it.

"The only way you can recover is to push the rudder bar in the direction opposite the spin," he explained. "You'll have to use both feet on one side to move it, due to the side pressure of the spin. This action will check the spin, so that your machine will just go into a straight nose dive, and it's easy to recover from that. Any volunteers?"

There were plenty. He had imbued them with "that lonely impulse of delight," and he trained some of the best pilots of the Navy Aeroreserve.

As soon as the United States entered the war, he persuaded the Navy to take him on the first naval air operations with the U.S. Fleet in Guantanamo Bay. He was explaining to an incredulous captain how an aerial torpedo could be launched from a battleship when suddenly he was doubled up by stabbing pains in his stomach. He was operated on at sea for acute appendicitis and sent back to New York on inactive duty.

Conservative commanders and captains were glad to "retire" this twenty-five-year-old madman. He talked about sinking submarines with depth charges, catapulting flying bombs from ships, all sorts of wild ideas that sounded more like crackpot science fiction than fact. Jules Verne stuff. It was still a commonly held belief that aviators were a little crazy.

But there were a few officers, Jimmy Doolittle and Billy Mitchell, for example, who had the same vision as Lawrence. They foresaw the "aerial navies grappling in the blue" and the day when a battleship would be a sitting duck for an airplane.

The concept of inactive duty was not congenial to Lawrence's temperament. He had adhesions from his appendicitis scar when he embarked on the most dangerous experiments of his hair-raising career. He would personally prove the efficacy of his invention, the aerial torpedo. And he wanted to do it on his own without let or hindrance. He needed to cut the umbilical cord with the Company, "the Sperry Religion" that now had more than three thousand acolytes. He loved his family, but he was impatient with their anxieties. He admired his father, whom he so closely resembled in genius if not in temperament, but he wanted to get away from a company bureaucracy that now included a finance division, an engineering division, a factory division, a contracts division, an accounting department, a legal department, an estate department, a research department, a compass department, a searchlight department, a drafting department, a service department, a production control department, a methods department, separate departments for purchasing, personnel, service and maintenance, merchandising, sales, advertising, publications, traffic, and, almost as an afterthought, his own Aeroplane Department.

Charles Colvin, his "test pilot," had already broken loose to found Pioneer Instruments. Now it was Lawrence's turn to "prove his mettle," to be on his own, to be free to devote himself to his soaring dreams of the wild blue yonder: aviation.

On May 5, 1917, with his father's reluctant blessing, he formed the Lawrence Sperry Aircraft Company, with a large workshop and hangar at Farmingdale, Long Island, and capital assets of $50,000. There was a loose agreement between Lawrence and his uncle Herbert E. Goodman of the Sperry Executive Committee, who shared Father Sperry's worries about Lawrence, not only about his recklessness, his "dash and bang," but about his impatience with such mundane matters as inventories, office equipment, capital stock, insurance, notes payable and receivable, and double-entry bookkeeping.

When Lawrence set up his own company, he drove the same kind of astute financial bargain with the Sperry Gyroscope Company that his own father had arranged with big corporations as a younger man, and for the same reason: to retain his independence. While his brothers, Edward and Elmer, were content to remain on the Sperry Company payroll as employees, Lawrence insisted on a $5,000 annual consultancy fee and on sharing in the royalties of all Sperry airplane inventions that he had patented himself or on whose development he had worked jointly with his father. He also demanded a 15 percent royalty on Sperry Gyroscope profits on Lawrence Sperry instruments manufactured by the parent company.

"Father Sperry was upset," Elmer Sperry III said as recently as May 31, 1975, "but he went along and set Lawrence up in business rather than have him as a competitor.

"My father idolized Lawrence," he added. "Could it have been because he was the only one of the three boys that dared to stand up to the Old Man?"

Elmer III put his finger on the source of the difficulty between Daedalus and Icarus. Although he said that his father, Elmer A. Sperry, Jr., never mentioned any friction between Lawrence and Father Sperry, there is some evidence to the contrary.

There is, for example, a memorandum from Father Sperry, dated March 12, 1918, with the rather arresting title "Suggestions in Treating with Lawrence."

The memo begins by recommending that business relations be separate and that Lawrence's business be entirely separate from that of the Company. It goes on to complain that "no contract exists with Lawrence, although a memorandum might have been drawn up by his uncle [Herbert Goodman], which I have never seen."

Inasmuch as Lawrence was in need of immediate cash for his enterprise, Father Sperry proposed a settlement of $50,000 instead of profit sharing, and that the Company pay Lawrence $5,000 down plus notes that he could discount.

> If we give him notes they might draw five percent and be negotiable, but I think a restraint on his immediately cashing any large sums would be good for him. In connection with this, I think we should advise Lawrence to be as saving and conservative as possible.
>
> I suggest that it seemed to be Lawrence's wish, which he himself expressed, to be put upon his mettle and to see if he could not make an enterprise of his own go from this time on, exactly as his father had to do before him, but in the latter case with no such backing as the above arrangement provides him with. . . .
>
> I should like very much if Lawrence would accede to some further clauses in the contract. For instance, he should return to the files of the Company all records, photographs etc. that have been

gathered in the past and keep them where they will be complete and fully available to ourselves as well as to him.

In this connection it should be a common wish of us all that he refrain from violence and violent denunciations and threats, especially to his father and mother. From now on it would be very desirable that the heartiest cooperation should exist with the family, and that we all work in the greatest harmony. I think Lawrence should also be urged to reject the counsel of those who are trying to separate and alienate him from his parents and his family.

It is expected that very little business will have to be transacted with the family. The relationship should be held as much as possible along social lines, but if business is to be transacted with members of the family it must be put in writing, and woven into this clause should be a reference about refraining from bringing up or referring to any and all matters that are in the past. . . .

At this time Lawrence should square himself with the world— whatever he owes the Company should be squared up. It may be possible that the Company can take his notes, constituting orders on the Company under the contract, so that it can repay itself when profits actually exist and these payments would not interfere with other things. Similar notes should be given to the family for that part of each of the checks that he has not returned, as per original agreement.

It is understood that all business with the Company shall be transacted through Mr. Gillmor, and all business with members of the family in writing.

As always, money would appear to have been the root of all evil. Lawrence wanted to "be put upon his mettle," and he was obviously one of the most mettlesome men who ever lived. But, with the end of the war, aviation went into the doldrums. The statement of assets and liabilities for the Lawrence Sperry Aircraft Company showed them just about breaking even, and it was difficult for Lawrence to pay back the sums that had been advanced by the giant Sperry Company to finance his fledgling corporation. The reference to Lawrence's wanting to make it on his own exactly as his father had to do before him, but with no such backing as his father was giving him, could only serve to widen the generation gap between the two.

No one has so far been able to discover the nature of the "threats" made by Lawrence toward his parents nor the identity of those who wished to alienate him from his family. Lawrence's sister Helen ascribed this role to Grover Loening, a close friend of Lawrence's, and one of the most distinguished figures in the history of aviation. Four years Lawrence's senior, Grover was the first American to receive a graduate degree in aeronautics, and he was inducted into the Aviation Hall of Fame, with Jimmy Doolittle as his sponsor. A prolific writer, Grover Leoning used Lawrence as the model for his hero, Gilbert Carey, in his novel *The Conquering Wing.* Despite his impeccable credentials, Helen disapproved of Grover Loening and his influence on Lawrence. He did not, in her opinion, lead Lawrence in the direction of "the finer things of life."

It is quite possible that Grover Loening aided and abetted Lawrence's desire to be independent of his family. In *The Conquering Wing* he depicts Gil Carey as "a slim, erect six footer with blond hair, fresh clear complexion, and keen blue eyes." Like Lawrence, Gil flies in spite of the objections of his father, has "a lack of esteem for all those who don't share his vision," and belongs to "that lonely fraternity in which you know that you may be killed shortly, so you go after all that life can offer at once."

In any event a contract was duly drawn up in 1918 between Lawrence as party of the first part and Elmer A. Sperry as party of the second part and the Lawrence Sperry Aircraft Company as the party of the third part and the Sperry Gyroscope Company as the party of the fourth part. Lawrence accepted a consultant's fee and agreed to assign the patents in his name as sole or joint inventor to the Company in return for 10 percent of the total net profits derived from the sales of marching compasses, altimeters, airspeed indicators, angle-of-incidence indicators, airplane compasses, automatic pilots for airships, servomotors for use on aircraft, aerial torpedoes, and "any apparatus in the aeronautic field manufactured by the Company in accordance with inventions of the first party, including banking indicators, bomb sights, special night-flying equipment, aeronautical maps and instructographs."

In the final clauses of the contract the first party agreed to return all documents to the files of the Company, and it was "the understanding that cooperative relations and friendly dealings will prevail between all parties to this agreement and that all matters relating in any way to the business relations between the parties will be discussed in an impartial, businesslike and impersonal manner."

In a subsequent contract in 1919 the Gyroscope Company granted Lawrence an exclusive, personal, and nonassignable license to manufacture and sell Aerial Torpedoes under the existing patents and under all future patents and applications, United States and foreign. Lawrence B. Sperry, Jr., still applauds this concession wrung from the Company by his mettlesome father, especially since Father Sperry, in a subsequent moment of philanthropy, decided to leave a large part of his fortune, one million dollars, to the Y.M.C.A. instead of to his grandchildren.

14

IN 1916, before setting up his own business, Lawrence Sperry had gone to Europe to volunteer for active service in the British and French air corps. Reginald Gillmor, in charge of Sperry business in England, dissuaded him.

"Our time will come," he said. "You have plenty of work to do at home."

So Lawrence dined at the officers' mess in both countries and sold his stabilizers to the Allies. A Japanese delegation wanted to buy them, too, but Lawrence declined their offer.

"There is little doubt in my mind," he wrote to his father, "that these gentlemen from Japan will attack us, should differences arise. They are getting ready."

It was a prophetic statement, twenty-five years before the event.

Even in wartime, France and England exerted their old spell on Lawrence. He was "fascinated with life over there," Zula noted in a letter to her brother, Herbert Goodman, after Lawrence's return. "If you could see Lawrence who never used to care how he looked! Now in his tailor-made trousers, fancy vest, derby hat, kid gloves, shoes actually blacked all over, necktie carefully tied, you would hardly recognize him. It's a transformation. He seems to be blossoming out all at once."

Zula was right about her blue-eyed boy. He was blossoming out in many ways. It is evident from photographs, newspaper reports, and personal memories of men and especially women who knew Lawrence that he was endowed with that animal magnetism which F. Scott Fitzgerald called one of the two most important things in life (the other being money). "Sex appeal" was much too bold a term to have been invented as early as 1916, but Lawrence was loaded with it, and it played a notable role, though quite unwittingly, not only in aviation but in women's liberation too. Women who yearned for something more than their "place" in the home also yearned to fly with "the handsome young aviator from Brooklyn." From 1916 on, the New York papers were full of items about society women who took flying lessons from Lawrence. A typical story from the *New York Times:*

> Lawrence B. Sperry, inventor of the Sperry stabilizer for aeroplanes, who arrived on Tuesday night at Amityville in his flying boat from Marblehead, making 200 miles in 185 minutes, completed his journey this morning by flying to Governors Island. He made the distance of 32 miles in less than 30 minutes, carrying a passenger, Miss Emily Rich of 16 Central Park West.
>
> Miss Rich is secretary of the Art Students' League, and is learning to fly under Mr. Sperry.

The reporters used that last phrase so consistently as to indicate a certain malice aforethought. By 1918, twenty-five-year-old Lawrence had more lady applicants than he could handle. He had broken loose from the family company, and when the Sperrys moved from their Greek Revival house on Marlborough Road to a grander house with traces of Norman castle architecture just a block away on Albemarle Road, Lawrence declined the offer of a princely room in the tower and took up bachelor quarters with Grover Loening in a ramshackle house in Massapequa, just south of his new airplane factory at Farmingdale, Long Island.

Here Grover and Lawrence entertained numerous women whom Helen Sperry considered "most unsuitable" for her younger brother. "Grover Loening was a young buck in a disordered state," she recalls, "just like Lawrence. Lawrence did not meet the right sort of girls in Massapequa. That Grover Loening was a dandy. He came to Thanksgiving dinner at our house wearing spats. He was a satyr in spats. He and Lawrence egged each other on. They were interested in only two things: flying and women. It's a good thing Mother didn't know about the goings on at Massapequa."

Helen, who was twenty-eight at the time of these "goings on," clings to a theory that Lawrence was so busy inventing and building things as an adolescent that he had never had a normal social life. He resolutely refused to attend dancing school, she recalls, "and since he didn't learn about girls earlier, he chased them later, or rather they chased *him*."

Helen divided Lawrence's female companions into two categories: suitable and unsuitable. The suitable ones vied quietly with each other to marry him. The unsuitable ones hung around the flying fields of Nassau County, awaiting an invitation to spend the night at Massapequa. There was a third category that Helen was not aware of until late in 1916. This group might have been described as "socially suitable" but "morally and matrimonially unsuitable." These were New York society ladies who, enjoying the time-honored privileges of rank and money, were not inhibited by Victorian moral standards that had been designed to keep the lower classes in line. Helen would find out about them in due course.

In the meantime she had not renounced her efforts to refine and civilize her brother. Her first choice as a suitable bride was "that nice Mary Bacon," for whose election at Erasmus Hall young Elmer had climbed the steeple of the Dutch Reformed Church. Mary had gone on to graduate *cum laude* and Phi Beta Kappa from Smith. She came from a good family. She was a bluestocking, dedicated to literature, art, all the finer things of life. Lawrence admitted that Mary Bacon was attractive and intelligent, but she had one insurmountable flaw in her character: she got airsick.

Lawrence's "social activities," as the Sperry family euphemistically described them, were normal enough, especially given his impetuous character and his extraordinary energy. It is quite probable that his sexual initiation took place in France under the sophisticated tutelage of Paul Jourdan. It was easier in those days for an American boy of good family to lose his virginity in Paris than at home. Lawrence could hardly have spent *all* his time in France selling stabilizers, flying French military planes, and dining in the officers' mess.

On his way back to New York on the *Olympic* in 1915, he and a lady passenger apparently shared a stateroom. This came out in a long interview that Lawrence Sperry, Jr., had with his father's associate, Charles Colvin. After Lawrence's return from France, Charley said, a fellow passenger from the *Olympic* came to call on Lawrence in his office. The office was merely a partitioned section of the Aeroplane Department. There was no auditory privacy, and the visitor had a loud voice, which all the employees could hear. The visitor had seen a lady sharing Lawrence's stateroom and had concluded, as one did in those days, that she must be his wife.

"And how, may I ask, is Mrs. Sperry?" he boomed.

"You may well ask," Lawrence shouted back, "and my mother is fine, just fine, thank you very much, it has been nice to see you."

Elmer Sperry, Jr., told his son, Elmer III, that Lawrence's *Olympic* girlfriend hung around Brooklyn until Father Sperry paid for her passage back to France.

While the "suitable" girls vied quietly for his attention, Lawrence was most democratic when it came to taking ladies for a ride. He would fly into Brooklyn from Massapequa for Sunday dinner with the family, land on the Prospect Park Parade Grounds, and promise his female admirers a ride in return for standing guard over his plane while he dined. One of these aerial flights to Flatbush was vividly described by an anonymous reporter in *Aerial Age Weekly:*

> Lawrence Sperry flew to Sunday dinner at the family home, 1505 Albemarle Road, in his big Curtiss triplane. It was a thrilling afternoon for Flatbush. A little before one o'clock the residents of Flatbush were roused from their Sunday papers by the whir of an aeroplane motor. Quickly the houses emptied and thousands of persons saw a big triplane doing the most daring stunts a thousand feet aloft.
>
> Mr. Sperry, who was accompanied by a mechanic, looped the loop several times above the Prospect Park Parade Ground, and then did a feat that made all on the ground hold their breath, especially his pretty sister, who had been awaiting him. From a height of about one thousand feet, Mr. Sperry stood his machine on its head and started to dive straight down. Everyone was certain he had lost control and that the aeroplane would be smashed and the occupants killed. But, a hundred feet from the ground, the

aviator straightened out and the aeroplane turned and floated away, then circled and made a perfect landing.

There are six football fields and 12 goalposts on the parade grounds. Mr. Sperry guided his plane skilfully among them, although he had to hop over one of them, and stopped close to the Park Department Building at the west end of the field. There Mr. Sperry shook hands with several aviation officers, autographed notebooks for alumnae of his school, Erasmus Hall, and then the party went off to the Sperry home for dinner while 20,000 persons flooded onto the Parade Grounds to have a look at the machine.

When he got back to the Parade Grounds, after the traditional Sperry Sunday dinner of roast beef and Yorkshire pudding, the plane watchers were lined up hoping for a ride. He accommodated as many as he could. Those he liked came back for more. The less attractive ones were treated to such hair-raising stunts, like upside-down flying, that they decided never to fly again, not even with Lawrence. One young woman, Ruth Craigin, literally had her hair raised; it got caught in the motor. Lawrence, who had very fast reflexes, whipped out a knife and hacked her hair off just in time to keep her from being scalped. Ruth Craigin must have been literally crazy about Lawrence or an incurable masochist: she came back for more—with her head swathed in a turban.

Two of the "suitable" ladies in Lawrence's life are still living in New York, attractive and lively women in their seventies: Mrs. William Hester and Midge Austin, to whom Lawrence proposed when she came out in Charleston at the age of eighteen.

Mrs. Hester, née Lillian Scharmann, was one of Helen's leading candidates to be her sister-in-law. Her picture appeared in the society pages and the rotogravure section of the Sunday *Tribune*, holding up the tail of Lawrence's plane. He took her up and looped-the-loop. She got airsick, bore Lawrence no grudge, but decided to marry a publisher.

"My first ride was also my last," she recalled in 1975. "Lawrence loved to loop-the-loop. Spiraling and tailspins were two other specialties. He had absolutely no realization of danger.

"He frightened us to death at Bellport," she went on. "He would go into the wildest ocean and plunge through those breakers when nobody else was even on the beach. In the bay he would go underwater and stay there for minutes, clinging to the barnacled piles of the dock to test his endurance. I can still see those blue eyes shining when he finally came up.

"He was terribly attractive. The Sperrys were all good-looking, but the other brothers didn't have his flair. Lawrence was young, blond, fascinatingly devilish. When he had that house in Massapequa he tooled around in a Marmon car with leopard seats. The police chased him, but he could always outdistance them. When they finally caught up with him they made him put a governor on the car.

"He did everything to the hilt. The old salts at Bellport said, 'If that there Sperry drives his aeroplane the way he drives his car and sailboat, I don't never want to fly with him.' "

Lillian Scharmann Hester, whose husband's family owned the *Brooklyn Daily Eagle*, remembers the episode in which Lawrence took the Marlborough Road house apart to remove his glider.

"Zula just got the giggles," she said. "What else could she do? But the family forgave him. They knew he was a genius. He was inspired and driven by genius. He was absolutely fearless. He was a force of nature. His conflict was with the elements. He really wanted to conquer everything."

He tried to conquer the heart of Midge Austin, one of New York's prettiest debutantes. Her memory of him is strikingly similar to Lillian Scharmann's.

"He had to conquer the elements," she said. "He would swim in a typhoon and hike through a blizzard.

"Lawrence had a one-track mind," she said. "Nothing got in his way. I was the track for a time. I was seventeen and he was twenty-three. I said no, but he was a terribly exciting personality, full of a rage to live, in love with love, in love with life.

"After I married Stewart King," Midge went on, "Lawrence came to see us at Bellport. Stewart had spent the entire day installing screens. It was raining, and when Lawrence arrived, the screen door stuck. Lawrence was terribly strong. He just yanked, and the door came out of the frame, hinges and all. Stewart didn't exactly appreciate this. There was a certain coolness between Stewart and Lawrence.

"He had a *lot* of girlfriends," Midge recalled. "In 1915, when he was twenty-two, he brought a mysterious woman to Bellport. Her name was Juanita. She was exotically dark and beautiful, a little older than Lawrence, and a real vamp. Juanita was rumored to have tooth marks on her breast from love bites. We were all fascinated by that, but nobody dared ask Lawrence if it were true. And Lawrence didn't dare bring Juanita to the Goldthwaite Inn; he didn't want his mother to know she was in Bellport."

Mammary tooth marks may seem like pretty tame stuff in these topless days, but it should be remembered that Lawrence's premarital "social activities" took place in a publicly prudish context. Ladies did not expose their "limbs" in public. A snapshot of the vamp Juanita, taken in 1915, shows her in a modest white summer dress extending to her wrists and insteps. There are other pictures of his other girlfriends in bathing costumes black as a nun's habit, in which every square millimeter of flesh is covered except for the face and hands. Some women bathers are alleged to have drowned, dragged down by the weight of waterlogged stockings and skirts, but at least they died modestly. Men were pretty thoroughly covered too. Their bathing suits extended from the neck and armpits to the knees. Nevertheless, in the summer of 1916, at the height of Lawrence's escapades, twenty men were arrested and spent the night in jail for having committed an "affront to public decency" by having appeared in bathing suits one block inland from the beach at Coney Island.

In that same year Margaret Sanger opened her first birth control clinic in Brooklyn. It was raided and closed by the police. Her magazine, *The Woman Rebel,* in which she had mentioned contraception, was seized and she was jailed for thirty days for "obscenity."

It was against this background of public prudery that Lawrence's amorous experiments reached a sensational climax on November 22, 1916. He had been giving flying lessons to a New York society woman, Mrs. Waldo Polk, who was crazy about flying, especially with Lawrence. She learned things from the bottom up, even donning overalls to work as Lawrence's mechanic. Cynthia Polk was a good-looking woman—her husband was away driving an ambulance in France—and when she and Lawrence alighted on the grounds of the Garden City Country Club and strode into the dining room in their overalls, the eyebrows of the assembled elite rose in horror. Both socially prominent, there they sat, eating caviar and sipping champagne, looking like two elegant grease monkeys in jumpsuits. The head waiter could hardly refuse to serve them; they were both members of the club.

While the Rules Committee convened in extraordinary sessions to discuss the matter of proper attire, Mr. Sperry and Mrs. Polk blithely continued their high-flying experiments. On the afternoon of November 22, 1916, they were flying above Babylon, Long Island, when Lawrence decided to put the gyroscopic stabilizer to a supreme test. He put the Curtiss flying boat on automatic control and turned his attention gallantly to his pupil.

"They almost made it," Grover Loening told me, "but something went wrong with the automatic pilot, and the plane fell five hundred feet into Great South Bay."

Duck hunters paddling to their rescue were surprised to find a lady and gentleman stark naked. The impact of the crash, Lawrence said, had divested them of their clothing.

They scrambled into their sodden garments, and the duck hunters took them to Southside Hospital. Cynthia Polk, carried in on a stretcher, kept saying to the reporters, "It's nothing at all. No need to mention it. I do not wish to worry my family."

Lawrence walked into the hospital. Upon examination their injuries were found to be less acute than their embarrassment.

"Too trivial to mention," Mrs. Polk kept insisting to the *Times* reporter.

"Only the news that's fit to print," Lawrence said, slapping the reporter on the back, and indeed the *Times* handled the story with great discretion:

MRS. W. POLK HURT
IN AIRSHIP'S FALL

Hunters Rescue Sperry and
Woman Passenger from Craft
Wrecked in Sound Marshes

BOTH TAKEN TO HOSPITAL

But Doctors Say Aviator and His
Companion Are Not Injured
Seriously and Will Be Out Soon

————————

Special to the New York Times
BABYLON, L. I. Nov. 22—Duck hunters in the marshes half a mile
west of town this afternoon saw something coming swiftly toward
them through the air from the direction of Amityville and finally
recognized it as Lawrence Sperry's hydroaeroplane, in which he is
accustomed to make flights over Great South Bay. The craft was
about 500 feet above the water when the hunters saw it descend
suddenly.

James Hyde, of the theatrical firm of Hyde & Behman, with
Schuyler Watts and James Wyckoff, were first to reach the flying
craft. They found Sperry and Mrs. Waldo Polk of New York clinging
to the boat part of the machine. The plane was buried nose down in
the mud a quarter of a mile from shore and half a mile from the entrance to Mud Creek.

Although they had been in the water only a few minutes, Sperry
and Mrs. Polk were nearly overcome by the cold. Mrs. Polk was
stunned, almost senseless. She and Mr. Sperry were lifted into a
power boat which raced them to the steamboat pier here, and
where an ambulance was summoned from the South Side Hospital.
Sperry was able to walk to the ambulance, with assistance, but Mrs.
Polk was carried on a stretcher.

In the hospital both recovered rapidly, and Dr. James S. Ames
found that no bones were broken and neither was hurt internally,
though both were suffering from exposure. Mrs. Polk asked that no
word of the accident be conveyed to her relatives in New York, as it
was trivial and she would soon be out of the hospital.

Sperry and Mrs. Polk both made light of the affair, and said there
had been nothing wrong with the machine, that it had not fallen nor
got beyond control of the aviator. They had intended to alight on
the water, Sperry said, and had done so successfully, coming to grief
when the craft, then afloat, struck a "syke," as the stakes holding flat
fishnets are called.

The boat was making better than forty miles an hour at the time,
and was wrecked at once, Sperry and Mrs. Polk being tossed from
their seats, which were instantly submerged as the boat buried its
nose in the mud.

Hunters who saw the craft come down had previously declared that it had fallen like a wounded duck, but Sperry insisted that this had not been the case.

Lawrence had two reputations to protect: Mrs. Polk's and the stabilizer's. Nothing wrong with the machine! It had not fallen nor got beyond control of the aviator: it was a gallant improvisation.

The sensational tabloid newspapers were less discreet than the *Times*. One of them featured a big black headline:

AERIAL PETTING
ENDS IN WETTING

Father Sperry, affecting not to see these blatant examples of yellow journalism on his employees' desks, was not amused. As for the culprits, Lawrence and Mrs. Polk, they thought it wiser not to sue such publications as the *Mirror* and the *Evening Graphic*. Everybody who was anybody knew they were scandal sheets, beneath contempt.

Still, Lawrence had perpetrated a scandal. The Sperry family tried to cover it up with two words: "Grossly exaggerated." But the notorious episode found its way into printed history in a number of distorted forms. One history of aviation describes this "aerial lovemaking" as having taken place at North Island in 1914; but Lawrence was not ready to put his stabilizer to such a definitive test at that time.

The truth of the matter came from Grover Loening, who got it straight from Lawrence. At his aviation museum on Key Biscayne in 1971, this distinguished airman, eighty-four at the time, recalled the hushed-up Polk episode explicitly:

"Cynthia Polk was a wild girl," he said. "She was ready for anything anytime. Lawrence's aim, quite frankly, was to be the first man to screw a girl in the air. They almost made it, but something went wrong with the stabilizer. Lawrence confessed that to me, though he would never have admitted it to the press. It was high society gossip for some time, this love affair in the air, and it was most embarrassing for Lawrence's Baptist family.

"But Lawrence was no aerial playboy," Grover went on. "During the six months that we lived in that house in Massapequa, he was performing very secret and dangerous experiments for the Army in developing the aerial torpedo. The tension was unrelenting and he had to do something to relieve it. We agreed to live dangerously, but he lived more dangerously than I. He had such go and daring: an eccentric and brilliant character. He was a real genius, a terribly hard worker, and equally strenuous in his leisure.

"To relieve the strain of the torpedo tests, Lawrence had a drinking companion at Massapequa, and they would go out every night drinking and wenching. Sometimes they would pick up as many as five or six girls in a single night. That little two-story red house in Massapequa was not in the best neighborhood. There were some pretty wild parties there, everybody naked, orgies. It was sort of like a sexual commune: lots of boys and girls together with no restraint at all."

Asked if she knew anything about a "drinking companion" who had led her younger brother astray, Helen Sperry Lea replied, "Of course I do. His name was Grover Loening!"

Grover said that Cynthia Polk, despite her lofty social position, was "a tough baby. She actually boasted about her aerial liaison with Lawrence."

The most recent report on the Polk episode came from Elmer Sperry III, son of Lawrence's devoted younger brother, Elmer A. Sperry, Jr. Lawrence confided in his brother and told him that in the confined space of the plane he had inadvertently bumped the gyro platform, which threw the automatic pilot out of whack and sent the plane into a dive from which he was "too entangled" to recover.

Thus the stabilizer was absolved!

It should be added that Cynthia Polk was more than the wanton of the wild blue yonder and more than a passing fancy in Lawrence's life. She was one of his star pupils. She obtained her pilot's license under his tutelage, and Lawrence became an unwitting pioneer of women's liberation by going to bat for her in Washington in 1917 shortly before the United States entered World War I. The *New York Times* recorded this in a special dispatch from Washington on January 4:

A plan for probationary enrollment of women aviators in the Army Aviation Reserve Corps for such service, back of the fighting line, as watching for enemy aircraft and submarine mines, in the guarding of cities and harbors, is under consideration by the Aviation Board of Engineers in the War Department. The plan was submitted by Lawrence Sperry, the young aviator of New York City, who said that Major Gen. Leonard Wood had indorsed the order and had granted to one woman aviator, Mrs. Waldo Polk, permission to fly at Governors Island. Mrs. Polk, who also came to Washington in advocacy of the plan, holds a pilot's license, and expects to go to France, where her husband is in the ambulance service, to take up military aviation, but would like to qualify as the first woman aviator in the American Army.

In submitting his plan, Mr. Sperry presented broad endorsement from Dr. Straton of the Bureau of Standards, Rear Admiral Robert E. Peary, Secretary Redfield and others, and today received a letter from Lieut. Col. Squier in charge of the Aviation Section of the Signal Corps, in part, as follows:

"I am much interested in the Sperry plan, and I have no doubt that there are thousands of women in this country that could successfully operate aeroplanes, in case of necessity, for both commercial and military purposes."

This was one aspect of Lawrence's connection with Mrs. Polk that Helen could approve of, but there was great relief in the Sperry family when Cynthia Polk *did* go to France to join her ambulance-driving husband.

It is obvious that, like most creative geniuses, Lawrence was endowed with great sexual energy. The important question, especially in those days and in Lawrence's milieu, was who would channel this energy, who would legitimize this force of nature?

On the night of December 15, 1917, friends of Lawrence's, Mr. and Mrs. William Scovill, invited Lawrence to dinner at the Algonquin Hotel, one of the smartest places in New York, frequented by literary lights and stars of the stage and screen. Billy Scovill was the heir and managing director of the Scovill Manufacturing Company, one of the most prosperous and diversified industrial goods firms in America. Lawrence was interested in Scovill industrial cylinders and control valves. He and Billy

Scovill had become close friends and golfing companions. Now the Scovills wanted Lawrence to meet another one of their favorite people, a twenty-one-year-old movie actress who lived in the Algonquin and who had "captivated" them. Her name was Winifred Allen.

She captivated Lawrence, too. Thanks to the Polk scandal, he had an almost Byronic reputation by this time, "mad, bad, and dangerous to know." Now, as they dined by candlelight on Russian caviar and lobster Newburgh (one dollar each for the caviar and seventy-five cents for the lobster; Billy was a lavish host), Lawrence was spellbound by a pair of dark brown eyes. The Scovills remarked that Mary Pickford and Douglas Fairbanks were two tables away, and Billie Burke was there dining with Florenz Ziegfeld, but Lawrence's attention was riveted on Winifred Allen. Suddenly, after the "orgies" of Massapequa and the scandal of Babylon, he was as tame as the unicorn when it laid its head to rest in a virgin's lap.

"He looks like a Nordic prince," Winifred Allen said to her hosts after dinner.

He called her the next day.

Ten days later, on Christmas Day, he offered her a brown diamond to match her eyes. She accepted. She also accompanied him obediently on December 26 to Abercrombie and Fitch, where she was fitted for fleece-lined leather flying togs.

On New Year's Day, 1918, Lawrence took Winifred on her first flight. He lifted her into the copilot's seat of his Curtiss triplane, climbed in beside her, and took her two thousand feet up into the icy air pierced by all the towers of New York. He circled Governors Island, flew across the steel-gray river to Brooklyn, where he buzzed the astonished ice skaters on the lake of Prospect Park, and pointed out the Norman-towered Sperry home on Albemarle Road.

"That's where my folks live," he shouted above the whine of the motor. "Would you like to meet them?"

Winifred nodded assent. She had never looked so pretty, her brown eyes reflecting all the winter sky, her tingling cheeks the color of a rose.

"Will you marry me?" Lawrence shouted.

"I will," she shouted back.

"When? Today? Tomorrow?"

"After a decent interval," she yelled.

A decent interval in 1918 was supposed to be at least nine months between engagement and marriage. Anything else, according to neo-Victorian etiquette, might imply unseemly haste, carnal incontinence, or premature babies in incubators.

Lawrence accepted this stricture for the time being, though he allowed the plane to go into a slight symbolic wobble. He was determined not to wait nine months.

His happiness was sufficient unto the day. Winnie had said yes. And she had passed the acid test: she was immune to airsickness; she loved to fly.

"She's perfect for you," Grover Loening told Lawrence. "Forget about all the others. Marry her."

This exhortation was superfluous.

15

WHO WAS SHE, this tiny bit of spirited protoplasm that, within two weeks, had so captivated Lawrence that he was now set on forsaking all others, clinging only to her?

Winifred Allen, "one of the prettiest girls I ever directed," according to that prince of producers, Allan Dwan, was already an established movie star at the age of twenty-one when she met Lawrence Sperry. He was twenty-five, New York's most celebrated aviator and one of the city's most eligible bachelors, despite the gossip about him and Mrs. Polk, which in fact added a certain piquancy to his eligibility. New York society writers knew all about the dashing, daredevil scion of the Sperry family, but they contented themselves with one sentence about Winifred Allen: "A star of Triangle Films, Miss Allen is an orphan."

That was enough. An actress and an orphan: it suggested avant-garde "fast" living and nineteenth-century pathos in a single phrase. If a girl was not from an old New York family, there was no point in going into genealogical detail.

Winifred Allen's family tree had its roots in Ireland. Her mother, Winifred Jessica Allan Barclay, was a high-spirited Anglo-Irish woman from Kilbrittain in County Cork. She traced her ancestry back to Lord Barclay, a seventeenth-century Cavalier who had moved to Ireland rather than knuckle under to the regicide Oliver Cromwell. The Barclays of Kilbrittain never referred to the Lord Protector without that prefix; he was a murderer, the Regicide Cromwell.

Winifred Barclay's father was a magistrate, a member of that impecunious Anglo-Irish gentry that lived off poor land and on rich legend and language. The poetry and the beautiful scenery of the Emerald Isle, however, were not enough to compensate for the perennial troubles and potato famines. In 1890, at the age of sixteen, Winifred Barclay had a chance to escape.

A branch of the family had migrated to America during the famine of 1879 and prospered in Wisconsin, where they raised dairy cows and grew every crop except potatoes. They sent young Winifred $50 and an invitation to visit them and earn her keep by helping with the children.

Presented with a frostbitten potato that presaged still another famine, Winifred said, "I'll not eat another crumb of this demoralizing spud."

Off she went to Queenstown, thence on a boat to New York, thence by train to Madison, Wisconsin, with never a backward glance. But the poetry of Ireland stayed in her heart, and she had the confidence that comes with good looks.

The American Barclays sent Winifred to the University of Wisconsin. She majored in literature. She had another Irish trait, the gift of the gab, and everything she said in the lovely, lilting language of Inishfallen and Kilbrittain sounded like poetry. She gave poetry readings at the university. Single-handed, she brought the sorrows of Ireland and the Celtic reawakening to Madison and Milwaukee. She had the power to transfix an audience. They had never heard anything like it:

> Shan-walla where a willow-bordered pond
> Gathers the wild duck from the winter dawn . . .

People sat entranced by this rhythmic evocation of Celtic mystery and were moved to tears of moral indignation when Miss Barclay keened on and on about the current troubles of the Old Country, immortalized in the verses of Wilfrid Blunt:

> Did ye not hear it? From those muffled windows
> The sound of wailing rises, not of mirth.
> These are our daughters—ay, our sons in prison
> Captives to shame with those who rule the earth.
>
> The silent river by those gardens lapping
> Tonight receives its burden of new dead
> A man of age sent home with his lord's wages,
> Stones to his feet, a gravecloth to his head.

Such poetry on the lips of an eighteen-year-old colleen elicited large contributions for Parnell's Land League and Home Rule for Ireland. The reader also exerted a magnetic attraction on Dr. John William Barry of Milwaukee. He and Winifred Barclay were married in 1892. It was a sweet and happy marriage, but short; Dr. Barry died that same year, shortly after the birth of their daughter, May.

Three years later Winifred Barclay married a handsome civil engineer and surveyor with the romantic name of Henry d'Arcy Kelly. Kelly was loaded with Irish charm, but he had a traditional Irish weakness for tippling. He had a good excuse, chronic mastoiditis, but he overdid the cure.

Winifred Allen Kelly was born on June 26, 1896, in New Rochelle, New York, an old Huguenot settlement whose boosters were now touting it as "a great little town only forty-five minutes from Times Square." When Winifred was three and May was seven, Henry d'Arcy Kelly's drinking problem had become so acute and his behavior so abusive that his wife took the then drastic step of leaving him and officially changing her own and her second daughter's name to Allen.

She had enough money from her first marriage with Dr. Barry to send May to a fashionable finishing school at Millbrook, which specialized in Greek drama. May, having inherited her mother's flair for histrionics, led the chorus in Euripides' *Hippolytus:*

> O Eros, O Eros, how melts love's yearning
> From thine eyes, when thy sweet spell witcheth the heart.

Her sweet spell witched the heart of a young man in the audience to such an extent that she eloped with him. He was the spoiled scion of a rich and socially prominent Boston family. In the early days of the twentieth century, parents still had the audacity to interfere in their children's lives. Neither family approved of schoolgirl brides, and May was returned to school in the chauffeur-driven Pierce Arrow of her would-be husband.

Remarking that May had definite histrionic talent but was "too good-looking for her own good," Miss Bennett, headmistress of the Millbrook Finishing School, sent Mrs. Allen an extra bill for "special surveillance."

That finished Mrs. Allen with finishing schools. She sent young Winifred to the New Rochelle Public High School. When she graduated at the age of sixteen she was voted the prettiest girl in her class and the girl most likely to succeed as an artist. She had her mother's black hair, vivid coloring, and vivacious brown eyes. She announced that she wanted to be a sculptress.

All these factors plus the stifling suburban atmosphere of New Rochelle made Mrs. Allen decide to move to New York. She took an apartment on the then fashionable West Side at Riverside Drive and 110th Street and enrolled Winifred in the famous Art Students League on West 57th Street.

Equally celebrated and in the same building was Daniel Frohman's School of Dramatic Art. In 1913 one of the great personalities of American show business, S. L. Rothapfel, known as "Roxy," was coming out of the Frohman School and, as they said in New York, "bumped into" the budding seventeen-year-old sculptress Winifred Allen. Roxy, whose unerring sense of spectacle and distributorship would create the Rialto Theatre, the Roxy, and Radio City Music Hall, was immediately struck by the appeal of this diminutive, dimpled, brown-eyed girl, who had the kind of pure and wistful charm that wowed America in 1913.

"There's a greater future in acting than in sculpture," Roxy assured Winnie, and he introduced her not only to Daniel Frohman but also to the man whom Winifred considered "the most peerless of producers," Allan Dwan.

With her mother's blessing, Winifred transferred from the Art Students League to Frohman's School of Dramatic Art. Mrs. Allen died of cancer in that same year, 1913, but had the satisfaction of seeing her older daughter married and of being assured by Daniel Frohman that Winifred had dramatic talent as well as good looks. He had sent her down to D. W. Griffith's studios on 14th Street for a screen test. She was highly photogenic. Her beauty appealed to Griffith, who was already grooming such future stars as Mary Pickford, Mae Marsh, and Lillian and Dorothy Gish.

Griffith moved to Hollywood and made that obscure suburb of

Los Angeles famous when he filmed *The Birth of a Nation* in nine weeks, with a cast of three hundred and a budget of $61,000, most of which he had borrowed in small sums from investors who subsequently got rich on the profits. There was no script for *The Birth of a Nation;* Griffith made it up as he went along. But the results convinced even so august a critic as the British historian George Macaulay Trevelyan that the twentieth century was the film age.

At seventeen, Winifred Allen was ready for a role in that age. Although she was now officially an orphan, she was neither destitute nor alone in the world. She was taken in by a devoted friend of her mother's, Mrs. Yerkes, who had an apartment in the same house on Riverside Drive.

She also had an officially designated chaperone, another of her mother's friends, Wyn Hope, whom Lawrence Sperry, Jr., remembers as "a big sentimental woman, full of affection." "Aunt Wyn," as Winifred called her, wrote children's plays and books, the most popular of which was *Friends in Bookland.* Aunt Wyn lived in the glamorous Algonquin Hotel in the heart of the theater district on West 44th Street. It was already a favorite haunt of writers, publishers, actors, and producers. Though Wyn Hope predated the famous Algonquin circle, sometimes known as "the vicious circle," she knew what temperamental creatures artists could be and she was an ideal surrogate mother, highly qualified to steer Winifred Allen safely through the shoals of show business.

Although she was well protected, the film and society reporters of New York clung resolutely to the word *orphan* when they wrote about "petite and winsome Winifred Allen." And it added a note of mystery and pathos to what was to be the most widely publicized wedding of 1918. It was especially touching, since the bride-to-be was physically tiny—four feet eleven inches tall in her stocking feet—and had the winsome appeal of a defenseless child, the kind that strong men yearn to take under a protecting wing. In the case of Lawrence B. Sperry, this metaphor had special overtones. She came to his armpit, and she could just touch the middle wing of his Curtiss triplane if she stood on the tips of her toes.

The movies knew how to exploit this waiflike charm, and Winifred Allen had been snapped up from the moment of her graduation from drama school in 1916.

"They're looking for extras over at Famous Players," Daniel Frohman said as he handed out the diplomas.

The whole class sprinted one block from the Frohman School to 128 West 56th Street, where Adolph Zukor was filming *When We Were Twenty-one.*

Diffidently and demurely, nineteen-year-old Winifred presented her diploma. The male lead, William Elliott, showed no interest in that document, but he nodded approval of the young graduate's good looks.

"You're hired," said Mr. Zukor. "Get your engagement voucher from Mr. Kaufmann."

Mr. Kaufmann filled out the Famous Players Film Company engagement voucher in pencil. Under Salary Arrangement he wrote, "Sixty Dollars per Week."

"Sign here, Miss Allen, where it says 'accepted.' "

Winifred signed her name. The document still exists in a family scrapbook, and the signature manages to be firm and shaky at the same time. She had not dreamed of such riches, and she walked on air from the studio to the Algonquin Hotel, eleven blocks south.

"Aunt Wyn, look at this," she said, showing the voucher to her chaperone.

"Brava, my dear," said Aunt Wyn. "Now I think you had better move in with me. And if Mr. Zukor or Mr. Elliott suggests any night work, you are to tell them that an artist needs her sleep. Alone," she added.

Winifred got the point.

She was such a success in *When We Were Twenty-one* that Famous Players engaged her for Booth Tarkington's *Seventeen,* starring Jack Pickford and Louise Huff. In this film she had a heady experience, involuntarily stealing the show as "the little girl who finally wins Jack."

She was given a similar role by Famous Players in *The Long Trail,* starring Mary Fuller and Lou Tellegen, the greatest matinee idol of the day, but she scrupulously followed the sage advice of Aunt Wyn: "Don't forget, my dear, that kisses on the screen are to be simulated. That is the mark of a good actress: to simulate emotion without getting emotionally involved."

Winifred got the point of that too. The movie critics were already writing about her extraordinary talent as an ingenue, but that is exactly what she was: an artless, innocent girl in spite of the world of artifice in which she was making her mark.

Early in 1917, at the age of twenty, her equilibrium was put to the supreme test. She was put under contract by Triangle Films, which announced that Winifred Allen was now a star.

This entailed a lot of work. The public's appetite for films was already insatiable. Loew's New York Theatre at Broadway and 45th Street, for example, showed films continuously from 11:00 A.M. to midnight, changed its bill every day, and had double features on Mondays and Thursdays. Tickets ranged from ten to twenty-five cents.

Winifred Allen helped feed this prodigious appetite for celluloid experience by making no fewer than six pictures in 1917 under the general supervision of Allan Dwan. Her name was on the weekly bill of Loew's film fare along with those of Alice Brady, Carmel Meyers, Theda Bara, William S. Hart ("The Buffalo Bill of the Silent Drama"), and Roscoe "Fatty" Arbuckle. Winifred Allen's name also flickered across the street on the marquee of Roxy's Rialto with those of Juliette Day, Helen Hayes, Norma Talmadge, Madame Olga Petrova, Mary Pickford, and Douglas Fairbanks.

Although Winifred yearned for a chance to play the role of a *femme fatale*, she was resolutely typed as the incarnation of pathos in parts where virginity, though often assaulted, was never violated.

"Virgins are the hardest roles to play," said Lillian Gish. "Those dear little girls—to make them interesting takes great vitality, but a fallen woman or a vamp: 75 percent of your work is already done!"

Winifred had the requisite vitality to make virtue interesting. The plots of her feature films recall the innocent pleasures of a lost paradise in which one went through four harrowing reels of conflict, secure in the knowledge that it would be happily resolved in the fifth.

Winifred's first star vehicle was *The Man Who Made Good.* Her costar, the man whom she was to make good, was Jack Devereaux, a handsome, wholesome athlete, who was, according to one critic, "the active, optimistic type of man that is grown in Ireland, where he was born twenty-eight years ago in County Clare." In 1917 it was an axiom of American philosophy that behind every man who made good, there was a good woman pushing him toward that goal. This was the role of winsome Winifred Allen. *The Man Who Made Good* was described by the distributors as "a brisk, up-to-the-minute comedy drama, dealing with a young man, Tom Burton, and a young woman, Frances Claton (Winifred Allen), who are determined to make good in New York City."

Movies were silent in those days, and the silver screen shimmered not only with dialogue but with philosophy and wit. In the first reel of *The Man Who Made Good,* for example, these precepts for success were emblazoned on the screen:

If you are a Burton, pick out the right kind of wife.
If you already have the right kind, start making good for her.

In this stirring sociological epic, Tom Burton and Frances Claton meet in a New York boardinghouse just off Broadway, eating prunes for dessert, a subtle challenge to press on quickly toward higher goals. Attracted to one another—you can see it in their smoldering eyes—Tom and Frances immediately decide upon matrimony, for we are back in the halcyon days of American romance where there is no love without marriage, no marriage without love. There is only one problem, an obstacle to be overcome: money. Tom, a biscuit salesman for the Whitney Cracker Company, has just enough cash to make the $500 down payment on the home to which every American couple aspires. He puts the money down, but his salary and commissions are not adequate to meet the monthly payments. After all, they have to eat; man cannot live by love alone.

Frances (Winnie) straightens her young husband's tie, gives him a convincingly simulated kiss (after all, they are man and wife in the film), and gazes at him with those liquid brown eyes that convey a subtle combination of wifely devotion and bourgeois ambition so determined as to assure the audience that prunes will eventually be replaced by strawberry shortcake.

Her beautiful lips carefully articulate inaudible words that are flashed onto the screen: "Tom, you just go right down to the office and ask Mr. Whitney for a raise. Demand it! You deserve it!! I know you will make good!!!"

Tom squares his shoulders, and off he goes.

Meanwhile, having told Tom that she is visiting a sick cousin, Frances obtains a position as a maid of all work in a great house on Fifth Avenue. She is determined that she will not be a handicap; she will help Tom make good.

Mr. Whitney refuses Tom's demand for a raise, showing him a chart of declining sales and disappearing profits. What Mr. Whitney doesn't know is that the regional sales manager, an odious type named Flash Lewis, is swindling the company, falsifying the sales records, and pocketing the profits. It is supremely ironical. The audience knows this, and so does Tom, but Tom cannot tell Mr. Whitney; nobody likes a tattletale. So, in one of the most dramatic moments of the film, Tom mouths three fateful syllables that almost burn a hole through the screen: "I RESIGN!"

Poor, misguided Mr. Whitney shakes his head more in sorrow than in anger. After all, nobody in his right mind could dislike Tom Burton.

Taking his salesman's supply of biscuits with him, Tom now embarks on one of those whirlwind picaresque tours of the nation that have delighted our American hearts from *The Song of the Road* to *Travels with Charlie*. Hobnobbing with hobos, he rides the rails, paying off the railroad dicks with Whitney Crackers, which immediately transform them into addicts. He washes dishes in restaurants, whose proprietors go mad for his cracker samples and place huge orders. He sleeps on park benches, dispensing biscuits to the birds—and to one early-bird equestrian who happens to be the head of the biggest chain of grocery stores in the nation.

In the meantime Frances is slaving away at washing, ironing, and scrubbing floors in the Fifth Avenue mansion, whose mistress spends all her time reclining on a chaise longue, eating chocolates and reading *True Confessions* magazine. What a contrast! It is especially trying for Frances when this employer scatters the chocolate papers all over the floor, and she, Frances, must pick them up.

Nevertheless Frances makes enough to meet the monthly mortgage payments on Tom's and her dream house, to which she returns each night with barely enough energy to fend off the obnoxious amatory advances of guess who: Flash Lewis, the corrupt, double-crossing, swindling sales manager of the Whitney Biscuit Company.

"Tom's no good," says Flash. "He's left you. Why don't you make it in the big time with me?"

"Never!" replies Frances. "Get out of my house. I loathe you!"

She expresses scorn and revulsion with every nerve of her body, but this only serves to inflame the lascivious ardor of Flash Lewis, as Tosca's disdain set Scarpia ablaze.

A wild chase ensues. Frances is terror-striken. She rushes through the house mouthing one monosyllable: "Tom! Tom! TOM!"

Here he is in the nick of time with a briefcase full of biscuit orders. Winnie's brown eyes brim with tears of love and relief. She falls into her husband's arms.

Flash Lewis takes advantage of their reunion to jump out the window and flee, but Tom is after him in a trice.

"It is during these scenes," wrote one critic, "that Devereaux displays the agility that made him one of the best sprinters on the cinder tracks of Phillips Exeter and Georgetown University. In this exciting climax he hurdles fences, leaps ditches, and shoots down the road at a centimeter rate."

That last phrase is not exactly clear; in fact it's quite baffling. In any event, Tom tracks his quarry down, drags him before the astonished Mr. Whitney, chokes a full confession out of the swindler, slams down the biscuit orders (which he has managed to keep intact throughout the chase), and is named sales manager on the spot.

"It gives a brisk, exciting finish to a lively story," the critic concluded, "one in which the beautiful new star, Winifred Allen, despite her extreme youth and petiteness, deserves unstinted praise for her dramatic talent."

The beautiful new star deserved better material, but being typecast was already an occupational hazard, and the plots of her movies got so silly that even the critics complained. She starred in five more films, "lifting them all above average," one critic said, and her exquisite profile became familiar in every town of America where Triangle films were shown. Thanks to Roxy's continuing interest, her films were always booked into "high-class neighborhoods."

"Her rapid rise to fame hasn't turned her pretty head in the least," wrote the movie critic of the *Cleveland Plain Dealer* after the release of her last film, a war epic, *For Valour*, with Richard Barthelmess, in November 1917. "And fame will never turn her head," the writer added, "because she is too busy studying and dreaming wonderful, healthy dreams about log cabins and open fires in mountain woods."

She was dreaming of that and more. Interviewed by the *Philadelphia Record* late in 1917, she said, "I don't want to be a fussy, frilly, sweet young thing. Anybody can play with a fan and flutter through five reels making eyes at the handsome hero. I want to interpret deeper emotions. I want to be tragic and passionate. I want to be a young wife. Being a wife is a very important business in this world, a very serious role, and that's what I want to play."

Deeper emotions, passion, tragedy, being a young wife, a serious role: she was to find all this in the improbable script of life. The script began on that night of December 15, 1917, in the dining room of the Algonquin Hotel in New York. Enter Lawrence Burst Sperry.

When Triangle Films offered Winifred a new contract to star in six more movies, she declined.

Why? Her director, Albert Parker, Roxy, Daniel Frohman, Allan Dwan, all the people who had played a role in her professional career wanted to know why she would refuse such an opportunity.

"I don't want to play at life," she said, "I want to live it. I'm going to marry Lawrence Sperry. That's more exciting than anything else I can think of."

16

IT WAS AGREED that Aunt Wyn Hope would announce the engagement of her "niece," Winifred Allen, to Lawrence Burst Sperry on January 19, 1918. A September wedding was envisaged, but Lawrence had other ideas, especially since engaged couples did not live together before marriage at that time.

He had not yet told his family about Winnie.

"As usual," said Helen, "he made all his plans to suit himself, then confronted us with a *fait accompli.*"

That is precisely what Lawrence did in this case. A week after Winifred had said yes and ten days before the official announcement of the engagement, he telephoned Zula.

"Mother, this is Lawrence. I'm fine, thank you, how are you? That's fine, fine, fine. Mother, I'm bringing a girl home for Sunday dinner."

"Of course, dear," Zula said. "We'll be delighted to see you."

"She's a movie actress," Lawrence added, and rang off.

A movie actress! After the Babylonian seduction of Cynthia Polk and the orgies of Massapequa, Zula and Helen feared the worst. Actresses still had a reputation for being "fast." Some of them had so little visible talent that they were commonly believed to have advanced their careers in bed. In general they were not the sort of girls who would make suitable wives.

"I wonder if she'll like her beef well done or à la Sperry," Zula mused as she helped Delia prepare a rib roast. It was a splendid piece of beef—and should have been at nineteen cents a pound; prices were getting out of line.

A la Sperry meant medium rare.

"Better serve it raw, Mother," said Elmer A. Sperry, Jr. "She's probably a man eater."

169

He still idolized Lawrence and could hardly wait to meet his latest conquest.

"What's her name?" Helen asked Zula.

"Oh, Lawrence didn't bother with a little detail like that."

"I'll just bet she smokes," Helen said. "Probably come slinking in here with a long cigarette holder."

"Now, Helen, let's not exaggerate," Father Sperry said. He had heard that certain women smoked, but he had never seen such a thing. It was hard to imagine.

"I can't understand it," Helen said, arranging the Sunday flowers on the dining room table, white and yellow chrysanthemums with tawny autumn leaves. "There's that darling Mary Bacon, Phi Beta Kappa at Smith. There's Betty Schuyler. There's Adele van Rensselaer. There's Emily Rich, so artistic. Lovely girls from lovely families. And Lawrence is bringing a movie actress to dinner, and we don't even know her name."

"The flowers are beautiful," Zula said soothingly. "Just perfect."

They were. Everything Helen touched was tinged with beauty. She had a genius for decor, for assembling lovely things in perfect harmony, for composed order and flower arrangement. The only thing she could not arrange was her brother's disorderly conduct, especially in his sentimental life.

"I bet Lawrence's girlfriend's gonna look just like Theda Bara," said Elmer Jr. hopefully.

At this point, having landed on the Prospect Park Parade Grounds and walked to Albemarle Road, Lawrence and Winifred strode into the living room in their flying togs, eyes brilliant, cheeks tingling with the cold, like two dazzling creatures from another sphere. There was a moment of silence, of silent appraisal: what is known in the French theater as a profound sensation. A far cry from Theda Bara, Lawrence's diminutive companion was as demure as Dickens's Little Nell.

"Why, she's . . . she's nice," Helen blurted out involuntarily, and immediately blushed scarlet. So did Winifred, so that she looked even more ravishing.

Helen's remark broke the ice. It started the whole family laughing.

"Who were you expecting?" Lawrence said. "Lady Macbeth?"

Then they laughed some more, in a kind of nervous relief, as though some disaster had just been averted.

"Well, I'm glad you approve," Lawrence said. "Mother, this is Winifred Allen. Winnie, this is my mother, my father, my sister Helen, and my kid brother Elmer.

"All your in-laws," Lawrence added casually in the midst of all the handshakes.

There was another profound sensation.

"Winnie and I are engaged to be married," Lawrence said gaily.

In the ensuing silence, the Sperrys looked Winifred over very carefully. Then they looked at each other, resigned to the inevitable as one is to the weather. Young Elmer was the first to react. In his eyes Lawrence could do no wrong, and it was obvious that he was doing all right, since this Winifred Allen was a knockout, even prettier in real life than on the screen.

"First time I ever kissed a movie star," he said, giving her a brotherly smack on her exquisite cheek. "Lawrence, I congratulate you."

Zula's reaction was quick and instinctive. She enfolded Winifred in a motherly embrace.

"I'm so happy," she said, "really very happy for Lawrence, for you both," and her eyes got a little moist, for she loved happy endings, and Lawrence's wild Long Island adventures were not conducive to happiness. Now he would settle down with this lovely young woman and they would live happily ever after. She could see that Winifred adored Lawrence. That was as plain as the perfect nose on her pretty face.

Father Sperry scrutinized his prospective daughter-in-law with his usual wonder at all the follies and vicissitudes of this wonderful and varied world. He saw no sign of any of the libidinous loose living that was generally associated with movie stars. She was obviously a wholesome little thing with a candid and innocent expression. The rosy flush on her cheeks came from the weather; it was definitely not rouge. She wasn't a vamp. She wasn't an adulteress. She was a really nice girl, in fact, adorable. He could see what Lawrence saw in her, so he kissed her too.

As for Helen, despite her having blurted out that Winifred was "nice," this was not enough to warrant wedding bells. Quite apart from her normal social prejudice against actresses, she was genuinely concerned about whom Lawrence should marry. There was no denying that this girl was terribly pretty. Winifred had the kind of natural feminine beauty that could awaken the unconscious jealousy of a prospective sister-in-law. Helen had always had the older sister's proprietary interest in her brothers, and especially in Lawrence, whose genius she recognized and tried to direct.

Like so many educated young women of her background, Helen had avant-garde ideas about the perfectibility of the human race. She believed that intellectuals had the responsibility of improving society and perfecting the species. She believed in positive eugenics. She had read Sir Francis Galton's *Hereditary Genius,* in which he coined the word *eugenics* from the Greek word meaning "good birth." That book convinced her that talent was an inherited characteristic that could and should be passed on through genetic selection. By 1917 eugenics was both a scientific and a social movement, concerned with improving future generations by mating persons of superior types and sterilizing those with hereditary defects. From Helen's point of view, Lawrence had obviously inherited their father's genius, and it was his responsibility to transmit this spark by selecting, or allowing her to select, a mate with complementary mental as well as physical traits.

Now, from Helen's point of view, Lawrence was undermining her whole program with a vengeance. Who, after all, was Winifred Allen? She had a pretty face. That was all they knew about her. It was true that she was independent, that she made her own living—Helen rather envied that—but in a highly suspect profession that pandered to the senses, not the mind. Eugenically speaking, Winifred Allen was not the most suitable mate for Lawrence.

So, as they all sat down to the Sperry Sunday dinner of roast beef and Yorkshire pudding, Helen had misgivings and reservations. And these were exacerbated when Delia, the maid, was presented to Winifred, Lawrence's fiancée.

Delia said to Lawrence, "Sure and I'm glad somebody gotcha at last, and somebody nice, you were always a wild gossoon, hiding yer books in the milk box and playing hooky from Erasmus Hall while you were flyin' your aeroplane out at Sheepshead Bay."

"Ah, you're Irish," Winifred said warmly. "And so was my mother—from Kilbrittain in County Cork."

Good heavens, Helen thought, she may even be a Catholic!

After dinner Zula put her arm around Winifred and invited her to her bedroom for a private talk.

"I wish you could have seen this room when Lawrence got through demolishing it to get his first aeroplane out of the window," Zula said, and she shared her reminiscences of Lawrence with his bride-to-be. The two women were instinctively drawn to one another, both affectionate, unswerving in fidelity, idealistic, but practical.

"You need a lot of courage to make a marriage work," Zula confided to Winifred, "especially when you're married to a genius.

"Lawrence has always been a fascinating boy," she added, "but he isn't easy. Very impetuous, very willful and headstrong."

"I think I can handle him," Winifred said.

"I'm sure you can," Zula said serenely. "I can assure you of one thing," she added.

"What's that?"

The older woman's eyes twinkled behind her rimless glasses. "You may get exasperated with Lawrence," she said, "but you'll never have a dull moment."

Lawrence began proving Zula's assertions the minute he got Winnie back into the plane and up in the air. Now that his family had been notified, he saw no reason why their engagement should drag on, and he was determined to shorten it.

"Nine months is much too long," he shouted to his bride-to-be, turning around to admire her, where she sat in the rear cockpit. "That's an *in*decent interval. Let's just trundle down to Governors Island, and I'll get Chaplain Smith to marry us."

"When?" Winifred yelled.

"Right now!" he yelled back.

"Lawrence, we aren't even officially engaged. And you don't have a marriage license. And I have nothing to wear. What are you doing?"

"I'm putting this plane on automatic pilot," Lawrence shouted.

With that he managed to turn around in his own cockpit, stand up on the seat, lean over, and kiss her. She closed her eyes.

"How do you like that?" he said.

"It's the nearest thing to waking up in heaven," she said.

The plane dropped sharply in an air pocket at that moment. Winifred opened her eyes very wide and held her breath.

"Lawrence," she said, "I don't really want to wake up in heaven. And I don't want to fall into the bay like your great friend Mrs. Polk!"

Winnie knew all about her. According to the mores of the day, Lawrence had already confessed his sexual peccadilloes to his virginal bride-to-be. He had brazenly boasted that he had had Cynthia Polk so well trained that she could find his collar button under the bed!

Lawrence resumed manual control of the plane. He banked, turned, circled Governors Island, and turned his head again to argue in a most passionate but rational way with his fiancée.

"Something might happen to me," he yelled, "in the game I'm in. Come on, Winnie! Nine months waiting is nine months lost."

Winifred looked at his profile, her Nordic prince. He turned all the way around, lifted up his goggles, and magnetized her with his sky-blue eyes.

"Eight months," she said. "We'll get married next August."

Lawrence circled Governors Island two more times.

"A June wedding would be nice," Winifred conceded.

"I may be running out of gas," Lawrence said, as he circled the island for the sixth time.

Winifred looked at the skyscrapers, the graceful bridges linking Brooklyn with Manhattan. The world had never looked so exciting, so sharply in focus. At one point she felt she could reach out and grab the torch of the Statue of Liberty, gazing down the harbor with eyes of green bronze. In the next instant Lawrence had soared back up and she was lost in the clouds with the most wonderful man in the world.

"Next month. Say February," Lawrence yelled.

"Your mother is right," Winnie yelled back. "You're impetuous, willful, and headstrong!"

"Say February!" Lawrence insisted. It was an imperious appeal. He was not to be resisted. She looked again at his profile, etched like a medallion against the winter sky.

"All right, February," she said. "Next month. Why not? Yes. Yes."

And he brought her down to earth.

17

"THE MARRIAGE of Winifred Allen and Lt. L. B. Sperry has set a pace for 1918 weddings that will be hard to follow."

So wrote the society editor of the *New York Evening World* in a long lead article on February 19. Subordinate news items in that same edition included the following:

4,000 KILLED AS REDS CAPTURE KIEV
Anarchists Dealing Death in Fiendish Ways

TWO GERMAN ARMIES INVADE RUSSIA
Expect Trotzky to Yield

The U.S. Marines were shown in the rotogravure section, sweeping the streets of the French village in which they were billeted, "thus repaying the hospitality of the natives."

Rudyard Kipling demanded Peace with Victory. "Civilization is at stake," he said. "If German thuggery is not ended, life on this planet will become insupportable for human beings."

Lt. Pat O'Brien, author of *Outwitting the Hun,* lectured at Carnegie Hall on "My Escape from a German Prison Camp. The Wildest Tales of Fiction, Fable and Fancy Outdone in Real Life."

German music was unpopular. Patriotic Americans preferred Tchaikovsky and Rachmaninoff, even Meyerbeer, to Wagner and Brahms. Caruso, idol of the Met, sang *The Prophet.* The *World* reported that he paid $59,000 in income tax from his nightly salary of $2,500 and his royalties from talking machine records.

The young stars of the New York Philharmonic, conducted by Josef Stransky, were Mischa Elman and Pablo Casals.

American citizens of German descent, including many employees of the Sperry Gyroscope Company, massed in Grand

Central Palace and urged the German people to depose the kaiser.

Mrs. Ellen O'Grady, a widow, became the first woman deputy police commissioner of New York.

Judge Leonard Snitkin of the New York Municipal Court was indicted for selling draft exemptions. He sent some registrants to Indianapolis, which New York wags claimed was worse than the front.

Lt. Billy Taylor played a concert piano wearing a gas mask to publicize this new defense mechanism.

Winifred Allen was starring in *For Valour* at the Rialto; John Barrymore, as Raffles, the Amateur Cracksman, was packing them into the Strand. *Tarzan of the Apes* at the Broadway Theatre "set female hearts beating with throbs of love."

Bonwit Teller advertised Georgette frocks at $22.50 and Riding Togs for the "Equistriene" (*sic*).

The New Art of Correct Corsetry promised more flexible stays to give women swinging, graceful lines.

Society girls enrolled in business college to fit themselves for government service in the war.

Mrs. Alfred G. Vanderbilt was wintering at Palm Beach with her sons, Alfred and George. The novelties of that season were surf mattresses and ladies' bathing suits that exposed the arms.

Army and Navy dances brightened the "penitential days" of Lent, and there was a "Lenten slump in marriages."

The Lenten slump spurred society writers to new efforts in describing the Sperry-Allen nuptials, which held the attention of readers for days. *The Evening World*, for example, proclaimed:

LIEUT. SPERRY FLIES
BRIDE TO ALTAR

HONEYMOON IN THE CLOUDS
SETS STYLE FOR 20TH
CENTURY WEDDINGS

PROPOSAL TO "TRUNDLE DOWN
AND GET MARRIED" CAME WHEN
2,000 FEET UP

"Here's the secret of the surprising honeymoon in the air, whereby the fashion was set today for all daring brides by a brown-eyed beauty in a sheepskin aviation jacket who changed her name from Miss Winifred Allen to Mrs. Lawrence B. Sperry in the Chapel of St. George the Centurion on Governors Island last night.

"She didn't know that this was to be her wedding day when she went up in the big Curtiss triplane with her flying suitor at Amityville field yesterday afternoon.

"Of course it wasn't a total surprise," Mrs. Sperry said. "We were engaged, but it was very sudden all the same. The date had not been set.

"We were up about 2,000 feet when Larry yelled over the roar of the engine: 'Win, how about trundling down to Governors Island and getting married right now?'

"Well, it took my breath away—what little I had left after jigging around the sky at 80 miles an hour. So all I could do was nod my head.

"'Gee up, January!' said Larry to his triplane, shooting a little more gas into the engine, 'and lope right on down to the parson's house.'

"With that we dropped down on Governors Island, said hello to Parson Smith, came over to N.Y. for the license and the trousseau and then went back to be married. Larry had arranged the whole thing, of course," the fashion-setting bride reported.

By special arrangement the Government Steamer General Hancock was waiting to take the bride and groom elect to Manhattan. Two hours later it was waiting at the Battery to take them back together with the wedding party of 20 including the bridegroom's two brothers, Edward and Elmer Jr., his sister, Miss Helen Sperry, Mr. and Mrs. William Scoville, Reginald E. Gillmor of London, Miss Wyn Hope, the bride's aunt, and Thomas Morgan of the Sperry Gyroscope Company, who played the Wagner and Mendelssohn wedding marches on a Hawaiian ukulele when the chapel organ broke down.

Governors Island hummed with excitement over its first aeroplane wedding. Lt. Sperry's fellow officers and the whole garrison cheered the bridal party when they arrived at the chapel, threw their caps in the air when Lt. Sperry, the first civilian to volunteer for the U.S. Navy in 1917, pronounced his vows, and they pelted the happy couple with flowers and rice as they left the chapel.

They also festooned the aerial wedding coach with red, white and blue ribbons and confetti.

After lunch at the Hotel Vanderbilt, Lieut. and Mrs. Sperry disappeared without telling anyone where they were going.

Since Lawrence's chief idea was to get to bed as soon as possible, they went upstairs to a suite in the hotel. Here Lawrence learned that winsome Winnie had a practical side to her romantic nature and a will as strong as his. When Lawrence took off his immaculate naval uniform, Winifred noticed a most unromantic aspect of her Nordic prince's trousseau: his long winter underwear was patched in some fifteen places.

"Lawrence," she said, "that is disgraceful."

"Never mind," he answered gaily, "I'm going to take them right off. What people don't see won't hurt them."

"But I do mind," the bride said, holding her ground. "And I can see those ugly patches. Just put your uniform back on."

Picking up the phone, she asked for the men's shop in the lobby.

"Lieutenant Sperry will be right down to buy some BVDs," she said. "Better get a dozen pairs," she said sweetly to Lawrence. "Patched underwear may have been good enough for Mrs. Polk, but it's not good enough for Mrs. Sperry."

Lawrence got back into uniform and went meekly downstairs. When he came back with a dozen pairs of snow-white long johns, his bride was Winsome Winnie once again, irresistible in a nightgown and negligée of white chiffon.

"I don't have any patches," she said demurely, "and neither should you."

This private glimpse of the taming of Lawrence Sperry came from the family archives; it was not reported in the newspapers, which carried more conventional details of the wedding in editions from coast to coast. The marriage was even reported in *Paris Soir*, whose New York correspondent, remembering Lawrence's popularity in France, interviewed the bride.

"The more I know my husband, the more mysterious and fascinating he becomes," Winifred told him. This came out in French as *"Au fur et à mesure que je connais mon mari, plus il devient opaque et fascinant."*

An opaque husband: French readers found that worthy of Colette.

If the wedding made a splash, the subsequent "Honeymoon in the Air" released a veritable flood of printer's ink. It was all a bit ridiculous, since Lawrence was on active and dangerous duty with the U.S. Navy at Massapequa and Copiague and could get only a few hours' leave for his marriage. The *New York Times* reported this sober fact correctly, but the rest of the press was hungry for romance. The fifteen-minute flight from Governors Island to Massapequa *was* the first aerial honeymoon, and they were determined to make the most of it. With the beautiful and winsome bride, "the orphan," they had something to work with. In the midst of the war, she was the incarnation of an abiding American dream of romance.

Lawrence did his bit.

"Aren't you afraid you might get lost in the clouds?" a reporter from the *New York Journal* asked him as he and Winifred were about to take off in their plane.

"Lost in the clouds?" Lawrence replied, looking dreamily at his bride. "I already am."

Off they flew to Massapequa, where Lawrence taxied right up to the front door of what the *World* called "the handsome home provided in advance by the indulgent bridegroom."

The indulgent bridegroom carried the winsome bride across the threshold and went at once to the hangar at Copiague where he "indulged" himself in the nerve-wracking project of hurtling out to sea strapped to his aerial torpedo.

In the meantime reporters flocked to the handsome home to interview its new mistress, who was teaching herself how to make good coffee ("Boil it with eggshells," her cookbook advised) and how to grill toast in a gas oven. These mundane details did not interest the reporters. They wanted to know about the honeymoon. Winifred complied from the depths of her romantic nature with the total sincerity that had given her such enormous appeal on the screen.

"It is hard to express the sensation of sailing around and through and over the clouds," she said, "of being able to reach out and hold part of a cloud, a piece of eternity in your hand.

"When I was a little girl, before I ever knew anything about aeroplanes, I used to spend hours dreaming. I would sit at my window, look deep into the skies, and have the most beautiful visions. Everything that was good and lovely would float before my gaze.

"It would always make me think of the greater and nobler things of life, and I would wonder and wish for a magic carpet to be up there in that bewitching atmosphere. That's why it was so thrilling when we slowly rose from the ground at Governors Island yesterday morning. As we went up, up, up until the houses were lost from view and even the great skyscrapers of New York looked like mere nothings, my mind unconsciously went back to the days and nights of my star gazing.

"I never thought of danger, not once as long as Lawrence was there, but I think of many other things, essential things that all people should think about: love, happiness, and what a wonderful and mysterious world we live in.

"The higher we went the more thrilled I became, and when we really were up among the clouds, when I could reach out and touch them with my hands, it was the greatest sensation I ever expect to experience. My happiness seemed absolutely complete. Utter peace. I was so far removed from the earth, from its troubles and tribulations, that I did not want to come down. I would have been content to remain there indefinitely. And if something had gone wrong with the big aeroplane and we had been dashed to earth thousands of feet below, I know I would have died happy.

"Ah, there is a light above, a lesson, a fascination in those unfathomable elements, a key to happiness. It came to me. It will stay."

It is evident that Winifred Allen Sperry did not have the blood of the Celts for nothing; she was a poet.

"But Mrs. Sperry," the *World*'s reporter said, "do you give the mysteries of the clouds all the credit alone? Do you think the experience, the sensation, would have been the same if the trip had not been a honeymoon?"

"But it is honeymooning in the skies that I have been talking about," she replied. "When a young girl star-gazes and dreams, she's not dreaming about a new dress, a pair of shoes, or a diamond. She's dreaming about the one man, the big, strong prince, the most wonderful and the only man in all the world to her. Then, as in my case, when this man comes along and takes her to her dreamland, can there be anything more glorious, more beautiful? Love on earth brings us all a little nearer to heaven, and it is only natural to believe that the further lovers get from earth the nearer they are to Paradise."

As if this romantic adoration were not enough, Winifred also put in a practical pitch for her husband's business.

"Quite seriously," she concluded, "anyone will, I'm quite sure, experience the glorious sensation I've tried to explain if they'll only take some of the money they throw away on useless trips to uninteresting places and spend it on a flying machine."

And what of the happy bridegroom, who must have been pleased with this plug?

"It would not be fair," the *World* concluded, "to end this story without a word about the man who has made his little bird-girl so happy.

"At first glance one would call Lieut. Sperry a handsome young man, full of nerve and red blood. But take a closer look and you will see something about this 25-year-old youngster who has braved death thousands of times that makes you think of the cave-man days. You don't know why. In general appearance he is very much like other young men of his age, but there is a firmness about the mouth and chin, a glint to the smiling eyes, that tell a story all its own.

"Look at his record for the last two days. Is it so far removed from that of the cave-man who was wont to steal forth with his club and take the woman of his choice? Different. Yes, of course. But not so much in method as in style. Centuries ago the world was new as compared to today, and the cave-man worked in a crude, coarse way. He didn't have an aeroplane to sweep down upon his prey as did the dashing and daring young Lieutenant. He had to do the best he could.

"And Mrs. Sperry admitted last night she had only known Lieut. Sperry a few weeks. She did not resent a suggestion that, when all had been said and told, his methods were nothing more and nothing less than those of the men of the early ages, except that he was a twentieth century model.

" 'I always, somehow, admired those cave-men,' she declared. 'All women do.' "

This is one of the first times that this cave-man concept, with its daring overtone of male sexuality, appeared in print. Lawrence's virility, decisiveness, recklessness made him the unwitting prototype of the ideal "cave man" of the 1920s.

The rest of the New York papers contented themselves with the aerial aspects of the Sperry wedding.

"AIRPLANE BRIDE" RELATES
THRILLING STORY OF HONEYMOON
HIGH ABOVE THE CLOUDS
            (*New York Evening Telegram*)

HONEYMOON TRIP IN SKY
AFTER AIRPLANE WEDDING
            (*New York Evening Sun*)

SPERRYS FLY AWAY
ON HONEYMOON TRIP
VIA SKYLARK ROUTE
Lieutenant Whisks Bride
Through Clouds to and from Altar
            (*Brooklyn Daily Eagle*)

HIGH SOCIETY WEDDING
Marriage Coach Was an Aeroplane
            (*New York American*)

Even the *Philadelphia Public Ledger* picked it up, eliminating one wing of the Curtiss triplane in the process:

HONEYMOON TRIP IN A BIPLANE
TAKES PAIR 100 MILES AN HOUR

An Aerial Romance
Love Above the Clouds
"Afraid With Larry?"
Laughs Bride: "Don't
Be Foolish"

Responding to all this free publicity, Triangle Films revived *The Man Hater* with an advertising campaign featuring "the Bird Girl, Winifred Allen." *For Valour* was booked from coast to coast, and full-page ads showed Winifred draped in the Union Jack and framed by the Victoria Cross, from which dangled the delta-framed *T* of Triangle Films.

"The story of a modern Joan of Arc," the advertisement said, "a martyr to Humanity's holy cause, starring Winifred Allen, the flying bride."

The inevitable offers came from Hollywood: surely Miss Allen would resume her professional career.

"But I'm not Miss Allen," Winifred said demurely. "I'm Mrs. Sperry."

So much the better, said her agent, to "the bird girl, the airplane bride."

Winifred declined without a moment's hesitation or regret.

"Life with Lawrence is more exciting than anything in the movies," she said simply, "and more amusing."

At the first breakfast of their married life, she burned the toast, undercooked the eggs, and served weak, watery coffee.

"That's all right, dear," said Lawrence. "Never learn to cook and you'll never have to."

On the first weekend of their married life, he gave Winnie a golf lesson and managed to hit her in the eye with a driver.

Clutching at her eye, she shrieked, "Lawrence, if you've disfigured me I'll divorce you."

"Better think twice about that," he replied, kissing the offended eye. "If you're disfigured you won't find another husband, at least not another cave man like me!"

Brandishing his golf club, he picked his wife up and carried her into the house.

"That's the end of today's lesson," he said.

Burned toast and a black eye: the honeymoon was over. Married life began. With Lawrence it had more alarums and excursions than the movies could dream up.

Within a week of their marriage, Lawrence was making sketches of a new invention, the first pack parachute that could actually be worn by an aviator or carried for immediate access on the seat. It was to be one of his most important contributions to aviation history. The parachutes then in use were too big and heavy for small planes, and the U.S. Air Service actually forbade their use to American fighter pilots, a fact that Eddie Ricken-backer, one of Lawrence's champions, bitterly deplored.

"It was absolutely criminal for our higher command to withhold parachutes from us," he said. "Men who could have lived on to serve America in war and peace perished in agony for lack of parachutes. What reward did Raoul Lufbery gain for his role in helping to develop American air mastery? Death on a picket fence when a parachute would have saved his life."

Lawrence was determined to make flying safe by inventing a small, light, workable chute of silk instead of the cumbersome canvas tents then in existence.

As always, he used the pragmatic approach. He wasn't going to patent anything that he himself had never tested. His practical research included jumping from the second story of the house, then from the roof, and rolling himself into a ball like a Chinese acrobat upon impact with the ground. This activity was nothing new to him; he had done it as a child in competition with his brother, Elmer, but never above the second story.

Naturally, it worried his bride.

"Larry," she protested, "why don't you wait until you *have* the parachute? I don't see the point of jumping without it. It's bad enough to be billed as the bird girl; I don't want to be the bird *widow*."

"I have to test the velocity of a falling body," Lawrence explained. "And I want to be in shape in case the parachute fails to open."

"What am I supposed to do?" Winifred sobbed. "Stand behind you like the Roman emperor's slave and say, 'Remember, Caesar, all men are mortal'?"

When Lawrence saw she was upset, he desisted for a while and assured her that he always drew the line between fearlessness and recklessness.

His daily work, flying out over the sea in the highly secret tests of the aerial torpedo, was so dangerous and nerve-wracking that even he slept badly.

"Winnie used to read Lawrence to sleep," her sister May recalls. "She had a beautiful, deep voice, and she knew how to project it. She loved poetry, and she read it to perfection, aware of every nuance.

"The evening was a success when Lawrence drifted off. That," May added, "is love. Greater love hath no actress than this: that she will give up her career to soothe one man to sleep."

18

THERE CAN BE NO QUESTION that Lawrence's company was more flexible, more manageable, and better prepared than the behemoths of the Sperry Gyroscope Company to test the aerial torpedo and to cope with military demands for it.

Ever since Lawrence had begun his experiments in 1917, he found himself in competition with a typical "company man" in testing and proving the first examples of the guided missile. This was Charles Kettering, whose somewhat overbearing personality was reflected in his nickname, "Boss." Boss Kettering, sixteen years older than Lawrence, had invented the self-starter for automobiles and was now vice-president of General Motors Corporation in charge of research.

Mr. Harold Talbot, who became secretary of the U.S. Air Force in the Eisenhower administration, said that Lawrence's attitude during the first aerial torpedo experiments at Carlstrom Field, Florida, was "independent and imaginative," whereas Mr. Kettering said that "he didn't care about the 'Bug job,' especially since his General Motors position really required that none of the high engineering talent of the firm should be spent on anything but work having to do with the interests of the General Motors Corporation."

That was laying it on the line, even though the Army had provided General Motors and Kettering with a quarter of a million dollars for the experiments. Lawrence found cooperation with Boss Kettering impossible. First Lieutenant Jimmy Doolittle, who would achieve fame in 1942 leading a daring bombing attack on Tokyo, and who was a great admirer of Lawrence, wrote the following description of the Kettering fiasco for the Air Service Test Board:

Mr. Kettering felt that the device had promise but that as being prosecuted [by the Lawrence Sperry Aircraft Company] could never be highly successful. He was told to go ahead and design one along his own ideas and immediately started the layout of a torpedo of simple design which could be quickly assembled in the field, all parts of which were readily obtainable, adaptable to quantity production and cheap so that it could compete with the large high explosive shell. Twenty torpedoes were delivered at a cost of 12,000 dollars each.

On September 4 twelve torpedoes were shipped to Carlstrom Field, Arcadia, Florida. On September 26 the first flight was attempted. The tail rose until the torpedo slid off the car and nosed into the ground. On October 3 the tail veered to the right while still on the car and the torpedo left the car and crashed. On October 10 the torpedo took off accidentally during a test run on track, zoomed and crashed. On October 11, the torpedo took off in a zoom, climbed to 200 feet, fell off and crashed. Elevators set for too steep a climb. On October 13 torpedo flew 1¾ miles and crashed due to motor failure. On October 15 torpedo flew 1¾ miles and wings came off due to lag in altitude control causing dives and zooms. On this date the Army and Navy inspection board arrived. On October 21 torpedo took off but settled, crashing. Second flight, tail rose and torpedo crashed in front of car. On October 22 torpedo took off and crashed. On October 24 torpedo flew two miles and wings came off. The cause was probably due to improper altitude control. Second flight, torpedo crashed immediately after takeoff due to engine not turning up properly. Third flight with new elevator control. Took off well but dove and zoomed, due to aneroid cutting in and out, until it went over on its back and crashed. On October 28 a new type of altitude control was put on and the last torpedo, constructed from salvaged parts of previous wrecks, flew about 16 miles. It was approximately on its course, the proper altitude was adhered to and the crash was caused by motor trouble.

Among Jimmy Doolittle's conclusions: "The motor is not sufficiently reliable to permit of the torpedo flying over friendly troops."

That was putting it mildly.

Meanwhile back at Farmingdale, Long Island, Lawrence was

having his own crashes, but he learned something from them because he actually rode his aerial torpedoes to see what made them tick. In the winter of 1917–18 Lawrence modified a Curtiss "flying bomb," equipped it with skids, and made flights from the frozen surface of Great South Bay.

He had three crashes on the ice. One of them, according to Commander Benjamin B. McCormick, inspector of naval ordinance, who was assigned to observe Lawrence's top-secret tests at Copiague, involved plane and pilot in an unexpected triple somersault. "The Curtiss flying bomb slammed down on the ice, a complete wreck," he reported. "Only the engine, the radiator, and Lawrence Sperry came out undamaged."

The fourth accident involved minor damages to Lawrence which he described in what was meant to be a reassuring letter to Father Sperry: "I got one machine all tuned up by flying from the ice," he wrote, "with all three controls working. This was accomplished after correcting about 20 different things of the automatic pilot. . . . My fourth smash in one of these little torps resulted in my breaking my nose—just two little bones broken. While the nose has been flattened a little it can be made to grow straight and will not be noticed, although the passages inside are too crowded for breathing and will have to be operated on."

By March 1 he was breathing normally and testing a new launching device he had contrived for the aerial torpedo. It was an inclined track with rails and an ingenious turntable so that he could take off in the torpedo in accordance with wind direction. The torpedo itself had been improved and streamlined. It had no cockpit. It was fully automated, but Lawrence, for financial reasons, didn't dare risk losing it. So, during the experimental stages, he monitored it himself by strapping himself to the fuselage. A more complete identification between man and machine would be hard to imagine. Lawrence would start the propeller, then strap himself to the belly of the plane. He could feel it straining at the leash. When he felt there was enough lift under the wings, he pulled back on the elevator until the nose of the torpedo lifted. Then he let her rip. The aerial torpedo rose, carrying Lawrence between its fuselage and its four-wheel carriage. In the final tests he would dispose of these encumbering wheels, but he needed them now to land at Mitchel Field. Unlike Kettering and his giant corporation, Lawrence had to keep costs down. The wanton loss of planes described by Jimmy Doolittle in his report on the Kettering fiasco would have bankrupted the Lawrence Sperry Aircraft Company.

On March 6, 1918, Lawrence pronounced his aerial torpedo ready. It had to fly alone in this crucial test, and it did, under complete automatic control to its target one thousand yards from the launching track. It registered a perfect bull's eye. Rear Admiral Delmar S. Fahrney, who witnessed this test, said it was "the first entirely successful flight of an automatic missile in this country if not in the world."

But on March 18, just three weeks after breaking his nose, Lawrence had a more serious accident. His aerial torpedo landed on the ice of Great South Bay, skidded out of control, did a double somersault, and was smashed to bits. The only identifiable objects on the ice were the engine, the radiator, and Lawrence with a broken pelvis.

Just a month after their wedding, Winifred found herself in constant attendance upon her husband in the Brooklyn Naval Hospital. Her readings, which she had begun at home to calm Lawrence's nerves, now became a nightly performance.

When Lawrence came out of the anesthetic in his hospital room, he said, "That wouldn't have happened if we'd had skids on that torp instead of wheels. Give me a pencil."

"Lawrence," said Winifred sternly, "you're to lie perfectly still. Doctor's orders."

It was like telling the ocean, a volcano, or some other force of nature to lie still.

"I have something to tell you," she said toward the end of his convalescence. "I too have been to see the doctor. He thinks I am in an interesting condition."

"You're always interesting," Lawrence said. "You mean . . . ?"

"You're going to be a father," Winifred said.

"Who? Me?"

He looked very pleased.

"Well, I think it's you," Winifred said wickedly, "but I'll be the only person who will ever really know."

Lawrence laughed, then clutched at his restored pelvis.

"Don't make me laugh, Winnie. It hurts."

"Poor darling. Shall I read to you?"

"Yes."

"Something serious?"

"Yes, serious. It's ridiculous, but it really does hurt to laugh."

Winifred adjusted the lamp so that the light fell on her book, leaving Lawrence in the penumbra, flat on his back as though he were lying in state. Her Nordic prince. There was a strange, silent light in the hospital room, like the northern twilight in which dusk breaks imperceptibly into dawn.

Winifred's voice, deep and vibrant with ancestral memory, broke the silence:

> I know that I shall meet my fate
> Somewhere among the clouds above;
> Those that I fight I do not hate
> Those that I guard I do not love.

"But I do love you," Lawrence said.

It moved her deeply, this simple statement, old as chivalry, old as the effigies of those recumbent knights who appear to be awaiting the Resurrection.

"Don't stop," Lawrence said.

> Nor law, nor duty bade me fight,
> Nor public men, nor cheering crowds,
> A lonely impulse of delight
> Drove to this tumult in the clouds . . .

"It's wonderful," Lawrence said. "Is that all?"

> I balanced all, brought all to mind,
> The years to come seemed waste of breath,
> A waste of breath the years behind
> In balance with this life, this death.

The words hung in the still air, as though graven on stone. Winifred clung silently to her husband's hand.

"Lawrence," she said, "do you remember Glenn Curtiss promised to give up flying when his son was born?"

"He didn't keep his promise," Lawrence said.

"Then I won't ask you."

"No," Lawrence said. "I do love you, but don't ask me to give it up."

19

WHEN LAWRENCE WAS RELEASED from the hospital late in May of 1918, it was assumed that he would stay on the ground and confine his activities to the drawing board, patent applications, and the problems of running the Lawrence Sperry Aircraft Corporation, which now occupied a fifteen-acre tract at Farmingdale. The Navy had officially grounded Lawrence by placing him, in spite of his protests, on inactive duty, so it began to look as though his flying days were over.

Father Sperry, Zula, and Winnie silently rejoiced in what appeared to be a new conservatism on Lawrence's part. This impression was strengthened when Elmer Jr., for whom his dashing older brother remained a model of manly behavior, volunteered to replace him in the dangerous, top-secret experiments with the aerial torpedo. Lawrence wrote a letter to his father on this subject which Father Sperry might once have written about Lawrence:

"If Elmer wants to fly the aerial torpedo, send him to the Curtiss School for a few months. Don't let him try it just after he has a few rides with some Curtiss pilot. I had four years of apprenticeship before I was able to properly fly a powered machine alone. I first started to fly in 1910. It was not until 1914 that I became good and not until several months later that I became really very good. Dash and bang is fine, but it's not enough. The army killed 17 men by letting inexperienced men fly. They are killing the inexperienced men off very rapidly. 3 smashes last Sunday."

Lawrence's apparently growing conservatism was reflected in another way. Anticipating children, he and Winnie bought a larger house at Garden City with a nursery suite on the top floor.

"If we have a girl, we'll have to have a boy," Lawrence said.

"And if we have a boy, we'll have to have a girl. Winnie, this sort of thing could go on forever."

"I suppose it could," Winnie agreed. She had disappointed her avant-garde friends from the Art Students League and Frohman Drama School by turning a deaf ear to planned parenthood and other ultramodern causes that they championed. Winifred was willing to let nature take its course, and she may have thought of each successive child as one more mooring to hold Lawrence down, as the Lilliputians bound Gulliver to the earth.

She noted with approval that Lawrence was no longer jumping out of windows. He now seemed to be content to conduct his parachute experiments with sandbags the weight of his own body.

His mania for speed was also confined to the ground for the nonce. Zula had said, "Anything that can shorten time and distance is the most important scientific problem for Lawrence to deal with." He now dealt with it on the ground by installing a sixty-horsepower airplane engine in his Marmon sports car. In the summer of 1918 it may very well have been the most powerful automobile in the world. It could outdistance anything on Long Island, and Lawrence delighted in eluding motorcycle policemen by dramatic bursts of speed that left them sputtering.

"That Marmon of Lawrence's was like Lawrence himself," Helen observed. "It did nothing moderately or gradually. It leaped from a standing position to sixty miles an hour.

"Lawrence didn't dare come into town in a car, especially in that Marmon with its leopard-skin seats; we called it 'The Yellow Peril.' The cops were on the watch for him," she said, "and when they could not nail him, they picked on me. I was the victim of my brother's recklessness."

Helen claimed that she was crossing the Manhattan Bridge at twenty-six miles an hour—only one mile above the New York City speed limit—when a motorcycle cop began tailing her air-cooled Franklin, known in the family as "the Brown Baby."

She slowed down prudently, but he overtook her on the Bushwick Extension of the bridge.

"Pull over! See yer license!"

"But officer," she replied, "I was not exceeding . . ."

"You were doing forty," the officer said.

"But I'm a volunteer in the Women's Motor Corps," Helen said. "And I'm late for an appointment to see our wounded sailors at the Brooklyn Naval Hospital."

"Make any difference," the cop said. "See yer driver's license."

When he saw the name of Sperry, he immediately wrote out a ticket charging her with being "the most reckless woman driver in the city."

"It was because of Lawrence," Helen insisted, fifty-eight years after the arrest. "I was fined a hundred dollars and put in the lockup because I was Lawrence's sister.

"Mother and Father were furious," Helen said. "My parents said I should never have been allowed to have a car. Mother had a chauffeur for her Locomobile. Father disapproved of women driving. He regarded it as Dr. Johnson regarded lady preachers, unseemly and incongruous. I suppose the women's libbers today would call my father a male chauvinist pig, but we didn't think of such a thing in those days. Mother and I were sort of on the sidelines; half the time we had to guess what the men in the Sperry family were talking about."

Helen was arrested a second time, a few weeks after her initial brush with the law. This time she made the *New York Times:*

FINES MOTOR CORPS DRIVER

Miss Helen Sperry Pays $50 in
Long Island City for Second Offense

Miss Helen Sperry, 29 years old, of 1505 Albemarle Road, Brooklyn, an active worker in the Women's Motor Corps, was fined $50 by Magistrate Doyle in the Long Island City Court yesterday after she had been found guilty of driving on the Queensboro Bridge at the rate of twenty-eight miles an hour. Earlier this summer she was fined $100 by Magistrate Nash, Brooklyn, on a charge of driving at a rate of forty miles an hour on the Manhattan Bridge.

When on the stand she denied that she was exceeding the speed limit, although she admitted that she had not been watching the speedometer and did not know how fast she was driving at the time.

Miss Sperry is the daughter of Elmer A. Sperry of the Sperry

Gyroscope Company and the sister of Aviator Lawrence B. Sperry, who holds several records for speed on land and in the air.

"That proves it," Helen said. "I was Lawrence's fall guy. He was the scapegrace and I was the scape*goat*. Lawrence could go as fast as he liked. My father just shrugged that off and said, 'Boys will be boys.' "

Father Sperry did take Lawrence to task, however, after an especially egregious example of traffic violations in Toronto, where Lawrence had gone to sell planes to the Canadian government:

                                                            Aug. 16, 1918

Dear Lawrence,

In your letter about Elmer's flying the aerial torpedo, you made a reference to "dash and bang." Now dash and bang usually sounds good to an American car and is splendid if not overdone. But let me say that you have overdone it in Canada, which is, after all, a foreign country. In Toronto you left in your wake a horrible nightmare of 19 traffic fines. These notices of delinquency have ended up on my desk. They are not the responsibility of the Sperry Gyroscope Company, and I enclose them herewith for your immediate attention.

The matter of parachutes is officially before the Naval Consulting Board [of which Father Sperry was a member] at the coming session to be held in Washington August 24. You better give me full details of any parachute that you would like to have brought to the attention of this meeting, as we are going to recommend strongly that parachutes be used. There are two or three forms of parachutes that are going to be presented at this meeting. Any device that adds 50% or even 25% toward the chances of saving life will be considered.

The parachutes considered will be demonstrated at the Dayton Air Show, McCook Field, next month. Since you are on inactive status, there is no question of your demonstrating your own chute. If it is considered, the Navy will choose a qualified aviator on active duty for this project. Make sure you send me all drawings and details of your parachute before I leave for Washington on the 22nd.

Your sister has now been fined twice for speeding. Please pay the enclosed fines promptly and set Helen a better example by de-emphasizing the dash and bang.

With love to Winnie,

E. A. Sperry

For Lawrence, one phrase in this letter stood out with the boldness of a challenge: "there is no question of your demonstrating your own chute."

He knew he had invented a foolproof seat-pack and back-pack parachute, one that would save thousands of lives. He sent a full description and twelve drawings of these devices to his father, details that would be incorporated in one of Lawrence's most important patents. Figure 1 showed two aviators in a monoplane. Figure 2 was a view of one of them leaping from the plane with the parachute opening free of the dreaded entanglement with the plane that had plagued airmen up to this point. Even in these working sketches, the aviators have expressions of fierce determination on their faces.

As soon as Lawrence had dispatched text and drawings to his father, he took the sample parachutes he had made and climbed, without the sandbags, to the roof of the Garden City house.

"Lawrence, what are you doing?" Winifred asked.

"Preparing to demonstrate my parachute at Dayton."

"Lawrence, you can't," she said. "You're on inactive duty."

"Says who?"

"The United States Navy," she said firmly. For once she was going to stand up to him. "Please come down and talk it over," she pleaded.

He let the parachute fill with air and pull him from the roof. He landed on the lawn in a tangle of cords and silk.

"You see," he said triumphantly, "it works perfectly."

"But please don't do it from a plane," Winifred pleaded.

Now there were tears in those winsome brown eyes that had melted the hearts of a million moviegoers; but Lawrence's blue eyes sought the sky.

"Jumping has nothing to do with flying," Winifred said, as though pressing an advantage. "Flying is safe."

"Until the day you have to jump," Lawrence said. "Do you

know how many aviators have lost their lives because they didn't
have chutes?"

"I don't want to think of it," Winifred shuddered. "I just don't
want you to jump.

"Your father is right," she went on. "Since you're on inactive
duty, there's no *question* of your demonstrating your own chute."

"My father?" Lawrence said, looking down at his diminutive
wife. "Are you taking his part against me? There's no such thing
as *in*active duty," he added. "This is something I *have* to do
myself."

There was a long pause. Lawrence held his wife in his arms, as
one might reassure a frightened child.

Then Winifred said, "Yes. You have to do it. I understand."

It was the reference to Father Sperry that did it. Winifred had
enormous respect for the old man. There was a bond of affection
between them. But Winifred herself had a strong and independent spirit, and she had sensed from the beginning that Father
Sperry's dominating presence could overwhelm a whole family
and that Lawrence would have to free himself of his father's control to realize his own potential.

As Grover Loening put it, "Winifred Sperry's role was harder
than Zula's, for Winnie had *two* geniuses to cope with: her husband and her father-in-law."

She coped. She took her husband's part, cleaving only to him,
even when it went against her own best interests. At such moments she resigned herself to living with danger, to a sense of fa-
tality. Dante Gabriel Rossetti had expressed it in one of her favorite poems:

> That day by water or fire or air
> My feet shall fall in the destined snare . . .

In the meantime she would submit to unavoidable necessity. She
was a stoic.

For Winifred, who had seen her mother die of cancer and who
had made her own way in the world, this stoicism was part of an
understated culture and a living philosophy. The Frohman Drama
School had enriched her romantic Celtic nature with the solid val-

ues of classical theater and thought. She was fascinated not only by Greek drama (she would have liked to play Antigone) but by the Stoic philosophers. They confirmed her instinctive faith in such old-fashioned ideals of human behavior as virtue, dignity, and self-sufficiency. Her favorite Stoic author was Seneca. Taking his philosophy literally, she was able to endure the darts of destiny, to put aside passion in moments of crisis, and to inculcate these virtues, by example, in her children.

Helen Sperry was astounded and gratified when her brother's "pretty little wife" turned out to have a brain. When Winifred referred, for example, to such matters as Seneca's influence on Shakespeare, Helen was both delighted and amazed. One reference of Winifred's to the consolations of Seneca's *Moral Letters* to Lucilius actually sent Helen to the Brooklyn Public Library. Seneca had not been included in the curriculum of the Packer Collegiate Institute, although the school was noted for its "refined and elevating influence."

"But I could have lent you that book," Winifred said; "it's one of my favorites."

Eventually Helen, who had tried to tame and civilize her wild brother, came to the grudging admission that Winnie had succeeded, at least partially, where she had failed.

On one occasion, when Lawrence scared the whole family by swimming too far out beyond the booming billows of Fire Island, Helen actually took her sister-in-law to task for not being "stronger" with Lawrence.

"You should put your foot down," Helen said. "You're as self-effacing as Andromache. Lawrence will make an absolute doormat out of you."

"No he won't," Winifred replied.

Then, drawing on a frame of reference that fascinated her bluestocking sister-in-law, Winifred added, "Remember the Andromache of Euripides: 'I know how to overrule Hector as well as obey him.' "

So she did, especially in domestic matters. The wedding-night underwear story was a case in point. And though she tended to model herself on her mother-in-law, adopting Zula's habit of reading aloud to her husband, for example, Winifred was not as self-effacing as Zula. Early in their married life Winifred noticed an atavistic trait in Lawrence that she determined to change. Father Sperry was notorious in the family for giving Zula "practical" presents, like a hot water heater or a radio, that the whole family could enjoy. This point of view did not suit Winnie's romantic Irish temperament at all, and when Lawrence presented her with a gift-wrapped Eureka vacuum cleaner one day, Winnie said, "Better exchange it for a Hoover, and never mind the fancy paper. A household appliance is not a present. A present is personal." Lawrence got the message, and expressed his adoration less mechanically with her favorite French perfume.

On another occasion, when Winifred said she would need a new evening dress for the Cherry Valley Country Club Spring Ball, Lawrence demurred on the ground that she already had a couple of dresses. As they were dressing for the dance, Winifred, who had learned more than Stoic philosophy at the Frohman Drama School, contrived to make herself look so dowdy and pathetic in an old dress that Lawrence was taken aback.

"Haven't you got something else to wear?" he asked.

"No," she said, looking as forlorn as both the *Orphans of the Storm*.

"It's all right," she sniffled. "People will just think that business isn't very good at the Sperry Aircraft Factory. I'll make do with this."

"Winnie!"

Lawrence was getting the point.

"As a matter of fact," Winifred said, brightening a bit, "I do have something else."

She went into her dressing room and emerged with a big box from Bonwit Teller.

"I thought you might like this," she said.

She opened the box, peeled off last year's old gray dress, and enveloped herself in a luminous cloud of crimson organza.

"Do you want me to send it back?" she said demurely.

"Mrs. Lawrence B. Sperry," the papers reported, "was the belle of the Cherry Valley Ball in a red evening gown designed by Worth."

"They were the most beautiful couple in New York," Grover

Loening recalled. "Perfect for each other. Winnie was one woman in a million; she knew how to handle Lawrence."

That she did, but she couldn't tame him out of the skies. And so she went to Dayton as her husband's champion and confidante in the fall of 1918 and went through the harrowing emotions of that famous parachute jump with that stoical outward calm that Archie Roosevelt preferred to call "the courage of a lion."

LIEUTENANT LAWRENCE B. SPERRY, U. S. NAVAL AVIATOR, AND HIS "AIR-
PLANE BRIDE," FORMERLY MISS WINIFRED ALLEN.
Who Were Married at Governors Island on Last Monday After Having Flown
to the Island From Massapequa, L. I., and Who, the Next Day, Spent a
Part of Their Honeymoon in the Clouds on Their Homeward Flight.

Opposite: Lieutenant and Mrs. Lawrence B. Sperry donned more conventional clothes for their "official" wedding portrait. Not shown is the patched underwear that Winifred made Lawrence change on their wedding night.

Above: "LIEUTENANT LAWRENCE B. SPERRY, U.S. NAVAL AVIATOR, AND HIS 'AIRPLANE BRIDE,' FORMERLY MISS WINIFRED ALLEN.
"Who Were Married at Governors Island on Last Monday After Having Flown to the Island From Massapequa, L. I., and Who, the Next Day, Spent a Part of Their Honeymoon in the Clouds on Their Homeward Flight." *Courtesy of The New York Times.*

Below: Winnie with Douglas Fairbanks, 1916.

Right: Billy Mitchell inscribed this photo for fellow maverick Lawrence Sperry, who shared Mitchell's advocacy of air power and his contempt for bureaucratic obstructionists.

Below: In 1922 Lawrence said, "I own both a car and an airplane. The initial cost of each is about the same, $5000, but the airplane, mile for mile, is pleasanter, easier, and cheaper to operate."

Lawrence fueling his own Messenger plane in July 1922. *Courtesy of International Newsreel.*

Lawrence gets a ticket from a Garden City cop for landing on a public highway.

Messenger plane equipped with the first detachable landing gear and skids. The wheels were dropped off after takeoff to lighten the plane and increase speed, and Lawrence designed skids for short landings. *Courtesy of Wide World Photos.*

Sperry M-1 Messenger on skis, inspired by General Mitchell to facilitate its use in winter.

Flying instruments invented or perfected by Lawrence.

A—Gyroscopic Unit
E—Air Compass
C—Hand Control Lever
D—Drift Indicator
E—Search Light
F—Anemometer
G—Servo Motor
H—Hand Cut Out Switch

Above: Lawrence flying in front of the Capitol, Washington, D.C., in March 1922. *Courtesy of National Photo Co.*

Below: Lawrence landing on the steps of the Capitol in his Messenger plane. *Courtesy of National Photo Co.*

Top: Sperry-Verville Racer, 1922, the first low-wing monoplane.

Above: Campaigning for the Liberal party in the English election of 1923.

Opposite: Lawrence with four-year-old Lawrence B. Sperry, Jr., in 1923.

20

TWO MONTHS after Lawrence's sensational parachute jump at Dayton, he was celebrating the Armistice with a series of exultant loop-the-loops. But the Allied victory plunged American aviation into the doldrums. Military minds resumed their customary peacetime state of arteriosclerosis. The U.S. Navy took umbrage when Brig. Gen. Billy Mitchell said that a single bomb could sink a battleship, and the Army ordered Mitchell not to rock the boat.

America went cheerfully back to the joys of a burgeoning consumerism, most of which were touted on huge billboards as one drove, perhaps in a $1,400, seven-passenger Chandler touring car "guaranteed to go faster than 99 out of 100 car owners would ever want or even dare to drive."

In the first summer after the war, Mum, "as easy to use as to say," prevented "hot weather embarrassment for only 25 cents." BVD underwear provided "cool comfort" and made "going away enjoyable and staying home endurable." Puffed Wheat, shot from guns, was twelve cents a box, and Si-Wa-Clo, a euphemism for Silent Water Closet, suppressed "a noise you do not want heard and do not want to hear."

As for the airplane, no less an authority than John Galsworthy consigned it to the dustbin of history.

"A thoroughly unpleasant machine with no possible civilian use," he said in a letter to the *London Times*. "It is time to ban all aircraft for any purpose whatsoever."

The profits of the Lawrence Sperry Aircraft Company for 1919 seemed to bear him out. They amounted to $1,930.

Lawrence Sperry decided that something must be done. His first step disquieted the Sperry family, still reeling from the shock of the Dayton parachute jump. Lawrence had new office stationery printed. At the top, against the engraved background of a steeply banking biplane, was a variant of his company's corporate name, printed in boldface like a newspaper headline:

SPERRY FLYING CORPORATION
LAWRENCE SPERRY, PRESIDENT

Running down the left-hand margin was an announcement certain to revive all the old anxiety about barnstorming:

SPERRY'S
AERIAL
CIRCUS
AND PARACHUTE
EXHIBITIONS
A Spectacular
   Aeroplane
Divertisement [sic]
For Special
Advertising
Campaigns
SPERRY'S
AERIAL
SIGHTSEEING
TRIPS

As if to alleviate the anxiety, there were additional headlines under the letterhead:

AN AERIAL EXHIBITION AND PASSENGER SERVICE
EQUIPPED WITH SAFETY PLANES, SAFETY PILOTS,
SAFETY SCHEDULES, SAFETY LANDING DEVICES
ORGANIZED TO OPERATE WITH DESPATCH AT SHORT
NOTICE IN ANY PART OF THE WORLD FOR THE TRANS-
PORTATION OF MERCHANDISE OR TOURISTS ON LONG
OR SHORT FLIGHTS

At the bottom of what was left of the page (it was obvious that Lawrence intended to write only the briefest of business letters), this emphasis on safety was reiterated:

ALL MACHINES PROTECTED BY SPERRY STABILIZERS
AND GRAVITY SAFETY INVENTIONS
THE MOST EXTENSIVE & COMPLETELY FURNISHED
FLIGHT ORGANIZATION IN AMERICA

In spite of these reassurances, Lawrence covered himself by
also printing an Agreement of Assumption of Risk, which all passengers were required to sign before flying. Most potential customers remained resolutely on the ground. With one notable exception—Lawrence won the Aero Club of America Prize in a
parachute contest at Atlantic City in May 1919—Sperry's Aerial
Circus was a flop.

It was a blessing in disguise. Lawrence's inventive powers and
dedication to flying were too great to be restricted to exhibitions.
On his fifteen-acre field at Farmingdale, where he built a plant
and an airdrome, he wanted to construct airplanes that embodied
his own ideas. He wanted to incorporate his fold-out retractable
wheels into a practical, foolproof amphibian plane, and he wanted
to manufacture the first sports aircraft in America, what he called
"the aerial flivver," which he felt would revolutionize air transport by bringing planes within the price range of the average automobile owner. He worked on these two projects at the same
time.

In the matter of the amphibian, he had an unexpected ally in
Franklin D. Roosevelt, assistant secretary of the Navy. Despite
the Sperry family maxim that the only good Roosevelts were Republican Roosevelts, Lawrence now approved thoroughly of
FDR's views on aviation.

On March 17, 1919, the assistant secretary of the Navy said,
"America originated the science of flying, only to have other
countries take its development and control out of her grasp. We
must regain supremacy of the air, not only for defense in event of
possible future conflict but for commercial and traveling purposes
as well."

Democrat or not, this was the right spirit, and Lawrence signed
a contract with the U.S. Navy for the construction of amphibious
triplanes on which the wheels could be folded out of the way

when alighting on water. The official name of this project, for which the contract was signed in 1919, was the Sperry Land and Sea Triplane with 48-foot Wing Span, Boat Hull, and Retractable Landing Gear. It was to be powered by a pusher-type Liberty engine, mounted on top of the middle wing.

The idea of the aerial flivver was even closer to Lawrence's heart, for this would put the joys of flying within reach of the average motorist. Here his chief ally was an old friend, the brilliant maverick Brig. Gen. William Mitchell, who, like Lawrence, was absolutely fearless about what he did and what he said.

Billy Mitchell, assistant chief of the U.S. Army Air Force, wanted an inexpensive, maneuverable little single-seat plane that the Army could use as a training ship for pursuit aviation. This coincided precisely with Lawrence's desire for a single-seater sports plane. He went to his drawing board and designed a small biplane whose lower wing was almost unnoticeable. Delighted with the design, Bill Mitchell ordered three of the planes, the first sports plane in American aviation, for the War Department. This plane was the famous Sperry Messenger; it was Billy Mitchell who gave it its name.

The Messenger went ninety-five miles an hour, had a twenty-foot wing span and a three-cylinder, sixty-horsepower radial engine, and flew thirty miles on a gallon of gas. Taking the first one up on a trial run, General Mitchell reported, "I am very much impressed by the construction of this little single-seater. I have never seen anything fly better."

Billy Mitchell was so impressed, in fact, that he persuaded the Army to quadruple its initial order of three planes. When Lawrence announced this news to his employees, they all cheered and quadrupled their efforts.

The maneuverable little Messenger became the star of the grande finale of Lawrence's efforts with the aerial torpedo.

In April 1920, the Army, thoroughly disenchanted by the Kettering fiasco, signed a contract with the Lawrence Sperry Aircraft Company to equip his Messenger airplanes with automatic pilots and to develop them as aerial torpedoes.

Major Guy L. Gearhart, mindful of the huge sum expended

on the Kettering experiments, proposed an $84,000 contract plus an ingenious bonus system that suited Lawrence's competitive temperament to a T.

In addition to the contractual guarantee, he would get the following incentive awards.

(a) For hitting a target at 30 miles' range once out of 12 flights, Five Thousand Dollars ($5,000.00)

(b) For hitting a target at 30 miles' range two additional times out of said 12 flights, Five Thousand Dollars ($5,000.00)

(c) For hitting a target at 60 miles' range once out of 12 flights, Five Thousand Dollars ($5,000.00)

(d) For hitting a target at 60 miles' range two additional times out of said 12 flights, Five Thousand Dollars ($5,000.00)

(e) For hitting a target at 90 miles' range once out of 12 flights, Five Thousand Dollars ($5,000.00)

(f) For hitting a target at 90 miles' range two additional times out of 12 flights, Five Thousand Dollars ($5,000.00)

(g) For making one successful launching into the air automatically and to automatically maintain continuously a predetermined direction for at least one mile without lateral deviation exceeding two degrees (2°), right or left, Five Thousand Dollars ($5,000.00)

(h) For making two additional successful launchings conforming to sub-division (d) of Section (3) of Article IV, Five Thousand Dollars ($5,000.00)

Forty thousand dollars in bonuses: it challenged Lawrence's young company to the limits of its capacity. After a typically hasty and optimistic agreement to fulfill the terms of the contract within a year, he ran into trouble keeping the automatic gyro controls exactly on target for such extended distances and was granted an extension until June 29, 1922.

The slight deviations of more than 2 percent of the target range and more than two degrees of lateral and longitudinal deviation continued to bug him as he rode out alone on his aerial torpedoes and brought them back himself to Mitchel Field. He had to keep costs down and simply could not afford to lose a single torpedo before the final test.

As June 29 approached he was worried about those slight but all-important deviations that meant the huge distance between success and failure. Then, on May 15, in one of those flashes of genius, Lawrence Sperry hit upon the solution that has been used ever since from here to the moon: accurate remote control of the missile by radio. It was typical of Lawrence that he could not only think this up, but put it into practice. He installed the radio controls in conjunction with the gyroscopic pneumatic controls of the aerial torpedo. He flew to the farthest target, ninety miles from Mitchel Field, receiving about a dozen correctional radio impulses from the ground, and he achieved a bull's eye. He was ready for the big test of his aerial torpedo, without a pilot, on June 29.

On that day the Sperry aerial torpedo hit the thirty-mile target twice, the sixty-mile target three times, and the ninety-mile target once.

The only flaw in this triumph with the aerial torpedo came from the chief of the Engineering Division. He complained to the chief of Air Services that the Lawrence Sperry Company had "installed radio control in one of these Torpedoes without my knowledge and thus on the last day of the fiscal year were able to hit the targets. I have investigated this matter and believe that bonus payments would be illegal under the terms of the contract as it was not contemplated that radio be used."

Lawrence had merely to point to the appropriate clause in the contract which stated that "articles under control shall function in flight test *without manual control.*"

"Radio control is not manual control," Lawrence told the chief of the Engineering Division. "Try to get that simple idea fixed in your little bureaucratic mind." He collected his $40,000 in bonuses and distributed the money to all the workers of the Sperry Aircraft Company who had made this triumph possible.

Lawrence was aware of the terrible potential power of his invention. He wrote an article on the subject, which appeared in the January 1926 issue of the *U.S. Air Service Magazines*, "hoping and praying" that aerial torpedoes would be a deterrent to war. The article was accompanied by Billy Mitchell's definitive statement on Lawrence's role in the evolution of guided missiles: "The aerial torpedo is, and will be, a weapon of tremendous value and terrific force to air power. Lawrence Sperry was its great developer."

It was ironical that the Sperry Messenger became the prototype of the guided missile. Lawrence originally designed this plane for pleasure, and he kept one in his garage. He could manage it alone without the help of the usual mechanics—another breakthrough—and he commuted in it daily, flying the ten miles from his Garden City home to the Farmingdale factory in less than five minutes. This was part of his ceaseless promotion of his aerial flivver. He flew everywhere in the Messenger. He wrote articles about it in *Aerospace Weekly* and *Motor Life*. He coined the expression "motorists of the air" and was a tireless propagandist for the advantages of air over motor travel.

"No traffic jams," he wrote in *Motor Life*, "no jaywalkers to contend with, no poor road surfaces or profane detours." He meant hellish detours, but in 1921 words like that did not get into print; it was sufficiently daring to have said profane.

"No officious traffic cops to bawl you out," Lawrence went on, "no constable to enforce freak speed laws to finance the village government." This was a slap at the Long Island police who had pursued him for years as he raced down the roads in his high-powered Marmon. Now these poor earthlings tried to follow his free-wheeling antics in the clouds. Sometimes, just to taunt them, he would land on a road, then take off as they roared up on their motorcycles. "Physical exertion is much greater in driving a car or a motorcycle," he wrote, "than in piloting an airplane." The panting Long Island police had to agree.

"I believe many women are as qualified to be pilots as men," Lawrence wrote magnanimously, and he gave Winnie lessons to prove this feminist point—though he had already proved it, she reminded him, with Cynthia Polk.

"It is child's play," Lawrence went on. "Give me any normal person between the ages of five and forty-five and I will teach him or her to fly in the same span of time as a novice masters the intricacies of driving an automobile."

He looked at his three-year-old son, Lawrence Jr., but Winifred held her firstborn child in a mother's anxious grip.

"You said five," she reminded Lawrence.

Lawrence kept insisting in print on the benefits of what he defensively called "alleged stunting."

"A program of stunting, the whole catalogue of aerial acrobatics makes for safety in flying," he wrote. "The first requisite is a strong, safe machine like the Sperry Messenger. The second is sufficient altitude to allow recovery from a dangerous position. A pilot with stunting ability is more capable in an emergency than a 'conservative' pilot who has never experimented with barrel rolls and flat spins. The conservative pilot is much more likely to crack up."

Lawrence had already proved that point by stunt-training his military pilots during the war, and although such training is officially credited with having saved many lives, the public regarded stunting with mixed, romantic emotions, as one might watch in terrified fascination a fearless daredevil in the act of crossing the Niagara River on a tightrope.

As Lawrence continued to make headlines with his Sperry Messenger, his father sent him an urgent plea:

> Please don't encourage your brother Elmer to fly. One flying "Simoleon" in the family is already as much as your mother can stand, not to mention,
>
> Your devoted father,
E.A.S.

The Sperry Gyroscope Company reflected its founder's fears and his attitude toward his son's aerial antics. In an official bulletin it referred approvingly to newsreel films that showed Lawrence demonstrating the Sperry stabilizer. "But the other films have nothing to do with stability," the bulletin added. "They show Lawrence using his Messenger plane for all sorts of mad stunts."

The most famous—or notorious—of these "mad stunts" took place on March 22, 1922. A direct consequence of Lawrence's impatience with bureaucracy, it shocked his father deeply, but it must be seen in the context of Lawrence's "business career" and his relations with the U.S. government, especially with regard to his manufacture of amphibian planes.

The creation and early development of amphibian planes have been attributed to Glenn Curtiss, whose *Triad* (so named for the three elements, land, sea, and air) and *Flying Fish* had been tried out on Keuka Lake as early as 1912. Igor Sikorsky and Grover Loening have also been credited with major roles in amphibian engineering, but it was Lawrence Sperry who officially designed and built the first amphibian planes in America. The work was begun under U.S. Navy contract in 1918, just after Lawrence's epoch-making demonstration of the first blind-flying instrument, the turn-and-bank indicator.

The Navy had long been aware of Lawrence's experience with flying boats. They knew about his triumph at Bezons, and he was also famous for his daredevil stunts, such as looping the loop, in these bulky machines. The Navy had also taken note of Lawrence's almost casual invention of the first retractable landing gear back in 1915. So it was logical, when they wanted to order fifteen two-cockpit amphibians, that they should turn to Lawrence. The Navy wanted a plane that could land and take off on both land and water, and in heavy seas if necessary; previous demonstrations had been confined to Lake Keuka and the shallow water of the Spanish Bight.

Lawrence had just opened his Lawrence Sperry Aircraft Company when the Navy contract came through. He had a team of two hundred workers who were eager to get started. This was their first big order. Glenn Curtiss, Lawrence's mentor and close personal friend, was delighted to support the fledgling company, and he agreed to provide the motors.

The design was Lawrence's improvement on the Curtiss flying boat with which he was so familiar, though he had tested it only on the relatively placid waters of Lake Keuka, the Spanish Bight, and the Seine. The new boat must be capable of coping with the billowing Atlantic. Lawrence designed the largest and strongest hull that had yet been seen, strengthening this wooden shell with crossbeams to withstand the lateral pounding of ocean waves. The locking mechanism of the retractable landing gear would have to be above the waterline, Lawrence realized, to minimize resistance when the huge plane took off or landed on water.

The design of this landing gear was the most revolutionary aspect of the Sperry amphibian; it was an improvement of his

1915 invention and it became the prototype for all subsequent retractable landing gear. Lawrence made a separate right and left strut-and-wheel assembly that could be locked in the extended or down position for terra firma landings without fear of splaying outward and collapsing. For water landings the wheels had to be retracted well above water level. Lawrence solved this by lifting them up under the lower wing by means of a hand crank and cable, easily manipulated by the pilot. The disk wheels with their solid rubber tires were made of alloy steel, the supporting struts of high tensile steel, light as a sea gull's leg but strong enough to resist any longitudinal stress.

As usual, Lawrence performed all the experiments himself, putting his strut-and-wheel assemblies through a series of severe tests until he was sure that they would withstand the shock of landing without any tie rod connecting the wheels. He designed the first wheels in history to operate without a tie rod. Photos of all previous planes indicate this tie rod, which made retraction of the wheels impossible. Dispensing with the rigid, intractable tie rod was the most important innovation of Lawrence's amphibian plane.

The weight of landing gear, engines, fuel, and a flight crew of two had to be taken into account in designing the wings and struts of the Sperry amphibian. Since wind tunnels did not exist at the time, Lawrence had to test each of his designs under actual flying conditions. Climbing into the cockpit of the wingless hull, he had himself towed by speedboat so that he could determine the speed at which the hull, loaded down with dummy weights to simulate the burden of wings, fuel, engine, and wheels, would reach the "planing step" stage, that moment when the heavy boat would surge upward in its effort to take off.

Lawrence tested the plane almost daily for several months on both land and water, noting its ground maneuverability, its stability, the vibration of the engine in its mounting. As usual, he became almost literally a part of the plane's mechanism, the nerve center of its system. Faster and faster runs were made on both land and water. Sensitive to every throttle change, Lawrence tested his new baby in almost every conceivable condition of wind, terrain, and sea.

While all this was going on he was bugged, as usual, by Navy technical "experts" and their endless paperwork, but he had to put up with them; bureaucracy was a necessary evil when one accepted a Navy contract.

Finally, shortly after the New Year of 1919, Lawrence was satisfied with his new amphibian. As Navy officials and two hundred Sperry employees stood on the shore of Great South Bay, Lawrence and a Navy copilot took off, flew over Fire Island, and landed in the Atlantic amid heavy ocean swells that would have swamped any previous plane. Then he took off again, churning through the furrows of the ocean, rising up in a geyser of salt spray, triumphantly aloft. Above Farmingdale, he cranked down his retractable landing gear and made a perfect landing on the field of the Lawrence Sperry Aircraft Company. The employees of the company pulled their boss and the Navy pilot out of the cockpits and carried them around the field on their shoulders. The naval pilot pronounced himself satisfied. The Sperry amphibian was a success, and production began on the fifteen-plane order.

Getting the Navy to pay for it was another story. It was here that the maddest stunt with the Sperry Messenger became necessary, at least to Lawrence's way of thinking. The original contract for the Navy order had been signed by Franklin D. Roosevelt, undersecretary of the Navy. Now, in 1922, there was another undersecretary, Franklin's cousin, Theodore Roosevelt, Jr., who was demurring about payment on the order signed by his predecessor.

Politically speaking, as far as the staunchly Republican Sperry family was concerned, to be Theodore Roosevelt, Jr., was tantamount to being the son of God. But, though Junior did his best to live up to his father's swashbuckling reputation, the task was beyond him.

Now, since Lawrence himself was a good Republican; since he was a former schoolmate and abiding personal friend of young Teddy's brother, Archie; since Lawrence was a reserve officer in the United States Navy; and, above all, since he needed the promised money for the amphibians to keep his business going, he did not hesitate to write a personal letter to T.R. Jr., requesting prompt payment of this overdue bill.

There was no reply. Young Teddy enjoyed an almost dictatorial position in the realm of naval aeronautics. He wished everything to go out over his signature so that the beneficiaries would know that he was the source of government manna, and this mania slowed down the already cumbersome processes of government procurement and payment to an almost paralytic state.

Lawrence had to pay his workers, so he sent his general manager, Bill Stoermer, to Washington to discuss the matter with T.R. Jr. Stoermer had a firm date, but when he got to the undersecretary's office, he was told that T.R. had had to attend a more important meeting and would be unable to see him as planned. Stoermer, an old-line Navy man himself, took a pretty dim view of this sort of "irregularity."

He had also been an investigative officer and he found out that T.R.'s "more important" engagement was on the golf course of the Burning Tree Country Club. He pursued the assistant secretary to those exclusive precincts, only to be told by a subaltern that "the secretary would not see him at any time for any reason."

When Lawrence got this message back in Farmingdale, he almost went through the corrugated roof of his airplane factory. A statement from the assistant secretary of the Navy that he would not authorize final payment on the Sperry amphibians until he had reviewed all the contracts and orders did nothing to calm Lawrence down.

He decided to take direct action. He packed all the necessary papers, endorsements, and supportive papers into the baggage compartment behind the cockpit of his Messenger plane. Then he called reporters of the *Times*, the *World*, the *Evening Journal*, the *Sun*, the *Telegram*, and the *Brooklyn Daily Eagle*. "It's the first day of spring," he notified them. "I am flying to Washington tomorrow, but it won't be to see the cherry trees. I invite you all to meet me on the plaza in front of the Capitol steps."

On March 22 Lawrence descended on the nation's capital to strike a memorable blow against bureaucracy. The reporters were there, all right, and as Lawrence circled the dome of the Capitol, he could see that the crowd was too thick in the plaza to permit a landing.

Paul Garber, former director of the Air and Space Museum of the Smithsonian Institution, was an eyewitness to the stunt. "People sensed that something unusual was happening," he reported. "Lawrence flew right up South Capitol Street. Hearing the motor, people rushed out of their offices. Even the United States Senate stopped its deliberations. Lawrence saw there was no other place to land, so he landed on the Capitol steps. Bump, bump, bump! That little Sperry Messenger plane ran up the steps like a baby carriage. Then it stopped, perfectly intact.

"Lawrence got out, smiling, but looking very determined. I realized I was in the presence of an extraordinary man. He was no common clay.

"He spoke calmly to the newspaper reporters. 'Gentlemen,' he said, 'come with me. We are going to the office of the assistant secretary of the Navy.' And they all followed him like the Pied Piper."

Accounts differ as to the precise nature of the ensuing confrontation between Lawrence Sperry and Theodore Roosevelt, Jr. One persistent rumor is that Lawrence actually marched into T.R.'s office and called him "a little fifth-rate tin replica of your father."

Lawrence *could* have said that; it has a "Lawrencian" ring. But more credible is the report that when Lawrence and his press entourage reached T.R. Jr.'s office, they were met by a secretary who told Lawrence that "Mr. Roosevelt *had* been able to get at the matter, that Mr. Sperry's bill *had* been approved for payment, and that, if Mr. Sperry would go to the Treasury, the money was waiting for him."

In any event, after a few more landings in Washington in front of the Lincoln Memorial and on the Mall, Lawrence flew back to Farmingdale with his money.

The landing on the Capitol steps was duly reported in the nation's leading newspapers the following day.

"That's the kind of advertising money can't buy," said Bill Stoermer, happy to be the manager of a solvent company and very pleased with the comeuppance of Theodore Roosevelt, Jr.

Back in his oak-paneled office in Brooklyn, Father Sperry was not so pleased. He dictated a letter to the Honorable Theodore Roosevelt, Jr., assistant secretary of the Navy:

Dear Sir:

I have just been informed of an extremely embarrassing occurrence in your office, in which I am told my second son, Lawrence B. Sperry, took a leading part. It should be remembered that he was not representing this company in any way, but was representing his own company, known as the Lawrence Sperry Aircraft Company, Inc.

I am writing this to say that we most sincerely regret this occurrence, although neither this company nor any of its personnel has, or ever had, any interest in or connection with the Lawrence Sperry Aircraft Company, which is a private enterprise of his own, located out on the Island at Farmingdale, and does not represent us in any way. Since both the Sperry Gyroscope Company and the Aircraft Company have business with the Government, it is highly desirable that they be kept entirely separate and distinct in the minds of those who have dealings with them.

I am hoping that if occasion arises, you will do us the very great favor of letting the Secretary of the Navy, Mr. Denby, have this same information.

Respectfully yours,
Elmer A. Sperry
President

The assistant secretary of the Navy answered in due course on April Fools' Day:

April 1, 1922

My dear Mr. Sperry:

Thank you for your nice letter of March 31st. Don't worry for a moment. I understand the situation perfectly. Insofar as your son Lawrence B. Sperry is concerned, I in no way connect him with you and with the Sperry Gyroscope Company. As far as he goes personally, it makes little difference to this office what he says or does not say. He will receive the same fair treatment that is due any American citizen, and his own remarks and actions will not prejudice the judgment either one way or the other.

With best wishes, believe me,
Very truly yours,
Theodore Roosevelt, Jr.

If the Lawrence Sperry Aircraft Company got rather short shrift from the Navy after Lawrence's direct dunning of Theodore Roosevelt, Jr., Gen. Billy Mitchell made up for this negligence by ordering fifty more Sperry Messenger planes for the U.S. Army.

21

TWO MORE MAD STUNTS with the Messenger took place in 1922, but again there was a method in the madness of the manufacturer of America's first sports plane.

In October of that year, Lawrence entered the "On to St. Louis" cross-country race for civilian planes from New York to St. Louis. He climbed into his Messenger at Garden City, Long Island, at 5:00 A.M. on October 19, stopped over for some business in Washington, then flew to McCook Field in Dayton, Ohio, for dinner, leaving afterward by bright moonlight for St. Louis.

He flew over the silent city at midnight, landed in the deserted streets, and startled the night staff of the Trocadero Hotel by taxiing straight up to the front door of that elegant hostelry. The manager was awakened. The night reporter of the *St. Louis Post Dispatch* came to photograph the surrealist sight of the Sperry Messenger parked in front of the Trocadero. A crowd gathered in the morning. The manager was rather pleased, especially when Mrs. Sperry arrived by train to join her dashing husband.

The judges of the "On to St. Louis" contest admitted that Lawrence was the first to arrive, but, after much deliberation they reduced him officially to fourth place by claiming that his starting point had been Washington, D.C., and that he had landed on the asphalt of downtown St. Louis instead of on the grass of Jefferson Barracks, official terminal field of the contest.

"Those judges don't know the difference between a starting place and a stopover," Lawrence told the press, "and they don't know their grass from a hole in the ground."

"Lawrence!" Winnie remonstrated.

"They don't know their grass from their asphalt," Lawrence went on gaily.

"You are absolutely incorrigible," Winifred Sperry said to her husband.

"Of course, you're not going to print that," she said to the reporters, giving them the appealing smile they remembered from her films. She had the newspapermen eating out of her hand. Soon she and Lawrence were posing for pictures, "the birdman and his bride."

Winifred was in on the next mad stunt in the promotion of the Messenger. Lawrence had invented a kind of aerial rumble seat by converting the baggage compartment behind the pilot's seat into a second cockpit. He bundled Winnie into it and took off for Chicago, where he was arrested for landing in Grant Park. How inhospitable! While the Chicago police were writing out the summons, Lawrence leaped out of the plane, spun the propeller, and took off for Detroit.

"What can you expect from the hog butcher of the world?" he said, but he circled once above the lakefront of Lake Michigan and waved to the baffled cops to show he bore them no ill will. Earthbound creatures, they were just doing their duty as they saw fit.

Detroit was less stuffy, more welcoming, as befits the automotive capital of the world. Lawrence landed his Messenger neatly on the lawn of Grand Circus Park at the junction of Washington Boulevard and Bagley Avenue and taxied up to the entrance of the Detroit Statler Hotel. "Every Detroit paper had us on the front page," he wrote home.

He and Winnie attended the marriage of Billy Mitchell to a Detroit society girl.

"Best wedding I ever went to except my own," Lawrence noted. "It was just wonderful; there were aeroplanes overhead at the reception."

One of the wedding guests, Edsel Ford, expressed great interest in Lawrence's aerial flivver. "You ought to be able to sell this to the same type of people who bought our first cars," he said, "to pioneers who are going to break unbroken ground and fly, despite all obstacles.

"My father would be very much interested in seeing your little airship," Edsel added.

"When? Where?" Lawrence wanted to know.

"Why don't you come to tea tomorrow?" Edsel said.

He described the location of the Ford family estate in Dearborn. "East of the River Rouge, north of the railroad tracks to Chicago," Edsel said. "I'll put a sheet on the ground, showing you where to land."

So Lawrence and Winnie took off on a beautiful October Sunday to meet one of the most famous men in the world.

"It was a thrilling ride," Winifred Sperry recalled later. "It was always a thrill to fly with Lawrence, but this was an especially exciting day; all the wheat fields looked like gold. We followed Lake St. Clair and the St. Clair River, crossed the Canadian border, then flew to the mouth of the River Rouge and followed the river, flying above that enormous Ford plant. Even a factory is beautiful from the air.

"Then we spotted the estate, and the white sheet on the front lawn, sloping down to a beautiful lake."

"The lawn was rather narrow," Lawrence recorded, "about 1,500 feet, so I had some apprehension about chavalling into the trees. With Winnie in the rear seat, I didn't want to cut up Mr. Ford's lawn with my tail skid. So I circled and landed from the lake side on an uphill slope."

Edsel, Henry, and Mrs. Henry Ford gave the flying couple a warm welcome. The rest of the visit is best described in Lawrence's own words. Henry Ford's interest in the Sperry Messenger and his practical suggestions were everything that the young aviator could have hoped for:

"Mr. Ford's eye immediately went to the motor, and he began asking questions. I explained to him that the cylinders had a steel lining inside and blocks of bronze were cast in the head for the valve seats. He thought this was a very clever idea. He criticized the fact that the fins were machined, as he said he believed that sand blasting would do the trick, as well as be a better radiator. He then looked at the rocker arms and said that these could be eliminated by use of a small L-type head.

"Mr. Ford wanted to know why the rest of the airplane was not made of metal, and I told him it would be profitable to go into metal production if large numbers were produced, but that in small numbers the present type construction was all right.

"He then looked at the motor again, and said that he could

mass produce motors for $50 apiece; that the whole job should
not cost as much as a Ford, as it was so much simpler than the automobile, there being no such things as a clutch, change speed
gears, universals, drive shafts, and rear end.

"I then told him that the biggest difficulty was to sell to people
who could learn to fly, the airplane being of no use to anyone
unless that person knew how to fly it. He said, 'Sell to the city
boys. They will take it up much quicker than the country lads.
We had the same trouble with our tractor.'

"Mr. Ford asked me how much my motor weighed, and
thought that 175 pounds was very light. I told him that the weight
was a highly important factor in an airplane. If 50 pounds could
be saved in the motor, a total weight of 125 pounds could be
saved in the whole outfit, as it was necessary to have 1½ pounds
of plane for every pound of motor. He said this was quite true,
that it is true of all vehicles of transportation, that he always followed the principle in his cars, and that nature recognized the
theory by making the bones of a bird hollow.

"In stepping around the plane, I showed Mr. Ford how the
machine, which was a single-seater, could be made into a two-
seater by taking the cover off the rear cockpit, which immediately
could be used as the back of the rear seat by pushing it into place.
That impressed him very favorably because of using the cover for
two purposes.

"The airplane part of my ship seemed not to interest Mr. Ford
as much as the motor. He asked me if my father was associated
with my enterprise, and I told him 'No.' He replied, 'That's quite
right.' He thought that I should not be handicapped in any way
by the prejudices of the older generation, as he said this was a
part of transportation, not for his generation but for mine and future generations to come."

This was music to an aviator's ears, though it must be admitted
that Father Sperry's "prejudices of the older generation" were
beginning to melt in the radiant energy of his son's enthusiasm.
The old man was mellowing. It almost seemed that Lawrence,
having conquered the automotive king of the world, could now
get away with all the dash and bang he wanted to.

"Lawrence has been full of his activities," Father Sperry wrote to Zula's niece ("dear, splendid Jean Goodman") on October 23, 1923. "At a wonderful aviation meet at St. Louis he quite won the hearts of the people. So far as I can gather, he was easily the most popular in the airplane line in St. Louis. They allowed him to light on their boulevards and the more general havoc he wrought in their rules and regulations, the more they seemed to pat him on the back and tell him to go to it.

"He is easily doing more to popularize flying than anyone else in the United States. All the people who know seem to agree on this point. He flew to St. Louis in his little tiny plane, so small that he wanted it under a huge 40,000 lb. bomber to be photographed to show the enormous contrast. Then he flew to Chicago and was arrested for coming down in the park. He was given some trouble, I think, but got out of it.

"After Lawrence and Winnie attended General Mitchell's wedding in Detroit, Lawrence did an extremely daring thing. They called at Henry Ford's place, lighting on the front lawn. In a nice interview he surprised Ford by showing him that he could go between two and three times as far in the air flivver on a gallon of gas as Ford can go with a land flivver. Ford was interested in the little engine that propels the machine. Mrs. Ford and Edsel served tea and they were all in high feather."

They must have been—surely Lawrence was—for Henry Ford's parting remark had the confident ring of prophecy: "The world is on wheels," he said; "it will soon be on wings."

Edsel Ford provided Winnie with an extra sweater and muffler. Mrs. Ford kissed her good-bye and Lawrence lifted her into the rear cockpit.

"I stepped around the left wing," Lawrence told the reporters, "threw the motor over once, whereupon it started. We took the air, taking straight off down the lawn and over the little lake. I turned to the right and waved again from a height of five hundred feet, and we were off on our flight to New York."

"It was our happiest flight together," Winifred Sperry told her children, little Winifred ("Bam") and Lawrence Jr., years later. "We flew over Cleveland and Buffalo, then landed at Hammondsport and spent the night on the shores of Lake Keuka where Lawrence got his pilot's license. Next morning we buzzed

all the buildings of Cornell and landed on the campus for gasoline. Then home. We had a westerly wind all the way; we were
only six hours in the air from Detroit to Garden City, a distance
of some seven hundred miles.

"Lawrence was completely happy on that flight. He kept looking around at me, his eyes as blue as the sky overhead, and he
kept repeating Henry Ford's parting shot: 'The world is on
wheels; it will soon be on wings.'"

22

FROM 1922 ON, fulfilling Henry Ford's prophecy was Lawrence's mission in life. Five years before Lindbergh's flight to Paris, Lawrence was the most romantic figure in American aviation. At twenty-eight he was at the height of his physical and inventive powers. He had a devoted wife, as beautiful as he was handsome. He had a son, a daughter, and a record of achievement that might well have satisfied a less dedicated and driven man. He had invented and perfected the automatic pilot for airplanes, the turn-and-bank indicator, source of all instrument flying, and the aerial torpedo, first of the guided missiles. He had also patented the first practical parachute, in the demonstration of which he had symbolically freed himself from the devoted but inhibiting dominance of his powerful father and the gigantic Sperry Gyroscope Company. Now in his *Wunderjahre*, 1922 and 1923, running his own aircraft company, he was determined to "put the world on wings."

During his experiments with the amphibians, Lawrence had become increasingly aware of the flying boat's heavy, wind-resistant body, its bulkiness and ungainliness. Although he had dared to loop-the-loop in it and had pushed it to new heights of performance, he was one of the first aviators to realize that the flying boat was doomed to obsolescence. He longed for a swifter, lighter plane, one that would offer the least possible resistance while passing through the air.

This desire coincided exactly with the wishes of his friend and fellow maverick, Billy Mitchell, who had helped him launch the Sperry Messenger. General Mitchell now wanted a maneuverable fighter plane for the Army. He was tired of what he called "squirrel-cage" airplanes. He was referring to the external struts

and wires that supported the wings of biplanes and triplanes, giving them the look of giant box kites.

"I couldn't agree with you more," Lawrence told Billy. "Sometimes I feel like getting out on the wings and giving a harp reci-
tal."

The two friends talked about a whole new concept: the possibility of a single-winged aircraft that would dispense with the
squirrel-cage effects.

"A cantilever monoplane," Mitchell said. "Is it possible? Is it
practicable?"

Lawrence's blue eyes looked off into space, that blue indifferent space where past and future meet.

"What are you thinking of, Gyro?" Billy Mitchell asked.

"Funny thing," Lawrence mused. "I was thinking of Arizona,
the desert, the buzzards out there where I went to school. Talk
about aerodynamics: they could stay aloft all day, gliding, banking, turning at will.

"The wires could be built into the wings as spars," Lawrence
went on. "The spars would be concealed under the skin of the
wing like the bones of those birds.

"They have pretty thick wings, those buzzards," he continued.
"If we built the wires into the wing as spars, the wings would
have to be thicker, thick enough to accommodate the spars."

"Why not?" said Billy Mitchell.

"Yes," Lawrence said excitedly. "Why not? That would eliminate the air resistance of your squirrel-cage struts and wires. A
bird doesn't need four wings," he concluded. "Why should a
plane?"

Billy Mitchell already had the services of a first-rate designer,
working for him under U.S. government contract. His name,
Alfred Verville, was to become indissolubly linked with that of
Lawrence Sperry in the history of aviation. Born in 1890, he was
two years older than Lawrence. Like Lawrence, he had started in
aviation with Glenn Curtiss and had helped with the design of the
Curtiss "Jenny." Unlike Lawrence, however, he was essentially
an air service engineer, preferring the drawing board to the cockpit. Verville's genius in aerodynamic design was matched and
complemented by Lawrence's in aeromechanics. Billy Mitchell

chose Lawrence as the implementing contractor for the new racing monoplane that Verville was designing. Lawrence eagerly agreed to manufacture three of these revolutionary monoplanes for starters.

Verville was at the Lawrence Sperry Aircraft Factory every day, watching every move Lawrence made, afraid that this pragmatic "flying fool" might modify his specifications by a single millimeter. But there was no problem. Lawrence knew a good design when he saw one. He was fascinated by the aerodynamic potential of the monoplane and highly satisfied with the three planes that emerged from his factory. Although they were officially tested by a consortium of U.S. Army pilots, Lawrence, in typical fashion, took one up on a Sunday morning, when Verville and the pilots were absent from the plant, and he had the thrill of gunning the monoplane up to its maximum speed of 230 miles per hour, which was actually 14 miles an hour faster than the official world record established by the Sperry-Verville Racer when it won the Pulitzer Race at Dayton, Ohio, in 1924.

The "Sperry-Verville" Racer: Verville was highly annoyed by this inevitable compound. He wrote a letter to Lawrence demanding an apology for the fact that the Verville Racer was now called the Sperry-Verville Racer. Lawrence replied that he was sorry for anything he might have done to give that impression. He congratulated Verville wholeheartedly on the success of this first cantilever monoplane, and he did not try to claim any credit for its design, though the final product did incorporate Lawrence's retractable landing gear, which retracted, as it does today, into wheel wells in the wings. Another innovation of this first streamlined strutless plane was the antivibration engine, mounted on rubber shock absorbers to reduce the shaking, noise, and bodily discomfort of older planes. This was also Lawrence's idea, but he made no claim to having assisted in the design of the plane. No disclaimer, however, could keep the public and even the experts from calling this revolutionary monoplane the Sperry-Verville or the Verville-Sperry Racer. It is called the Verville-Sperry Racer to this day in the Military Aerospace Museum of the Wright-Patterson Air Force Base in Dayton.

By any name, Billy Mitchell was delighted with the results of this three-man collaboration, combining his own dreams with the reality of the low wings designed by Verville and the Sperry landing gear. He called this beautiful and speedy monoplane "the motorcycle of the air" and was typically annoyed when the U.S. Army kept this prototype of all subsequent planes under wraps for another year.

Lawrence turned to promoting the nation's first easy-to-fly sports plane, the Sperry Messenger.

"It was a product well worth promoting," Gen. Ira Eaker recalled as recently as 1971. "It was one of the toughest planes ever made in those early days of flying.

"I actually saw a Sperry Messenger land *upside down* at Mitchel Field," he said. "A ne'er-do-well barnstormer was fond of flying low over the hangars, buzzing the ground crews. He drank. One day he flew a little too low upside down, and he flopped. We rushed out expecting to pick up the pieces. This guy got up, brushed himself off, and walked away. The propeller was broken; otherwise that little Sperry Messenger was as good as new.

"Lawrence did more to popularize flying than any man I ever knew," General Eaker continued. "He was so earnest he could sell you anything. He never had a negative thought."

Lawrence's propaganda for the Messenger was not limited to dramatic landings and takeoffs in the city streets of America. For a boy who had flunked English at Erasmus Hall, he was making a reputation as a popular "essayist," to use his father's term. His most ambitious essay was an article, "My Car and My Airplane," published in 1922 in one of the most literate and influential of American magazines, *Vanity Fair.*

"People as a whole look upon the airplane as a means of achieving a thrill, a recipe for publicity, an easy method of breaking one's neck," he wrote. "It will, of course, do any of these things, but its real purpose is to become the means of long distance travel—just as the automobile is today the universal vehicle for short distances."

After this prophetic statement, he proceeded to tout the superior safety factor of the airplane over the auto, which, already in 1922, was responsible for one death every three minutes in the United States. He contrasted these statistics with the record of the Aerial Mail, "traveling day after day and night after night for thousands of miles in all sorts of weather without a single fatal accident.

"I own both a car and an airplane," he went on, "and the airplane, mile for mile, is pleasanter, easier, and cheaper to operate. My little sport plane has a high speed of 97 miles per hour and a gasoline economy of 20 miles to the gallon, due to its light and truly remarkable sixty horse power, air-cooled motor. The total width of this little Messenger Plane is only twenty feet, so that I can easily keep it in an ordinary two-car garage. . . . I fly daily from my home to my factory, ten miles away. I do this in preference to using a car not only because it saves time, but also because it costs less, requires less labor, and is far more enjoyable."

After railing against "the old opposition and skepticism, the antiquated antagonism to progress, the old reluctance to accept what is new," Lawrence became lyrical about the novelty and joy of flying:

"You can land on a country road or drop in at any gasoline station and be certain of prompt service because you are not just one of a stream of banal motor cars. No tolls to pay. No new tires to swell the upkeep.

"Then there is the sheer joy of flying and the moments of exhilaration which come to one in the air. Compared with the physical exertion of driving a car, the energy expended in flying is almost nil. . . . Once the motor is started—and in the Messenger the motor is so small that it can be turned over with one hand—the driver has nothing to do but set the ship in the desired direction, occasionally touch the control, and spend the rest of the time leaning back comfortably and enjoying the exhilarating air and glistening scenery.

"If you try flying you will find that the more you do it the better you will like it and the easier it will become—the fascination of it will lead you on and on to the discovery of a quaint village caught between two hills, of an uncharted lake in the Sierra Nevadas, or a level stretch of prairie that is romantic as well as excellent for landing. And wherever you land, your vehicle will serve as a passport and admit you to the warm hospitality that is always accorded the pioneer."

Lawrence enjoyed a great deal of this warm hospitality, often in rural American communities, whose inhabitants had never seen an airplane. Bored with business details, factory routine, and books that were hard to balance, Lawrence was happiest after work when he could follow the open road of the sky and indulge in his "sheer joy of flying."

It was a measure of Winifred Sperry's devotion that she accepted the fact that these twilight flights often involved a night away from home.

"It was complete relaxation for Lawrence to take off and travel the skies for hours," wrote S. Paul Johnston, director of the Institute of Aeronautical Sciences. "If night fell he would pick out the dim lights of some isolated village and land in a nearby field. Farmers came running, followed by wives and children, all amazed to see a man drop from the sky. Always there was a good dinner for the pilot, a long chat—about flying, of course—a bed for the night and, next morning, a friendly send-off."

On one occasion, in July 1923, he landed at dusk on a farm near Taylorstown, Pennsylvania. The farmer and his wife, Mr. and Mrs. A. D. Miller, found him lying under the wing of his Messenger in a state of great fatigue. A local doctor prescribed whisky (then legal only for medical purposes) and a week in bed.

"It was like taking care of a perfect son," Mrs. Miller, who was childless, later wrote in a letter to Zula Sperry.

By the end of the week, everyone had fallen for this aviator who had suddenly dropped from the clouds. He was an object of great curiosity. People came from miles around to see him, and the local kids took turns standing guard over the Messenger so it would not be demolished by souvenir hunters.

"This was a most attractive and gallant young man," the attendant country doctor wrote to Mrs. Sperry. "You have every right to be proud of such a son. He dropped out of the clouds in his Messenger, and then, after a week of Mrs. Miller's homemade scrapple and sausage, he disappeared back into the sky!"

Scrapple and sausage: what a diet for a sick man! No wonder he thought he was immortal.

"Now," the doctor continued, "on the rare occasions when a plane flies over Washington County, we all run out of our homes, hoping that it's 'our Mister Sperry' coming back to see us."

Lawrence had become a local legend.

Back at the factory in Farmingdale, he gave his accountants and bookeepers as wide a berth as possible and concentrated on improving the Messenger and showing the world what this versatile plane could do.

He modified the original design to include releasable landing gear, a dual skid landing arrangement, full-span wing flap modifications, and finally a "skyhook" that made it possible, for the first time, for aircraft to make direct contact with each other in the air.

Aeronautics magazine reported:

SPERRY DROPS LANDING GEAR, LANDS ON SKIDS

Lawrence Sperry has added to his other achievements, the invention of a skid device so constructed that by a simple mechanical means the whole landing gear of his airplane is released and dropped to the ground and a landing is made on skids. Mr. Sperry in a Messenger plane that has a usual run of 400 feet had landed in one tenth of the distance.

The high speed of the Messenger, which is normally 99 m.p.h., was found to be 105 m.p.h. with the landing gear released.

The demonstration took place on August 21st at the Sperry field, Farmingdale, L.I. in the presence of Brigadier-General William Mitchell, Assistant Chief of Air Service. . . . While in flight Mr. Sperry released the entire wheel and landing gear by parachute so that it fell clear of the airplane, thus relieving the craft of extra weight and interference.

He then made a perfect landing bringing the machine to a dead stop 50 feet from the place where the skid first struck the turf.

General Mitchell expressed himself as highly gratified with the outcome of the experiment.

The new landing gear was developed by Mr. Sperry at the suggestion of officers of the Army Air Service.

A technical description of the new invention followed, along with a close-up view of the Sperry releasable landing gear with auxiliary skids.

The *New York Times*, which always found Lawrence prime copy, ran a popular account of this latest exploit with the Messenger on the front page of its edition of August 26, 1922.

SKIDS AID AVIATOR
IN QUICK LANDING

Lawrence B. Sperry Uses
Parachute and Drops to
Earth With New Device

SLIDES ONLY 50 OR 75 FEET

His Invention Said to Permit
Landing on Top of Buildings
or in Rough Country

A stroller on the road outside Farmingdale, Long Island, if he had looked into the air at the right moment yesterday morning, would have seen a pair of wheels falling slowly to earth beneath a parachute and an airplane just starting its groundward swoop for a landing, and might have feared that the plane was coming to pieces like the one-hoss shay. But it was just Lawrence B. Sperry dropping his landing gear preparatory to "sliding home" on his lately-invented wooden skids.

For instead of rolling seven or eight hundred feet to a stop, Mr. Sperry just slides for fifty or seventy-five, and doesn't have to be particular whether he hits a field of grass or a plain dirt road. His two-part invention has four distinct purposes, which he thus described to a group of reporters yesterday afternoon after one of his impromptu landings.

"In the first place," said Mr. Sperry, who is President of the Lawrence Sperry Aircraft Company, "the dropping of the landing-gear, which is done by moving a lever at the right of the fuselage, will enable an aviator, through decreased air resistance and carrying weight, to increase his speed by about ten miles an hour. In the second place, by landing on wooden skids he does not need a smooth landing place. Third, these skids may be used to enable an airplane to descend on water, and fourth, they may let a seaplane down on dry land."

The adjunct of wooden runners, he said, permits landing on the tops of buildings and other confined spaces, or in rough country in emergency descents.

The two runners, each about two feet in length, were attached to the lower wing of a Messenger airplane in yesterday's demonstration by interlocking metal parts, fitted front and rear with heavy elastic cording as a shock absorber.

Personal promotion of the Messenger continued that summer at Bellport, Long Island, where Lawrence consented to spend a couple of weeks with Winnie and what Father Sperry always referred to as "her beautiful babes" at the family summer home. The house, built by the senior Sperry, was, and remains, one of the loveliest "summer cottages" on the South Shore. It had a living room forty feet long, six master bedrooms, each with private bath, and a great veranda overlooking Bellport Bay.

Things were more relaxed between father and son, now that Lawrence had made such a success with his Messenger. The old man even forgot Lawrence's insult to Theodore Roosevelt, Jr., and he wrote a personal letter to Henry Ford, thanking him for his hospitality to Lawrence and Winnie and proudly announcing that Lawrence had licked the problem of landing his Messenger "on a dime."

Winifred Allen Sperry was a joy to her in-laws, "another daughter," Zula called her, and Helen was happily married to Robert Lea, a brilliant engineer with the Sperry Gyroscope Company; he had been a classmate of Edward Sperry's at Cornell.

So all was relaxed. It was the Indian Summer of the Sperrys. Lawrence was exceedingly popular, having modified his Messenger into a two-seater, and there was a waiting list of potential passengers. He would fly them one by one from the family lawn across Bellport Bay to Fire Island, whose rolling sand dunes provided perfect terrain to show off the prowess of his new skids.

There was only one flaw in the tranquillity of those golden vacation days. Lawrence, who was a powerful swimmer, insisted on diving through the booming breakers of Fire Island, even in stormy weather, and he would swim out into the Atlantic until he was literally out of sight. At the dock in Bellport Bay, he would disappear like a steeplejack in reverse, descending underwater hand under hand on the barnacled piers. He would remain underwater for minutes that seemed hours, holding his breath, testing his lungs to the limits of their capacity; then, just as Winnie thought she couldn't stand it for another second, bobbing up to the surface, his face almost as blue as his eyes.

"Darling, is that really necessary?"

"It's a matter of training," he said. "You never know when you might have to do it."

"Father and Mother Sperry have asked me to stay on a few days with the children after Labor Day," she said.

"That's okay," Lawrence said.

"It's a matter of training," Winifred said. "Getting used to being without you. I never know when I might have to do it."

.

23

WHEN WINTER CAME, Lawrence devised a new diversion for his versatile Messenger and became as popular as the Pied Piper with the school kids of Long Island, who modified one of the ancient juvenile jingles of America:

> Ladies and gentlemen, isn't it nice,
> Mr. Sperry's latest device?
> Put on your britches and slide on the ice!

What Lawrence did was to add a new dimension to skijoring. The *New York Times* reported it thus:

SKI-PLANING BRINGS NEW THRILL TO SPORT

Lawrence Sperry Tows Boys at
Cherry Valley at Sixty Miles
an Hour

GARDEN CITY, March 9—A new thrill was added to American outdoor sport today when Lawrence Sperry, inventor of the Sperry Messenger plane, demonstrated to movie cameramen and newspaper photographers his latest sport—ski-planing. It's a near relative to aquaplaning, only one uses an airplane and a pair of skids instead of a motor boat and water sled. Spectators crowded the links of the Cherry Valley Golf Club this afternoon and watched boys of the neighborhood being towed on skis across the snow-covered inclines of the golf park by the diminutive Messenger plane. At times the skiers were swept along at a speed of more than sixty miles an hour.

Sperry succeeded in holding his airplane as low as five feet above the earth as he sped along the course, but was forced to rise higher when approaching the grove that lines the outer bounds of the club's property. The skiers would release their hold on the ropes tied to the wings and tail skid of the plane as they approached the trees.

To demonstrate the unusual qualities of the small plane Sperry went down the side of a forty-foot embankment, almost perpendicular, without turning over. The machine was outfited with skids during the demonstration.

A more significant development for aviation was "Project Zodiac: Experiments Carried Out by Lawrence B. Sperry Under Contract for United States Air Service Division, U.S. Army 1922–1923." This project realized Lawrence's dream of making midair contact between "parasite" and "mother" airplanes for purposes of midair refueling, carrying of short-range aircraft by longer-range aircraft for observation and tactical missions over extended ranges, and carrying of a remote-controlled pilotless aircraft by a mother aircraft. It was in connection with this project that a number of Lawrence's Messenger aircraft were converted to pilotless, radio-controlled aerial torpedoes or guided missiles.

The idea of the "skyhook" or "aerial trapeze" had been germinating in Lawrence's mind since the 1918 experiments that the U.S. Navy had undertaken to effect a contact in the air between the dirigible airships *Akron* and *Macon*.

"None of the 1918 experiments," wrote Richard K. Smith of the United States Naval Institute in Annapolis, "contemplated the airplane's returning to the airship; a means for retrieving the airplane on board the flying aircraft carriers had to wait upon the genius of Lawrence B. Sperry."

Lawrence mounted a hook on the upper wing of his Messenger, designing it to engage the bar of a trapeze suspended from the airship. The hook-on apparatus was produced and demonstrated by the spring of 1923. On March 18 of that year, the Sunday *New York Herald* published a spectacular photograph of two planes making contact in the air with Lawrence's skyhook, mounted on his Messenger, latching onto the trapeze of a larger biplane flying about twenty feet above him.

"Playing tag 2,000 feet in the air at sixty-five miles an hour," the caption read; "Lawrence B. Sperry in an eighteen foot Sperry Messenger plane establishing contact with a big De Havilland Six, piloted by Lt. Clyde V. Finten, in a series of aerial tests at Mitchel Field."

Below this photo was another of Lawrence and Lieutenant Finten, both in full flying fig: "Principals in the contact tests for airplanes in the clouds."

The *Aeronautical Digest* confirmed this information in its April issue, featuring photos of the Messenger and De Havilland planes and reporting that they had "touched one another eight times while in flight at Mitchel Field, L. I. to demonstrate how messages and fuel could be exchanged high above the earth."

Another photo showed Lawrence in his flight regalia standing next to his Messenger plane on the ice of Great South Bay and reported that this first successful coupling of planes in the air had involved the use of Lawrence Sperry's hook in conjunction with a twelve-foot metal ladder swung from the De Havilland plane. Captain Eddie Rickenbacker, who had watched this historic exploit from the ground, is alleged to have said, "It's a wonder Lawrence didn't just climb up that ladder."

The thought had undoubtedly entered Lawrence's mind, but this time he consented to limit himself to the phases he had outlined in his contract with the U.S. Army. In the initial phase his Sperry Messenger liaison aircraft was equipped with a dummy "touching pole." This was used for making touch-and-go contact during flight with a trapeze suspended from a De Havilland DH-4B. In the second stage, a hook was mounted on top of the Messenger. This enabled the Messenger to hook onto the trapeze and be carried by the mother airplane. Thanks to a secret patented device, the pilot of the Messenger could disengage the hook at any time he chose.

"These first two phases," the official Army report said, "proved conclusively that mid-air contact, mid-air capture and release were feasible. . . . Soon after the Sperry experiments, actual mid-air refuelling was accomplished between two planes."

The *Cyclopedia of American Biography* was more precise: "Lawrence Sperry was the first to successfully accomplish the feat of transferring fuel and other materials from one plane to another in flight when on March 8, 1923 he made contact eight times between his own Messenger plane and an Army De Havilland, piloted by Lt. Clyde D. Finten."

These aerial prodigies did not escape the attention of the air-minded British. In the summer of 1923, Lawrence received an official invitation to bring his Messenger to England, all expenses paid, to demonstrate it for the Royal Air Force.

24

DELIGHTED THAT HIS MESSENGER had attracted international attention, Lawrence booked passage for himself and his
plane on the *Mauretania,* sailing October 30, 1923, from New York
to Southampton.

But how were they going to get the plane to the ship, Father
Sperry wanted to know.

"That's duck soup," said Lawrence, and he flew the Messenger
right down West 53rd Street to the Cunard Line pier, landing on
his newfangled skids in front of the dock.

A policeman attempted to arrest him for violation of a recent city
ordinance that forbade flying over New York at a height of less than
two thousand feet.

"Wait a minute, officer," Lawrence said as he attached ropes to
the plane so they could hoist it onto the deck of the steamer.

The cop wrote out a summons and handed it to Lawrence, while
Father Sperry looked on, mildly perturbed at his son's latest brush
with the law.

The summons ordered Lawrence to appear in court within a
week.

"I've got more important business than that," Lawrence said
airily, handing the ticket to his father. "Take care of it, Dad," he
said. "I suggest you fix it up with our fellow member, Rodman."

Rodman Wanamaker, deputy police commissioner of New York,
and a founding member of the Aero Club of America, was among
the dignitaries seeing Lawrence off.

Elmer Sperry diffidently handed the ticket to Wanamaker, who
had recently ordered "prosecution to the limit as a warning that the
city would not tolerate flying at low altitudes."

By this time, as thousands cheered, Lawrence was in the cockpit
of his plane being swung up onto the aft deck of the *Mauretania,*

amid more than the usual swirls of confetti that celebrated a big New York sailing.

On the pier, Mr. Wanamaker commended the policeman for his vigilance. "But unfortunately," he said, "we do not have a treaty of extradition with Great Britain. The case is closed."

Joining Lawrence on the deck, Winifred and Father Sperry posed for photographers, bidding their blue-eyed boy a fond farewell.

"The *Mauretania* sure is a tremendous roller," Lawrence wrote home, thus confirming the seasick memories of thousands who remember crossings on this elegantly narrow, constantly rocking liner and her sister ship, the *Aquitania*. These boats gave a new dimension to the song "Rocked in the Cradle of the Deep."

"The *Mauretania* sure could use a couple of extra stabilizers," Lawrence added. He passed this opinion on to the captain, at whose table he was invited to sit, but this suggestion went over like a lead balloon, and Lawrence marveled at the capacity of the English to cope with sliding chairs, crockery, and glassware as though nothing were happening, instead of applying a little practical science to the problem.

Socially speaking, sitting at the captain's table was like a temporary elevation to *Burke's Peerage*. Lawrence found himself the object of much attention. Traveling with one's own plane was the greatest of novelties. The Messenger was a conversation piece. Lawrence took all the ladies at his table on guided tours of the plane, allowing them to sit in the cockpit while he explained the controls.

"I've never flown," said Lady Diana Mainwaring, "but with you I'd rather like to try."

Her name was pronounced "Mannering"; the British had odd habits like that, and they tested Lawrence's phonetic spelling method to the limit.

Diana Mainwaring was a vamp. She had the daring new "boyish" haircut. Her bosom had been strapped flat. The waistline of her dress had descended to her thighs and the hemline was at the knee. It was the rage of 1923. She got Lawrence to take her tea-dancing in the Palm Court of the *Mauretania*. The deck, heaving about at a forty-five-degree angle, now to port, now to starboard, was not conducive to dancing. Lady Mainwaring clutched and clung to Lawrence as to a lifebuoy as they staggered around the deck, while the English Salon Orchestra, sawing away imperturbably amid the swaying potted palms, played "Roses of Picardy."

Lawrence was more concerned about the safety of his Messenger. It too was swaying back and forth like a slow-tempo metronome with the incessant rolling of the ship. He spent most of his time checking the hawsers and the wheel blocks that held her to the heaving deck. He sat in a deck chair and heard the North Atlantic wind whining through the struts and wings of his plane and twanging the taut shrouds that held her down.

The Messenger was like a person to him. She wants to fly, and I want to fly, he thought.

On the sixth day out, sea gulls appeared. They followed the *Mauretania* like a perfectly deployed aerial cortege. Each gull seemed conscious of its own air space. Lawrence watched them cleaving the sky with their white wings, gliding at the same speed as the ship, rolling and swooping at will, accommodating themselves to every caprice of the wind. What grace! What freedom! What a lesson in aerodynamics! These birds were masters of every current in the ocean of the air. He longed to join them. He had gone an entire week without flying. The boat was maddeningly slow. Someday I'll fly across this pond, he thought. No one on the *Mauretania* was happier to sight land than Lawrence B. Sperry.

But the British could be difficult, especially with an impetuous aviator who was accustomed to flying when, where, and how he pleased. When the Messenger was lowered onto the pier and rolled down to the roadway at the end of Southampton docks, Lawrence was all set to take off immediately for London. But, as he was about to spin the propeller, a restraining hand was placed on his arm.

"Just one moment, sir."

It was a British bobby, affable, bland, polite, and, thanks to his helmet, a figure of some authority, even taller than Lawrence.

Then Lawrence noticed that there were two other persons to contend with, one in an overcoat and bowler hat and clutching a tightly furled umbrella, the other turned out in full military fig, complete with swagger stick.

"Mr. Lawrence Sperry, I presume," said the civilian, like Stanley encountering Livingstone in darkest Africa.

"Righto," said Lawrence.

"I beg your pardon," the civilian said.

"What for?"

"I am Mr. Parrott of the Avro Aviation Company, and this is Major General Sir William S. Brancker, chief of civil aviation for His Majesty's Ministry of the Air."

"How do you do?" said Lawrence, removing his hand from the propeller and shaking the hands of Mr. Parrott and Sir William. Then, for good democratic measure, he also shook hands with the bobby, who seemed both pleased and taken aback by this unexpected attention.

"How d'you do?"

"How d'you do?"

"Good crossing?" said Mr. Parrott affably.

"Fine. Fine," said Lawrence.

"Don't like the look of the weather," Sir William observed, looking at the sky with an obviously practiced eye. "Cooking up a bit of a blow, I should think.

"So this is the Sperry Messenger," he added. "We know quite a bit about her. Span, twenty feet four; length, eighteen six; empty weight, 581 pounds; dihedral, one and one-half degrees; radial engine, sixty horsepower, air-cooled."

Impressed and gratified by Sir William Brancker's familiarity with the Messenger, Lawrence was thunderstruck by his next remark.

"Now," said Sir William, "we shall have to see if she's airworthy."

"Airworthy!" Lawrence exploded. "Of course she's airworthy. I've flown this baby twenty thousand miles myself."

"Yes, yes, of course," Mr. Parrott said, "but not in *British* air."

This statement left Lawrence momentarily speechless. He stared at Mr. Parrott and Sir William with his blue eyes and put his hand back on the propeller. The only way to show these strange, skeptical Englishmen that the Messenger was airworthy in British air was to take off at once and fly.

Gently but firmly, the bobby again interposed the restraining hand of the law.

"If you will permit me to explain," Mr. Parrott said, "you cannot fly in British air, I mean you *may* not fly until such time as you and your plane have been issued a certificate of airworthiness by the Department of Civil Aviation.

"In England," he added, "we have sane and serious air laws."

Lawrence was becoming annoyed. For one thing, he resented the implication that flying was not a sane and serious matter in America. And he did not like the prissy, sibilant way in which Mr. Parrott pronounced the word *issued*, as though it were two words: *iss* and *you'd*.

Since both Mr. Parrott and Sir William seemed to be on their high horses, Lawrence decided he must mount his. He had a devastating knack of mimicry, and he now adopted the exact, high uvular intonation of Mr. Parrott.

"Mr. Parrott," he said, "I have been *invited* to your country *offiss-ially* by the Royal Air Force to demonstrate the qualities of the Sperry Messenger as a pursuit plane and as an aerial torpedo. There was not the slightest question when this invitation was *iss-you'd* as to the *airworthiness* of the plane. Now, if you will be so kind as to step to one side, I shall be happy to give you an immediate demonstration of airworthiness, both the plane's and mine.

"I had hoped," Lawrence added sarcastically, "to see more of your country than the Southampton Docks."

This show of wit elicited a warm response from Sir William Brancker. He had one regret and one ambition. The 1918 armistice had come too soon to suit him, just two months before he had planned to lead a squadron of planes to bomb Berlin. His ambition was to go to the United States and lecture on aviation. He could see that this young American aviator, high-spirited and thoroughly impatient with the restrictions of bureaucracy, was a man of his own stripe.

"Come, come," he said, touching Lawrence affectionately on the shoulder with his swagger stick, as though he were conferring a knighthood on him. "This is a mere matter of routine. Of course your Messenger is airworthy. We shall simply transport her by truck to the Avro aerodrome at Hamble, grant the certification of airworthiness to pilot and plane, and then you can fly to your heart's content all over England—and Europe too, for that matter."

Lawrence did fly all over Britain and, like every civilized traveler, fell in love with England's green and pleasant land.

"It was necessary to go through a few formalities before flying," he wrote to his parents. "As soon as I got permission, I flew from Southampton to London in 25 minutes. There happened to be a very strong southwest wind. I had never flown in England of course, so I just got a map and it was great fun finding my way to Croydon.

"Croydon is a joy," he went on, "and a wonderful example. I landed there with my ship, and instantly three gas companies wanted to put gasoline—they call it petrol—in my tank. I wanted to go to Harewood Down Golf Club and it didn't take me five minutes to get a map and get the thing straightened out. It is just like touring England in a Rolls Royce. The men assist me with my baggage, and I store my aeroplane for fifty cents a day. Imagine storing a plane in the United States for fifty cents a day! You can buy gasoline at any aerodrome in England.

"When I flew over to Harewood to play golf, the golf people were waving a big American flag to indicate that it was the right club.

"When I stayed at the Golf Club overnight, the Croydon people got on the telephone to inquire if I was coming back, as they were keeping their lights on all night and all their night flying equipment ready for me."

"These English Golf clubs are splendid," he wrote later, after sampling a few more of them. "You can play all through the winter on them, as England does not get as cold generally as the United States. Their putting greens are perfect, as a much finer grass grows on them than we can grow in the United States on account of the burning out in summer time.

"I have seen a great many of the different aeroplane people, and have also had the opportunity of getting better acquainted with the British people, as the last time I was here was during the war, and things were rather upset. The British are surely a great race, and I like the country very much. There is only one thing I have against it, and that is, when you have to go into your bedroom, it is icy cold!"

Lawrence loved the London theater: "I have been to Shakespeare," he wrote. *"Twelfth Night*—and it was wonderfully good. It is almost impossible to believe it was written so far back because of the modern way it is done."

He was doing some business: "The British Air Ministry have made us a definite offer on the aerial torpedo, but it takes a little time to conclude the negotiations because a tremendous election is going on over here, and everybody's time is entirely taken up with it."

The "tremendous election" followed the resignation of Lloyd George's government in 1922 in the face of rising unemployment and the failure of his Liberal government to solve the latest dispute between Greece and Turkey. The Conservative opposition, under Stanley Baldwin and Bonar Law, had withdrawn from the coalition government, forcing Lloyd George to call for a new election.

Lawrence, who had met Lloyd George's campaign manager on the *Mauretania,* was asked to distribute Liberal party leaflets from his Messenger. It was the first time in history that anyone had thought of using an airplane in a political campaign. Jumping at the chance to add a new function to the Messenger's possibilities, Lawrence found himself in the headlines of the *London* and the *New York Times:*

AMERICAN AVIATOR AIDS LIBERALS

LONDON, Nov. 30—Lawrence Sperry, American Aviator, and his "aerial flivver" have been enlisted by the Liberal Party for the election campaign.

Mr. Sperry's aid to the Liberals is due to his friendship with Sir Alfred Cope, ex-Premier Lloyd George's campaign manager, formed during their crossing on the Mauretania. Mr. Sperry awaits orders at Croydon Aerodrome, where he is supplied with campaign literature. On receiving telephone orders he will jump off with leaflets or carry communications to distant constituencies.

In the ensuing outcry from the Conservatives, Lawrence kept his cool. He was, after all, not a politician. He was an aviator—in the empyrean, above all the broils of petty politics. Four days later another news item appeared:

SPERRY OFFERS AID TO CONSERVATIVES

LONDON, Dec. 4—Lawrence Sperry, the American airman, who
has been running aerial errands for the Liberal party's election
campaign, offered his services today to the Conservatives.

Mr. Sperry's friends objected to the American's taking sides in
British politics. He explained that his only interest was to demonstrate how practical his "aerial flivver" was for election purposes,
and he would just as soon see England helping the Conservatives
as helping the Liberals.

The most amusing episode of Lawrence's brief foray into British
politics came when he flew a Liberal candidate, Miss Ursula Williams, to her remote Yorkshire constituency of Annfield Plain. He
packed Miss Williams into the baggage compartment that doubled as a second cockpit, and when the Messenger alighted on
Annfield Plain, a large crowd of farmers and the local gentry came
to hear what Miss Williams had to say from this unusual aerial po-
dium.

In the midst of her speech she was interrupted by a heckler.

"What the hell do you know about farm problems?" shouted
this rude Conservative bumpkin.

"Many things," the candidate replied.

"Well, how many ribs has a pig got?" said the heckler.

"I don't know offhand," retorted Miss Williams, "but if the gentleman will step up on the platform, I shall be happy to count
them."

"No more was heard from that heckler," the *Times* reported.

"That was pretty keen," Lawrence said to Miss Williams as
they took off for London.

Since Lawrence so cheerfully accommodated both sides, the
crushing defeat of Lloyd George and the ruin of the Liberal party
cannot be ascribed to his aerial electioneering. He had not been
involved in such activities since the election of Mary Bacon to the
student presidency of Erasmus Hall.

But he had succeeded in his principal aim: the promotion of the
Sperry Messenger, whose fame now crossed the English Channel
as Lawrence's pictures were published in the newspapers of
France, Holland, and Germany.

French aviation buffs had not forgotten Bezons, and their

monthly illustrated aviation magazine, *L'Aeronautique*, hailed Lawrence's imminent arrival in France. They called him *un pilote hors de pair*, a pilot without equal, and they had obviously kept abreast of his exploits: "Sperry made a point of keeping abreast of all the fine points of airmanship and became celebrated for his landings and takeoffs in streets and public parks, for his first experiment of contact between two airplanes in flight, his pioneer work with detachable landing gear, skids, etc. A remarkable technician, he has created a number of interesting technical innovations, notably the automatic stabilizer and the aerial torpedo."

Invited by both the French and the Dutch to demonstrate the Messenger, Lawrence took off from Croydon Airdrome on the morning of December 13, 1923, for Amsterdam. He told newspapermen he was going to show that the flight could be made on eight gallons of gasoline at a cost of only $2. A group of his English friends and all the mechanics of Croydon were on hand to see him off, together with a movie photographer for Universal Newsreel.

It was a terribly cold day. His cheeks tingling in the frosty air, Lawrence flew south over Tunbridge Wells, the Weald, the patchwork fields of Sussex, sharply defined under a transparent silver glaze of hoarfrost. He dipped low over the historic battlefield of Hastings, glittering with a million tiny needles of frozen dew. Some witnesses thought Lawrence had intended to land there; his wheels nearly touched the ground. Then, banking to starboard, he soared upward and eastward over the Sussex Downs and out to sea, fascinated by the gray waves that spent themselves in fans of white foam on the beaches of Winchelsea and Rye. The Channel was unusually calm, as though the tide had been momentarily frozen in that treacherous Strait of Dover where the North Sea and the surging Atlantic collide in endless struggle.

Lawrence was about three miles out from the Kentish coast, about a thousand feet above the water, when his engine sputtered and stopped. A local coast guard saw the Messenger descend, "as gently as a bird, vanishing briefly in a cloud of mist, before it actually touched the water." The witness proceeded to Rye and gave the alarm. The local lifeboat and a motor launch put to sea, but the mist had thickened and they couldn't find the plane.

At 2:45 that afternoon, almost two hours after Lawrence's perfect water landing, the plane was found two miles from the beach of Rye. Its top wing was on a level with the water.

"It's a wonder we ever saw it," a coast guardsman observed.

The Messenger was towed ashore. It was in perfect condition when they pulled it out of the icy water up onto the ice-encrusted beach. There was no sign of the pilot.

25

WHILE THE BRITISH COAST GUARD began to comb the English Channel from Beachy Head to Broadstairs, the news of Lawrence's disappearance was flashed around the world by wireless, and the Sperry family, back in Brooklyn and Garden City, had the shock of reading it on the front page of the *New York Times* of Friday, December 14, 1923. It was—and remains—an almost hallucinating experience to see those headlines spread out over two columns under the masthead like an epitaph on a tomb:

SPERRY BELIEVED DROWNED IN ENGLISH CHANNEL;
WRECK OF BABY PLANE FOUND, FLIER MISSING
LONDON, Dec. 13—It is feared that Lawrence B. Sperry, the American aviator, has been drowned in the English Channel, says The Daily Mail.

Sperry left the Croydon Airdrome this morning in his small one-seater airplane, intending to fly to Amsterdam, Holland. Coast Guards found the airplane at sea three miles off Rye this afternoon, but no trace of Sperry was seen.

The Coast Guards at Pett, five miles from Rye, saw Sperry about noon flying seaward at a height of about 500 feet. Soon afterward he turned and flew about one mile inland, but after making a wide circle went seaward again.

A workman on shore near Pett says that at 12:50 o'clock he saw the machine crumple and fall into the water. The cause for the fall of the aircraft was not apparent. No flames were observed coming from the machine.

The Coast Guards of Pett notified the guards at Rye, and a lifeboat was sent out. The wrecked machine was recovered and the men searched vainly for four and a half hours for the airman. They found only his air jacket about a mile away from where the machine fell.

A chart and other property marked L. B. Sperry were found

floating near the wreckage. The Coast Guards did not find the engine of the plane, which had apparently fallen out of the machine when it struck the water.

The weather was clear, and there was no wind when the accident happened. Coast Guards all along the coast have been notified and are watching for the body of the aviator. It is believed improbable that the airman was picked up as no boats were near the scene of the accident.

There followed several paragraphs recounting Lawrence Sperry's inventions, adventures with the Messenger, and other exploits, including the facts that his home was in Brooklyn and that "he first attracted attention in 1911, when 17 years old, he built and operated an airplane."

This first newspaper report of Lawrence's disappearance is at variance on numerous points with a more personal account written to Father Sperry four days later by Sir William Sefton Brancker. In the Brancker letter, the weather was not mild, the machine did not "crumple and fall into the water," there was no "wreckage," and the engine was not missing from the machine.

"The machine is in perfect condition in every way," Sir William wrote, "except that I believe the tailplane is slightly damaged through the landing on the water."

Sir William's statement was corroborated by photographs of the Messenger after it was pulled up onto the icy shingles of the beach at Rye. These appeared in the *Sussex Daily News* and the *Illustrated London News* with similar captions: "Practically intact, but with no sign of the airman; Mr. Lawrence Sperry's aeroplane recovered from the sea by Rye lifeboat men." The British license of airworthiness assigned to Lawrence stands out in bold relief on the top wing and the fuselage of the tiny biplane: G-EB IJ; and it is obvious that the tailplane, emblazoned with a huge *G*, is not materially damaged.

"We are examining the engine," Sir William's letter continued, "but the investigation has not been completed. The sea was quite calm at the time, and the weather was very cold. I fear that there is no doubt that your son made a perfect landing on the sea on account of engine failure, and then, as the water poured into the cockpit, climbed on the top of the plane, until he became so numb with the cold that he must have slipped off and been drowned. The local coastguard gave it as his opinion that no one could have existed in the prevailing temperature for as long as half an hour on the aeroplane as it was found floating."

So, from the beginning, there was a certain ambiguity, an air of mystery and speculation about the disappearance of Lawrence Sperry. The suspense and the speculation continued for a month. It was front-page news:

NO TRACE OF SPERRY; PLANE FOUND INTACT

the *New York Times* reported on December 15.

Machine Landed Neatly in the
Calm Sea and He Could
Have Clung to It

MAY HAVE TRIED TO SWIM

Hunt is Abandoned, but His
Wife and Friends Here Are
Still Hopeful

LONDON, Dec. 14 (Associated Press)—Up to a late hour tonight no trace had been found of Lawrence B. Sperry, the American aviator whose "baby" airplane was found in the waters of the English Channel yesterday three miles off Rye.

P. R. Jackson, London manager of the Sperry Company, returned tonight from Rye, where he had gone when word reached him that the aviator was missing, reporting that an all-day search had failed to find the body and that searching parties had abandoned their attempts. The plane, which has been towed into Rye, is believed by Mr. Jackson to be in satisfactory condition.

Mr. Jackson is at a loss to account for the disappearance of Sperry, as the plane evidently landed on the water neatly. It was in an upright position when first sighted, the lower plane and tail being awash. He believed it would have been an easy task for Sperry to climb onto the upper part of the plane or hang onto the sides, as the sea at the time was perfectly calm.

A lifeboat reached the plane an hour and a half after the accident and made a search of the vicinity but there was no trace of the aviator.

Mr. Jackson is inclined to the belief that the missing airman attempted to swim around to the tail, but became so numbed by the cold water that he was unable to climb up or hang on. He thinks it impossible that Sperry jumped from the plane, on account of its position in the water, or that the body was washed out of the pilot's seat.

At this point an inevitable question arises: on what basis did Mr. Jackson think it impossible that Lawrence jumped from the plane, since Jackson saw the plane empty only after it had been towed to Rye? Apparently it did not occur to anyone to experiment with the plane, to see if it would sink or stay afloat under a man's weight.

To continue with the AP dispatch:

Sperry, just before he set off yesterday, told a newspaperman he expected to fly to Amsterdam on eight gallons of gasoline and to return to London on Monday, making the round trip at an expense of little more than two dollars.

The trip was neither for pleasure nor experimental, but was for business purposes, he explained.

"I am surprised that English businessmen do not make greater use of flying, now that it is so economical," said Mr. Sperry. "They could fly their own planes to any one of the important Continental cities at less than the railroad fare and in one-fifth of the time."

Saw Sperry in Difficulties

HASTINGS, England, Dec. 14 (Associated Press)—Detective Inspector Milton, who was shooting game on the coast at the place where Lawrence B. Sperry flew seaward, says that the aviator's engine was running badly just before the plane disappeared from view. Sperry, according to Milton, circled at a low altitude, apparently seeking a suitable landing place, but finally decided to venture oceanward.

"As I was on leave yesterday," said Milton, "I took the opportunity to have a day's shooting, and went to a place between Fairlight and Pett, near Hastings, where the country is very flat.

"Between noon and 1 o'clock I noticed an airplane coming from inland which held my attention because of the fact that the engine was running very badly, spitting and making a great noise. I was the only person within sight and my view must have been better than anyone's. The plane was quite low and I could distinctly see its number and colors. As the airman came overhead he seemed to get into worse difficulties.

"It circled around twice, and on the first circle was apparently about to land. I was quite sure of this and had started to run toward it when the plane rose and began a second circle. Obviously, the airman was looking for a place to land, but afterward he decided to attempt the sea passage.

"The spot was quite suitable for landing, as the fields there were covered with short grass.

"The engine was still running in fits and starts when the airman turned his machine toward the sea and disappeared over the water into the rather thick mist. I could hear the motor running after the plane had disappeared. It seemed extremely unwise for the aviator to cross alone under such circumstances. I know very little of mechanics but was perfectly convinced it was most unsafe in the state in which the engine of the plane was running.

"So convinced was I that when I reached home I mentioned the subject to my wife and said I should not be surprised to hear that the airman had fallen into the sea. By a curious coincidence a few fields further on I met Constable Hoadley of the Hastings force, who was walking there. He had seen much the same as I had, although not quite so well, as he was not so near. His first words were: 'Wasn't that engine running badly?' "

The ear- and eyewitness report of Detective Inspector Milton raises another query. If Milton admittedly knew very little about mechanics, Lawrence knew a great deal; in fact he was a mechanical genius. If Lawrence's engine was really defective, why did he not land in a field, he who was accustomed to bringing his Messenger safely down on boulevards, in public parks, and on private lawns? The observation that the engine was "spitting and making a great noise" could suggest a blockage of the exhaust, leaking valves, or a faltering magneto. But no one could have been more conscious of these dangers than Lawrence, and, although he was fearless, he was not suicidal. If he really was in mechanical trouble, what lonely, reckless impulse would have sent him out to sea?

This long dispatch ended on a desperately hopeful note:

Mrs. Winifred Sperry refused yesterday to believe that Lawrence B. Sperry, her husband, had been drowned in the English Channel.

"My husband has been through so many things that I do not believe anything serious has happened to him," she said. "I feel he is safe somewhere."

Officials of the Sperry Gyroscope Company were also hopeful.

"Sperry was always prepared for emergencies and never took chances, as commonly believed," said C. O. Jobson, a company official. "He was a strong swimmer and trained in aquatic sports just for such an emergency."

Garden City, where Sperry resided, was stunned by the cable dispatches indicating he might have been drowned in the English Channel. Just before leaving for England Mr. and Mrs. Sperry gave a dance at the Cherry Valley Club, attended by scores of his friends in aviation circles. They all wished him good luck on his trip to England.

Sperry kept his miniature plane in tip top shape and daily used it to commute to work in Farmingdale and New York, as if by automobile. Each morning about 8 o'clock his motor could be heard overhead and his neighbors could almost set their watches by the time he took off. At night he would alight in a little field hardly big enough to navigate a truck comfortably.

Last Winter he initiated the sport of airplane skiing at the local country club, towing several sportsmen behind his plane, as well as children on sleds.

The days passed slowly. Contrary to the December 15 report that "searching parties had abandoned their attempts," the search was widened and intensified.

STILL HOPEFUL FOR SPERRY

the *Times* headlined on December 16:

Friends Here Think He May Have
Been Picked Up by Ship

It was said at the offices of the Sperry Gyroscope Company at 40
Flatbush Extension, Brooklyn, yesterday that hope had by no
means been given up for Lawrence Sperry, whose Messenger
plane was found floating in the English Channel together with its
pilot's coat. The British Air Ministry and Coast Guard are co-
operating with the French authorities and it is held extremely
likely that Sperry was picked up by some ship without wireless.

If Mr. Sperry came down to get his bearings, he would doubtless throttle the engine, said the officials. In a large plane with at
least six cylinders there would in this case be a fairly continuous
roar. It was doubtless this sound which to the observer seemed to
be lacking. A three-cylinder motor, throttled down, might fire
somewhat irregularly for a time, whereas there might be nothing
seriously wrong at all.

This would seem to indicate the most logical reasons for
Lawrence's hesitation about landing and subsequent decision to
cross the Channel; he must have throttled the engine and been
satisfied that he had things under control before heading out to
sea.

Three days had now passed since the first news of Lawrence's
disappearance. On December 17, still clinging to the hope that
her husband had been picked up by some small ship without a
wireless, Winifred accompanied the Sperry family to Mitchel
Field, where they occupied a box at an air show celebrating the
twentieth anniversary of the Wright Brothers' first flight. The
family sat silently in their box, their faces like masks of self-con-
trol. Only one stunning, physiological change betrayed the desperate burden of anxiety that weighed them down: Zula's hair had
literally turned white overnight.

Winifred had decided to take young Lawrence with her. Her
four-year-old son had not been told that his father was missing.
He sat with the family, his eyes riveted on the sky as the pilots of
the National Aeronautics Association flew in formation to mark
this anniversary, proclaimed as Aviation Day.

"Look," Lawrence shouted, "those are Daddy's planes!"

The boy recognized the familiar silhouettes of three Sperry

Messengers which led the squadron of planes, wheeling and dip-
ping like birds in honor of the Wrights.

"And there's the Sperry-Verville Racer," Lawrence yelled.

He was very excited. Why did the rest of the family look so solemn?

Two groups of Martin bombers flew above the stands. Then the
De Havillands roared by, the biggest planes in America.

"Here come the Messengers again," the boy said, as the three
tiny sports planes volplaned down and flew over the crowd.
"Those are my father's planes," he said proudly.

"Yes," Winifred said, "those are your father's planes."

"When he comes home I'll fly with him. I can, can't I?"

"Of course you can," his mother said. "When he comes home.
He will be so pleased."

The Aviation Day flyover was written up in the *Times* next day
with comparisons between the 30-mile-per-hour speed of the first
Wright plane and the astonishing 266 miles per hour attained by
the Sperry-Verville Racer.

At the bottom of the column there was a smaller headline:

Airplanes to Search for Sperry
HASTINGS, England, Dec. 16—During the weekend coast guards
kept a sharp watch between here and Dungeness for the body of
Lawrence B. Sperry, the American aviator who disappeared last
week when his plane fell in the English Channel. A search along
the coast will be made tomorrow by men in airplanes.

The continuing search was reported now in a series of daily
bulletins:

Continue Search for Sperry
LONDON, Dec. 17—The Coast Guards along the English Channel and other agencies are continuing their search for Lawrence B.
Sperry, but so far without being able even to determine the cause
for the fall of his baby airplane into the Channel last week or obtain any further clue to the airman's fate. P. R. Jackson, London
manager for the Sperry firm, declared today he had no idea of
abandoning the search until every hope was exhausted.

Every hope was finally exhausted twenty-five days later on January 11, 1924. On January 12 the *New York Times* gave the news in the center columns of its front page:

Sperry's Body Is Found on Channel Coast;
Brooklyn Aviator Identified by Clothing

LONDON, Jan. 11—A body believed to be that of Lawrence Sperry, the American aviator who has been missing since his plane was lost in the Channel on Dec. 13, was washed up by the sea between Dungeness and Rye, in Sussex today. P. R. Jackson, representative here of the Sperry Gyroscope Company, who saw the body this afternoon, said it was Sperry's, judging from the build and the clothing.

The body was found on the beach about 120 yards from the high-water mark and the clothing included trousers, waistcoat, undervest, silk shirt and two pairs of socks, all bearing the name of a New York firm. A few one pound notes were in the pocket of the waistcoat.

At the office of the Sperry Gyroscope Company in Brooklyn, Vice President Charles S. Doran stated yesterday that the family of Lawrence Sperry were convinced it was his body that was washed ashore in England. Edward Sperry, a brother, will leave today on the Majestic to bring the body home.

Mr. Doran told of two cables received from Mr. Jackson in London giving a description of clothing on the body. Elmer A. Sperry, head of the firm and father of Lawrence, saw the cablegrams and went to his home at 1505 Albemarle Road in Flatbush, positive of the identification. The news was also conveyed to the airman's widow, now ill in the Peck Memorial Hospital.

Lawrence Sperry lost his life on Dec. 13 in an attempted flight from England to Holland. A workman reported seeing Sperry's machine, a twenty-foot "flivver," crumple and fall into the Channel. Coast guards found his airplane at sea, and since that time a search has been made for his body.

One of Sperry's greatest achievements in the field of military aviation was his development of the aerial torpedo. He was a pioneer in the field of aviation, and one of its most brilliant inventors, in spite of his youth. He was the first to take a woman passenger aloft over New York and the Statue of Liberty, the first to loop the loop in a hydroplane, the first to land in city streets, the first to experiment in night flying, was a pioneer in parachute development, and the first to make contact in the air with another plane.

26

EVEN BEFORE EDWARD SPERRY identified his brother's sea-changed body, newspapers and magazines prepared their eulogies, and letters of condolence reached Brooklyn and Garden City from the farthest corners of the world. The obituaries and letters deepened the mystery that still cloaked Lawrence's death.

What really happened and how did it happen to "this truly extraordinary contributor to the history of aviation, an expert pilot with over 4,000 flying hours, much of it devoted to risky testing of experimental equipment"?

How, on a calm day and over a calm sea, could such a thing have happened to "one of the most brilliant figures in aviation of his era, a man who, with his auto pilot, had flown consistently in weather no other pilot would attempt"?

The magazine of the U.S. Air Services posed such questions in its issue of January 1924, prefaced by an editor's note: "At the time of going to press all efforts to find a trace of one of America's most dashing, capable, and lovable aeronautical men have failed."

"From all facts so far gathered," the writer, O. B. Whitaker said, "it would appear that his life was not lost due to any misapplication of his remarkable air senses, but that he was apparently forced down by some mechanical failure of his equipment; and even under these adverse circumstances he apparently accomplished a good landing. When his machine was reached by a rescue party it was found that the top wing of his small biplane was practically awash which would indicate that he had got wet upon landing and, not seeing any aid putting off from shore and after waiting a reasonable length of time, that he stripped off his excess clothing and endeavored to swim in, but succumbed to the chill of the water and possible adverse currents for which the English Channel is famous. The fact that he was a powerful swimmer and practiced aquatic feats in preparation for just such an emergency lends considerable strength to this theory.

"Lawrence, as he was familiarly known by even those who had never come personally in contact with him, was a flyer whose air instincts rivaled even those beings whom God naturally endowed with facilities for flying. His directional and stability senses were developed almost beyond comprehension and he practiced 'stunts' which many people believed to be 'dare-devilish,' but a more intimate acquaintance with Lawrence indicated at once that it was not his ambition to be spectacular. His main concern in doing these things was to prove or disprove theories regarding various flying conditions and to popularize flying.

"If a plane crashed from some peculiar and unknown cause, Lawrence invariably endeavored to find a solution by putting his plane through manoeuvers as nearly as possible parallel to those causing the crash. It was in this way that he aided in gathering much valuable data for the use of aviators in bringing their planes out of precarious attitudes. He was known, in at least one or two cases, to seek permission of Army flying officials to be permitted to fly a plane exactly duplicating, in all respects, one which had recently crashed from some unknown cause. With these planes he would prove to his own satisfaction the cause of the casualty, barring, of course, the mechanical failure of some vital part."

A mechanical failure: that was the most likely reason. But there was no Lawrence to succeed Lawrence in duplicating the conditions of his last accident.

While the British Air Ministry continued its autopsy of the sixty-horsepower Lawrence radial engine, fresh speculation about the cause of Lawrence's death was stirred by an unexpected letter to his mother, from Mrs. A. D. Miller, the woman in Taylorstown, Pennsylvania, who had taken care of Lawrence after his crash landing on her property in July of 1923.

The letter, semiliterate but full of sensitivity, touched Zula deeply. It is undated:

Taylorstown Pa

To the Mother of Larance B. Sperry
Dear Mss Sperry.

No doubt you will be surprised to get a Letter from one you have never seen and perhaps never herd from But we had the pleasure of Intertaning your Son. Last July when he was flying on his way to Daton Ohio and when he was pasing over our little town he had trouble with his Plain and Became very Sick and had to Land Just a Little ways from our homr. My Husband was the first to get to him and we Invited to our home to stay until he would gett better and get his Plain fix we had the Pleasure of having him for a week and during that time we became grate friends and O Mss Sperry I cannot tell you how sorry we are to hear of his ofle Death it has caused you the Loss of a Good Son Because he must have Been one or he could not have been so nice in our home he spoke of you and his Wife and Babbies so often we feal we have Lost a good friend and Mss Sperry I could not help But rite to you. We have watched every Paper hoping to hear that he has been found alive Mr. Sperry made friends with every one he came in contact with while in our Little Town. God Bless his Wife and his Dear Little Children and Mss Sperry if you feal you can I would like to hear from you and of what you can tell us of your Son. we are so sorry for All you people But we all have our Troubl. But I feal that God Is with you and will put his Arm about you and Comford you so no one Elce can. Dear Mss Sperry I must bring this to a close so when you are reading it you will know it is from Stranger to you. But friend of your Son and ones who thought a goode eal of him

> With Love to the family
> Mrs. A. D. Miller

Zula's reply cannot be found, but Mrs. Miller's answer to it was dated January 3, eleven days after Lawrence's disappearance and eight before the finding of his body.

My Dear Mss Sperry.

Just reseaved your very welcome Letter and will try to an it and tell you all I know about what caused Mr Sperry Illness when with us. he sayed after he Passed over Washington Pa. he Discovered his Plain was not working very good and that he had ran out of Oil and the Fumes from the Plane was making him very sick and he thought he was going to faint and would have to Land soon or his Plane would be on fire so he made the Landing All right. and so I told you in My Letter that Mr. Miller was the first to get to him he found him a very sick Man and of corse got a Dr right away the Dr Said he was overcome with the Fumes from the Plane so we broughted him to our home and did all we could for him but Mss

Sperry I do not know what caused them But Mr Sperry would take weak Spells and would have to Lie down where ever he was one day he was Siting talking to Mr. Miller in the Dineing Room and took one and he Layed down on the flor. I ask him if he was sick and he sayed no Just Weak and I wanted to do some thing for him but he sayed he would be all righ a Little while and he took them several times when working with the Plane and had to Lye down on the Grass. He did not seem sick But just weak. Mr Miller would not let him walk over to the Plain and took him in the Machane I was so worried the day he Left hear for fear he would not Land home safe But he send us a Litter stating that he Landed O.K. and I cannot tell you how glad we were to hear from him and that he was all right. Mss Sperry we have no Children and of corse I do not know what the Wonderful Love is and what it is to loose one But I have Lost Both Father and Mother My Mother Just a few days before Mr Sperry was hear so I know what you are Passing through you have our Deepest Sumpethy in your Sad house if it had not Been for the Faith I had in God and Gods word I could not have stood it when I lost my Mother we all have these Sad Hours but it seames to me your is so Sad But God gives us that Wonderfull Promis that where he is ye may Be Also—and while you do not have your son with you hear you know he is waiting for you on the other side.

Mss Sperry you did not say Wheather you had found any trace of your son or not if you have would you care to Let us know we get al the papers we can to see if there is anything in them about him Being found But have not been able to see any thing I have some Pictures that was taken of him and his Plan when hear and whin I get them finished will send you them well Mss Sperry I think I have told you all I know about his Illness when hear—and sometimes I wonder if he had taken one of those Weak Spells and that was the cause of his Death of corse we will never know. . . .

Mrs. Miller's speculation that a spell of weakness may have caused Lawrence's death was shared by Lawrence's father, who, surprisingly enough, given his scientific spirit, appears to have turned Mrs. Miller's conjecture into a theory. On January 3, 1924 (Lawrence's body still had not been found), Father Sperry wrote to Maj. L. W. McIntosh, a friend of Lawrence's at McCook Field in Dayton:

"We are not at all sure that the engine was working badly. On one other occasion, after experiencing night after night of hospitality, Lawrence has been known to be taken sick in the air and forced down immediately, making quite a wonderful landing by side slipping, smashing up some, and taking a week in which to recover. This was down in Washington County, Pennsylvania, an incident in his life that he never told anyone about, not even his wife. It would never have come to light had not the mother of the lovely family that took care of him written a wonderful letter of condolence to Lawrence's mother. The swinging in towards the shore makes me think that he was again taken with one of those attacks, but that he felt somewhat better and changed his mind, thinking that he could go another 25 miles before he was compelled to come down.

"Someone has expressed it that the poor fellow was caught in an inextricable trap between two 'lows'—low, almost negligible buoyancy of the little plane and very low temperature of the water. The plane was found with only about 4 inches of the tail sticking out, and the top wing level with the surface of the water. It was very difficult to pick up and almost a wonder that they found it at all."

There is a mystery and ambiguity in this letter too. The phrase "smashing up some, and taking a week in which to recover" is totally at variance with the information in a letter written to Father Sperry himself on January 14, 1924, by an eyewitness of Lawrence's landing in Taylorstown, a woman named Mary W. Crocthers.

"I can well believe your son made a perfect landing on the water," she wrote. "I shall never forget the perfect landing he made in our field, above the house. The plane seemed to come so close to our house and the top of the trees that I asked him if he thought he was going to strike the house—and the look of amusement when he said, 'Not for one minute, I knew exactly how I was going to land.' And afterward in looking at the plane I could see how well he had landed. Just above where the plane stopped was a row of sugar maples—one had died and been removed, leaving a space, and the plane just went right through that opening. When we arrived at the machine he had climbed out and was lying in the shade under one wing. A doctor was with us and soon had a stimulant ready for him—and he was soon up trying to get the plane started."

How curious, in the light of this letter, that Father Sperry ascribed Lawrence's convalescence in Taylorstown as a recovery from a smash! Perhaps he was thinking of those crash landings in the past, so numerous that Grover Loening, in an access of hyperbole, said that Lawrence had "broken every bone in his body at least twice!"

Even more curious, psychologically, was another theory that the senior Sperry seems to have accepted about his son's death. The source of the information on which the theory is based remains unknown. But Father Sperry propagated the idea in a letter written on April 3, 1924, nearly seven weeks after Lawrence's funeral, to Howard E. Coffin in Detroit, a colleague of Lawrence's in the Air Service Reserve Corps.

"My dear Howard," the old man wrote, "little did we think when we saw Lawrence at St. Louis that his end was so near. It seems it all came from being entirely misdirected as to how to reach Dover from the Croydon airdrome. He was simply told to follow the railroad. That is one of the menaces of people who are not 'oriented,' as I put it. This instruction should have been accompanied by the statement that at one point this railroad goes through a long tunnel, and just at that point a branch of the line bears off to the right, which branch should not be followed as it leads to a very wide, unfrequented part of the Channel. It seems all crossings are made at Dover, where fast motorboats with observers are in readiness on either side. Poor Lawrence went down and mistook Hastings or some other town for Dover, and finally started across where there was no hope of his being rescued."

This idea, born of wishful thinking and a perhaps unconscious impulse to assert parental criticism and control even beyond the grave, is patently absurd. Up to that point in the history of aviation, no one had done more for aerial cartology than Lawrence Sperry. He knew the importance of maps and could certainly tell the difference between Hastings and Dover. "Poor Lawrence": Is there something unconsciously patronizing in that? The implication is clear: this brilliant, dash-and-bang Icarus would not have come to grief if Daedalus had been there to guide him, to save him from the "menace" of not being "oriented."

This is not to imply that Elmer Sperry was in any way untouched by the death of the son who most resembled him and who most opposed him.

"He never really got over Lawrence's death," Preston Bassett said. "And neither did Zula."

A laconic entry made every December 13 in Elmer A. Sperry's diary records his almost speechless grief: "the day Lawrence was lost."

So much of the speculation about that loss seems to have been animated by a desire to reverse it, to have rewritten the scenario of his life so that he would not have died in his thirtieth year at the height of his powers. *If* he had landed on terra firma at Hastings, *if* he had not followed the wrong railroad track, *if* he had lashed himself to the plane, things would have been different.

Speculation could not alter the irrevocable fact of death. On April 15, 1924, after an exhaustive examination of the engine of what the papers called the "death plane," the British Air Ministry issued its official report. "BLAMES SPERRY'S ENGINE," the *New York Times* announced:

> English Air Ministry Finds Its
> Failure Caused American Flier's Death
> LONDON, April 15—The result of the investigation made by the
> Air Ministry's Inspector of Accidents into the cause of the death of
> Lawrence B. Sperry, the American aviator who fell with his air-
> plane into the English Channel on Dec. 13 last and was drowned,
> was announced by the Ministry today. The announcement read:
> "The pilot was forced to alight in the sea owing to the complete
> failure of his engine. He was subsequently drowned in an attempt
> to swim ashore. The failure of the engine was due to warping and
> the consequent seizure of the valves of the top cylinder, followed
> by a displacement of the tappet rod."

The Messenger did not sink but remained half submerged under the combined weight of Lawrence and the water that engulfed the cockpit. The temperature of that water was a blood-congealing forty degrees Fahrenheit. The air temperature on that

December day was thirty-two, precisely freezing. It was a fatal combination. There must have been a few moments of agonizing indecision as Lawrence's hands and feet became numb. His clothes were soaking wet and beginning to stiffen with the cold. With no help in sight, he must have peeled off his fleece-lined jacket, unlaced his shoes with fingers that had almost lost their feeling, and started to swim for shore. It probably never occurred to him that he would not make it. He was a swimmer of legendary strength, but he was now the victim of hypothermia, the lethal lowering of the body's inner temperature. In a few minutes the violent, involuntary shuddering and shivering began: the body's desperate automatic effort to restore its warmth. That effort itself involves a cruel loss of energy, and the heat loss continued. As the core temperature continued to drop, Lawrence's brain became numb and the motor control of his beautifully coordinated body failed. His arms and legs, unbearably heavy now, refused to respond to his will. The vision of the distant shore, the frosty fields, the frozen shingles of the beach, the gleaming ice-white cliffs, flickered, faded, darkened, then vanished altogether as the light of fierce determination was finally extinguished in a pair of blue eyes. Doctors have confirmed that no man could survive immersion in that cold water for more than half an hour, not even Lawrence Sperry. It is said to be a merciful death, as painless as it is sudden, an almost soporific heaviness, a feeling of overwhelming weariness, then the blackout of the long and dreamless sleep.

27

AS FOR WINIFRED SPERRY, home they brought her airman dead, in a glass-lined walnut coffin. The love of her life: her Nordic prince.

"It's best not to see him, Winnie," her dead husband's brother said.

She agreed. The casket was sealed.

She spent a few minutes with it alone with her children, Lawrence Jr., four, and Winifred, two, before the public was admitted to the Protestant Episcopal Cathedral of the Incarnation in Garden City.

In the beautiful low voice in which she had so often read Lawrence to sleep, she recited one of their favorite poems—for herself and their children.

> Count me not with those who whine for what is over—
> All that once was good is good for evermore.
> All we had of joy endures, a joy within us;
> All the rest of life is lovelier for years before.

"When will we see Daddy?" young Lawrence wanted to know.

"Always in your mind's eye," Winifred said, "every time you see an aeroplane, you'll think of him. He'll be with you. All your life."

"She was perfectly marvelous," Father Sperry said. "The way she stood up to it filled everyone with wonder and admiration."

Now men and women in black thronged into the cathedral, and voices resounded in the Gothic vaults, celebrating the ultimate mystery of death, so that the lilies, the flickering tapers around the coffin, the swelling, melancholy music of the organ became an affirmation of the brief, bittersweet beauty of life.

"Nothing seems so tragic to the old as the death of one that is young," the minister, Dean Oscar Treder, said. "This proves that life is good."

It was a striking statement, worthy of the great, pathetic, poetic palliatives with which the human race attempts to annul the fact of death.

". . . Though he were dead, yet shall he live: and whosoever liveth and believeth in me, shall never die. . . . So when this corruptible shall have put on incorruption and this mortal shall have put on immortality, then shall be brought to pass the saying that is written, Death is swallowed up in victory. O grave, where is thy victory? O death, where is thy sting?"

Winifred and her children, Father and Mother Sperry, the brothers and sister of the fallen airman sat motionless as figures in a medieval frieze while the minister intoned these ancient consolations.

Apart from their private emotions, the funeral was a public affair. The leaders of world aviation were there among the five hundred people who overflowed the church. There were floral offerings from the Bureau of Aeronautics, the Aero Clubs of Britain and the United States, the Aeronautical Chamber of Commerce, the British Navy, the Mitsui Aviation Company of Japan, the Sperry Gyroscope Company of England, whose wreath depicted the American and British flags, and, perhaps most touching of all—for one can imagine the love that inspired it—a replica of the Sperry Messenger airplane in white and lavender sweet peas, offered by the employees of the Sperry Aircraft Company to their beloved boss.

Two formations of five airplanes from Mitchel Field circled overhead while the choirs sang the hymns of Resurrection: "The Fight is O'er, the Battle Done" and "The Day Thou Gave Us, Lord, Is Ended."

Then the funeral party entered twenty waiting limousines, and the airplanes slowly circled over the cortege, accompanying it fourteen miles to the Brookville Cemetery. Here the aviators dropped hundreds of carnations on Lawrence's grave. The casket was lowered into the earth, Lawrence committed at last to the ground, as the mourners stood at the edge of the grave and heard that final ritual:

"We commit *his* body to the ground; earth to earth, ashes to ashes, dust to dust . . . O Lord, Jesus Christ, who by thy death didst take away the sting of death . . ."

A marble slab was placed over the grave in its pine-hedged plot, carpeted with pine needles, withered oak leaves, and the crimson carnations that had rained down from the sky.

Under Navy wings incised into the marble, the following information was carved:

LAWRENCE B. SPERRY
SON OF
ELMER A. SPERRY
AND ZULA G. SPERRY

———

BORN DEC. 21, 1892
DIED DEC. 13, 1923
AVIATOR AND
ENGINEER
LOST WHILE FLYING OVER THE
ENGLISH CHANNEL

That was the official end of this life, this death.

It continued to be evoked in family memories, in genetic resemblances: the immortality of the bloodstream. Lawrence Jr. became a pilot at nineteen, too late to fly with his father, except in spirit. His mother's assurances in the cathedral proved most accurate.

Then there were the eulogies that were credited by some writers and some members of the Sperry family with helping Winifred to bear the pain of her husband's loss. These memories of Lawrence, treasured in family archives, vary from flights of poetry to the most down-to-earth prose. They have one thing in common: a deep personal feeling and affection for the lost aviator they celebrate. These valedictories help to re-create him in his habit as he lived.

"Always, Lawrence demonstrated his exuberant sense of humor," wrote Sir William Brancker in the British aviation maga-

zine *The Aeroplane*, "and everything he did was to him a huge joke
with a serious purpose behind it. His faith in the future of flying
and in himself was unbounded.

"Recently he came to England, happily ignorant of our sane and
serious air laws, and intended to fly off the roadway of the Southampton Docks to Croydon. He was met on arrival by Mr. Parrott
of the AVRO firm who explained some of our laws to him and accommodated the 'Messenger' at the AVRO aerodrome at Hamble.
Thence, after a little innocent wrangling which resulted in certification of air-worthiness being granted to him and his machine by
the Department of Civil Aviation, he flew to Croydon, did some
excellent business for the Sperry Aircraft Co., flew to play golf, and
flew on missions for both the Liberal and Conservative Parties during the Election. His plans for a European tour were cut short by
his death.

"Lawrence Sperry was a singularly attractive personality. He was
an ardent student of psychology and got immense entertainment
out of studying himself and his fellow men. Sperry discoursing on
the conscious self trying to humbug the subconscious self into a
proper state of obedience was as good as any psychological play.
He was a peculiar combination of the man of ideas and the man of
action.

"The best valedictory to him was spoken by a famous British Aviator in the Aero Club one evening. An older member had la-
mented the death of so young and promising a man. The aviator,
who has lived in suffering for years past, said, 'Can you imagine a
more satisfactory way of going out? He had youth, energy, enthusiasm, faith. He had great schemes ahead with every prospect of success. All his future was as bright as it could be. And then annihila-
tion, no disappointments, no suffering. Finish!'

"It was probably as Lawrence himself would have wished. He
was a good lad, just as agreeably crazy as an aviator should be, and
we will miss him greatly. For him there need be no mourning. All
our sympathy must go to his mother, his father, and his young
wife. And even they have the consolation of pride in all that
Lawrence accomplished in his short and brilliant life."

This personal reminiscence was preceded by a tribute by the editor of *The Aeroplane* which sums up the British view of Lawrence's character and achievement:

TO LAWRENCE B. SPERRY

"In an unusually significant way Lawrence, from early boyhood, was essentially a child of the air. He literally 'ate and drank in' all the myriad aspects of human flight from motive power to the subtleties of wing form, from stability to aspect ratio. He personified the bird man in every wakeful moment and dreamed dreams of the future far beyond the ordinary. Lawrence was a lovable chap while being unusually imbued with the true pioneer spirit. The characteristic feature of his dreams was that no matter how irrational and visionary they might seem at the start, he had the daring and skill to presently transform them into actualities. So, as Kipling says, 'When the thing that couldn't had occurred,' his beloved art had achieved a definite advance and he was exuberantly happy. Thus he lived and thus he died amidst almost bewildering activities, holding to his ideals with intense application, and so crowded very much result into the short span allotted him. Certain it is that the intrepid soul of this boy of the air flies on and on."

The most eloquent of the French obituaries appeared in *L'Aeronautique* in the March 1924 issue after Lawrence's funeral:

La Mort de Lawrence Sperry, Perte Immense
pour l'Aviation

"The death of Lawrence Sperry is an immense loss to aviation. An engineer and inventor of the highest quality, he was one of the lights of American aviation. A peerless pilot, a remarkable technician, he created numerous 'firsts': notably the stabilizer and automatic pilot, the aerial torpedo, detachable landing gear, the first contact between planes, etc.

"A profound philosopher with a charming and happy character, Sperry leaves a void that will not be filled."

This sentence had its echo across the Atlantic in a valedictory by Billy Mitchell, who was one of those most deeply touched by Lawrence's death:

"When Lawrence Sperry was drowned in the English Channel, world aviation lost one of its most brilliant minds, one of its greatest developers, a splendid pilot and airman. In my attempts to develop new adjuncts to air power, I felt Lawrence's loss more keenly than that of any other individual. His loss is irreparable."

The Aeronautical Chamber of Commerce of America made this sense of irreparable loss official in a resolution of January 26, 1924:

"The art and science of aviation represent the mechanical mastery by man over the most difficult and stubborn forces of nature. This science requires for its ultimate achievement sacrifices that are indeed hard to bear—none more so than the loss of Lawrence Sperry with all his name leaves as a stimulating example of the highest order of progress, skill, integrity and enthusiasm.

"The world has lost another great genius and pioneer in aviation whose sacrifice, however, strongly fixes the determination of his associates in aviation to achieve mastery of the elements that have caused so great a loss."

This determination would have warmed the heart of Lawrence, whose loss had left an unfillable void in so many hearts.

Quite apart from the newspaper obituaries, the magazine articles, and the official resolutions, the Sperry family received more than four hundred letters and telegrams of condolence from men as famous as Glenn Curtiss and Henry Ford, from people as obscure as Mrs. Miller of Taylorstown, Pennsylvania.

Anne Lloyd, the poet of Bellport, wrote a poem called "Icarus," dedicated to "Lawrence Burst Sperry, unafraid of death":

> Questing he went, and only sky and sea
>   Bore witness to his passing. Who shall tell
> The secret of his summons? Blest are we
>   Who know it was the hampering sheath that fell,
> And that his fleet-winged spirit now is free
>   To storm the furthest starry citadel.

There were other memorials. The citizens of Farmingdale named the village square Sperry Place in honor of the fallen aviator. At Amityville, Long Island, scene of so many of his pioneering experiments, a plaque was unveiled on the shore of South Oyster

Bay commemorating "Lawrence Sperry's successful demonstration in September 1916, to representatives of the U.S. Navy, of the first Guided Missile—then known as the Aerial Torpedo."

So much for plaques and village squares. Lawrence lived on vividly in the memories of people who knew him, and his widow kept him alive in the minds of their children, Lawrence Jr. and Winifred ("Bam"), who were four and two years old respectively when their father died.

Young Lawrence's only direct memory of his father remains indelible. "I was four," he recalls, "and I was disobeying my father's orders by sliding down the banisters between the third and second stories of our house in Garden City. I lost my balance and fell about twenty feet down the stairwell. Fortunately Bam's perambulator was parked at the bottom. I guess that saved my life. I can still hear the sound of splintering wicker and metal springs snapping as I hit that pram. My father was furious. He was all set to give me a spanking, but my mother intervened.

" 'He was only doing what you would have done at his age,' she told him.

"When she had calmed us both down, my father carried me out into the yard and put me in the cockpit of the Messenger. I remember feeling very insecure. The seat belt was miles too big for me. My father asked me if I wanted to go up with him.

" 'Not in that crate,' I replied.

"I had heard other people call it a crate," Lawrence Jr. remembered, "but I'm sorry I said that now. That 'crate' was the prototype for every subsequent small plane in the history of aviation. In 1928, when I was ten, Clarence Chamberlain made a thirty-thousand-mile air tour of the United States in a Sperry Messenger.

"That same year my mother took me to Paris, and Ambassador Myron T. Herrick pinned a bronze medal on my chest. It had been given by the king of the Belgians, a friend of my father's, and was presented to me 'as a token of the admiration of aviators in all parts of the world for Lawrence Sperry's contributions to the progress of aviation.'

"I was very proud of that medal, but I'm still sorry I didn't fly with my father when I was four. I think he wrote me off as a loss at that moment. And I didn't feel that I had redeemed myself until I got my own wings when I was nineteen. Then it was too late, but I was glad when my mother assured me he would have been proud of me."

Winifred Sperry died in 1943 and was buried next to her husband in Brookville Cemetery.

Going through her effects, Lawrence Jr. came across a volume of Seneca's letters. In it he found a picture of his father, a still from a Universal newsreel, the last photo of him ever taken, as he was leaving Croydon Airdrome to fly across the Channel.

"Full of courage as always," the caption read, "Lawrence Sperry on his last flight."

On the page where the photo was inserted, Winifred Sperry had underlined a passage in one of Seneca's *Moral Letters:*

"Life is like a play; it is not the length but the excellence of the performance that counts. When you stop is not important."

THE PATENTS OF
Lawrence B. Sperry

Patents of
Lawrence Burst Sperry

UNITED STATES PATENT OFFICE

LAWRENCE B. SPERRY, OF BROOKLYN, NEW YORK, AS-
SIGNOR TO THE SPERRY GYROSCOPE COMPANY, OF
BROOKLYN, NEW YORK, A CORPORATION OF NEW YORK

1,239,837   UNIVERSAL CONTROL-HANDLE
            Application filed February 25, 1915
            Serial No. 10,457
            Patented September 11, 1917

1,309,489   DOUBLE-GYRO INCLINOMETER
            Application filed April 18, 1918
            Serial No. 229,467
            Patented July 8, 1919

LAWRENCE B. SPERRY, OF BROOKLYN, NEW YORK, AS-
SIGNOR TO THE LAWRENCE SPERRY AIRCRAFT COM-
PANY, INC., OF NEW YORK, N.Y., A CORPORATION OF
NEW YORK

1,339,006   AEROPLANE HEIGHT-INDICATOR
            Application filed July 13, 1917
            Serial No. 180,268
            Patented May 4, 1920

1,353,544   TWIN-PROPELLER AEROPLANE
            Application filed October 19, 1917
            Serial No. 197,388
            Patented September 21, 1920

LAWRENCE BURST SPERRY, OF MASSAPEQUA, NEW YORK

1,369,139   PARACHUTE AND SAFETY-BELT
            Application filed May 17, 1918
            Serial No. 235,188
            Patented February 22, 1921

LAWRENCE B. SPERRY, OF BROOKLYN, NEW YORK, AS-SIGNOR TO THE SPERRY GYROSCOPE COMPANY, OF BROOKLYN, NEW YORK, A CORPORATION OF NEW YORK

1,378,490   TRANSMISSION-GEARING
            Application filed February 25, 1915
            Serial No. 10,458
            Patented May 17, 1921

1,384,867   AIR-CURRENT INDICATOR FOR AEROPLANES
            Application filed October 9, 1916
            Serial No. 124,448
            Patented July 19, 1921

1,390,653   STEERING DEVICE FOR AIRCRAFT
            Application filed March 24, 1915
            Serial No. 16,721
            Patented September 13, 1921

LAWRENCE BURST SPERRY, OF BROOKLYN, NEW YORK, ASSIGNOR TO THE SPERRY GYROSCOPE COMPANY, OF BROOKLYN, NEW YORK, A CORPORATION OF NEW YORK

1,418,605   AERIAL TORPEDO
            Application filed December 22, 1916
            Serial No. 138,485
            Patented June 6, 1922

LAWRENCE B. SPERRY, OF GARDEN CITY, NEW YORK, ASSIGNOR TO THE SPERRY GYROSCOPE COMPANY, OF BROOKLYN, NEW YORK, A CORPORATION OF NEW YORK

1,433,102   TURN INDICATOR
Application filed May 21, 1920
Serial No. 383,106
Patented October 24, 1922

LAWRENCE B. SPERRY, OF FARMINGDALE, NEW YORK

1,479,013   DISTANCE-MEASURING   INSTRUMENT   FOR AIRCRAFT
Application filed May 5, 1921
Serial No. 467,158
Patented January 1, 1924

LAWRENCE B. SPERRY, OF FARMINGDALE, NEW YORK, ASSIGNOR TO THE SPERRY GYROSCOPE COMPANY, OF BROOKLYN, NEW YORK, A CORPORATION OF NEW YORK

1,521,132   GYROSCOPIC APPARATUS FOR AIRPLANES
Application filed November 25, 1921
Serial No. 517,482
Patented December 30, 1924

LAWRENCE B. SPERRY, OF FARMINGDALE, NEW YORK; THE BANK OF AMERICA, OF NEW YORK, N.Y., AND WIN-IFRED ALLEN SPERRY, OF HEMPSTEAD, NEW YORK, EX-ECUTORS OF SAID LAWRENCE B. SPERRY, DECEASED

1,573,100   MEANS FOR GUIDING AEROPLANES ON THE GROUND
Application filed June 8, 1922
Serial No. 566,702
Patented February 16, 1926

LAWRENCE B. SPERRY, OF FARMINGDALE, NEW YORK, ASSIGNOR TO THE SPERRY GYROSCOPE COMPANY, OF BROOKLYN, NEW YORK, A CORPORATION OF NEW YORK

1,579,670   MEANS FOR DETERMINING RANGE
Application filed April 13, 1921
Serial No. 460,933
Patented April 6, 1926

LAWRENCE B. SPERRY, OF GARDEN CITY, NEW YORK; THE BANK OF AMERICA, OF NEW YORK, N.Y., AND WIN- IFRED ALLEN SPERRY, OF HEMPSTEAD, NEW YORK, EX- ECUTORS OF SAID LAWRENCE B. SPERRY, DECEASED

1,594,478   PARACHUTE
Application filed March 24, 1919
Serial No. 284,755
Patented August 3, 1926

LAWRENCE B. SPERRY, OF MASSAPEQUA, NEW YORK; THE BANK OF AMERICA, OF NEW YORK, N.Y., AND WIN- IFRED ALLEN SPERRY, OF HEMPSTEAD, NEW YORK, EX- ECUTORS OF SAID LAWRENCE B. SPERRY, DECEASED, ASSIGNORS TO WINIFRED ALLEN SPERRY

1,629,978   FLYING BOAT
Application filed July 26, 1918
Serial No. 246,832
Patented May 24, 1927

LAWRENCE B. SPERRY, OF FARMINGDALE, NEW YORK; THE BANK OF AMERICA, OF NEW YORK, N.Y., AND WIN- IFRED ALLEN SPERRY, OF HEMPSTEAD, NEW YORK, EX- ECUTORS OF SAID LAWRENCE B. SPERRY, DECEASED, ASSIGNORS TO WINIFRED ALLEN SPERRY

1,641,700 AIRCRAFT
Application filed October 21, 1922
Serial No. 595,920
Patented September 6, 1927

LAWRENCE B. SPERRY, OF MASSAPEQUA, NEW YORK,
ASSIGNOR TO THE SPERRY GYROSCOPE COMPANY, OF
BROOKLYN, NEW YORK, A CORPORATION OF NEW YORK

1,670,641 MECHANICALLY-PILOTED DIRIGIBLE DEVICE
Application filed April 18, 1918
Serial No. 229, 466
Renewed October 10, 1927
Patented May 22, 1928

LAWRENCE B. SPERRY, OF FARMINGDALE, NEW YORK;
THE BANK OF AMERICA, OF NEW YORK, N.Y., AND WIN-
IFRED ALLEN SPERRY, OF HEMPSTEAD, NEW YORK, EX-
ECUTORS OF SAID LAWRENCE B. SPERRY, DECEASED,
ASSIGNORS TO THE PIONEER INSTRUMENT COMPANY,
INC., OF BROOKLYN, NEW YORK, A CORPORATION OF
NEW YORK

1,697,293 SEXTANT
Application filed September 28, 1923
Serial No. 665,492
Renewed May 22, 1928
Patented January 1, 1929

LAWRENCE B. SPERRY, OF GARDEN CITY, NEW YORK,
ASSIGNOR, BY MESNE ASSIGNMENTS, TO SPERRY GYRO-
SCOPE COMPANY, INC., A CORPORATION OF NEW YORK

1,707,690 AUTOMATIC PILOT FOR AIRPLANES
Application filed September 13, 1919

Serial No. 323,464
Renewed December 13, 1928
Patented April 2, 1929

LAWRENCE B. SPERRY, OF FARMINGDALE, NEW YORK,
ASSIGNOR, BY MESNE ASSIGNMENTS, TO SPERRY GYRO-
SCOPE COMPANY, INC., A CORPORATION OF NEW YORK

1,713,930 PITCH INDICATOR
Application filed April 14, 1922
Serial No. 552,464
Patented May 21, 1929

LAWRENCE B. SPERRY, OF FARMINGDALE, NEW YORK,
ASSIGNOR, BY MESNE ASSIGNMENTS, TO LAWRENCE
SPERRY AIRCRAFT COMPANY, INC., OF FARMINGDALE,
LONG ISLAND, NEW YORK, A CORPORATION OF NEW
YORK

1,716,670 DEVICE FOR LAUNCHING AND LANDING
AEROPLANES FROM AND UPON SUSPENDED
POSITIONS
Application filed June 27, 1922
Serial No. 571,252
Patented June 11, 1929

LAWRENCE B. SPERRY, OF BROOKLYN, NEW YORK, AS-
SIGNOR, BY MESNE ASSIGNMENTS, TO SPERRY GYRO-
SCOPE COMPANY, INC., OF BROOKLYN, NEW YORK, A
CORPORATION OF NEW YORK

1,757,096 GYROSCOPIC PILOT FOR AEROPLANES
Application filed August 1, 1916
Serial No. 112,505

Renewed January 2, 1930
Patented May 6, 1930

LAWRENCE B. SPERRY, DECEASED, LATE OF GARDEN
CITY, NEW YORK, BY WINIFRED A. SPERRY AND BANK
OF AMERICA, CO-EXECUTORS, OF NEW YORK, N.Y.

1,887,335   AUTOMATIC PILOT FOR AIRCRAFT
Continuation of application Serial No. 638,781, filed
March 30, 1923
This application filed November 9, 1929
Serial No. 405,939
Renewed February 17, 1932
Patented November 8, 1932

UNITED STATES PATENT OFFICE.

LAWRENCE B. SPERRY, OF BROOKLYN, NEW YORK, ASSIGNOR TO THE SPERRY GYROSCOPE COMPANY, OF BROOKLYN, NEW YORK, A CORPORATION OF NEW YORK.

DOUBLE-GYRO INCLINOMETER.

1,309,489. Specification of Letters Patent. Patented July 8, 1919.

Application filed April 18, 1918. Serial No. 229,467.

To all whom it may concern:

Be it known that I, LAWRENCE B. SPERRY, a citizen of the United States of America, residing at 1505 Albemarle road, Brooklyn, in the county of Kings and State of New York, have invented certain new and useful Improvements in Double-Gyro Inclinometers, of which the following is a specification.

This invention relates to inclinometers, more specifically to inclinometers of the type employing a rotating wheel or top to establish a reference line and especially adapted for use on aeroplanes.

I have discovered that while a rotating wheel or top will maintain its rotational axis substantialy vertical when the aeroplane, or other device on which the top is employed, is turning in azimuth in the same direction as the top is rotating, the rotational axis of the latter drops out of vertical position when the vehicle is turning in the opposite direction. The last mentioned action renders the device unreliable and under the conditions assumed practically destroys its utility.

While the problem presented under the above assumed conditions might be solved by employing a damping force impressing or other similar means, it should be noted that by the provision of any such means the device would lose its chief characteristic, *i. e.*, simplicity. I solve the problem by employing two oppositely rotating wheels or tops, so that at least one will furnish a true reference line at all times.

Referring to the drawings in which, what I now consider to be the preferred form of my invention, are shown:

Figure 1 is a plan view of the device constructed in accordance with my invention, the cover of one of the gyroscopes being removed.

Fig. 2 is a cross section on approximately line 2—2 of Fig. 3.

Fig. 3 is a diagrammatic view, partly in section and on a smaller scale, of my invention showing the means used to continuously withdraw air from the interior of the casing.

Fig. 4 is a plan view showing the graduations on cover 8.

Each top is shown as comprising a rotor or flywheel 1, having a heavy ring 2 and a cut-out under portion 3. In the center of the top is a point 4 which supports the top

for rotation about a normally vertical axis and at the same time allows the top freedom of movement about both horizontal axes intersecting at said point. While in the common or ordinary form of top the center of gravity is located above the point of support I prefer to so design the tops, employed in my invention, that the center of gravity is located very close to but slightly below the point of support 4. By virtue of this design each top stands substantially in neutral or indifferent equilibrium when at rest whereby a long period of oscillation is secured.

Each top is preferably provided with a spindle 5 which acts as a pointer or indicator, and coöperates with radial graduations 6 and with circular graduations 7 on the transparent covers 8 to indicate both the angle and direction of inclination of the vehicle on which the instrument is mounted. Each cover is secured within a cap 9 threaded into the top of the casing proper 10 or 10', the joint 100 being tightly packed. Illuminating means such as lamps 70 and 71 may be provided, if desired. Each casing surrounds its rotor and supports the same on a post 11 secured to the bottom of the casing. Casing 10, together with companion case 10' are shown as resiliently supported from a ring or frame 12 by means of a plurality of rods 13, 13' and 13'' which are adjustably threaded to said frame and locked thereto by lock nuts 14, the casings being supported on said posts by springs 15 resting on washers 16 or the like. Preferably a downwardly acting spring 17 is placed above said ring and acts between the cap 18 and the ring so that jars will not affect the apparatus. Preferably three such supporting rods are provided for the gyroscopic device. A bracket 72 secured to ring 12 may be used to attach the apparatus to the aeroplane or other vehicle.

For revolving each rotor I prefer to provide means for continuously withdrawing air from the interior of its casing, relying upon the entrance of air into the casing in a proper direction and location to revolve the rotor. For this purpose I have provided valves or other openings 18' 18'' through which the air is exhausted from the casings in any manner, preferably in the manner hereinafter described.

One or more openings shaped in the form

of approximately tangential nozzles 19, 20, 21 and 22, are provided in the casing 10 in the plane of the rotor 2. The rotor in casing 10 is provided with buckets or vanes 23 located in the plane of said nozzle and adapted to receive the jets of air issuing therefrom. Preferably said vanes are formed by incisions in the periphery of the rotor. The casing 10' and its rotor 3 are provided with nozzles 19' to 22' and buckets 23' similar to the corresponding structure of casing 10 and its rotor 3 except that the former extend in a direction opposite the last mentioned nozzles and buckets. Thus the rotors 2, 2 will be rotated in opposite directions.

Each post 11 is shown as comprising a central supporting stem 20 having an axial bore 21 in which is located a spring 22 supporting a rod 23. Said rod is provided adjacent its top with a tapered or concave recess 24 in which the point 4 attached to the top 1 rests. Preferably said recess is flat at the bottom portion 80 at which point the wall 81 is substantially perpendicular for a short distance.

As above stated I employ a plurality of tops 1 and 1' which are driven in opposite directions as indicated by the arrows in Fig. 1. The reason for employing two oppositely rotating tops is, as previously stated, to insure having at least one of the tops correct at all times. For instance, if the aeroplane on which the apparatus was mounted was turning in the direction of arrow C (Fig. 1) top 1', which is shown as rotating in the opposite direction, would have a tendency to flop over, as indicated, while top 1 would remain unaffected. Similarly, if the aeroplane were turning in the other direction, top 1' would straighten up, while top 1 would tend to turn over. The casings 10 and 10' inclosing the two tops may be formed as one or connected by pipe 50. Each casing may be provided with an outlet valve 18' and 18'', which may be connected to the air exhausting device.

For exhausting the air from the casings, I prefer to employ a device 55 somewhat similar to a Venturi tube. Said device may comprise a tubular member with a restricted passage 56 therein, each end of the member tapering outwardly. Fig. 3. If the aircraft is flying in the direction indicated by the arrow a in said figure, the air will flow with great speed through the said tube and restricted passage, thereby reducing the pressure to a marked extent adjacent said passage. At or adjacent said restricted passage is located a second small tube 57 which is connected to the valves 18' and 18'' by means of a pipe 58 having a branch pipe 59. Pipe 58 is shown tapped into tube 57 adjacent a restricted passage 60 therein as indicated in Fig. 3, whereby a double rarefaction of air, so to speak, is produced. By properly manipulating the valves 18', 18'' and a valve 110, provided in the pipe 50 either or both of the tops may be disconnected from the air exhausting device.

In accordance with the provisons of the patent statutes, I have herein described the principle of operation of my invention, together with the apparatus, which I now consider to represent the best embodiment thereof, but I desire to have it understood that the apparatus shown is only illustrative and that the invention can be carried out by other means. Also, while it is designed to use the various features and elements in the combination and relations described, some of these may be altered and others omitted without interfering with the more general results outlined and the invention extends to such use.

Having described my invention, what I claim and desire to secure by Letters Patent is:

1. An inclinometer for aeroplanes comprising a pair of point-supported gyroscopic rotors having normally vertical spinning axes and air turbine means for driving said rotors in opposite directions.

2. An inclinometer for aeroplanes comprising a pair of tops, an inclosing casing for each top, means for withdrawing air from said casings, oppositely positioned buckets or vanes on the tops and a nozzle adjacent each top connecting the interior of the casing with the outside air.

3. The combination with an aeroplane, of a Venturi tube thereon, a casing connected to said tube, a plurality of tops within said casing, buckets or vanes on said tops and openings through the casing adjacent each top and oppositely directed whereby opposite rotation of the tops is secured.

4. In gyroscopic apparatus, the combination with a plurality of rotors, communicating inclosing means for said rotors, a plurality of outlets from said casing at least one for each rotor, means for exhausting air through said outlets and an air admitting nozzle for each rotor.

5. In gyroscopic apparatus, the combination with a plurality of rotors, communicating inclosing means for said rotors, a plurality of outlets from said casing, means for exhausting air through said outlets and means for shutting off that portion of the casing adjacent a rotor from a portion of the apparatus adjacent another rotor.

In testimony whereof I have affixed my signature.

LAWRENCE B. SPERRY.

L. B. SPERRY.
DOUBLE GYRO INCLINOMETER.
APPLICATION FILED APR. 18, 1918.

1,309,489.

Patented July 8, 1919.

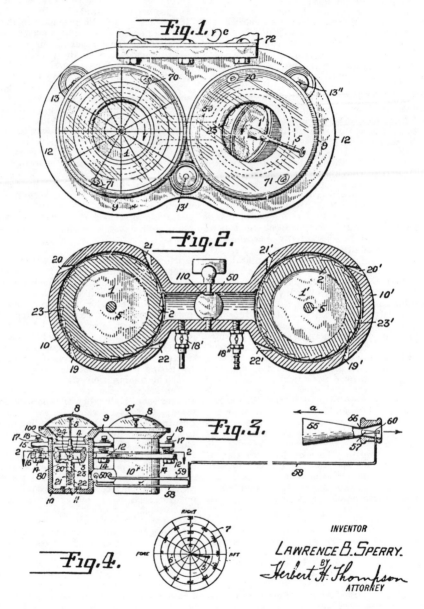

Fig.1.

Fig.2.

Fig.3.

Fig.4.

INVENTOR
LAWRENCE B. SPERRY.
BY
Herbert H. Thompson
ATTORNEY

UNITED STATES PATENT OFFICE.

LAWRENCE BURST SPERRY, OF MASSAPEQUA, NEW YORK.

PARACHUTE AND SAFETY-BELT.

1,369,139. Specification of Letters Patent. Patented Feb. 22, 1921.

Application filed May 17, 1918. Serial No. 235,188.

To all whom it may concern:

Be it known that I, LAWRENCE B. SPERRY, a citizen of the United States of America, residing at Massapequa, L. I., in the county
5 of Nassau and State of New York, have invented certain new and useful Improvements in Parachute and Safety-Belts, of which the following is a specification.

This invention relates to parachutes, and
10 especially to parachutes adapted to the use of aviators in escaping from aeroplanes or other aerial craft.

One object of the invention is to provide a safety belt or support which may be easily
15 put on, and which the aviator cannot fall out of.

Another object is to provide means for insuring the opening of the parachute when falling through the air.

20 Referring to the drawings wherein I have shown what I now consider to be the preferred form of my invention:

Figure 1 is a side elevation of a parachute in its open condition.

25 Fig. 2 is an elevation of the parachute just before opening.

Fig. 3 is a view of the safety belt or support.

Fig. 4 is a view showing a method of ar-
30 ranging the parachute to be placed on the aircraft.

Fig. 5 is a fragmentary detail showing possible points of attachment of the parachute ropes to the parachute body.

35 In the drawings, 1 represents the body or inflation portion of the parachute, having an opening 2 at its top and a cord 3 attached to the top. The lower edge of the body may comprise a strip 4 of comparatively stiff fab-
40 ric which is preferably cut on the bias. The parachute ropes or cords 6 may be secured directly to the main part of the body 1 as at 7, Fig. 5, or to the strip 4 as at 8, Fig. 1. All of the cords 6 are shown as terminating
45 in a ring 9, to which may be fastened a sling 10, shown as comprising a pair of ropes or straps 11 and 12 spread by a member 13. Any suitable means such as snap hooks 14 may be provided on the straps 11 and 12 for
50 attachment to a support 15 adapted to be secured to the body of the aviator.

The said support 15 may comprise a belt 16, a seat portion 17 and a pair of looped members 18 adapted to serve as straps to fit
around the legs of the aviator. The belt 16 55 is preferably provided with a suitable quick locking means, which may comprise a pair of interfitting members 20 and 21, each fastened to one of the ends of the belt and adapted to be locked together by a pin 22. 60 The seat member 17 may comprise a strap of suitable width, fastened at its two ends 24 and 25 to the belt 16. The leg members 18 may be integral with or fastened to the seat strap 17, and while they may be pro- 65 vided with buckles for fastening them around the legs of the aviator, I have shown them as being completely closed. This necessitates stepping into the loops, but affords a saving of time which would other- 70 wise be consumed in securing the buckles. It also lends a greater element of safety to the device by minimizing the number of parts to be fastened, thereby reducing the possibility of some of the parts being inad- 75 vertently or carelessly left unsecured. A pair of rings 26 may be provided on the support for attachment to hooks 14.

The aviator will of course wear the safety belt or support while occupying his place in 80 the aircraft and should be prepared to jump quickly from the craft should occasion require. The parachute should therefore be so disposed that it will follow the aviator with minimum danger of being caught. To 85 facilitate this, the parachute may be folded back and forth as at 27, Fig. 4, and placed within a bag or other container 28. A ring 29 is shown attached to the top of the bag for attaching the same to the aircraft. The 90 bottom of the bag is shown as provided with a opening 30, large enough to pull the parachute through.

When the aviator jumps out of the craft, he will drag the parachute out from the bag. 95 In order to cause the body portion of the parachute to stream out as in Fig. 2 so as to facilitate its opening to the air instead of bundling up and falling unopened to the ground, I prefer to attach the cord 3 at the 100 top of the parachute, to the top of the bag or to ring 29 by means of a light cord 31. This will hold the top part of the parachute back until the weight of the aviator exerts a sudden pull on the said cord 31 and breaks 105 it. The position of the parachute and attached parts will then be as shown in Fig. 2.

The stiffness of the lower edge 4 of the

parachute as well as the biased condition of the fabric will tend to cause the lower part to flare outwardly as shown at 5. This will cause air to enter the parachute and force it open.

In accordance with the provisions of the patent statutes, I have herein described the principle of operation of my invention, together with the apparatus, which I now consider to represent the best embodiment thereof, but I desire to have it understood that the apparatus shown is only illustrative and that the invention can be carried out by other means. Also, while it is designed to use the various features and elements in the combination and relations described, some of these may be altered and others omitted without interfering with the more general results outlined, and the invention extends to such use.

Having described my invention, what I claim and desire to secure by Letters Patent is:

1. In a parachute, an inflation portion, a strip of diagonally cut fabric secured along the edge thereof and cords attached thereto.

2. In combination, a parachute, including an inflation portion, a strip of diagonally cut fabric secured along the edge thereof, a plurality of cords attached thereto and a belt member attached to said cords.

3. A device for suspending an aviator from a parachute, comprising a belt portion adapted to be placed around the waist of the aviator, means for locking said portion in closed position, a seat strap attached to said belt portion and a pair of looped members attached to said strap and adapted to fit around the legs of the aviator.

4. A device for suspending an aviator from a parachute, comprising a belt portion adapted to be placed around the waist of the aviator, means for locking said portion in closed position, a seat strap attached to said belt portion, and means for attaching said device to the strings of a parachute.

5. In a parachute, an inflation portion, a strip of diagonally cut stiff or coarse fabric secured along the edge thereof for tending to open said inflation portion and cords attached to said parachute.

6. In a parachute, an inflation portion, the edge of said portion comprising a strip of biasly cut fabric and a plurality of cords attached to said portion.

7. In a parachute, an inflation portion, an edge piece on said portion comprising a strip of biasly cut coarse fabric, a plurality of cords attached to said edge and a common attaching means on said cords.

In testimony whereof I have affixed my signature.

LAWRENCE BURST SPERRY.

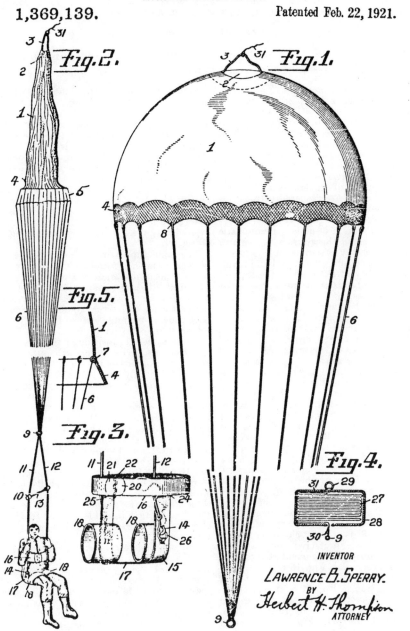

Fig.2.

Fig.5.

Fig.3.

Fig.1.

Fig.4.

INVENTOR

LAWRENCE B. SPERRY.

BY

Herbert H. Thompson

ATTORNEY

UNITED STATES PATENT OFFICE.

LAWRENCE BURST SPERRY, OF BROOKLYN, NEW YORK. ASSIGNOR TO THE SPERRY
GYROSCOPE COMPANY, OF BROOKLYN, NEW YORK. A CORPORATION OF NEW YORK.

AERIAL TORPEDO.

1,418,605.　　　　Specification of Letters Patent.　　**Patented June 6, 1922.**

Application filed December 22, 1916.　Serial No. 138,485.

To all whom it may concern:

Be it known that I, Lawrence B. Sperry, a citizen of the United States of America, residing at 1505 Albemarle Road, Brook-
5 lyn, in the county of Kings and State of New York, have invented certain new and useful Improvements in Aerial Torpedoes, of which the following is a specification.

This invention relates to means whereby
10 all of the controls of an aeroplane, dirigible balloon or the like are rendered entirely automatic whereby an operative automobile aerial torpedo may be produced. In carrying out my invention I employ an automatic
15 device for steering the aircraft in azimuth which is preferably of a gyroscopic nature, a means for maintaining the lateral and longitudinal stability of the craft if the type of craft used is not inherently stable, means for
20 governing the height at which the craft flies and means for discharging either directly or indirectly the explosive charge at a predetermined point in the flight of the torpedo.

Referring to the drawings in which what
25 I now consider to be the preferred form of my invention are shown: Fig. 1 is a diagrammatic view illustrating the various controls employed. Fig. 2 is a detail section of an instrument termed a "revolution counter"
30 which controls the point at which the explosive is discharged. Fig. 3 is an end view of the same. Fig. 4 is a section of the gears of Fig. 2 on line 4—4. Fig. 5 is a vertical section of the instrument used to govern the
35 height at which the torpedo flies. Fig. 6 is a plan view of the same. Fig. 7 is a plan view of a modified form of the instrument for controlling the point at which the explosive is discharged. In this instance the instru-
40 ment is in the form of a chronometer. Fig. 8 is an elevation of the same, partly broken away. Fig. 9 is a side elevation partly in section of the preferred form of generator for supplying current to operate
45 the various controls. Fig. 10 is a diagrammatic side elevation of a torpedo mounted on a launching track. Fig. 11 is an end elevation partly in section of the gyroscope used to control the steering. Fig. 12 is a section
50 on line 12—12 Fig. 11. Fig. 13 is a section on line 13—13 of Fig. 1.

My invention is shown as applied to the aeroplane type of aircraft. It may be of any desired construction although of course as no passengers are carried it may be much 55 smaller than the ordinary passenger aeroplane. It may be either of the inherently stable or of the neutral-stable type. If of the former type, or if a dirigible balloon is employed. the stabilizing devices hereinafter 60 described need not be employed.

The aeroplane is shown in Fig. 10 as consisting of a body portion 1 on the forward portion of which is mounted an explosive charge 2 and the propeller 3. A cap 4 may 65 be used to ignite the explosive on striking an object.

The main supporting planes of the aeroplane are shown at 5 and 6 while the vertical rudder, horizontal rudder and ailerons are 70 shown at 7, 8 and 9 respectively. The torpedo may be driven from any source of power such as an internal combustion engine (not shown) mounted within the body 1.

One of the most important elements in se- 75 curing a successful torpedo of this character is a steering device which will unfailingly keep the aeroplane on the course upon which it was originally set. To provide such a means I prefer to employ a gyroscope 10 80 (see Figs. 1, 10, and 11). Said gyroscope preferably comprises an electrically driven rotor 11, journalled within a rotor bearing frame or casing 12 which in turn is mounted for oscillation about horizontal axis 13 with- 85 in a vertical ring 14. The said ring in turn is swiveled about a vertical axis on pivots 15—16 within framework 17. The gyroscope is preferably non-pendulous or perfectly balanced and is, as will be seen, provided with 90 three degrees of freedom. It may be provided with an adjustable weight 18 if desired to compensate for variations in latitude.

The steering mechanism is controlled by 95 variations which take place in the angular position of the gyroscope and aeroplane. For this purpose electrical contacts 19—20 may be secured to the vertical ring 14 while a cooperating trolley or brush 21 is mount- 100 ed on some relatively fixed portion of the aeroplane. Preferably the said trolley is mounted on a rotatable worm gear 22 or the like which is adapted to be set so as to move the trolley to various portions with respect to the gyroscope for purposes hereinafter described. The worm wheel 22 may be set by means of worm 24 and knob 25. Trolley 21 is preferably pivotally mounted at 21′ on a lever 121 which in turn is mounted on gear 22 on pivot 23 so that the trolley may be moved with reference to the gear by means of connecting members or wires 23′, forming a follow-up connection from the steering mechanism. Said contact and trolley are in circuit with coils 25—26 on a servo motor 27. The servo motor is shown as comprising gears 28 and 29 which are continuously driven in opposite directions from a wind mill or fan 30 on shaft 30′ by means of inter-meshing pinions 32, 33. A clutch disc 34 mounted upon shaft 35 is positioned between said gears 28, 29, the gears being provided with clutch faces with which the disc is adapted to engage. As either magnet 25—26 is excited the corresponding gear will be thrown against the discs 34 and the shaft 35 revolved to actuate the vertical rudder 7 through bevel gears 37 and connecting wires 38. From the drum 40 follow-up wires 23′ above referred to lead back to the trolley 21.

As the details of the preferred form of my servo motor, for this and similar uses, are set forth fully in my co-pending application No. 87,434 for automatic pilots for aeroplanes, filed March 29, 1916, further elaboration of the exact construction of the servo motor need not be presented here.

For controlling both the longitudinal and lateral stability I prefer to employ one or more gyroscopes 41 of the type set forth in the above mentioned application. As there explained the gyroscopic unit comprises a pendulous gyroscope mounted on a vertical spinning axis and controlling both the longitudinal and lateral controls by two sets of contacts 42—43 positioned so as to be moved by the relative movement of the gyroscope about either axis. The contacts 43 which with the aeroplane flying in the direction of the arrow 44 would govern the longitudinal stability are shown as mounted on the horizontal gimbal ring 45 while the contacts 42 are secured to a swinging loop 46 connected to the gyroscope so as to receive motion about the longitudinal axis.

As is the case with the steering gyroscope I prefer to provide the cooperating brushes with a follow-up system. For this purpose the arm 46′ which supports the plurality of brushes 47 is shown as pivotally mounted and secured to a pulley 48 around which the follow-up wires 49 from the horizontal rudder 8 extend. Similarly bush 42′ is connected to a pulley 51 over which follow-up wires 52 are placed leading from the ailerons 9. The brush 54 is normally in circuit and is so positioned as to cause the machine

to climb rapidly. Means are provided to shift the effective position of the brushes as soon as the aeroplane rises to or above the predetermined height. For this purpose I place in circuit with brush 54 a relay 55 which, when operating magnet 56 is excited, breaks the circuit of brush 54 at point 57 and places the second brush 157 in circuit. The latter brush may be located so as to cause the machine to be positioned in a substantially horizontal position or in other words, so that it will descend slightly while flying, or at least not rise. Magnet 56 is operated by means of barometric device 58 which may assume the form shown in Figs. 5 and 6. This device comprises an aneroid barometer, comprising the usual expansion chamber 59 multiplying mechanism 60 and index 61. On the said barometer and preferably attached to the index stem 62 is a contact member 63 adapted to come into contact with a second member 64 when a predetermined altitude is reached or exceeded. Preferably member 64 is made adjustable so that the instrument may be set for flying at different heights. For this purpose it may be secured to a ring 65 rotatably mounted on the top of the casing 66 of the barometer.

It will be seen that the excitation of magnet 56 will close contacts 67 and throw brush 54 out of circuit and place brush 157 in circuit. In series with said relay is preferably placed a second relay 68, having contacts 70 and 71. When the relay is in normal position as shown the two brushes 54 and 157 are operated as above described. But when the operating magnet 69 is excited contact 70 will be broken and contact 71 made, which will place a third brush 72 in the circuit and throw out both of the other brushes. Brush 72 is set for a steep and rapid descent of the aeroplane and is only designed to be thrown in circuit when the aeroplane has reached a point near the target at which it was originally aimed.

The problem to be solved in devising a successful aerial torpedo will be seen to be somewhat different from an under-water torpedo, as in the latter type the torpedo is usually fired merely by contact without any reference to how far or how long it has traveled before striking the object. In the air, on the other hand, it is usually necessary to fly the torpedo at a much greater height than the object at which it is aimed extends so that it would never strike the object unless means are provided to alter its course or elevation when it nears the object.

To excite the said magnet 69 any means for indicating or measuring distance may be employed. In one form of the invention I have shown a revolution counter 75 designed to be driven from the propeller shaft 76 (see Fig. 2). Such a counter will indicate with comparative exactness the distance through the air or medium through which the torpedo is driven and since the air currents are of relatively slow velocity compared with the speed of the aeroplane, such indicator will designate the approximate distance traveled. The exactness of this indication, of course, may be increased by noting the direction and the velocity of air currents before launching the torpedo and making due allowance therefor in the setting of the counter. Said counter is rotated through gears 77 and flexible shaft 78. The counter comprises preferably a plurality of multiple reduction gears 178 designed to produce an extremely slow rotation of the last pinion 79. The last large gear 80 is mounted on a slidable sleeve 81 so that it may be withdrawn from engagement with the said pinion by pulling out knob 82. While said gear is disengaged it may be set to any desired relation with the pinion 79. Gear 80 is provided with a contact 83 adapted to engage a fixed contact 84 on the casing 85 or other part of the revolution counter. A notch 86 may be provided in said gear so that the pinion 79 will run into it and the gear 80 be stopped when the contacts 83 and 84 are engaged. By this or a similar method I provide means for making sure that the aeroplane will continue to descend when the descent is once started. Contacts 83 and 84 are of course, in circuit with magnet 69. Instead of employing a revolution counter or the like I may employ a chronometer 101 for indicating distance. As the normal speed of the aeroplane is known, a chronometer may be used to advantage for this purpose. The chronometer is provided with contacts 83' adapted to be operated after a predetermined period of time has elapsed, in a manner similar to that described in the revolution counter. I may provide a switch 87 on the aeroplane so that either the revolution counter or the chronometer may be used at will.

As above stated, I prefer to drive the servo motor by a windmill 30. I also prefer to generate the electricity necessary for operating the various controls above described by a wind driven fan. A desirable form of dynamo electric machine is shown in Fig. 9 and consists of a tubular body portion 90 having a tapering stream line tail 91. The forward portion is closed by the enlarged hub 191 of the turbine blades 92.

Preferably the said machine is designed to furnish both alternating and direct current. As shown, two separate generators are provided for this purpose, the direct current generator being indicated at 95 and the alternating current machine at 96. The direct current machine is employed to actuate the servo motor and operate all other devices in the torpedo for which such current is suitable, while the A. C. generator is used for

driving the stabilizing and steering gyroscopes (see Fig. 1). The field 102 of the A. C. generator may be excited from the D. C. machine. The alternating current apparatus is shown as a three phase type, the generator being an inductor alternator while the gyro motors are three phase induction motors; the rotor 11 forming the gyro wheel while all the windings are placed on the stator 196.

As I find it desirable to have both gyroscopes in full operation before the torpedo takes the air, I prefer to place the generator 90 in the stream line of the propeller 3, so that the wind caused by the propeller as soon as the engine is started will quickly bring the generator up to speed. The servomotor, also, may be similarly positioned.

The operation of my invention is as follows:

The torpedo is preferably launched from a track 99 or the like so that the direction in which it takes the air will be known. If desired the track may be mounted on a turntable 100 so that the torpedo can be fired in any desired direction. The torpedo body may be made without wheels and a launching carriage 200 provided upon which the torpedo rests. Blocks 201 and 202 are attached to the torpedo body and rest in shallow pockets 203, 204, on carriage 200. When the torpedo starts to move forward it takes the carriage with it, but as soon as it starts to rise it leaves the carriage on the track. If such a turntable is not provided or circumstances are such that the torpedo cannot be launched in the direction in which it is desired to fly, for instance, if it is found desirable to always launch the torpedo into the wind, I may make use of the knob 25 above referred to which shifts the position of the trolley 21 with respect to the gyroscope. It will readily be seen that if it is desired that the torpedo should fly on a course at right angles to the launching track all that is necessary is to set the trolley at 90° to the line of the track or to the fore and aft line of the aeroplane. Upon being launched, therefore, the trolley 21 and the contacts 19—20 on which it is placed will operate the rudder 7 and turn the aeroplane until it brings the trolley back to the insulated section between the contacts.

Upon taking the air the torpedo will rise rapidly since as shown in Fig. 1 contact 54 is normally in circuit with the servo motor. As soon, however, as the torpedo reaches the desired height the aneroid barometer contact will operate the relay to throw brush 157 in circuit and thereby cause the aeroplane to slightly descend. This will continue until the barometer contact is again broken and the plane will rise again. The flight will continue until the predetermined distance has been traveled, or in other words, until the revolution counter or the chronometer compels the contact to operate relay 68 whereupon brush 72 be thrown in circuit and the aeroplane caused to descend sharply. As soon as it strikes an object the charge will be exploded by contact or by a time fuse in the usual manner. A time fuse, if used, might be connected to chronometer 101 so as to be exploded at a predetermined interval of time after the torpedo is set to the descending position. To this end the solenoid 151 is placed in circuit with a second contact 152 on the chronometer 101 (Fig. 7). Said solenoid serves to withdraw catch 153 thereby releasing trigger 154 to fire the cap 150 and charge 2.

In accordance with the provisions of the patent statutes, I have herein described the principle of operation of my invention, together with the apparatus. which I now consider to represent the best embodiment thereof, but I desire to have it understood that the apparatus shown is only illustrative and that the invention can be carried out by other means. Also, while it is designed to use the various features and elements in the combination and relations described, some of these may be altered and others omitted without interfering with the more general results outlined, and the invention extends to such use.

Having described my invention, what I claim and desire to secure by Letters Patent is:

1. In an aerial torpedo, the combination with longitudinal control means, of a gyroscope for normally maintaining said means in an ascending position, a barometric device and means brought into operation by said device and acting through said gyroscope for setting said control means to a substantially horizontal position.

2. In an aerial torpedo, the combination, with longitudinal control means, of a pendulous device for normally controlling said means, a barometric device, and means connecting said barometric pendulous devices whereby the former alters the effective relation between the latter and the control means without disturbing the former and a follow-up connection between the gyroscope and said control means.

3. In an aerial torpedo the combination with longitudinal and vertical control rudders of a gyroscope for normally controlling said longitudinal rudder, a gyroscope for controlling said vertical rudder, a source of power for continuously spinning said gyroscope and a barometric device also effecting said longitudinal rudder.

4. In an aerial torpedo the combination with longitudinal control means, of a pendulous device for normally controlling said means, and a distance responsive device also affecting said means.

5. In an aerial torpedo, the combination, with a longitudinal control member of a pendulous device for normally controlling said member, a distance responsive device and means connecting said devices whereby the former alters the effective relation between the latter and the control member.

6. In an aerial torpedo, the combination with longitudinal and vertical control rudders, of a pendulous device and a distance responsive device for normally controlling said longitudinal rudder, a gyroscope for controlling said vertical rudder and a barometric device also affecting said longitudinal rudder.

7. In an aerial torpedo, the combination with a longitudinal control member. of a barometric device for normally controlling said member, and a distance responsive device for turning said member to a new position.

8. In an automobile dirigible device, means for steering it through its enveloping medium at a predetermined altitude, a distance responsive device, and means for altering the altitude of flight actuated by said device.

9. In an aerial torpedo, in combination, an electro-motor stabilizing gyroscope, an electro-motor steering gyroscope, a servo-motor electrically controlled from said gyroscopes, and a dynamo electric machine for driving said gyroscopes and exciting the servo-motor, said machine being wind driven.

10. In an aerial torpedo, the combination with the explosive charge, of an aeroplane structure for carrying the charge, means for causing said torpedo to fly at a predetermined height, means for causing the same to maintain its course, and distance responsive means for causing descent and detonation of said charge.

11. In an aerial torpedo, the combination with a pendulous device, of a longitudinal control means, a barometric device for normally controlling said means through said pendulous device, and a distance responsive device for causing detonation of said torpedo.

12. In an aerial torpedo, the combination with a rudder and a device adapted to maintain a predetermined position in azimuth, of a two part means responsive to relative turning of the torpedo and device for controlling the rudder, a follow-up connection between the rudder and said device, and means whereby the relative position of said means may be varied to cause the torpedo to change its course.

13. An aerial torpedo, including longitudinal, lateral and azimuth control means, a plurality of electrically driven gyroscopes, a wind driven generator for said gyroscopes, and a servo-motor connected to

said means and actuated electrically from said generator by said gyroscopes for controlling said means.

14. In an aerial torpedo, the combination with a longitudinal control means, of a barometric device for normally controlling said means, and a distance responsive device also affecting said means.

15. In an aerial torpedo, the combination with a longitudinal control member, of a gyroscopic device, means on said device and on an adjacent part of the aeroplane for operating said member, a barometric device, and means brought into operation by said barometric device for shifting the effective relation between said two means without disturbing the gyroscopic device.

16. In an aerial torpedo the combination with a longitudinal control member, of a gyroscope, means on said gyroscope and on an adjacent part of the aeroplane for operating said member, a distance responsive device, and means brought into operation by said device for shifting the effective relation between said two means.

17. In an aerial torpedo the combination with a longitudinal control member, of a gyroscopic pendulum, means on said pendulum and on an adjacent part of the aeroplane for operating said member, a barometric device, a distance responsive device, and means responsive to each of said devices for shifting the effective relation between said two means.

18. In an aerial torpedo, the combination with an explosive charge and longitudinal control means, of a means responsive to the happening of a predetermined event for causing said control means to cause the descent of the torpedo, and means for detonating said charge at a predetermined interval after said descent is caused.

19. In an aerial torpedo, the combination with a longitudinal control means, of a pendulous device for normally controlling said means, a barometric device affecting said means, and a distance responsive element also affecting said means.

20. In an aerial torpedo, the combination with longitudinal and azimuth control members, of a pendulous device and a device adapted to maintain a predetermined position in azimuth, alterable governing means operable between said members and said devices, respectively, and means for altering said means whereby in launching said torpedo will both ascend and turn in azimuth before reaching its final course.

21. In an aeroplane, the combination with longitudinal control means, of a gyroscope, an altitude responsive device, alterable means operable by a relative inclination of the aeroplane and gyroscope for governing said control means and means controlled by said device for shifting the effective relation between said other two means whereby said control means causes ascent of the aeroplane to a predetermined height and substantially horizontal flight at that height.

22. In an aerial torpedo, the combination with an explosive charge and longitudinal control means, of means for causing said control means to cause the descent of the torpedo at a predetermined point in the flight of the torpedo, and means adapted to detonate said charge at a predetermined point in its descent.

23. In an aerial torpedo, the combination with a longitudinal control plane, of means responsive to the height of the torpedo for normally controlling said plane, and an auxiliary element adapted to be brought into action at a predetermined point in the flight of the torpedo for causing said control plane to move to a descending position.

24. In an aerial torpedo, the combination with a launching runway adapted to be set in any desired direction, of a direction maintaining device on the torpedo, means responsive to a change in the relative positions of said device and torpedo for steering the same and means permitting the altering of the relations of said means whereby the torpedo may be set to any desired course irrespective of the direction of launching.

25. In an aerial torpedo, the combination with a pendulous device, of a longitudinal control means, a barometric device for normally controlling said means through said pendulous device, and a distance responsive device also affecting said means.

26. In an aerial torpedo, the combination with a pendulous device, of a longitudinal control means, a barometric device for normally controlling said means through said pendulous device, and a distance responsive device also affecting said means through said pendulous device.

27. In an aerial torpedo, comprising a body adapted to contain an explosive charge, propelling means for said body, an elevating plane for said body, automatic means for governing the position of the same, means responsive to the distance of travel of said body, and means operated by said last named means for changing the normal position of said elevating plane.

28. In an aerial torpedo, a body adapted to contain an explosive charge, propelling means and controlling surfaces therefor, means for normally maintaining said surfaces in a predetermined position, and means responsive to the happening of a predetermined event and having connection with said surfaces and charge for causing descent of the torpedo and exploding said charge.

29. In an aerial torpedo, a body adapted to contain an explosive charge, propelling means and controlling surfaces therefor, means for normally maintaining said sur-

L. B. SPERRY.
AERIAL TORPEDO.
APPLICATION FILED DEC. 22, 1916.

1,418,605.

Patented June 6, 1922.

3 SHEETS—SHEET 1.

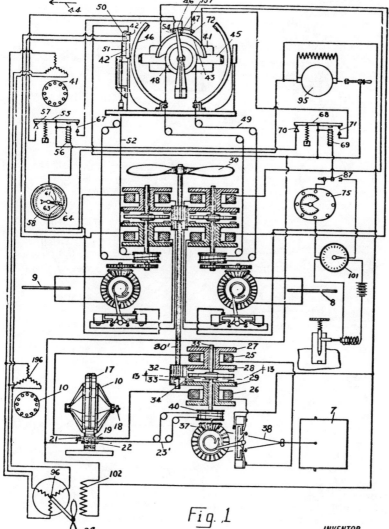

Fig. 1

INVENTOR
LAWRENCE B. SPERRY.
BY
Herbert H. Thompson
ATTORNEY.

L. B. SPERRY.

AERIAL TORPEDO.

APPLICATION FILED DEC. 22, 1916.

1,418,605.

Patented June 6, 1922.

3 SHEETS—SHEET 2.

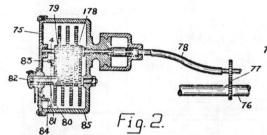

Fig. 2.

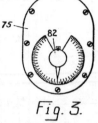

Fig. 3.

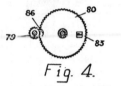

Fig. 4.

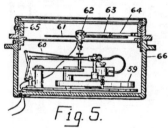

Fig. 5.

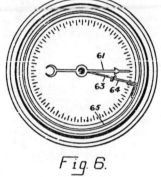

Fig. 6.

Fig. 7.

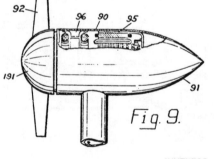

Fig. 9.

Fig. 8.

INVENTOR
LAWRENCE B SPERRY
BY
Herbert H. Thompson,
ATTORNEY.

L. B. SPERRY.
AERIAL TORPEDO.
APPLICATION FILED DEC. 22, 1916.

1,418,605.

Patented June 6, 1922.
3 SHEETS—SHEET 3.

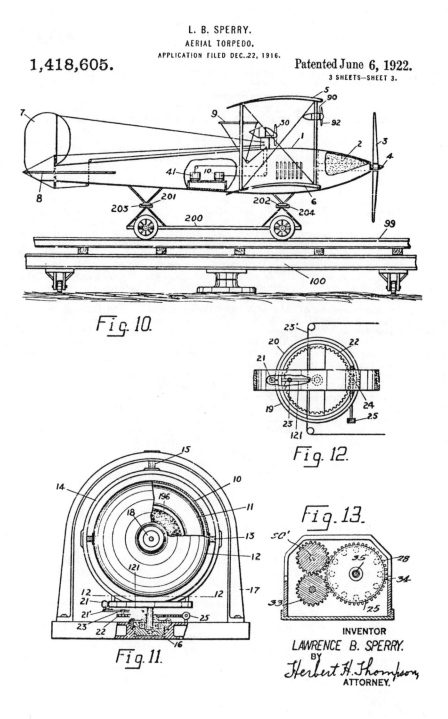

Fig. 10.

Fig. 12.

Fig. 11.

Fig. 13.

INVENTOR
LAWRENCE B. SPERRY.
BY
Herbert H. Thompson,
ATTORNEY.

UNITED STATES PATENT OFFICE.

LAWRENCE B. SPERRY, OF GARDEN CITY, NEW YORK, ASSIGNOR TO THE SPERRY
GYROSCOPE COMPANY, OF BROOKLYN, NEW YORK, A CORPORATION OF NEW
YORK.

TURN INDICATOR.

Application filed May 21, 1920. Serial No. 333,106.

To all whom it may concern:

Be it known that I, LAWRENCE B. SPERRY, a citizen of the United States of America, residing at Garden City, Long Island, in 5 the county of Nassau and State of New York, have invented certain new and useful Improvements in Turn Indicators, of which the following is a specification.

This invention relates to gyroscopic turn 10 indicators for aircraft or other dirigible vehicle and more particularly to the improvements in the apparatus shown and described in the copending application of Elmer A. Sperry for turn indicators, Serial No. 15 353,739, filed January 20, 1920.

According to this invention a small gyroscope mounted for precession about a horizontal axis upon turning of the craft upon which it is mounted is made use of to in- 20 dicate turning by means of a suitable indicator. Such an instrument has been found to be very sensitive but in its original form many defects appeared, the purpose of this invention being to overcome the defects in 25 the original instrument.

A further object of the invention is to provide means for use in conjunction with the turn indicator proper for showing the banking angle of the airplane.

30 Referring to the drawings in which are now considered preferred forms of the invention are shown:

Fig. 1 is a horizontal section of one form of turn and banking indicator.

35 Fig. 2 is a vertical section of the same.

Fig. 3 is a detail in section of the controlling valve for exhausting the air in the casing.

Fig. 4 is a front elevation of a modified 40 form of indicator.

Fig. 5 is a vertical section of the same.

Fig. 6 is a sectional detail of the regulating valve.

The turn indicator comprises preferably 45 a closed casing 1 in which is pivotally mounted a frame 2 supported on horizontal pivots 3 and 4. Said pivots are preferably in practice placed fore and aft of the airplane. In said frame the rotor proper 5 50 is journalled in suitable anti-friction bearings 6 and 7. Said rotor is preferably built up of a plurality of parts comprising a central flat disc 8 shrunk or otherwise secured to the shaft 9 and a pair of heavy rings 10 and 11 riveted or otherwise secured near the 55 periphery of said disc. The face of said disc is preferably provided with suitable buckets 12 or vanes adapted to receive the impulse of the air jet from nozzle 13.

The bearings for the rotor shaft 9 are 60 shown as roller bearings 19 mounted in threaded blocks 20 which may be adjusted for taking up the end play of the shaft and then locked in place by lock nuts 21. Balls 22 may be placed between the ends of the 65 shaft and the bearing members for reducing end thrust friction. The bearings may be lubricated by oil wicks 24 and 25 extending throughout the length of the frame as shown in Fig. 1. Suitable passages 26 and 27 may 70 lead from said wicks to the frame bearing 3 and other passages 76, 77 may lead from said wicks to the rotor bearings. By such construction the bearings remain oiled indefinitely and water is excluded therefrom. 75

As shown in Fig. 1 the air is introduced into the casing through a hollow pivot 14 communicating with the exterior of the casing at 15. Said pivot may be made in the form of a separate closure 16 threaded in an 80 aperture in the end of the casing and having a tube 17 constituting pivot 14 secured to, or integral with, the same. A screen 18 may also be secured to the outer end of the casing for preventing foreign matter 85 from being carried into the casing with the air.

At the forward end of the frame 2 is shown secured a gear 28 which meshes with a pinion 29 on the shaft 30. A light paddle 90 or blade 31 is shown as mounted on said shaft for the purpose of damping the oscillations of the gyroscope. Also mounted within said frame 1 is a simple pendulum 32 or other pendulous device. Said pendu- 95 lum is shown as having secured thereto a gear 33 meshing with pinion 34 also carrying a blade or paddle 35 for damping purposes. Also secured to said gear and pendulum are a pair of normally horizontal in- 100 dicators 36 and 37 secured to the outer ends of oppositely extending arms 38 and 39. Said indicators are readable upon a stationary dial or index 40 which has marked thereon reference indications 41 and 42 to simu- 105 late the horizon line, in other words, to simulate the line the aviator normally employs as indicating horizontality. The gyroscope also has secured to the frame 2 thereof an arm 44 bearing a normally vertical indicator 45. Said indicator is preferably readable upon the same dial 40. Said dial is preferably marked in such a manner as to indicate roughly the outline of the radiator or hood of the airplane since it is the cap on the radiator which is usually observed by aviators with reference to a distant object to ascertain whether the airplane is turning or not. A number of graduations 47 may be provided to indicate the rate of turning of the airplane.

Suitable stops 50 are, of course, provided within the casing for preventing the gyroscope from turning too far or from turning over. Said stops are shown as pieces of rubber tubing mounted on transverse lead 80 and adapted to cooperate with the bearing frame 2 of the gyroscope. Also it is important that a centralizing means be employed for normally holding the gyroscope in the vertical or other predetermined position and only permitting turning or precession thereof upon turning of the aircraft. Spring or springs as ordinarily secured to the gyroscope are unsuited for this purpose owing to the fact that if made weak enough to permit sufficient sensitiveness of the gyroscope to indicate a slight turn, when a sharp turn is taken the gyroscope will immediately precess over and strike the stop from whence it will start oscillating back and forth and become useless. On the other hand if the spring is made stiff enough to prevent its being too sensitive under the conditions stated it will not be sensitive to slight turns of the aircraft and will not fulfill its complete function.

For the purpose of overcoming these difficulties I have shown one or more sensitive spiral springs 51 and 52 secured between opposite points 53 and 54 on frame 2 and points on the casing. The springs are preferably in line with each other and under little tension when the gyroscope is in the normal position. It will readily be seen that with this arrangement very little force will oppose the initial precession of the gyroscope so that it will be very sensitive to slight turns of the airplane. On the other hand the force exerted by the springs will rapidly increase with the angle of precession of the gyroscope so that not only will the gyroscope be prevented from striking the stops but also the angle that the gyroscope is able to turn against the springs will furnish a ready indication of the rate of turning of the aircraft in a similar manner that a spring balance shows the acceleration of gravity upon a mass hung thereon, since gyroscopic effort is directly proportional to the rate of turning of its precession axis.

Preferably means are provided for adjusting the tension of one or both springs 51 or 52. For this purpose at the outer end of the spring 52 is secured a thread 57 which in turn is secured to the rotatable rod 58 mounted in the casing. Said rod has fixed thereto at its forward end a combined thumb piece and indicator 59 readable on scale 60 so that the tension of the spring may be readily adjusted to any desired extent. A second thumb piece and indicator 61 is mounted preferably at the lower part of the casing, being readable upon the scale 62. Said thumb piece is mounted on a shaft 63 to which is secured a rotary valve 64 for closing and opening the outlet passage 65 from the casing. Said outlet passage is preferably connected to a low point on the casing 1, as shown, so that any condensed vapor may be readily withdrawn therefrom. The valve 64 is journalled in the valve fitting 66, said fitting being provided with an extension 67 to which a flexible hose may be secured. It will be understood that in operation, air is exhausted from the casing through the opening 65 and fitting 66 by coupling any suitable type of exhaust pump thereto, such as a Venturi tube mounted on the airplane, as illustrated in the aforesaid copending application of Elmer A. Sperry.

Preferably also the casing is provided in connection with the valve or separate therefrom with a safety or speed limiting device such as valve member 38 consisting of a fitting 69 and a ball or other closure 70 adapted to normally close the aperture 71 thereby preventing the ingress of atmospheric air. Said ball is normally held on its seat by spring 72 but in case the pressure within the casing becomes too low, atmospheric pressure will force the ball off its seat and admit enough air to bring the pressure up to the desired amount for maintaining the proper speed of the gyroscope. By this means the speed is maintained comparatively constant irrespective of the variations in the rate of exhausting due to changes in the speed of the airplane or other cause.

While the principal features of the turn indicator shown in Fig. 5 are the same as already described, a modified form of damping means for the pendulum 32' is illustrated. In this form of the invention the pendulum illustrated is suspended within the closed casing 74 filled with liquid as a damping medium. At the same time the fan for damping the gyroscope, as well as the fan on the pendulum, is also omitted. The damping action of the bearings and the centralizing springs are depended upon in this instance to damp the gyroscope. In addition only one centralizing spring 51' is shown. Also, instead of bringing in the air through the hollow trunnion 3 of the frame 2, it is in this instance brought through a separate nozzle member 75 in the top of the casing so as to impinge upon buckets 12 at a point approximately in line with the horizontal bearings 3', 4'.

Having described my invention, what I claim and desire to secure by Letters Patent is:

1. In a gyroscopic turn indicator, the combination with a gyroscope mounted for precession about an axis, of yielding centralizing means therefor which increasingly opposes precession of the gyro as it becomes further displaced from its normal position, and means for adjusting said yielding means.

2. A flying indicator for aircraft comprising a reference member, a movable normally horizontal member symbolizing the horizon adjacent thereto, a second normally vertical indicator, a pendulous device connected to the first mentioned member and a gyroscope mounted for precession on turning of the aircraft connected with said vertical indicator.

3. In an air driven gyroscope, the combination with the rotor, of a closed casing, a tube communicating with the interior thereof and connected to the same at a low point on the casing to draw air and condensed vapor therefrom, and an intake nozzle adjacent the rotor.

4. In a banking indicator, the combination with a pendulous device, an indicator connected thereto a dial on which said indicator is readable, and a gyroscopic turn indicator readable on the same dial.

5. A gyroscopic turn indicator comprising a gyroscope, means for mounting the same for precession about a normally horizontal axis, said gyroscope being fixed about the vertical axis, yielding centralizing means connected to the gyroscope about said horizontal axis which opposes precession of the gyroscope about said axis with increasing force as said gyroscope becomes displaced from its normal position and means for damping the oscillation of said gyroscope about said axis.

6. A turn indicator comprising a gyroscope, means for mounting the same for precession about an axis at an angle to the vertical, said gyroscope being fixed about the vertical axis, and means comprising a spring under a slight initial stress when the gyroscope is in its normal position for offering very little force to small precessional movements of the gyroscope but for opposing further precession with greater force whereby the extent of precession of the gyroscope furnishes an indication of the rate of turn.

7. In a turn indicator for dirigible vehicles, a gyroscope mounted for precession about an axis at an angle to the vertical in response to turning of the vehicle in azimuth, and a plurality of springs connected with said gyroscope in line with each other each of which opposes precession of said gyroscope about said axis in each direction.

8. In a turn indicator for aircraft, a frame, a support, pivots connecting said frame and said support for permitting movement of said frame about an axis at an angle to the vertical, a rotor mounted in said frame for rotation about another axis, a spring connected to said frame adjacent one of said pivots for opposing movement of said frame in either of opposite directions about said axis and means for adjusting the tension of said spring at will.

9. In a flying indicator for aircraft, means including a reference member for indicating when the aircraft turns about an axis, and means including the aforesaid reference member for indicating when the aircraft turns about another axis.

10. In a flying indicator for aircraft, a pendulous device, an indicator connected thereto, a reference member in connection with which said indicator is readable, a second indicator readable in connection with said reference member, a gyroscope mounted for precession upon turning of the aircraft, and connecting means between said gyroscope and said second indicator.

11. In a turn indicator for aircraft, a frame, a support, pivots connecting said frame and said support for permitting movement of said frame about an axis, at an angle to the vertical, a rotor mounted in said frame for rotation about another axis, and a spring connected to said frame adjacent one of said pivots for opposing movement of said frame in either of opposite directions about said axis.

12. In a turn indicator for dirigible vehicles, a casing, a gyroscope mounted for precession within said casing about an axis at an angle to the vertical, a passage for a current of air through one end of said casing, and means for causing said current of air to rotate said gyroscope.

13. In a turn indicator for dirigible vehicles, a gyroscope mounted for precession about an axis at an angle to the vertical, yielding means for opposing said precession, and means comprising a rotatable member for altering at will the resistance offered by said yielding means to said precession.

14. In a turn indicator for aircraft, a casing, a gyroscope mounted in said casing for precession about an axis, a tube connected to said casing to conduct air therefrom, a passage for the entrance of air into said casing, means for directing the air to drive said gyroscope as the air is drawn through the casing, a valve in said tube and means for adjusting said valve at will to vary the speed of rotation of the gyroscope.

15. In a turn indicator for aircraft, a cas-

ing, a gyroscope mounted in said casing for precession about an axis, a tube connected to said casing to conduct air therefrom, a passage for the entrance of air into said casing, means for directing the air to drive said gyroscope as the air is drawn through the casing, a valve in said tube, a stem connected to said valve for adjusting the latter to vary the speed of rotation of the gyroscope, an indicator connected to said stem for movement therewith, and a reference member adjacent said indicator for cooperating therewith to show the extent of adjustment of said valve.

16. In a gyroscopic turn indicator for dirigible vehicles, the combination with a gyroscope mounted for precession about an axis at an angle to the vertical, of yielding centralizing means therefor which is very sensitive when the gyroscope is near its normal position, but which opposes precession about said axis with greater force when the gyroscope is further displaced from its central position and indicating means associated with said gyroscope for showing the rate of turn of the vehicle.

17. In a turn indicator for dirigible vehicles, a gyroscope mounted for precession about an axis at an angle to the vertical, yielding means for opposing said precession, means comprising a rotatable member for altering at will the resistance offered by said yielding means to said precession, and a rate of turn indicator associated with said gyroscope.

In testimony whereof I have affixed my signature.

LAWRENCE B. SPERRY.

1,433,102.

Patented Oct. 24, 1922.

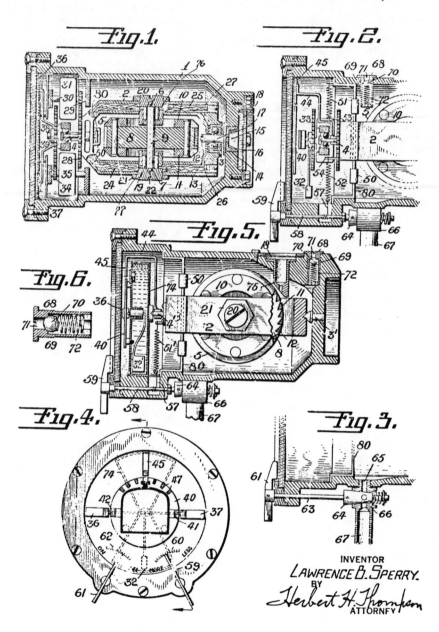

INVENTOR
LAWRENCE B. SPERRY.
BY
Herbert H. Thompson
ATTORNEY

Patented Aug. 3, 1926.

1,594,478

UNITED STATES PATENT OFFICE.

LAWRENCE B. SPERRY, OF GARDEN CITY, NEW YORK; THE BANK OF AMERICA, OF NEW YORK, N. Y., AND WINIFRED ALLEN SPERRY, OF HEMPSTEAD, NEW YORK, EXECUTORS OF SAID LAWRENCE B. SPERRY, DECEASED.

PARACHUTE.

Application filed March 24, 1919. Serial No. 284,755.

This invention relates to parachutes, more particularly to parachutes adapted to the use of aviators in escaping from air craft, and especially from rapidly moving craft such as aeroplanes.

One of the great difficulties in the use of parachutes for escaping from aeroplanes is that the slip stream from the propeller is apt to catch the parachute and tear it or to blow it against the tail parts of the plane, or otherwise foul it so that it will fail to function properly.

The main object of the invention is to devise a method and means whereby a parachute may be mounted on an aeroplane, being always ready for quick attachment to the aviator, and adapted to function with a high degree of reliability.

Referring to the drawings wherein I have shown what I now consider to be the preferred forms of my invention.

Fig. 1 is a side elevation of an aeroplane, showing one method of carrying the parachutes in accordance with my invention.

Fig. 2 is a fragmentary section of the fuselage of an aeroplane illustrating one method of carrying the parachute; showing also one of the stages in the releasing of the same.

Figs. 3, 3ᵃ, 4, and 5 illustrate further stages in the releasing and opening of the parachute.

Fig. 6 is a detail of the double set of cords adapted to be attached to the aviator's belt.

Fig. 7 is a view of a belt adapted to be used with my invention.

Fig. 8 shows a modified method of carrying the parachute.

Fig. 9 is a section taken on line 9—9, Fig. 2.

Fig. 10 is a section of the bag shown in Fig. 8.

Fig. 11 is a view of an aviator escaping from an aeroplane.

Fig. 12 shows a modified form of bag.

In the drawings the aeroplane is shown at 1 having a fuselage 2, within which are shown pits 3 and 4 for two persons, a pilot and an observer or passenger. Set within the fuselage through openings in the bottom 5 thereof are shown two receptacles 6 (see also Fig. 2). The receptacle is provided with a removable cover 7, and may be oval in shape as shown by the shape of the cover

in Fig. 3ᵃ. This shape will permit the receptacle to be inserted end first into the fuselage, and then adjusted into position with cover 7 substantially flush with the bottom of the fuselage 2. A strip of quarter-round moulding or the like 8 may be fastened to the receptacle 6 to serve as a shoulder to rest against the inside of the fuselage for holding the receptacle in place. Screws 9 passing through the bottom of the fuselage and into the quarter-round moulding 8 may be provided to secure the receptacle in place.

The cover 7 may be fastened in position by any suitable means which will permit ready separation when a substantial pull is exerted thereon. In Fig. 2 this means is shown as comprising several elastic bands 10 fastened at 11 to the inside of the receptacle and passing over pegs 12 formed in the edge of the cover by making slits 13 therein. Another means is shown in Fig. 6 comprising a separable fastener, the ball 14 of which is shown secured to the cover 7 and the socket 15 to a projection 16 integral with the receptacle 6.

The parachute 17 is preferably contained within a bag 18, within receptacle 6. The top of the bag is secured by means of a cord 19 to the receptacle at 20. The bottom of the bag may be provided with a plurality of slits 21. The several ends 22 thus formed being fastened together around the protruding cords 23 as shown at 24 in the dotted line position. The cords 23 are shown as folded back and forth under resilient strips 25 (Fig. 3ᵃ) secured to the inside of cover 7, and fastened at their ends to said cover at four points 26.

On the outside of cover 7 I have shown four cords 27 (Fig. 6) attached at points directly below the aforesaid points 26, so that said last mentioned cords will be in effect continuations of the four parachute cords 23 (Fig. 5).

When in position on the aeroplane the cords 27 may be carried around the fuselage to a position convenient to the aviator, being secured as by means of an elastic cord 28 to a peg 28′, the fastener 29 at the end of the cords being snapped over the elastic cord 28 or otherwise supported where it may be readily reached by the aviator.

In order that the aviator may escape from

either side of the aeroplane, duplicate cords 27' carrying a snap hook 29' may be carried around the other side of the fuselage and fastened in a similar manner to that in which cords 27 and hook 29 are fastened. If desirable, in order that one set of cords and hook will not hang in the way of the aviator when the parachute is being used, the cords 27 and 27' may be continuations of each other passing through eyelets 30 (Fig. 6) in cover 7, so that when one set is used the other will be drawn up out of the way as shown in Fig. 5, knots or the like 31 being provided in the cords so they will be properly centralized, and so that any one thereof may be pulled upon without further sliding through eyelets 30.

The aviator may be provided with a belt (Fig. 7) comprising a strap 32 adapted to fit around the body, being buckled or otherwise secured to a front plate 33 and provided with a strap 34 adapted to pass over the shoulder. Straps 35, 36 may also be attached to front plate 33 and adapted to fit around the legs of the aviator. This constitutes a belt out of which the aviator can not fall. A bail 37 may be provided on the front plate 33 to which the snap hook 29 is attached.

While flying the aviator may have one of the hooks 29 attached to his belt, or he may permit them to remain in their places, reaching for one when he intends to jump from the plane or anticipates a possible necessity for doing so. He will, of course, reach for the hook on the side of the fuselage from which he desires to jump.

Having the hook attached to his belt, when the aviator jumps from the plane the fastening 28 will break so that the cords 27 may hang directly from the cover 7 in the bottom of the fuselage. The elastic bands 10 or separable fasteners 14—15 will obviously permit cover 7 to be readily pulled out, while the cords 27' and hook 29' on the opposite side of the fuselage will also separate therefrom and be drawn in toward cover 7 as shown in Fig. 5. A partition 38 of fabric fastened at its edges to container 6, may be spread across the inside of said container, between bag 18 containing the parachute, and the cover 7 with the cords 23, the cords passing through the partition at 41 so that said cords 23 will be withdrawn from under strips 25 before the bag 18 leaves container 6.

Said partition 38 may be slit in several places 39 and held in normal position by any suitable means as, for instance, by lacing 40, so that as soon as cords 23 are drawn out from under said strips 25 the pull on the bag will cause partition 38 to open allowing the bag to be pulled out of the container 6. As soon as cord 19 reaches its full length it will check the fall of bag as shown by the

dotted line position 18', 19' in Fig. 2. The bag will then be torn open at 24 (Fig. 2) so that the parachute will be free to fall out as seen in Fig. 3. In order that the parachute will not fall in a bundle and fail to open a light cord 42 may be fastened to the top of the parachute 17 and to bag 18 as shown in Fig. 4. As soon as the parachute reaches full length the cord 42 will break. The opening of the parachute during the continuation of the fall is thus insured.

As shown in Fig. 5, the four cords 23 may be divided into several smaller cords 23^a, which in turn are shown as divided into several still smaller cords 23^b; the latter being attached to the parachute. By this method each of cords 23 controls one-fourth of the parachute. As previously pointed out each of cords 27 is in effect a continuation of one of cords 23, so that the aviator may, by pulling down on one of said cords 27, cause the parachute to tilt in a desired direction and thus glide in such direction. In this way the aviator may within reason choose a spot of landing, and thereby avoid falling into trees or upon other undesirable objects.

In order to absorb the shock produced when the parachute opens, elastic material 43 may be used as shown in cords 27, or in any other suitable place.

Returning now to the purpose of the bag 18 and the cord 19; it has been found that where the parachute begins to unfold near the fuselage it is apt to be torn open by the propeller blast, or to be carried thereby against the tail parts of the aeroplane. By the use of the bag and cord the parachute may be dropped in a compact bundle (Fig. 11) a sufficient distance below the aeroplane to escape the propeller blast 47 and there permitted to unfold.

The cord 19 may be elastic so that after the parachute breaks away, the bag 18 may be drawn back to the fuselage. Thus, if one of several persons leaves the aeroplane, the others continuing to fly, the bag will not be left dangling and apt to foul the steering elements of the plane.

The container 6 with the parachute and all of its parts contained therein, may constitute a complete parachute unit which may readily be put in place in a manner hereinbefore described, so that when a parachute has been used a new unit may be inserted.

In Fig. 8 I have shown a modification of my invention, wherein instead of showing the parachute fitted in the bottom of the fuselage as hereinabove specified, it may be carried in any other suitable place. In this instance the bag 18^a is shown as constituting a cushion for the aviator's seat 44, fastened by means of a cord 19^a to the aeroplane, as for instance to the leg 45 of seat 44. Cords 23^a are shown hooked to bail

37 of the aviator's belt. Obviously the bag may be carried under the aviator's seat or in any other place where it may readily be reached by the aviator, who would grab it by a handle 46 and jump overboard with it. As shown in Fig. 10 the bag may have a partition 38' similar to partition 38 (Figs. 2 and 9), the parachute 17 being carried in the upper compartment and cords 23 in the lower case as shown, so that cords 23 and the parachute 17 will be drawn out successively.

As shown in Fig. 12, the bag 18^b may be provided with flaps 50, 51. In such case partition 38' may be dispensed with. The pair of flaps 51 may be closed over the parachute within the bag and fastened by means of light lacing 52. The cords 23^a may be folded between outer flaps 50 and inner flaps 51 and tucked under strips attached to either pair of flaps. I have shown the strips 53 on flaps 51. Flaps 50 will close over said cords 23^a and be laced. In operation, the bag having passed without the propeller slip stream as in Fig. 11, flaps 50 will be torn open, the cords 23^a will then pay out after which the inner flaps 51 will open to permit the parachute to fall out as in Fig. 4.

In accordance with the provisions of the patent statutes, I have herein described the principle of operation of my invention, together with the apparatus, which I now consider ·to represent the best embodiment thereof, but I desire to have it understood that the apparatus shown is only illustrative and that the invention can be carried out by other means. Also, while it is designed to use the various features and elements in the combination and relations described, some of these may be altered and others omitted without interfering with the more general results outlined, and the invention extends to such use.

Having described my invention, what I claim and desire to secure by Letters Patent is:

1. In combination, an aeroplane fuselage having an opening through the bottom, a parachute within said fuselage adjacent said opening, a cord for said parachute passing from said opening around the outside of said fuselage to a point adjacent the aviator's seat, said cord being attached to the fuselage at such point and adapted to become released in response to a predetermined strain.

2. In combination, a fuselage having an opening in the bottom thereof, a bag within said fuselage adjacent said opening, a parachute within said bag, cords for said parachute, said cords passing from adjacent said opening around the outside of the fuselage to a point adjacent the aviator's seat.

3. In combination, a container adapted to be carried by an aircraft, a cover for said container separably fastened thereto, a bag within said container and attached thereto by a cord, a parachute within said bag, cords for said parachute, said cords being fastened to said cover, and additional cords attached to said cover and adapted to be secured to an aviator's belt.

4. In combination, a container adapted to be carried by an aircraft, a cover for said container separably fastened thereto, a bag within said container and attached thereto by a cord, a parachute within said bag, cords for said parachute, the ends of said cords being fastened to said cover, means on said cover for receiving portions of said cords, and means on said cover adapted to be attached to an aviator's belt.

5. In combination, a container adapted to be carried by an aircraft, a cover for said container separably fastened thereto, a bag within said container and attached thereto by a cord, a parachute within said bag, cords for said parachute, the ends of said cords being fastened to said cover, and resilient strips attached to said cover for tucking the slack of said cords under.

6. In combination, a parachute and cords therefor, means for containing said parachute and cords, said means having a removable cover to which said cords are fastened, and a partition in said containing means for separating said parachute from said cords for retaining the parachute within said first mentioned means while said cords are being paid out from said removable cover, said partition having an opening therethrough through which said cords extend.

7. In combination, a cushion for an aircraft seat, means adapted to suspend said cushion from the aircraft without the propeller blast thereof, and a parachute adapted to be contained within said cushion.

8. In combination, a bag, a parachute within said bag, cords for said parachute, means for holding said parachute within said bag until said cords have paid out, means for attaching the top of said parachute to said bag until said parachute has unfolded, and resilient means for attaching said bag to an aircraft for withdrawing said bag to the fuselage when the parachute is detached therefrom.

9. An aviator's belt comprising a front plate, a band attached thereto and adapted to encircle the body of the aviator, a strap attached to said band adapted to fit over the aviator's shoulder, a pair of straps attached to said plate adapted to fit around the aviator's legs, and attachment means on said plate.

10. In combination, an aeroplane fuselage having an opening through the bottom, a container for a parachute within said opening, and a resilient connection between said

container and said fuselage for tending to retain said container within said opening.

11. In combination with an aeroplane, a container for a parachute, a detachable parachute within the same for supporting an aviator, and a resilient connection between said container and said aeroplane, whereby upon release of said parachute from said container the container is withdrawn to the aeroplane

12. In combination with an aeroplane fuselage having an opening therein, a parachute within said opening, cords secured to said parachute, connecting means extending from said cords to points on opposite sides of said fuselage, said means being so attached to the fuselage at such points as to become detached in response to strain in excess of a predetermined value.

13. In combination with an aeroplane fuselage having an opening therein, a parachute within said opening, cords secured to said parachute, extensions on said cords reaching to opposite sides of said fuselage and attached thereto, either of said extensions being adapted to become detached from the fuselage when the other thereof is brought into use, and said extensions being so interconnected that the free end of the one so detached is withdrawn to inoperative position.

14. A parachute for aircraft comprising a foldable fabric, said parachute being folded into the form of a seat cushion on which the aviator sits.

15. A parachute for aircraft comprising a foldable fabric, said parachute being fold-ed into the form of a seat cushion on which the aviator sits and means for connecting the parachute to the aviator's body.

16. A parachute for aircraft comprising a foldable fabric, a cover in which the folded fabric is positioned to form a cushion on which the aviator sits, means for connecting the parachute to the aviator's body, and means for releasing the parachute from said cover when the aviator jumps out of the aircraft.

17. A parachute for aircraft comprising a foldable fabric, a cover in which the folded fabric is positioned to form a cushion on which the aviator sits, means for connecting the parachute to the aviator's body, means for connecting the cover to the aircraft, and means for releasing the parachute from said cover when the aviator jumps out of the aircraft.

18. A parachute for aircraft comprising a foldable fabric, a cover in which the folded fabric is positioned to form a cushion on which the aviator sits, means for connecting the parachute to the aviator's body, and means for connecting the cover to the aircraft, said means permitting the cover and parachute to drop below the slip-stream of the propeller when the aviator jumps out of the aircraft, and means for releasing the parachute from said cover when said cover and parachute have dropped below the slip-stream.

In testimony whereof I have affixed my signature.

LAWRENCE B. SPERRY.

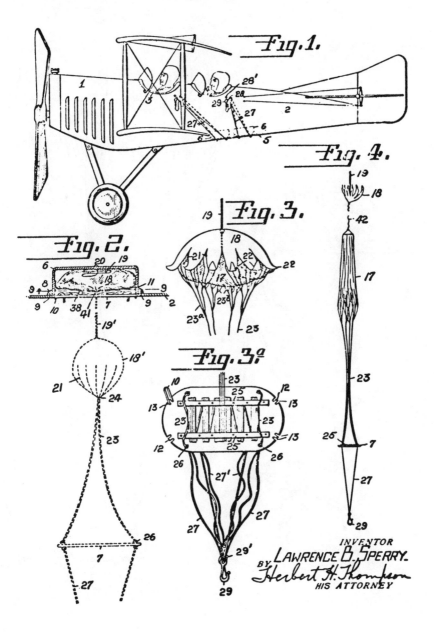

Fig.1.

Fig. 4.

Fig. 3.

Fig. 2.

Fig. 3ª

INVENTOR
LAWRENCE B. SPERRY.
BY *Herbert H. Thompson*
HIS ATTORNEY

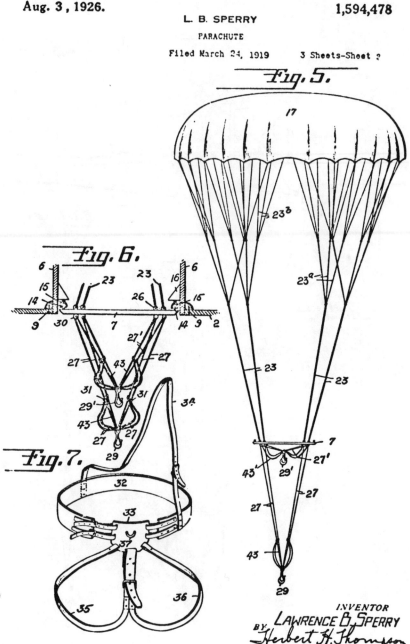

Fig. 5.

Fig. 6.

Fig. 7.

INVENTOR
LAWRENCE B. SPERRY
BY Herbert H. Thompson
HIS ATTORNEY

Aug. 3 , 1926.

L. B. SPERRY

PARACHUTE

Filed March 24, 1919

1,594,478

3 Sheets—Sheet 3

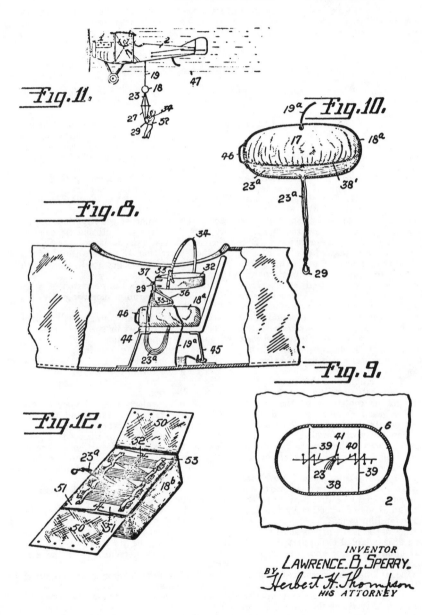

INVENTOR
LAWRENCE. B. SPERRY.
BY Herbert H. Thompson
HIS ATTORNEY

UNITED STATES PATENT OFFICE.

LAWRENCE B. SPERRY, OF FARMINGDALE, NEW YORK; THE BANK OF AMERICA, OF
NEW YORK, N. Y., AND WINIFRED ALLEN SPERRY, OF HEMPSTEAD, NEW YORK,
EXECUTORS OF SAID LAWRENCE B. SPERRY, DECEASED, ASSIGNORS TO WINIFRED
ALLEN SPERRY.

AIRCRAFT.

Application filed October 21, 1922. Serial No. 595,920.

This invention relates to aircraft, and has for its principal object the provision of a heavier-than-air flying machine of maximum efficiency in flight, or in rising from or alighting upon land or water.

Further, the invention has for its object the provision of an aircraft having a detachable landing gear whereby an aviator may rid his machine of said gear after rising in the air. The advantages of such construction are many. In the first place, it obviously reduces the weight of the machine by ninety or one hundred pounds and will thus enable an aviator to increase the speed of his machine ten miles an hour or more. Secondly, the air resistance of the machine is lessened by the removal of projecting parts. Thirdly, landing of the machine upon a body of water is greatly facilitated. Heretofore, the landing gear has proven a severe hindrance to the landing of the machine upon water, the landing gear tending to capsize the machine upon striking water. And finally, it may be desirable to land on a more convenient mechanism than wheels, such e. g., as skids, which are effective for traveling over rough ground.

It is a further object of this invention to provide a detachable landing gear, as aforesaid, and means controlled by the aviator whereby the gear may be rapidly and easily released from its attachment to the machine without possibility of jamming.

A further object is the provision of means for preventing too rapid falling of the detached landing gear. This means may take the form of a parachute normally in closed position and carried by said aircraft, but which is adapted to be detached from the aircraft and rendered effective by the falling of the landing gear.

A further object is the provision of means, such as a float, adapted to support the landing gear upon the water and prevent sinking thereof.

When the landing gear is removed from an aircraft, it may be the case that the body of the machine is so low that the propeller, upon landing, may strike the ground in rotating. It is a further object of this invention, therefore, to provide means for stopping the propeller in substantially horizontal position and for maintaining it in said position.

A further object is the provision of landing skids which take the place of the detached landing gear. These skids carry the machine easily over rough ground and are to be preferred in many instances to the wheels of the usual landing gear for the purpose of alighting upon solid, and especially rough, ground.

A further object in employing skids is to prevent the machine from capsizing or turning over on its nose when landing on land, as it is possible to place the skids so far ahead of the center of gravity that nosing over in bad places will be impossible whereas with wheels, it is not possible to put them more than 15 degrees ahead of the center of gravity, and get good results with them.

A further object is the provision of a resilient, shock-absorbing mounting for the landing skids.

Other objects and advantages will in part be obvious and in part be specifically pointed out in the specification.

In the accompanying drawings,

Fig. 1 is a side elevation of an aeroplane embodying one form of my invention.

Fig. 2 is a front elevation thereof with the propeller removed.

Fig. 3 is an enlarged detail view of the landing gear releasing means and the operating mechanism therefor.

Fig. 4 is another view of the landing gear releasing mechanism still further enlarged.

Fig. 5 is a section taken on the line 5—5 of Fig. 7 and showing the skid and skid-supporting means.

Fig. 6 is an enlarged front elevation of the airplane showing the skids.

Fig. 7 is a vertical section taken on the line 7—7 of Fig. 5.

Fig. 8 is a view showing the landing gear at the beginning of its downward flight, after having been detached from the airplane.

Fig. 9 shows the landing gear supported by a parachute.

Fig. 10 is a view showing the detached landing gear with a buoyant member attached thereto for supporting it in the water.

Fig. 11 is a front elevation of the aircraft floating upon a body of water, the propeller being held in substantially horizontal position.

Fig. 12 is a side elevation of a brake operable for holding the propeller shaft in fixed position.

Fig. 13 is a front elevation of the brake shown in Fig. 12.

Fig. 14 is a vertical section through the cylinders of an airplane engine showing means for stopping the engine so that the propeller shaft driven thereby occupies a predetermined position.

Referring to the drawings, there is illustrated in Fig. 1 an aircraft 10 of ordinary construction having the usual rudders 11, propeller 12, wings 13 and operator's enclosure 14. The machine is provided with a landing gear comprising a pair of wheels 15 mounted upon an axle 16 supported upon the machine by struts or hangers 17. A pair of struts is shown, in the present case, at each side of the machine.

As hereinbefore stated, it may be desirable to rid the machine of its landing gear after the former has left the ground. For this purpose the gear is detachably connected to the machine, so that it may be disconnected at the will of the operator. One suitable form of connection is illustrated in Figs. 1–4, and comprises a latch 20 slidable in a holder 21 in the form of a track or guideway fixed to the fuselage of the machine. Said latch has a slot 24 cut therein and extending from the bottom edge thereof obliquely upward and then substantially horizontally to form a prong or finger 22 adapted to engage an eye (not shown) near the upper end of a hanger or strut 17. A vertical guide-slot 25 is formed in the track 21 to permit the strut to be raised above the prong 22 so that the latter may pass through the eye in said strut.

Since two struts 17 are provided at each side of the machine, two latches 20 of the same construction but oppositely disposed are provided. To operate the latches to effective (locking) and ineffective (unlocking) positions, the latches 20 may be provided at their inwardly disposed ends with links 30 which may be pivoted at one end upon ears 31 on said latches and at their other ends upon opposite ends of a balanced lever 32 fixed upon a shaft 33 journaled in the machine. Said shaft carries also a sprocket wheel 34 over which operates an endless chain 35. The other end of said chain operates over a similar sprocket wheel 36 mounted upon the side of the machine, and a handle 37 is provided to move integrally with said wheel 36. The handle 37 is positioned adjacent the aviator's seat so that he may readily swing handle 37 forwardly or rearwardly to operate lever 32 through the chain and sprocket connection, and hence operate the latches into or out of the apertures in the upper ends of the hangers 17.

The shaft 33 extends through the machine to the other side thereof where the locking mechanism is duplicated so that all of the latches (in the present case) on both sides of the machine are operated simultaneously. It will be apparent that when the lever 32 is in substantial alignment with the links 30, the prongs 22 will project through the struts, but when the handle 37 is operated to rotate lever 32 out of alignment with links 30, the prongs will be withdrawn.

As hereinbefore stated, the slot 24, outwardly from the prong 22, inclines downwardly so as to form a cam surface 36. As the prong 22 leaves the aperture in the upper end of hanger 17, the cam surface 36 comes in contact with the upper edge of said hanger and cams the latter downwardly out of the slot 36. To prevent the hanger from being jammed between the prong 22 (before the latter has left the aperture in the hanger) and the cam 36, the outward tip of the prong may be cut off to form a cam 37 substantially parallel to cam 36. It will thus be apparent that not only are all the hangers released simultaneously, but a positive force is introduced for ejecting them from the holders. All possibility of sticking or jamming of one or more of the struts or hangers in the holders, due to some force such as wind, is thus avoided.

To prevent damage to the landing gear which would ordinarily result from dropping thereof, there may be provided a small parachute 40 normally held in folded position in a stream-line case 41 in the bottom surface of the fuselage. The parachute is connected to the four struts by cords 42 which are in turn connected by a cord 43 to the cords 44 of the parachute. When the landing gear starts to drop, it pulls upon cord 43 and breaks a cord 39 tying together the ends 45 of a bag enclosing the parachute in case 41, permitting the parachute to drop. The ends of the latter are tied together by a light cord 46 having one end fixed to the case at 47. The cord 46 is broken by the fall of the landing gear and parachute, permitting the latter to open. Thereafter the landing gear drops slowly.

A cross-bar 49 is interposed between struts 17 to prevent distortion thereof during the fall of the landing gear. The cords 42 are subjected to a heavy strain during the fall of the landing gear, and if the cross-bar 49 were not provided to hold the struts rigidly in position, there is possibility that the struts on opposite sides of the landing gear would be bent together and rendered useless for co-operation with the latches.

Where the landing gear is to be dropped over water, there may be substituted for the parachute a buoy 50 attached to the landing gear by a cable 51 wound upon a reel 52 which may be mounted upon cross-bar 49.

The reel may be spring-pressed so as normally to wind up the cable. When the buoy . 0 strikes the water, the cable will be unwound to the extent where the spring neutralizes the weight of the submerged landing gear.

The usual rubber tires of wheels 15 may serve to float the landing gear upon the water while the parachute attached thereto serves to indicate the position of said gear. In the case where a buoy is used, it may be painted white for the same purpose. It is apparent that both a parachute and a buoy may be employed in some cases.

The purpose of dropping the landing gear may be, as hereinbefore explained, to facilitate alighting of the machine upon water. In this case the body of the machine is constructed as a water-tight unit capable of floating. The usual lower wing may also be dispensed with in this case.

Another purpose of dropping the landing gear is to permit the use of more efficient landing gear upon very rough ground. In the present case skids 55 are employed, since the latter travel easily over very rough ground and permit the machine to be brought to rest in a quarter of the distance usually required when wheels are employed. The skids are shown as operating in channels, slots, or guideways 54 in the fuselage extending from the front end almost to the rear thereof. The skids may be shaped somewhat like the runners of sleighs, and each may comprise an upper member 57 a lower member 58 formed preferably integral with the upper member, and brace rods 59 connecting said members to form a sturdy frame which is the preferred construction of skid. The skids are guided to move substantially parallel to the walls of the channel 54 by means of a plurality of links 60 pivoted at one end at 61 on a wall of the channel and at the other end on an adjacent side of the skid-frame. The relatively long length of links 60 and the small angular distances through which they move insure movement of the skids practically parallel to the walls of the skids. Said movement is resisted by heavy resilient members or rings 64 adapted to engage over arms 65 on the skid-frame and cross-bars 66 on the fuselage. The arms 66 are positioned back of each wall of the channel 54, and arms 65 extend through slots 67 cut in the channel walls so that said arms 65 overlie the respective arms 66, and the resilient bands 64 may engage the respective bands at substantially right angles.

A plurality of such sets of arms 65, 66 and rings 64 are provided throughout the length of the skids and the channel. It will be apparent that upon landing on any portion of the skids, that portion will be pressed upwardly in the channel, thus stretching the resilient members 64. Not only is the shock of landing fully absorbed, but the movement of the skids relative to the machine is resisted to damp the movement and guard the fuselage from injury which might be caused by coming in contact with the ground.

When the machine with the landing gear detached alights upon the water, the watertight body acts as a floating unit, and when the machine lands upon the skids, the body of the machine is so low with respect to the surface of the water and the ground, respectively, that it may be necessary to stop the propeller in horizontal position before alighting. For this purpose there may be provided the device which is more fully described in my co-pending application, Serial No. 581.287, filed August 11, 1922. This device comprises a lever 70 connected to each exhaust valve 71 of the cylinders 72 of an internal combustion engine employed for driving the machine. A linkage 73 is connected to all the valve stems in such manner that when operated by the aviator, certain of said valves are opened and certain valves are closed, the fuel supply to the engine having previously been cut off. This would tend to hold the pistons 74 in the same relative positions within the cylinder every time the linkage was operated, and the propeller is fixed to its shaft to occupy the horizontal position whenever the pistons occupy said relative positions.

To hold the propeller firmly in horizontal position there may be provided a brake comprising a band 80 encircling the hub 79 of the propeller shaft and split at one point in its periphery, the portions of the band adjacent the split being bent off to form flanges 81. A shaft 85 extends through said flanges, said shaft being screw-threaded on its lower end and clamped in position against lower flange 81 by a lock-nut 86. A ratchet-member 87 is fixed upon the upper flange 81 and has teeth 88 meshing with teeth 90 of a ratchet-member 91 journaled on the upper end of shaft 85. Said ratchet-member 91 has an arm 92 fixed thereto to the end of which is pivoted one end of a link 93 having its other end pivotally connected to one end of an operating lever 94 pivoted upon the machine adjacent the aviator's seat. By operating lever or handle 94, the aviator rotates ratchet 91 to cause the teeth 90 thereof to cam downwardly the teeth of ratchet 87 and hence also move the upper flange 81 toward the lower flange 81 (which is fixed relative to ratchet 91) and cause the band to tighten about the hub 79 of the propeller shaft. Movement of the flanges 81 relative to each other is against the action of a spring 95 positioned between and normally tending to separate said flanges. To maintain the band centralized so that all parts thereof are out of contact with the hub 79 when the brake is released, centralizing springs 98 fixed at one end to brackets 99 on the body of the machine and at the other end to said band are provided.

In accordance with the provisions of the patent statutes, I have herein described the principle of operation of my invention, together with the apparatus, which I now consider to represent the best embodiment thereof, but I desire to have it understood that the apparatus shown is only illustrative and that the invention can be carried out by other means. Also, while it is designed to use the various features and elements in the combination and relations described, some of these may be altered and others omitted without interfering with the more general results outlined, and the invention extends to such use.

Having herein described my invention what I claim and desire to secure by Letters Patent is:

1. In combination, an aircraft having a landing gear, said gear having a plurality of struts, connections between said struts and said aircraft, and means for releasing all of said struts simultaneously to permit detachment of said landing gear.

2. In combination, an aircraft having a landing gear, said gear having a plurality of struts, connections between said struts and said aircraft, means for releasing all of said struts simultaneously to permit detachment of said landing gear and means for ejecting said struts from said aircraft.

3. In combination, an aircraft having a landing gear, said gear having a plurality of struts, connections between said struts and said aircraft, and means for releasing all of said struts simultaneously and ejecting said struts from said aircraft.

4. In combination, an aircraft having a landing gear, said gear having a plurality of struts, connections between said struts and said aircraft, means for releasing all of said struts simultaneously to permit detachment of said landing gear, said means comprising latches engaging said struts, and means for operating said latches simultaneously to ineffective positions.

5. In combination, an aircraft having a landing gear, said gear having a plurality of struts, connections between said struts and said aircraft, means for releasing all of said struts simultaneously and ejecting said struts from said aircraft, said means comprising latches engaging said struts, and means for operating said latches simultaneously to ineffective positions, said latches having cams adapted to engage said struts when said latches are moved to ineffective positions to force said struts out of said machine.

6. In combination, an aircraft having a landing gear, said gear having a plurality of struts, connections between said struts and said aircraft, means for releasing all of said struts simultaneously, and means for ejecting said struts from said aircraft, said means comprising members having cams adapted to engage said struts to force said struts out of the machine.

7. In combination, an aircraft having a landing gear, said gear having a plurality of struts, said aircraft having holders, means in said holders normally engaging said struts, and means operable during flight for rendering said first named means ineffective so as to release said struts.

8. In combination, an aircraft having a landing gear, said gear having a plurality of struts, said aircraft having holders, means in said holders normally engaging said struts, means for rendering said first named means ineffective so as to release said struts, and means for ejecting said struts from said holders after said struts are released.

9. In combination, an aircraft having a landing gear, said gear having a plurality of struts, said aircraft having holders, latches in said holders normally engaging said struts, and means for operating all of said latches simultaneously to release said struts from said holder.

10. In combination, an aircraft having a landing gear, said gear having a plurality of struts, said aircraft having holders, latches in said holders normally engaging said struts, and means for operating all of said latches simultaneously to release said struts, said latches having cams adapted to engage said struts to eject said struts from said holders.

11. In combination, an aircraft having a landing gear, said gear having a plurality of struts, connections between said struts and said aircraft, means for releasing all of said struts simultaneously to permit detachment of said landing gear, said means comprising latches engaging said struts, and means for operating said latches simultaneously to ineffective positions, said last named means comprising a plurality of links connected to said latches, an operating handle, and gearing between said links and handle.

12. In combination, an aircraft having a landing gear, said gear having a plurality of struts, connections between said struts and said aircraft, means for releasing all of said struts simultaneously to permit detachment of said landing gear, said means comprising latches engaging said struts, means for operating said latches simultaneously to ineffective positions, a plurality of links connected to said latches, an operating shaft, connections between said link and shaft whereby rotation of said shaft operates said links to effective and ineffective positions, an operating handle, and gearing between said handle and said shaft.

13. In combination with an aircraft having

a propeller shaft, a propeller mounted thereon, means for enabling said aircraft to land
upon water including a detachable landing
gear, and means for stopping the propeller
5 in substantially horizontal position, a brake-
band substantially surrounding said shaft
and normally spaced therefrom, and means
for clamping said band around said shaft to
hold said propeller in substantially horizontal position.   10

In testimony whereof I have affixed my
signature.

LAWRENCE B. SPERRY.

Sept. 6, 1927.

L. B. SPERRY

1,641,700

AIRCRAFT

Filed Oct. 21, 1922

4 Sheets—Sheet 1

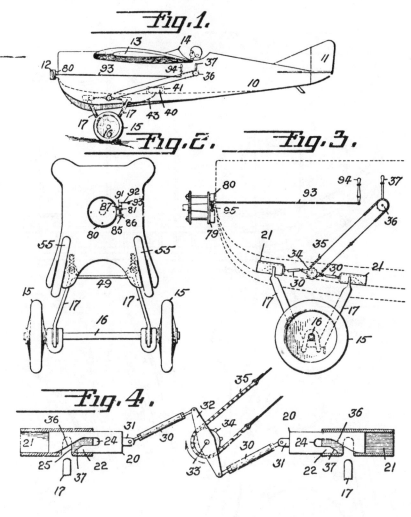

Fig.1.

Fig.2. *Fig.3.*

Fig.4.

Inventor

LAWRENCE B. SPERRY.

By his Attorney

Herbert H. Thompson

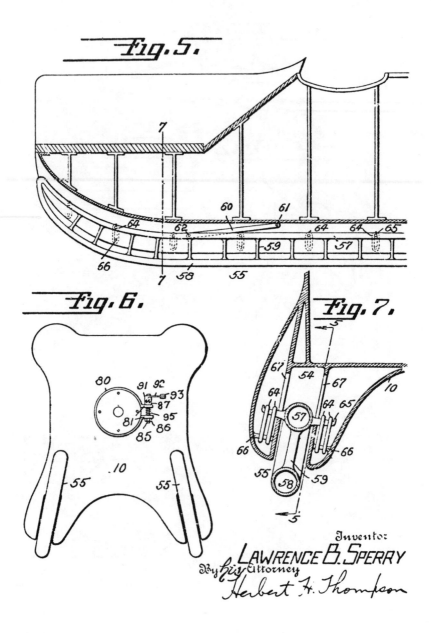

Fig. 5.

Fig. 6.

Fig. 7.

Inventor

LAWRENCE B. SPERRY

By his Attorney

Herbert H. Thompson

Sept. 6, 1927.

L. B. SPERRY

1,641,700

AIRCRAFT

Filed Oct. 21, 1922

4 Sheets-Sheet 3

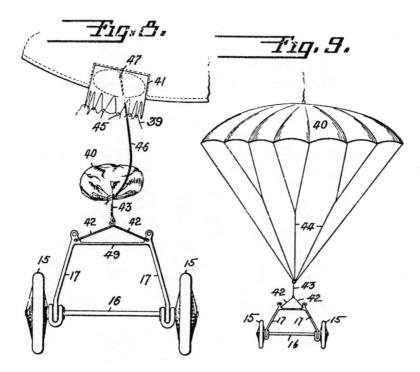

Fig. 8.

Fig. 9.

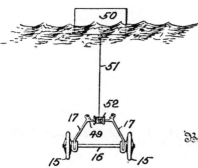

Fig. 10.

Inventor

LAWRENCE B. SPERRY.

By *his Attorney*

Herbert H. Thompson

Sept. 6, 1927.

L. B. SPERRY

1,641,700

AIRCRAFT

Filed Oct. 21, 1922

4 Sheets—Sheet 4

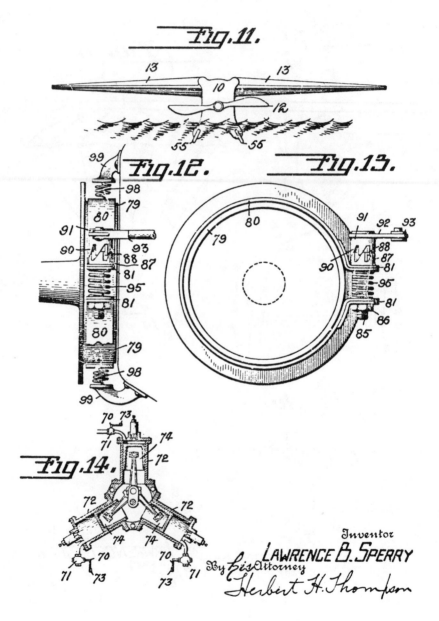

Fig.11.

Fig.12.

Fig.13.

Fig.14.

Inventor

LAWRENCE B. SPERRY

By His Attorney

Herbert H. Thompson

UNITED STATES PATENT OFFICE

LAWRENCE B. SPERRY, OF BROOKLYN, NEW YORK, ASSIGNOR, BY MESNE ASSIGN-
MENTS, TO SPERRY GYROSCOPE COMPANY, INC., OF BROOKLYN, NEW YORK, A COR-
PORATION OF NEW YORK

GYROSCOPIC PILOT FOR AEROPLANES

Application filed August 1, 1916, Serial No. 112,505. Renewed January 3, 1930.

This invention relates to steering devices for dirigible vehicles, such as aeroplanes, torpedoes and the like. The main object of the invention is to devise a simple automatic 5 steering gear which will relieve the aviator of the major portion of the work involved in steering the aeroplane, and at the same time enable it to be brought under the instant control of the aviator.

10 A further object of the invention is to provide means whereby an aircraft may be flown upon a predetermined course and also with means whereby the said course may be changed at will.

15 The principal elements of my device comprise a small gyroscope of simple design, adapted to maintain a constant position in azimuth for a fairly long period of time, and a servo-motor controlled from said gyroscope 20 and connected with the rudder. In navigating aircraft it is not necessary to provide an extremely accurate azimuth indicator such as the Sperry gyroscopic compass, as the shifting currents of air will carry the aviator off 25 his course sooner or later, even if the aeroplane is under the control of the most precise gyroscopic compass. I therefore propose to make use of a comparatively small compass, which will maintain its position in azimuth 30 with a fair degree of accuracy, and to make use of correcting or setting devices controlled by the aviator for periodically placing the machine upon the required course and resetting the gyroscope, or for altering the 35 course at will.

Referring to the drawings in which what I now consider to be the preferred form of my invention is shown, Fig. 1 is a side elevation, partly in section, of a gyroscopic unit, de-40 signed according to my invention for use in steering an aeroplane or other dirigible vessel.

Fig. 2 is a front elevation of the same, a few parts being in section.

45 Figures 3 and 4 are a plan and side view respectively of a spring washer used in the gyroscope.

Fig. 5 is a detail, and Fig. 6 a front elevation of a device which I term a centralizing 50 member.

Fig. 7 is a longitudinal section of the solenoid adapted to control said centralizing member.

Fig. 8 is a diagrammatic view and wiring diagram illustrating the application of my 55 invention to an aeroplane.

Taking up first my preferred form of gyroscopic unit:—1 denotes a suitable base on which is mounted a vertical bracket 2. Within vertical bearings 3 and 4 in the ring and 60 base respectively is rotatably mounted a vertical or gimbal ring 5, within which the rotor bearing casing or gimbal 6 is pivotally supported on horizontal pivots 7 and 8. All of the pivots mentioned are equipped with anti- 65 friction bearings 9, and each set is provided with a special take-up device adapted to compensate for wear in the ball bearings and to thereby prevent any end-wise play in the pivots. This device may comprise a set screw 70 10 or other adjustable device adapted to clamp upon a ball 11 situated between said screw and the end of the pivot 12 on the ring or casing. The other end of the bearing is also supported on a ball 11'. An index 120 may 75 be attached to ring 5, if desired for indicating changes in the heading of the aircraft by cooperating with a suitable scale 121 on base 1.

The gyroscope proper is mounted within 80 the casing 6 and is preferably constructed as an integral part of a polyphase induction motor. The stator of said motor is placed upon a fixed shaft 13 supported within the casing, and upon said stator are placed all 85 of the polyphase windings. The rotor may be of standard squirrel cage construction as far as electrical features are concerned. Mechanically it is made, however, in the form of a heavy fly-wheel 14 journalled upon said 90 shaft 13 on anti-friction bearings 15. It will be seen in this construction that the rotor completely encloses the stator and thus gives a maximum moment of inertia to the rotating parts. The wires 16 are brought into the 95 stator through one end of shaft 13, which is made hollow for the purpose. I find it important that all end play of the rotor upon shaft 13 be prevented. For this purpose I mount between the rotor and a fixed portion 100 of the shaft or stator a small washer 22 which is split and sprung apart somewhat as indicated in Fig. 4, so that the resilience of the washer will take up any end play that may exist, or that may be caused by the wearing down of the ball bearings.

An adjustable weight 17 is shown threaded upon a shaft 18 secured to the ring 5 for the purpose of adjusting the balance of the gyroscope about the vertical axis. The balance about the horizontal pivots 7 and 8 is adjusted by means of a threaded weight 19 mounted upon shaft 13 or an extension thereof. Weight 19 may also be used to adjust the balance of the gyroscope for different latitudes in order to cause precession of the gyroscope at the required rate to keep up with the earth. A ring 20 provided with a series of holes 21 may also be used for adjusting the balance by placing small weights in the various holes. These refinements are very essential to the proper operation of the gyroscope, it being important that the gyroscope be balanced about each of its three axes. The aeroplane is controlled from a gyroscope indirectly by means of electric contacts which operate a servo-motor connected to the rudder. The contacts are shown as consisting of a pair of conducting segments 23 and 24 mounted on an arm 25 secured to the vertical ring 5. A trolley or brush 26 bears upon said segments and is adapted to complete a circuit through one or the other of the windings 27 or 28 on the servo-motor 29. The servo-motor is shown diagrammatically only and comprises a pair of gears 100 and 101 continuously driven in opposite directions by a pair of intermeshing pinions 102, 103. One of the pinions 102 is shown as mounted on the same shaft 104 as a fan or windmill 105, which is driven by the air currents caused by the flight of the aeroplane. The windings 27 and 28 are adapted to force the adjacent gear into contact with a clutch disc 106 secured to shaft 129, so that it may be driven in either direction. Follow up wires 32 from drum 34 are wrapped upon a drum 108 driven from shaft 129 through suitable gearing 109, while the rudder wires 31 and 32 engage a similar drum 110.

The servo-motor is not only connected to the rudder 30 by means of wires 31 ard 32, but is also connected with the gyroscopic unit so that a follow-up connection is provided between the two. The principal object of the follow-up connection is to reduce or prevent hunting of the aeroplane, in azimuth, about its predetermined course. This connection may consist of a wire 33 extending from the servo-motor around a drum 34 mounted adjacent to the gyroscope. Secured to said drum is one emember 35 of an electro-magnetic clutch, the other member 36 of which is normally held disengaged therefrom by spring 37, but is clutched thereto on excitation of

winding 38. Member 36 is provided with a pinion 39 meshing with a gear segment 40. The said segment is connected to the block 42 carrying trolley 26 by means of a link 41 so that when the clutch is engaged a follow-up motion will be imparted to the trolley from the servo-motor or other part of the steering apparatus.

The trolley block 42 is mounted upon an arm 44 pivotally supported on a boss 43 extending from base 1. Also mounted on or near said base are a pair of spaced leaf springs 46 which engage over an upwardly extending pin 47 on said base and downwardly extending pin 48 on the arm 44. The pins are so located that the trolley is normally positioned between the two contact strips 23, 24. It will be seen that as long as the clutch is engaged the trolley 26 will follow the movements of the servo-motor, but as soon as it is disengaged the trolley will be returned to its centralized position with respect to said reversing contacts by springs 46.

On the opposite side of the gyroscope from the drum is shown a special device which I employ to bring the gyroscope quickly back to a predetermined relation or centralized position with respect to the aeroplane at the will of the aviator. This device consists of tapering or conical shaped member 50 adapted to be moved toward the gyroscope and to engage a stem 51 extending from the casing or inner gimbal 6 of the gyroscope. Member 50 is preferably provided with inwardly extending radial blades or fins 52 which perform the important function of stopping the precessional movements of the gyroscope. Without some such means any attempt to move the gyroscope directly to a new position would only result in precession of the gyroscope at right angles to the application of the force, but by applying a force in the required direction and at the same time stopping the precession, the gyroscope may be brought quickly to any desired position.

Member 50 is controlled by means of a solenoid 53, the said member being secured to an extension 54 of the core 55 of the solenoid. A spring 56 is provided to hold the member 50 normally in the engaged position. On excitation of the solenoid, member 50 is quickly withdrawn out of the path of the stem 51. I prefer to provide means for reducing the current flowing through the solenoid after the core has been drawn fully within it, since a greater current is required to bring the core to this position than to hold it there. For this purpose we have provided a switch 57, which is opened when the core is in the innermost position as shown in Fig. 7. This switch is connected so as to cut out or short circuit a resistance 58, which is otherwise connected with the winding 60 of the solenoid (see Fig. 8).

The means directly controlled by the aviator for actually controlling the rudder is represented in Fig. 8 at 61. As far as this invention is concerned, said means may comprise any suitable form of handle, foot pedal, or other controlling means, but which has incorporated therein a novel form of switch. The controlling means is shown as a foot pedal made in two parts, 62 and 63, hinged together at 64. One half of a two part contact button 65 is placed upon each lever so that when the levers are rotated in opposite directions a slight distance from the position shown in figure 8 the circuit will be opened. A strong compression spring 66 is provided to hold the contacts normally closed. It will be seen, however, that as soon as the aviator pushes upon either or both levers to rotate the rudder, the compression spring will yield and the button open. This will not, however interfere with the steering of the craft as there is always sufficient give to the wires 67 and 68 extending from the pedal to the rudder 30 to allow for this slight lost motion.

Button 65 is in circuit not only with magnetic clutch winding 38, but also with the servo-motor and the solenoid 60, so that the effect of opening the button will be:

1st, to sever the follow-up connection between the servo-motor and the gyroscope.

2nd, to cut out the servo-motor and render it inoperative.

3rd, to automatically centralize the gyroscope.

I find in practice, however, that it is not necessary to disconnect the follow-up connections between the servo-motor and the gyroscope so that clutch 38 and associated parts may be omitted if desired.

By a further movement of the foot pedals the aviator can then shift the rudder 30 directly to a new position. Upon release of the rudder in this position the servo-motor will again be energized, the following-up connection completed, and the gyroscope released, so that the automatic pilot will take up the steering of the aircraft where the aviator left it, and maintain it on its course until the aviator again desires to change the course or to correct for side drift.

Another system for correcting for side drift which may be effectively employed is to couple the gyroscopic unit or some part connected therewith to a drift indicator such as disclosed in my copending application— Steering device for aircraft, filed March 24th, 1915, now matured into Patent No. 1,390,653, dated September 13, 1921. For this purpose the entire gyro-unit may be pivotally mounted on a base 100' so that it may be readily rotated from a sighting device 101' by means of wires 102' or the like. As shown in Fig. 2, wires 102' are wound about base 1 to turn the latter on base 100'. The turning of base 1, of course, shifts brush or trolley 26, while contacts 23

and 24 are maintained relatively stationary by the gyroscope. As the effect of such a rotation of base 1 is to shift the relative position of contacts 23, 24 and to brush 26, the wires 102' are shown as connected to the contacts in Fig. 8. The sighting device consists in a small telescope 103' rotatably mounted about a vertical axis in a bracket 104'. The telescope is provided with a line or cross hairs 105' adapted to be turned in the direction of the true line of flight, as observed by the direction of the stream lines seen through the telescope. The telescope is connected to a compass 106', so that when it is turned, the lubbers line 107 of the compass will be correspondingly shifted to a position 107', say. Without a connection such as wires 102', the observer would then move the pedals 61, 62 so as to turn the machine back through an angle approximately equal to the angle through which line 107 has been moved. Wires 102' are so connected, however, that the gyro-unit, is turned backwardly through the angle, so that, as the telescope is being turned the unit is turned in the opposite direction and the rudder 30 turned by means of the servo-motor through the correct angle to bring the machine to the correct course.

It should also be observed when the base 1 is rotated by wires 102' by the observer through his rotation of the sighting device that the reading of pointer 120 on its scale 121 is changed, since the latter is mounted on base 1 and the former is held stationary by the gyroscope. When the gyroscope of my invention is being used as a flight indicator, the observer at the sighting device may readily show the pilot at the gyroscope when to make the desired change of course. The pilot thereupon brings the aeroplane around until the pointer again reads at the proper reading on the scale. If no pilot is used, this function is accomplished automatically as described.

In accordance with the provisions of the patent statutes, I have herein described the principle of operation of my invention, together with the apparatus, which I now consider to represent the best embodiment thereof, but I desire to have it understood that the apparatus shown is only illustrative and that the invention can be carried out by other means. Also, while it is designed to use the various features and elements in the combination and relations described, some of these may be altered and others omitted without interfering with the more general results outlined, and the invention extends to such use.

Having described my invention, what I claim and desire to secure by Letters Patent is:

1. In an automatic pilot for aircraft, the combination with the vertical rubber, of a gyroscope for normally controlling the same to

maintain the craft on a course, means for altering the course of the craft including means for temporarily locking the gyroscope, and means for turning the rudder to bring the craft to a new course.

2. In an automatic pilot for aircraft, the combination with a rudder and means for controlling the same at will, of a gyroscope, a servo-motor connected with the rudder and controlled from said gyroscope, and means brought into action by movement of said first named means for centralizing said gyroscope.

3. In an automatic steering device for aeroplanes, the combination with a vertical rudder and means for controlling the same at will, of a gyroscope, a servo-motor, connections between the servo motor, rudder and gyroscope and means responsive to movement of said first named means for severing the connections between said servo-motor and the gyroscope, whereby the course may be altered, and means for restoring said connections after said movement to maintain the new course.

4. In an automatic pilot for aircraft, in combination with a rudder, a gyroscope, servo-motor, connections between the servo-motor, rudder and gyroscope including a primary connection and a follow-up connection between said gyroscope and said motor, and means for changing the course of the aircraft comprising means for turning the rudder and means for severing said connections between the servo-motor and the gyroscope while the rudder is being turned.

5. In an automatic pilot for aeroplanes, the combination with a rudder and a manual control device therefor, of a gyroscope, a servo-motor, connections between the servo-motor, rudder and gyroscope and means responsive to movement of said manual device for severing the connections between said servo-motor and the gyroscope, and for centralizing said gyroscope.

6. In an automatic pilot for aeroplanes, the combination with a rudder and a means for actuating the same at will, of a gyroscope, a servo-motor, connections between the servo-motor, rudder and gyroscope and means responsive to movement of said first named means for severing the connections between said servo-motor and the gyroscope, for centralizing said gyroscope and for rendering said motor inoperative.

7. In gyroscopic apparatus for dirigible craft, the combination with a gyroscope having a plurality of degrees of freedom, of means for centralizing said gyroscope comprising a projecting member and a hollow tapering member for engaging the same, one of said members being mounted on the gyroscope the other on a fixed part, means for imparting relative movement to said members and means controlled by the relative posi-

tion of said craft and gyroscope for governing the course of the craft.

8. In gyroscopic apparatus for dirigible aircraft, the combination with a gyroscope having a plurality of degrees of freedom, of means for centralizing said gyroscope comprising a projecting member and a hollow tapering member for engaging the same, having inwardly projecting ribs, one of said members being mounted on the gyroscope the other on a fixed part, means for imparting relative movement to said members and means controlled by the relative position of said craft and gyroscope for governing the course of the craft.

9. The combination with a gyroscope mounted for oscillation about a vertical axis, a member mounted for movement about the same axis, a plurality of electric contacts mounted on said gyroscope and on said member, said contacts comprising a contact segment and a co-operating brush, a clutch member adapted to engage and disengage said member, means for oscillating said clutch member, and resilient means for bringing the said contacts to their neutral position when said clutch is released.

10. In an automatic pilot for aeroplanes, the combination with a vertical rudder and control device therefor, operable at will, of a gyroscope, a servo-motor, means including a follow-up connection connecting said servo-motor, rudder and gyroscope and means responsive to movement of said device for breaking said follow-up connection.

11. In a steering device for aeroplanes the combination with a vertical rudder, of a servo-motor for controlling the same, a gyroscope, means for supporting the same for turning about a vertical axis and for oscillation about a horizontal axis, means operable by relative turning of the gyroscope and areoplane about said vertical axis for controlling said motor, a follow-up connection from the rudder to the second mentioned means, means for breaking said connection, and means for changing the relation between said rudder and said second mentioned means while said connection is broken.

12. In a steering device for aeroplanes the combination with a vertical rudder, of a servo-motor for controlling the same, a gyroscope, means for supporting the same for turning about a vertical axis, means operable by relative turning of the aeroplane and gyroscope about said axis for controlling said motor, a drift indicator, and means connecting said indicator and said other means for shifting the effective relation of said means, whereby the aeroplane is automatically brought on a true course.

13. In a steering device for aeroplanes the combination with a vertical rudder, of a servo-motor for controlling the same, a gyroscope, means for supporting the same for

turning about a vertical axis, means operable by relative turning of the aeroplane and gyroscope about said axis for controlling said motor, a drift indicator, and means connecting said indicator and said gyroscope, whereby the effective relation of said other means is shifted and the aeroplane turned to correct for side drift.

14. In an automatic steering device for aircraft, the combination with a rudder and a servo-motor for controlling the same, of an azimuth indicator, means brought into action by relative turning of the aeroplane and indicator for actuating the servo-motor, a drift indicator, and means connecting said indicators whereby the said first means are shifted to change their effective relation.

15. In a steering device for aeroplanes the combination with a vertical rudder, of a servo-motor for controlling the same, a gyroscope, means for supporting the same for turning about a vertical axis, means operable by relative turning of the aeroplane and gyroscope about said axis for controlling said motor, a drift indicator, a compass connected therewith so as to have its readings affected thereby, and means connecting said indicator, and said other means for shifting the effective relation of said means, whereby the aeroplane is automatically brought on a true course.

16. The combination with an aeroplane, of a steering rudder therefor, a gyroscope, a servo-motor connected to said rudder, means displaceable by relative turning of the aeroplane and gyroscope for governing said servo-motor, and means for altering the relation of said other means and the rudder to turn the aeroplane.

17. A control system for aircraft comprising, in combination, means for automatically maintaining the aircraft headed in a predetermined direction, means for determining the true course of the air craft and connections between said two first named means for automatically changing the heading of the aircraft.

18. In an automatic pilot for aircraft, the combination with the vertical rudder, of a gyroscope for normally controlling the same to maintain the craft on a predetermined course, means for altering the course of the craft, including means for temporarily rendering the gyroscope control ineffective and centralizing said gyroscope, and, means for turning the rudder to bring the craft to a new course.

19. In an automatic steering device for dirigible craft in combination, a gyro rotor, a rotor bearing casing therefor, a ring rotatable about an axis, said ring supporting said casing for turning about a second axis, and means for centralizing the gyro casing about both axes comprising a member adapted to engage said casing and cause rotation thereof toward the central position about one axis while preventing movement away from the central position about the other axis and means controlled by the relative position of said gyroscope and craft to govern the course thereof.

20. In an automatic pilot for aeroplanes, the combination with a rudder and a control device therefor of a gyroscope, a servo-motor connected with said rudder, means operable by relative turning of the gyroscope and aeroplane for controlling said motor, a follow-up connection from said rudder to said means, and means responsive to movement of said control device for severing said follow-up connection and rendering said servo-motor inoperative.

21. In an automatic pilot for aeroplanes, the combination with a rudder and a control device therefor, of a gyroscope, a servo-motor connected with said rudder, means comprising a control member connected to said gyroscope and an independently mounted co-operating control member for governing said servo-motor from said gyroscope, and means brought into action by movement of said device for rendering said servo-motor inoperative and for moving the second mentioned control member into a definite position with respect to the other control member.

22. In a steering device for aeroplanes, the combination with a vertical rudder, of a servo-motor for controlling the same, a gyroscope, means for supporting the same for turning about a vertical axis and for oscillation about a horizontal axis, means operable by relative turning of the gyroscope and aeroplane about a vertical axis for controlling said motor, means for shifting the relation between the gyroscope and rudder, for changing the course of the aeroplane, and a follow-up connection from the rudder to the second mentioned means.

23. In an automatic pilot for aircraft, the combination with the vertical rudder, of a gyroscope for normally controlling the same, to maintain the craft on a predetermined course, control members mounted respectively on the gyroscope and aircraft, a servo-motor controlled therefrom and connected to the rudder, and means for altering the course of the craft including means for turning the rudder to bring the craft to a new course, means for throwing out of action the gyro-control, and means for centralizing the control members while the gyro control is out of action.

24. In a steering device for aeroplanes, the combination with a vertical rudder, of a servo-motor for controlling the same, a gyroscope, means for supporting the same for turning about a vertical axis and for oscillation about a horizontal axis, means operable by relative turning of the gyroscope and aeroplane about said vertical axis for controlling said motor, a follow-up connection from the

rudder to the second mentioned means, and means including a centralizing device for the gyroscope for changing the course steered by the gyroscope during the flight of the aeroplane.

25. The combination with a gyroscope including a gimbal ring provided with an axial projection, of a member arranged to reciprocate in a predetermined path coincident with a line extending through the center of said gimbal ring for resetting said gyroscope into a predetermined position.

26. The combination with a gyroscope having a gimbal ring provided with an extension, of a member having diverging walls movable into and out of engagement with said extension through a predetermined path for controlling the operation of said gyroscope, and a power system arranged to move said member into and out of engagement with said gyroscope.

27. In gyroscopic apparatus for use in navigating aircraft, the combination with a ground observing sight, means for turning the same, a gyroscope, an indicating means connected to said gyroscope, and means operated from said first named means for altering said indicating means when it is desired to change the course.

In testimony whereof I have affixed my signature.

LAWRENCE B. SPERRY.

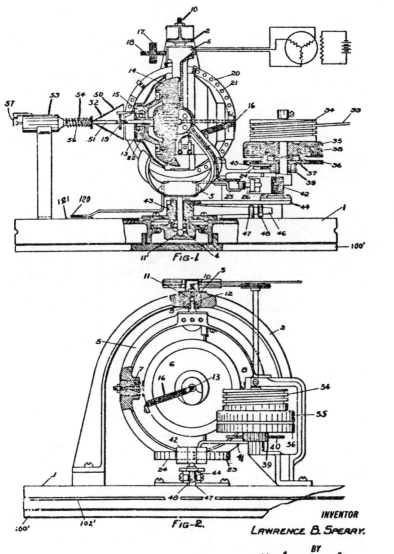

FIG-1

FIG-2.

INVENTOR

LAWRENCE B. SPERRY.

BY

Herbert H. Thompson

ATTORNEY

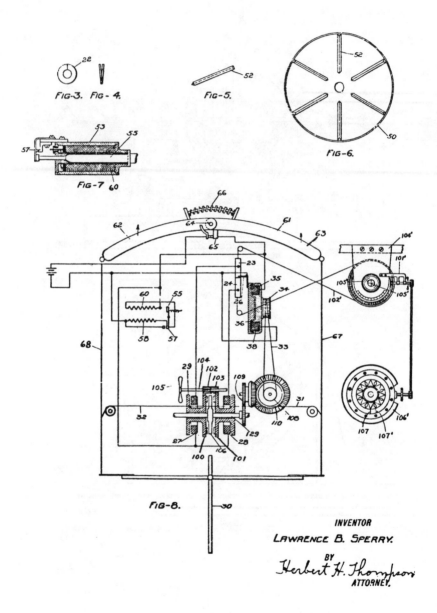

FIG-3. FIG-4.

FIG-5.

FIG-6.

FIG-7

FIG-8.

INVENTOR

LAWRENCE B. SPERRY.

BY

Herbert H. Thompson

ATTORNEY.

UNITED STATES PATENT OFFICE

LAWRENCE B. SPERRY, DECEASED, LATE OF GARDEN CITY, NEW YORK, BY WINIFRED A.
SPERRY AND BANK OF AMERICA, CO-EXECUTORS, OF NEW YORK, N. Y.

AUTOMATIC PILOT FOR AIRCRAFT   REISSUED

Continuation of application Serial No. 628,781, filed March 30, 1923. This application filed November 9,
1929, Serial No. 405,939. Renewed February 17, 1932.

This invention relates to an automatic control system for aircraft, aerial torpedoes, or other dirigible vessels and has for its object the provision of an improved device of this character. This application is a continuation of copending application filed March 30, 1923, Serial No. 628,781, certain parts thereof, however, having been divided out.

More specifically, the invention relates to such an automatic aircraft in which one or more gyroscopes are employed in the control system. Usually one gyroscope having a horizontal spinning axis is employed to control the vertical or steering rudder for the movement to the right or left of the craft, and a second or stabilizing gyroscope having a vertical spinning axis is employed to control the horizontal rudder, generally known as the elevator, or up and down movement of the craft, and the ailerons, or the banking of the torpedo. Such a system is shown in the copending patent of Elmer A Sperry, No. 1,792,937, dated February 17, 1931, for wireless controlled aerial torpedo. The invention is applicable to an airplane provided with either of said gyroscopes, or both of them. In conjunction with the gyroscopes, is employed an air system, which may have either a negative or a positive pressure, having control valves for the several elements to be actuated, which valves are in turn controlled by the gyroscopes. It is, of course, understood that the steering gyroscope preferably has three degrees of freedom, and, therefore, maintains its position in space, while the stabilizing gyroscope is preferably in the form of a gyroscopic pendulum. There is also provided a novel follow-up system for said gyroscopes. With the apparatus thus far mentioned, in flight the airplane will automatically maintain its direction, in both the vertical and the horizontal planes.

For the purpose of changing the direction of the aircraft in either the horizontal or vertical plane, banking the craft or actuating other local devices, the same air system is employed, which, for purposes of illustration, is shown as a vacuum system, connected to a master valve. This valve has separate connections to several air motors which work through respective gyroscopes in a manner to be fully described hereinafter, which connections are normally closed.

The invention will be better understood from the following description taken in connection with the accompanying drawings and its scope will be pointed out in the appended claims.

In the drawings, illustrating what is now considered the preferred form of the invention,

Fig. 1 is a plan view of the steering gyroscope for controlling the steering rudder, with a diagram illustrating the air system and connections.

Fig. 2 is an elevation of the gyroscope shown in Fig. 1, showing the details of the follow-up system.

Fig. 3 is a side elevation of the stabilizing gyroscope for controlling the horizontal rudder and ailerons, with a diagram illustrating the air system and connections.

Fig. 4 is a diagrammatic showing of a modification of Fig. 1, in which an electrical control system is shown.

Referring now to the drawings, the numeral 1 in Fig. 1 indicates the steering gyroscope unit for controlling the vertical rudder 2. This unit comprises a gyroscope mounted on a horizontal spinning axis, 100, 101 in casing 102', which is mounted for oscillation about a horizontal axis 102, 103 in vertical ring 3, journaled in frame 10 on vertical axis 104, 105, and may be of the type disclosed in Patent No. 1,521,132, dated December 30, 1924 for gyroscopic apparatus for aeroplanes. Such a gyroscope is designed to possess three degrees of freedom, so as to maintain its position in space. Frictionless means are preferably employed to transmit the position of the gyroscope to a distant point for effecting the control of the aerial device. For this purpose there is suitably mounted on the vertical ring 3 of the gyroscope, a segment 4 curved about the pivotal axis 104 of the gyroscope as a center, the ends 5, 6 thereof being sharpened to knife edges. Adjacent the ends 5, 6 are nozzles 7, 8, respectively, which are substantially radially directed with reference to segment 4 and which are connected with any suitable means for creating negative or positive air pressure, as will be described hereinafter. The nozzles 7, 8 are spaced so that they may be partially or almost entirely closed simultaneously by the ends 5, 6, respectively, a small clearance remaining to permit a slight leakage. Said nozzles are fixed to a base 9 which is rotatable about the axis of the gyro frame 10. By the construction of segment 4 and nozzles 7 and 8 as described, the lateral reaction or thrust from the air entering the nozzles on the gyroscope is minimized.

From the foregoing, it will be seen that as either nozzle is uncovered by the adjacent knife edge, air will pass therethrough at a greater rate than through the other, since as one nozzle is uncovered, the other will be covered. However, in the normal position shown in Fig. 1, the same volume of air may leak through both nozzles. For the purpose of illustrating my invention, I have shown a negative air pressure system, a vacuum reservoir or tank being shown at 11, having an air pump 12, which may be of any standard type. The tank 11 is connected by passages 13, 14 to the opposite ends of a closed cylinder 15, which is provided with a reciprocating piston 16. The opposite ends of the cylinder 15 are also connected by flexible passages 17, 18 to nozzles 7, 8 respectively. It will, therefore, be readily understood that when the knife edges 5 and 6 are in their normal position, the piston 16 will assume a middle or neutral position, as shown in Fig. 1, and that when either of the nozzles 7, 8 are uncovered, an unbalanced condition is set up in the cylinder 15 and the piston 16 moves accordingly. The piston 16 is provided with a stem 19, which is secured to the valve 20. The latter valve is, therefore, actuated by the reciprocation of the piston 16. As shown, the piston valve 20 is within an open ended cylinder 21, and is in the form of a double piston, the faces 22, 23 of which are united by a small neck 24. The chamber of cylinder 21 formed between the faces 22, 23 is connected by a passage 25 with the tank 11. The cylinder 21 is also connected with similar bellows 26, 27 by passages 28, 29, respectively. The passages 28, 29 are located at opposite ends of the cylinder 21, and are spaced to be evenly covered by the piston faces 22, 23 when the piston 16 is in its neutral position, so that in such a position a slight leakage is permitted, which will maintain the bellows 26, 27 in a balanced condition. When the piston 16 is moved to the right, the valve 20 uncovers passage 28, connecting it to the atmosphere, and connects the passage 29 entirely with the tank 11. When piston 16 moves in the opposite direction, passage 29 is connected to air, and passage 28 is connected to the tank 11. The lower sides 30, 31 of bellows 26, 27 are rigidly mounted on a fixed base 32 and are placed at an angle to each other. The upper sides of the bellows are united in a single flat element 33, pivoted to rock about a center at which the sides 30, 31 meet. The passages 28, 29 are flexible to permit the free movement of the member 33. The rudder 2 is provided with a cross piece 34, the opposite ends of which are suitably secured to the respective opposite ends of element 33 by wires 35, 36.

The follow-up system is represented as shaft 37, pivotally connected to the element 33 at one end, and at its opposite end engaging the rotatable base 9. The engaging means comprises a U-shaped bracket 38 pivotally connected to shaft 37, which bracket is slidably mounted on a shaft 39 of an air motor 40. Between the arms of the bracket 38, is a worm 41 meshing with a gear 42 on the periphery of base 9. The worm is slidable on the shaft 39, but rotatable therewith for a purpose hereinafter to be described. Therefore, any motion of shaft 38 reciprocates worm 41 on shaft 39 and thereby rotates the base 9 accordingly.

From the foregoing it will be seen that if the aerial carrier deviates from its course to the right or left, in accordance with well known gyroscopic principles, the gyroscope maintains its position in space, and the base 9 turns relatively to the gyro. Assuming that the craft has turned counterclockwise, the base 9 moves counterclockwise with respect to the gyro, causing nozzle 8 to be uncovered and nozzle 7 to be covered by segment 4. This causes piston 16 to move to the left, thereby moving valve 20 to the left to connect passage 28 with tank 11 and passage 29 to air. This causes bellows 26 to collapse whereby element 33 through the medium of wire 36 moves rudder 2 counterclockwise. When the bellows 26 is collapsed, the element 33 is rocked counter-clockwise, thereby moving the shaft 37, which through its connection to rotatable base 9, moves said base clockwise until the segment 4 reassumes its normal position with respect to nozzles 7, 8. In this manner the aircraft torpedo may be automatically maintained on the course controlled by the vertical rudder, but a graduated movement of the rudder is secured instead of the "hard over" system employed on under-water torpedoes.

In Fig. 3 is shown the stabilizing gyroscope unit 43 for controlling the ailerons 44, or the banking of the aerial torpedo and the horizontal rudder 45, or the up and down movement of said torpedo. The gyroscope is shown as mounted in a casing 110 on a spinning axis 111, the casing being pivoted in gimbal ring 46 on horizontal axis 112, 113. Said ring in turn is pivoted in brackets 48 on horizontal axis 114. The segment 4' for controlling the ailerons is carried by the gimbal ring 46, and the segment 4'' for controlling the horizontal rudder 45, by the loop or bail 47, pivoted outside of the ring 46 on brackets 49 and 49'. The devices controlled by the segment 4' are identical with those shown in Fig. 1 and above described, and, therefore, need not again be described. The similar parts have been given similar reference numerals, those relating to the ailerons being primed and those relating to the horizontal rudder being double-primed. Due to the different planes of operation, the gears 42' and 42'' are respectively pivoted on vertical standards 48 and 49 instead of on the base 9 as shown in Fig. 1. For the same reason, it has been necessary to connect the rods 37' and 37'' to their respective bellows controlled elements 33' and 33'' by wires 50 and 51. A single element 33' is provided to operate both ailerons 44, which are connected to move oppositely in a manner readily understood. From this it will be seen that the airplane may also be automatically maintained on the course controlled by the ailerons and horizontal rudder.

For controlling the course of the airplane after it is once in flight valves may be provided for operating the motors 40, 40' and 40''. These three motors respectively control the vertical rudder or the right and left movement, the ailerons or the banking movement, and the horizontal rudder or the up and down movement. in a similar manner, which will be understood from Fig. 1. As there shown the motor 40, which may be any suitable type of air motor, drives the shaft 39 in either direction which shaft carries the worm 41, as hereinbefore described. The worm 41 meshes with gear 42 and rotates it clockwise or anti-clockwise, which of course displaces the nozzles 7, 8 carried by it, with respect to edges 5, 6. When this occurs, the device controlled by the respective motor 40 is actuated in the manner hereinbefore described. When the base 9 is rotated clockwise, the result is the same as if the follow-up rod 37 had been lengthened and when rotated anti-clockwise. the result is the same as if the rod 37 of the follow-up system had been shortened. With the arrangement described, it will be seen that by driving the motors 40, 40' and 40'', in either direction, the course of the aircraft may be altered, and that the follow-up system is simultaneously adjusted to the altered course, and, therefore, the aircraft is automatically maintained thereon. To this end there are shown four short pipes 54, 55, 56 and 57 in communication with a passage 53 connected to the tank 11 and which are open at their free ends. In practice these pipes are arranged along side each other as indicated in Fig. 1.

The passage 54 communicates with one end of air motor 40'' through passage 59 and passage 55 communicates with the opposite end of air motor 40'' through passage 60. The passage 56 communicates with one end of air motor 40 through passage 61, and passage 57 communicates with the opposite end of air motor 40 through passage 62. The motor 40' is connected at one end to passage 62 by passage 63 and at its opposite end to passage 61 by passage 64', that is, in parallel with motor 40. As above indicated, the motor 40 controls the right and left movement, and the motor 40' the banking movement, and as is well understood by those skilled in the art, the vertical rudder and ailerons are operated together. The motors 40 and 40' are accordingly connected for simultaneous operation. The open ends of passage 54 to 57 inclusive are normally closed by padded fingers 54' to 57' inclusive. The fingers 54' to 57' are each normally held in closed position by any suitable means, such as by springs 68. When it is desired to turn in one direction, one of valves 56' or 57' is opened either directly or indirectly through relays (not shown) by the operator. This alters the pressure in pipe 61 or 62 and thus causes the motor 40 to turn in one direction, thus turning the worm 41 and the base 42 slowly around the gyroscope as long as the valve is held open. As soon, however, as the valve is closed, the motor stops. The result is that the entire airplane is brought around to the new course through the operation of the jets 7 and 8 and the rudder 2, as above explained. At the same time the motor 40' is operated to automatically bank the plane. Similarly valves 54', 55' are operated to control the angle of attack of the airplane.

In Fig. 4 is shown a modified form of the device shown in Fig. 1, in which similar reference numerals have been applied to similar parts, but triple-primed. Herein the nozzles 7, 8 are replaced by cylinders 7'' ' and 8'' ', which are actuated by oppositely wound solenoids 83, 84, respectively. The circuit of solenoid 83 comprises a battery 85, conductor 86 to a movable trolley 87 on the follow-up element 88, contact 89, conductor 90, through the solenoid, and conductor 91. The circuit of solenoid 84 comprises battery 85, conductor 86, trolley contact 87, contact 92, conductor 93, through the solenoid and conductor 91 to the battery 85. The solenoids 83, 84 are provided with rods 83', 84' carrying pistons within chambers 7'' ', 8'' ', and said rods may be pivoted to the opposite ends of a rocker 94 pivoted on a center 95. In this case, the element 88 corresponds to the base 9 in Fig. 1, and the contacts 89, 92 are carried by the gyro ring 4, and move in a manner similar to the segment 4 in Fig. 1. This arrangement is well understood in the art. Otherwise the operation is similar to that described in connection with Fig. 1.

In accordance with the provisions of the patent statutes, there is herein described the principle of operation of the invention, together with the apparatus, which is now considered to represent the best embodiment thereof, but it is desired to have it understood that the apparatus shown is only illustrative and that the invention can be carried out by other means. Also, while it is designed to use the various features and elements in the combination and relations described, some of these may be altered and others omitted without interfering with the more general results outlined, and the invention extends to such use.

Having herein described the invention what is claimed and desired to secure by Letters Patent is:

1. In a control system for aircraft, a pressure source, means connected with said source for actuating a control surface, means connected with said source for controlling said actuating means responsive to pressure changes, a gyroscope for differentially effecting pressure changes in said latter means, and means for altering the relation between the gyroscope and pressure source for effecting changes in course through the gyroscope.

2. In an aerial control system for aircraft, the combination with a gyroscope, of means for automatically controlling a control surface therefrom comprising a pressure source, means for actuating said surface connected with said source, a valve for controlling the connection between said source and said surface actuating means, a cylinder and piston for controlling said valve, differential air flow ports connected with said cylinder and actuated by said gyroscope whereby differential pressure changes are effected on the two sides of said piston and follow-back means to said ports controlled by said surface.

3. In combination, a dirigible vehicle, a gyroscope mounted thereon, a pressure source, means for actuating a control surface connected with said source, means for controlling said actuating means responsive to changes in pressure, means for effecting pressure changes in said latter means controlled by relative movement between the vehicle and the gyroscope in the plane controlled by said surface, and means for also effecting the operation of said last-named follow-up means.

4. In combination, a dirigible vehicle, a gyroscope mounted thereon for freedom about a vertical axis, means for automatically maintaining the vehicle on a set course in azimuth comprising a follow-up connection between the gyroscope and the control surface, a differential pressure system for actuating the control surface controlled by the gyroscope, and means for changing the course of said vehicle by varying the effective relation of the follow-up connection to the gyroscope.

5. In a control system for a dirigible vehicle, the combination comprising a gyroscope, a pressure source, means for actuating a control surface connected with said source, means for controlling said actuating means comprising elements carried by the gyroscope and by the vehicle, the control being effected by the relative movement between said elements, a follow-up element connected with the control surface and the vehicle element, and course-changing means for relatively moving said elements to adjust the follow-up element to the new relation.

6. In a dirigible vehicle, the combination comprising a control surface, a plurality of control elements one of which is gyroscopically stabilized and the others of which are rotatably mounted, means for rotating the latter elements comprising an axially slidable and rotatable worm, a follow-up connection between said surface and said worm and a change course device also connected thereto.

7. In a gyroscopic control apparatus, the combination with a gyroscope, a pair of air ports mounted adjacent thereto, pivot means for rotatably mounting the same, a lead-out pipe for each port, an intercepting plate on the gyroscope adjacent said ports, a servo motor actuated from the differential air pressure in said pipes, and a follow-back connection to said pivoted air ports to turn the same.

8. The combination with a control gyroscope for dirigible vehicles mounted for turning about an axis, of means for automatically controlling the dirigible vehicle therefrom, comprising a plurality of substantially radially directed nozzles, a curved segment having sharpened edges, said nozzles and said segment being adapted to create a differential flow of air through said nozzles on relative angular displacement of said vehicle and gyroscope, and means brought into action by said differential flow through the nozzles for controlling the course of the vehicle.

9. The combination with a control gyroscope for dirigible vehicles mounted for oscillation about an axis, of means for automatically controlling the dirigible vehicle therefrom, comprising a plurality of air intake nozzles mounted on said vehicle, a segment on the gyroscope having sharpened edges lying adjacent said nozzles and curved about said axis as a center adapted to create a differential flow of air through said nozzles on relative angular displacement of said vehicle and gyroscope, and means brought into action by said differential flow through the nozzles for controlling the position of the vehicle.

10. The combination with a control gyroscope for dirigible vehicles mounted for oscillation about an axis, of means for automatically controlling the dirigible vehicle therefrom, comprising a plurailty of nozzles mounted on the vehicle and radially directed with respect to said axis, a segment

on the gyroscope having sharpened edges
lying adjacent said nozzles and curved about
said axis as a center adapted to create a differential flow of air through said nozzles on
5 relative angular displacement of said vehicle
and gyroscope, and means brought into action by said differential flow through the
nozzles for controlling the position of the
vehicle.

10 11. The combination with a steering gyroscope for dirigible vehicles mounted for
turning about a vertical axis, of means for
automatically controlling the dirigible vehicle therefrom, comprising a plurality of sub-
15 stantially radially directed nozzles mounted
on said vehicles, a curved segment having
sharpened edges on the gyroscope adapted to
create a differential flow of air through said
nozzles on relative rotation of said vehicles
20 and gyroscope, and means brought into action by said differential flow through the
nozzles for controlling the course of the
vehicle.

In testimony whereof we hereby affix our
25 signatures.
WINIFRED A. SPERRY,
BANK OF AMERICA,
By W. J. MONTGOMERY,
Co-Executors of the Estate of Lawrence B.
30 *Sperry, Deceased.*

CERTIFICATE OF CORRECTION.

Patent No. 1,887,335.   November 8, 1932.

WINIFRED A. SPERRY, ET AL.

It is hereby certified that error appears in the printed specification of the
the above numbered requiring correction as follows: Page 4, line 51, claim 3,
strike out the word "follow-up" and insert the same before " means" in line 49,
of said claim; and that the said Letters Patent should be read with this correction
therein that the same may conform to the record of the case in the Patent Office.
Signed and sealed this 5th day of March, A. D. 1935.

Leslie Frazer

(Seal)   Acting Commissioner of Patents.

55

60

65

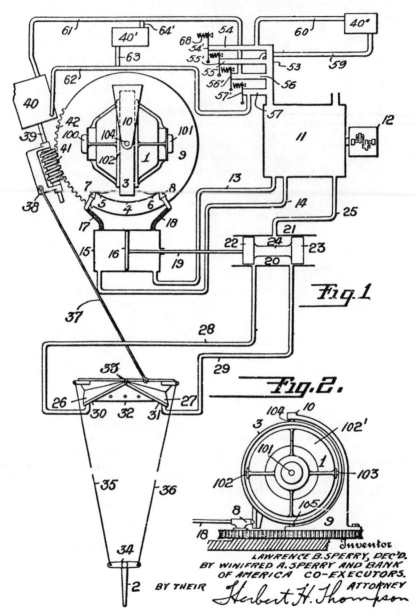

Fig.1

Fig.2

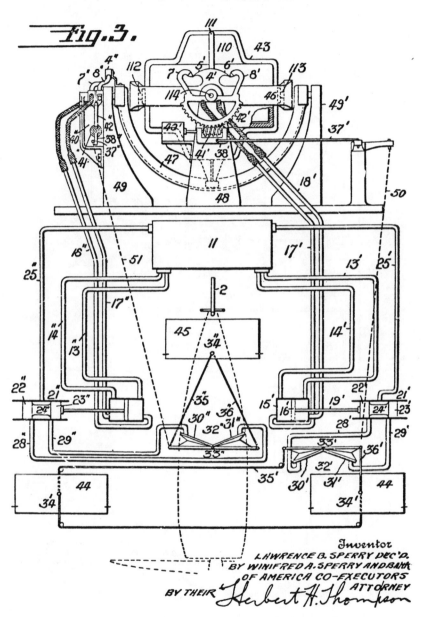

Fig.3.

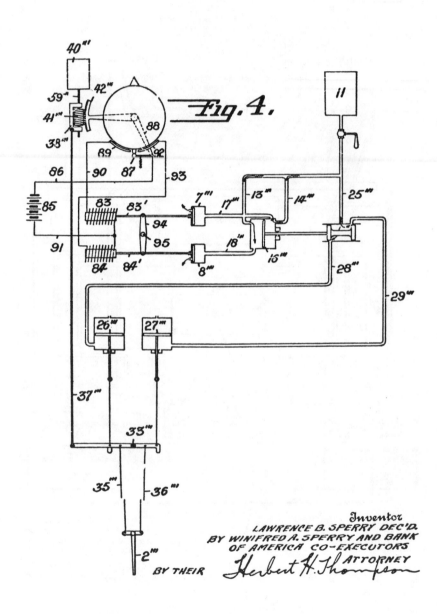

Fig.4.

Inventor
LAWRENCE B. SPERRY DEC'D.
BY WINIFRED A. SPERRY AND BANK
OF AMERICA CO-EXECUTORS
ATTORNEY
BY THEIR   Herbert H. Thompson

Index

Aerial torpedoes, 5, 185–88, 190, 192, 196, 215–17, 233

Airplanes
first airplane built by L. Sperry, 64–70, 78
See also Amphibian planes; Sperry Messenger; Sperry-Verville Racer

Airspeed indicator, invented, 136

Alexander III (Czar of Russia), 27

Allen, May (sister-in-law), 5, 11, 12, 14, 15, 160, 186

Allen, Winifred. *See* Sperry, Winifred Allen

Allen, Winifred Jessica Allan Barclay (mother-in-law), 158–61

Altimeter, invented, 136

Ames, James S., 152

Amphibian planes, development of, 214–15, 219–23, 233

Angle, Ed, 76

Austin, Midge, 148–50

Automatic stabilizer, development of, 78–79, 90–115, 117–19, 124, 233

Bacon, Mary, 47, 62, 146, 170

Baldwin, Stanley, 253

Bara, Theda, 164, 170

Barclay, Lord, 158

Barrès, Commandant, 107

Barry, John William, 160

Barry, May (sister-in-law), 5, 11, 12, 14, 15, 160, 186

Barry, Winifred (mother-in-law), 158–61

Bassett, Preston, 129, 130, 273

Beard, Dean, 31

Bell, Frank, 98

Bellinger, Lt. Patrick, 92, 95–98, 100, 102

Bennett (school headmistress), 160–61

Beveridge, Albert, 30

Blériot, Louis, 107

Blunt, Wilfrid, 159

Brady, Alice, 164

Brady, Major, 73, 74

Brancker, Gen. Sir William, 250–51, 258, 277

Bruce, Gordon, 118, 123

Burst, Mary (grandmother), 16

Burst, Mattie (aunt), 38

Cabot, Thomas D., 71

Cachin, Emile, 104–6, 108–10

Calvé, Emma, 21

Caruso, Enrico, 176

Casals, Pablo, 176

Cathcart, William L., 112

Chamber, Capt. Washington Irving, 78

Chamberlain, Clarence, 281

Chandler, Rex, 96

Cleveland, Grover, 19

Coffin, Howard E., 272

Coffyn (pilot), 76

Collins (race track manager), 58–59

Colvin, Charles, 128, 129, 136, 137, 139, 147

Conger, Will (uncle), 46

Corelli, Marie, 31

Coué, Emile, 3, 14

Craigin, Ruth, 148

Crocthers, Mary W., 271

Curtiss, Glenn H., 77, 79, 192
amphibian planes and, 220
development of stabilizer and, 79, 90–93, 99–102, 116, 119
Lawrence's death and, 280

Curtiss, Glenn, Jr., 99

Curtiss, Lena, 99, 100

Davenport, John, 16

Day, Juliette, 164

Deeds, Col. Edward A., 3, 1–12

Delia (maid), 45, 64, 66, 172

Denby, Edwin, 225

Devereaux, Jack, 165

Doolittle, Gen. Jimmy, 8, 138, 187–88, 190

Doran, Charles S., 265

Doyle (magistrate), 195